INCIDENTS

AND

ANECDOTES OF THE WAR:

TOGETHER WITH

LIFE SKETCHES OF EMINENT LEADERS,

AND NARRATIVES OF THE

Most Memorable Battles for the Union.

EDITED BY

ORVILLE J. VICTOR,

AUTHOR OF "HISTORY OF THE SOUTHERN REBELLION," "LIFE OF GARIBALDI," "LIFE OF WINFIELD SCOTT," "LIFE OF ANTHONY WAYNE," &C. &C.

New York:

JAMES D. TORREY, PUBLISHER,

13 SPRUCE STREET.

INTRODUCTION.

WHEN Cassius M. Clay offered his services to the Secretary of War, to raise a regiment of Kentucky volunteers, or to serve as a private in the ranks, the Secretary expressed his surprise, saying: "Sir, this is the first instance I ever heard of a foreign Minister [Clay had been nominated as U. S. Minister to Russia,] volunteering for service in the ranks." "Then let us make a little history!" exclaimed the gallant Kentuckian.

Clay only typified the spirit which prevailed in almost all conditions of life at the North, when the tocsin was sounded in April, 1861. The world never before witnessed such an uprising. It was as if the whole current of thought and feeling had been changed in a day. Men met on the marts to forget all about stocks and market quotations, to prove the degree of their own loyalty to the Government. Congregations gathered in the Churches to forget creeds and theological differences in their absorbing devotion to the salvation of the Country. Women gathered to forget small-talk and social tribulations in the noble enthusiasm ever awakened in woman's bosom when great emergencies come. Schools were listless, and the eyes of both teachers and pupils turned longingly to the streets where the people were gathering. The solemn tread of regiments was answered by the acclamations of the gathered thousands who everywhere thronged the highways. Men met friends changed to soldiers, and with a benediction bade them adieu. Fathers, mothers and sisters sat down to the evening meal to find one chair vacant, and the prayer which went up from that family circle called down God's blessing on the absent one. It was, indeed, the season of sorrow, but it was also the carnival of patriotism. The world may never witness its like again. Let us pray that an overruling Providence may spare the country from another such visitation of treason, when citizens shall fly to arms to protect with their lives and fortunes their beloved country. So let us pray!

The incidents of joy and sorrow, of pleasure and pain, connected with that Great Awakening, would fill a book—would make a volume to become the treasured tome for to-day, for to-morrow, and for the long years to come. It will only be made by time. When the war is past, and the soldier returns to rejoin the home he has so long forsaken—alas! how many homes will never have their doorway darkened again by the forms of their loved ones!—then will come forth the incidents of that patriot-service, to make their way over the community and become a part of the neighborhood's treasures. Those treasures, time will surely gather and present in a folio, which each loyal home will love to call its own. It will be our purpose to go over the field and glean what we may. Enough already has been recorded to make such a volume as we now propose. We shall devote a few weeks to gathering the scattered leaves—thus to contribute our share to the store from which the Home-Tome of the War shall be made hereafter, by some loving and competent hand.

We have superadded Life Sketches of Ellsworth, Winthrop, Baker, Lyon—all offered up as sacrifices upon the altar of Liberty. May their memory ever be held dear! Also biographies of General Scott and General McClellan. Also concise but explicit accounts of those conflicts which stand forth in the History of the War as "representative" events.

CONTENTS.

INCIDENTS AND ANECDOTES OF THE WAR.

I.

THE AWAKENING.

April 19th, 1775, the blood of the Men of Massachusetts, the first martyrs in the cause of American Independence, was shed at Lexington.

April 19th, 1861, the blood of the Men of Massachusetts, the first martyrs in the cause of the American Union, was shed at Baltimore.

How the news flew over the land to arouse the already awakening vengeance of the Men of 1775! The blood of Lexington had not become dry ere the beacon-fires of alarm gleamed from the hills. While the young men flew to arms, the old men leaped into the saddle, to herald the tragedy and call the country to its defense. The message flew from lip to lip, from hill-top to hill-top, "until village repeated it to village; the sea to the backwoods; the plains to the highlands, and it was never suffered to droop till it had been borne North and South, and East and West throughout the land. It spread over the bays that receive the Saco and the Penobscot. Its loud reveille broke the rest of the trappers of New Hampshire, and ringing like bugle-notes from peak to peak, overleapt the Green Mountains, swept onward to Montreal, and descended the ocean river, till the responses were echoed from the cliff at Quebec. The hills along the Hudson told to one another the tale." The summons hurried to the South. In one day it was at New York; in one more at Philadelphia: then it flew to the South, to the West—was borne along the sea-coast to awaken the answering shout from bays, and sounds, and harbors—was hurried over the Alleghanies to awaken the note of response in the solemn wilds of the pathless West.

How sublimely did the men of that time respond to the call! The ferries over the Merrimac swarmed with the men of New Hampshire. Three days after that cry "*to arms!*" John Stark was on the Boston hills with his invincible battalion. From Connecticut came Putnam, the man of iron, riding his horse one hundred miles in eighteen hours, and gathering as he ran a troop of followers, each armed with a rifle as true in its aim as the heart of its owner was loyal to Freedom. Little Rhode Island had a thousand of her resolute and hardy sons before Boston ere the oppressor had retreated from his sacrifice at Concord, and Nathaniel Greene was Rhode Island's leader. Thirty thousand patriots in a few days hemmed in the city of Boston, where the British had taken up their defiant stand; and the tragedy of Bunker's Hill was soon enacted before her gates.

How all this sounds like the rush to arms in 1861! Sounds like it because the cause was the same—the defense of Constitutional Liberty and Inalienable Rights; because the loyal men of '61 were worthy sons of the sires of '75; while the enemy of '61 were the degenerate sons of their sires, bent upon the destruction of those institutions which the heart of Liberty and the hand of Freedom had built. It was a cause worthy of the devotion lavished upon it; and history will never tire of recording the generous deeds of those who answered the call for men to "suppress treasonable combinations and to cause the laws to be duly enforced."

The Diary of Events, from the fall of Sumter to May 1st, deserves to be preserved in every man's memory. The events were so extraordinary in themselves, the spirit in which the people acted was so astonishingly alive with devotion to the country and the sustenance of its laws, that another generation will study the story with amazement. As preliminary to our work, we may offer the record of that remarkable Awakening.

April 13th, 1861. The attack upon Fort Sumter, and its surrender, instead of depressing, fires and animates all patriotic hearts. One deep, strong, overpowering sentiment now sweeps over the whole community—a sentiment of determined, devoted, active loyalty. The day for the toleration of treason—treason to the Constitution! defiance to the laws that we have made!—has gone by. The people have discovered that what they deemed almost impossible, has actually come to pass, and that the rebels are determined to break up this Government, if they can do it. With all such purposes they are determined to make an end as speedily as may be.

—The Pennsylvania Legislature passed the war bill, last evening, without amendment. Previous to its passage the news of the bombardment of Fort Sumter was announced, and produced a profound sensation. The bill appropriates five hundred thousand dollars for the purpose of arming and equipping the militia; authorizes a temporary loan; provides for the appointment of an Adjutant-General, Commissary-General, and Quartermaster-General, who, with the Governor, are to have power to carry the act into effect.

April 15th. The President of the United States called by proclamation for 75,000 volunteers to suppress insurrectionary combinations; and commanded "the persons composing the combinations aforesaid to disperse and retire peaceably to their respective abodes within twenty days." In the same proclamation, an extra session of both Houses of Congress was called for the 4th of July.

—Large Union meetings were held at Detroit, Mich., Westchester and Pittsburgh, Pa., Lawrence, Mass., and Dover, N. H. At Pittsburgh the meeting was opened by the Mayor, who introduced the venerable William Wilkinson. Mr. Wilkinson was made President of the meeting. About twenty-five Vice-Presidents were also appointed. Resolutions were adopted, declaring undying fealty to the Union, approving the course of the Legislative and Executive branches of the State Government in responding to the call of the President, disregarding all partisan feeling, and pledging their lives, fortunes, and sacred honor in the defense of the Union, and appointing a Committee of Public Safety.

—Governor Yates, of Illinois, issued a proclamation to convene the Legislature at Springfield, on the 23d of April, for the purpose of enacting such laws and adopting such measures as may be deemed necessary upon the following subject, to wit: The more perfect organization and equipment of the militia of the State, and placing the same upon the best footing, to render efficient assistance to the General Government in preserving the Union, enforcing the laws, protecting the property and rights of the people, and also the raising of such money, and other means, as may be required to carry out the foregoing objects.

—At Philadelphia the Union pledge is receiving the signature of all classes of citizens. It responds to the President's proclamation, and declares an unalterable determination to sustain the Government, throwing aside all differences of political opinion.

—An excited crowd assembled this morning before the printing office on the corner of Fourth and Chestnut streets, where the *Palmetto Flag*, a small advertising sheet, is published, and threatened to demolish it. The proprietor displayed the American flag, and threw the objectionable papers from the windows—also, the *Stars and Stripes*, another paper printed at the same office, restoring the crowd to good-humor. The crowd moved down to the *Argus* office in Third street, opposite Dock street, ordering that the flag should be displayed.

—After visiting the newspaper offices and Government property, they marched in a body up Market street, bearing a flag. At all points on the route, well-known Union men were obliged to make all haste to borrow, beg, or steal something red, white, and blue, to protect their property with. Searches were made for the publication rooms of the *Southern Monitor;* but as that paper had suspended, the mob were unable to carry out their intention of destroying the forms. They satisfied themselves with breaking the signs to pieces. The ring-leaders were furnished with ropes, with which to hang the editor if caught.

2

During the afternoon, General Patterson's mansion, corner of Thirteenth and Locust streets, was mobbed and threatened with destruction. A servant answered their call, and unfortunately slammed the door in their faces. The crowd became uproarious and violent, and made an attempt to force open the door. General Patterson finally appeared at the window, bearing the colors of the regiment. The crowd then moved away. It is understood that General Patterson, who is charged with secessionism, intends throwing up his commission.

They then visited General Cadwallader, who made a Union speech and threw out a flag. Several prominent Southerners, with secession proclivities, including Robert Tyler, have received warnings from a so-called Vigilance Committee.

The following is the speech that was made by Mayor Henry to the excited mob which threatened the *Palmetto Flag* building:

"*Fellow Citizens:* By the grace of Almighty God, treason shall never rear its head or have a foothold in Philadelphia. [Immense cheering.] I call upon you as American citizens to stand by your flag and protect it at all hazards—at the point of the bayonet, if necessary; but, in doing so, remember the rights due your fellow-citizens and their private property. [Immense cheering.] That flag is an emblem of the Government, and I call upon all good citizens who love their country and its flag, to testify their loyalty by going to their respective places of abode, leaving to the constituted authorities of the city the task of protecting the peace, and preventing every act which could be construed into treason to their country." The Mayor then hoisted the Stars and Stripes.

—Seventeen vessels were seized in the port of New York from ports in southern States, their clearances being improper, and not signed by United States officers. They were fined $100 each, and some were held subject to forfeiture.

—Albany, New York, has presented an unwonted appearance all day to-day. The Capitol has been thronged with citizens who have apparently left their business to gather at head-quarters, and watch eagerly the progress of events. The spirit of the masses is decidedly aroused, and, from present indications, Albany will be behind no city in the State or Union in evincing her patriotism and her determination, as the crisis has come, to stand firmly by the Government of the country, without pausing to charge upon any the responsibility of the present terrible events.

—The Directors of the Bank of Commerce, of Providence, R. I., advanced a loan of $30,000 to the State, for aiding in the outfit of troops. Large offers from private citizens have also been made to Governor Sprague for a similar purpose. The Globe Bank tendered to the State a loan of $50,000.

—An enthusiastic Union meeting was held at Cleveland, Ohio. Speeches were made by Senator Wade, and other prominent gentlemen. Resolutions were adopted to sustain the Government, approving of the President's call for volunteers, recommending the Legislature to make appropriations of men and money, and appointing a committee to ascertain the efficiency of the Cleveland militia.

—Fernando Wood, Mayor of New York, issued a proclamation, calling upon the people of the city to avoid turbulence and excitement, and to rally to the restoration of the Constitution and Union.

—An immense Union meeting held in Troy, New York, adjourned in a body to the vicinity of General Wool's residence. In response to the patriotic address of the chairman, General Wool rejoiced at the glorious demonstration. Never before had he been filled with such a measure of joy. He had fought under the old flag, but had only done his duty. His appeal in behalf of his country's honor was very touching. "Will you," he said, "permit the Stars and Stripes to be desecrated and trampled in the dust by traitors now? Will you permit our noble Government to be destroyed by rebels, in order that they may advance their schemes of political ambition and extend the area of slavery? It cannot be done! The spirit of the age forbids. Humanity and manhood forbid it. The sentiment of the civilized world forbids it. That flag must be lifted from the dust and saved from sacrilege at the hands of apostates to truth, liberty, and honor. I pledge you my heart, my hand, my energies to the cause. The Union shall be maintained. I am prepared to devote my life to the work, and to lead you in the struggle."

—The Governor of Kentucky, in reply to Secretary Cameron's call for troops from that State, says: "Your dispatch is received. In answer, I say emphatically, Kentucky will furnish no troops for the wicked purpose of subduing her sister Southern States. B. MAGOFFIN."

—General visitation, by the populace, to newspaper offices in New York and several other cities. Newspapers regarded as of doubtful loyalty are compelled to run out the Stars and Stripes.

April 16th. A great Union meeting was held to-day at Tyrone, Pa. Ex-U. S. Senator Bigler expressed unequivocal sentiments of loyalty, and called upon the people to sustain the Government in the exercise of its energies to suppress rebellion.

—The Ringgold Flying Artillery, of Reading, Pa., Captain James McKnight, 180 men, with four field-pieces, received a requisition from the Governor this morning to set out this evening, at six o'clock, for Harrisburg, the place of rendezvous for the first Pennsylvanians in the field. Two military companies from Tyrone, two from Altoona, and two from Hollidaysburg, will leave to-morrow for Harrisburg.

—Four regiments, ordered to report for service in Boston, Mass., commenced arriving there before nine A. M. this morning, the companies first arriving not having received their orders until last night. Already about thirty companies have arrived, numbering over 1,700 men in uniform, and with these are several hundred who are importunate to be allowed to join the ranks.

—The City Government of Lawrence, Mass., appropriated $5,000 for the benefit of the families of those who have volunteered to defend the country's flag.

—Governor Buckingham, of Connecticut, issued a proclamation calling for volunteers, to rendezvous at Hartford.

—The Mechanics', Elm City, Fairfield County, Thames, and

other banks of Connecticut, voted large sums of money to assist in equipping the troops, and the support of their families.

—New Hampshire responds to the President's proclamation, and will furnish the troops required. The Concord Union Bank tendered a loan of $20,000 to the Governor, and all the Directors, with the Cashier, agree to contribute $100 each to the support of such families of the volunteers of Concord, as may fall in defending the flag of the country.

—The session of the New York East Methodist Conference was opened by the following prayer: "Grant, O God, that all the efforts now being made to overthrow rebellion in our distracted country, may be met with every success. Let the forces that have risen against our Government, and Thy law, be scattered to the winds, and may no enemies be allowed to prevail against us. Grant, O God, that those who have aimed at the very heart of the republic may be overthrown. We ask Thee to bring these men to destruction, and wipe them from the face of the country!"

—Governor Letcher, of Virginia, responds to the demand for troops: "I have only to say that *the militia of Virginia will not be furnished to the powers at Washington for any such use or purpose as they have in view.* Your object is to subjugate the Southern States, and a requisition made upon me for such an object—an object, in my judgment, not within the purview of the Constitution or the Act of 1795—will not be complied with. *You have chosen to inaugurate civil war, and, having done so, we will meet it in a spirit as determined as the Administration has exhibited towards the South.*"

—The Governor of North Carolina refused to comply with the call, expressing his doubts as to the President's authority to make the call. He, at the same date, made quick preparations to seize all Government property in the State, and to place the State on a footing of military efficiency.

—A large meeting of German workmen held in Newark, New Jersey. The Germans everywhere in the North evince a spirit of great devotion to the cause of the Union.

—General Cass, late Secretary of State, in a speech at Detroit, took the strongest ground for the Union. Every citizen, he declared, should stand by the Government.

—Great meetings are held to-day throughout the chief towns in the Western States. The people are represented as "all on fire,"—all parties "fusing" on the common ground of devotion to the Union. Intense enthusiasm prevails. A volunteer roll opened at Michigan City, Indiana, was first signed by a minister of the Gospel. The first company of Indiana Volunteers left Lafayette, to-day, for the rendezvous at Indianapolis. Over two hundred companies are represented as nearly formed in the State, ready for regimental organization. Illinois is not behind. Ohio has moved with alacrity. Captain McClellan will be made Major-General, to command the Ohio Volunteers.

—Virginia "seceded" to-day, and her Governor issued a proclamation acknowledging the Independence of the Southern Confederacy.

—Washington City is regarded as in great danger of seizure by the Secessionists of Virginia, aided by a mob of cut-throats from Baltimore. Colonel Ben McCullough is known to be chief of the organization for the seizure of the Capital. The Southern papers generally regard the seizure as certain, and it is proclaimed that the Davis Government will occupy the Capital. Great precautions are being taken by General Scott to guard the place. The city is under arms. Volunteer companies, comprising Members of Congress and Government employees, are organized, armed and on duty. The District militia is enrolled and in service, under command of Adjutant-General McDowell. Large numbers of Northern men, singly and in squads, are hurrying to the Capital to enlist in its defense. One entire battalion of Philadelphia troops reach the city—the first volunteers in the field.

—Jefferson Davis to-day issued his proclamation, initiating the privateer system.

April 18. Governor Harris, of Tennessee, replies to President Lincoln's call for two regiments of troops, by saying that "Tennessee will not furnish a single man for coercion, but fifty thousand, if necessary, for the defense of our rights, or those of our Southern brothers."

—Governor Jackson, of Missouri, answers Secretary Cameron by telling him that his "requisition is illegal, unconstitutional, revolutionary, inhuman, diabolical, and cannot be complied with."

—The Common Council of Boston appropriated $100,000 to provide for soldiers enlisting from Boston. The Lowell city government appropriated $8,000 for soldiers' families.

—The banks in Trenton, N. J., Chicago, Ill., Portland, Me., subscribed in support of the Federal Government. A meeting of the officers, representing all the Boston (Mass.) banks, was held this morning, when resolutions were adopted to loan the State of Massachusetts 10 per cent. on their entire capital for the defense of the Government. The capital of the Boston banks amounts to $38,800,000.

—At Pittsburg, Pa., an intense war feeling prevails. Business is almost suspended. Immense crowds throng all the prominent streets, flags are floating everywhere, and the volunteer companies are all filled and departing eastward. Liberal subscriptions are being made for the comfort of volunteers and the support of their families. Recruiting is still going on, although there are more than enough for the requirements of the State to fill the Federal requisition. A Committee of Public Safety held a meeting to-day, and organized. A large quantity of powder which had been sent down the river, was intercepted at Steubenville, it being feared it would fall into the hands of the Secessionists. Ropes were suspended to lamp-posts last night, by unknown persons, labelled "Death to traitors." Some assaults have been made on persons who have expressed sympathy with the Secessionists.

—Lieutenant R. Jones, of the United States army, in command at Harper's Ferry with forty-three men, destroyed the arsenal at that place and retreated. He was advised that a force of 2,500 men had been ordered to take his post, by Governor Letcher; and he put piles of powder in straw in all the buildings, and quietly awaited the approach of the enemy. When his picket-guard gave the alarm that 600 Virginians were approaching by the Winchester road, the men were run out of the arsenal and the combustibles fired. The people fired upon the soldiers, killing two, and rushed into the arsenal. All the works, munitions of war, and 15,000 stand of arms were destroyed.

—An intimation is given that the U. S. volunteers will be assailed, if any attempt is made to pass to Washington through Baltimore. The Baltimore *canaille* is being excited to a mob spirit by secession emissaries.

—The Sixth Massachusetts regiment pass through New York *en route* for Washington, *via* Baltimore.

—The Mayor of Baltimore and the Governor of Maryland unite in a proclamation, urging the people to preserve the peace. The Governor stated that no Maryland troops should be placed at the General Government's disposal, except for the defense of the Capital.

—An immense mass Union meeting was held in Louisville, this evening.

—Governor Morgan, of New York, issued his Proclamation for volunteers.

—Major Anderson and his command arrive in New York on the transport *Baltic*. They have an enthusiastic reception.

April 19. The President of the United States issues his Proclamation of Blockade of the ports in the rebellious States.

—A most important session of the New York Chamber of Commerce is held to-day. Perfect harmony prevailed. The Government was sustained, and a Committee of the leading capitalists appointed to insure the taking of nine millions of the Treasury loan yet on the market. The resolutions adopted fairly rung with decision and patriotism. As the Chamber represented over two hundred millions of dollars in actual reserve, the proceedings were regarded as of the highest importance. From that moment the men of wealth of the metropolis were almost unanimously committed to the policy of an overwhelming demonstration of the Government's power against its enemies.

—An American flag, forty by twenty feet, was run out on Trinity Church spire, New York. The church bells chimed national airs in honor of the occasion.

—An attack is made, by the Baltimore ruffians, on the Massachusetts Sixth and the Pennsylvania Seventh regiments, which were passing through the city *en route* for Washington. The Massachusetts men occupied eleven cars. Nine cars succeeded in reaching the Washington depot: the other two were cut off by the mob, when their troops alighted, formed a solid square, and, preceded by the Mayor and police, marched up Pratt street for the depot. Brickbats, stones, and pieces of iron were hurled at the troops, but, obeying orders, they withheld any demonstration against their assailants, notwithstanding several of the men were seriously injured. This leniency only served to inflame the mob to further violence. Attempts were made to seize the muskets of the men, and a pistol-shot from a window killed one of the soldiers. The ruffian who committed the deed was immediately shot by one of the soldiers. An immediate passage of shots followed—the solid square, with fixed bayonets, led by the Mayor, still pressing on to the depot, bearing their wounded and dead in their centre. The depot was at length reached, when it was found that two of the Massachusetts men were killed and eight wounded—one mortally. Eleven of the mob were killed and thirteen wounded. This affair so fearfully excited the people of Baltimore that, for several days, the mob virtually reigned uncontrolled, overawing the Mayor and Governor, and finding coadjutors in the Chief of Police and the Police Board. The Chief of Police sped a dispatch and sent runners over the country to hurry forward the secession emissaries to "drive back the Northern invaders." His dispatch, soon brought to light, proved the fellow to be one of the secret agents of the traitors.

—The Pennsylvania troops arrived in Baltimore a few minutes after the Massachusetts men, and remained at the

Philadelphia depot to await the issue of the attempt to pass. The mob fell back, after the tragedy in Pratt street, upon the Pennsylvanians, who were entirely unarmed. They gathered in the depot, and soon orders came from the city authorities and the Governor for the railway company to return the troops to the State line—an order soon obeyed.

—In view of the state of feeling at Baltimore, the Mayor and Governor united in a commission to the President to represent that no more troops could pass through their city unless they fought their way. The President decided to spare the effusion of blood by ordering the regiments to march around the city. The route by way of Perryville and Annapolis was soon opened by General Butler, with the Massachusetts Eighth, assisted by the New York Seventh.

—The entire North was fearfully excited by the news of the attack on the Massachusetts men. It only served to intensify the antagonisms existing. It was so potent in exciting the public that every recruiting rendezvous in the North was literally overrun with applicants for positions in the ranks. It is estimated that more men offered in Pennsylvania than would fill the entire requisition of April 15th.

—Governor Andrew, of Massachusetts, sent the following dispatch to Mayor Brown: "I pray you, cause the bodies of our Massachusetts soldiers, dead in battle, to be immediately laid out, preserved in ice, and tenderly sent forward by express to me. All expenses will be paid by this Commonwealth." This was complied with, and the Mayor wrote apologetically for that sad occurrence.

—The City Council of Philadelphia, at a special meeting, appropriated $1,000,000 to equip the volunteers and support their families during their absence from home. Fourteen thousand dollars were subscribed for the same purpose at Norwich, Conn.

—The Seventh regiment, N. Y. S. M., left for Washington at noon, amid the wildest enthusiasm. An innumerable throng cheered them on their way. News of the assault in Baltimore was received before they left, when forty-eight rounds of ball-cartridge were served out.

—The Rhode Island Marine artillery followed the Seventh. This superb battery reflected great credit on the State and its Governor. It was composed of 130 men, 110 horses, eight splendid field-pieces and all requisite accessories. The commander, Colonel Tomkins, was eager to open the route through Baltimore.

—The Massachusetts Eighth followed the Rhode Islanders. It was accompanied by Brigadier-General B. F. Butler, in general command of the Massachusetts forces.

—Anticipating the descent of the forces now gathered at Philadelphia, the Baltimore mob proceeded to Canton station, on the Philadelphia railway, and, stopping the evening train, compelled the passengers all to leave it. The engineer was then made to run the mob up to the Gunpowder bridge—a fine structure over Gunpowder Creek. The draw and shore sections of the bridge were burned. The train then returned to Bush River bridge, which was also burned. Then the Canton bridge was fired and consumed. After the work of destruction the mob returned to Baltimore, on the train, and were received with acclamations.

—Stupendous mass meeting of the people of New York City, called by citizens of all parties and religious denominations, to express sympathy with the Government. The entire demonstration was harmonious and satisfactory, and resulted in great good to the common cause. It is estimated that one hundred thousand people, directly or indirectly, participated in the proceedings. The "Union Defense Committee"—composed of twenty-six of the most wealthy and prominent men of the city [the number afterwards was increased to thirty-two,] grew out of the great gathering. Its business was to collect and disburse funds for arming, equipping, and placing in the field the New York City regiments—to care for the families of the volunteers—to co-operate with Government in whatever would tend to strengthen the National cause. It was one of the most beneficent and effective organizations of the war. Besides the large private subscriptions placed at its disposal, the City Government voted one million of dollars, to be expended under the Committee's direction.

—The Gosport (Norfolk) Navy-yard destroyed during the night of April 19–20. Government property to the amount of over eleven millions of dollars was committed to the flames and the water, "to keep it," as the officer in charge, Commander McAuley said, "from falling into the hands of the revolutionists"—then in considerable force at Norfolk, under command of General Taliaferro. Commodore Paulding sailed in, on the *Pawnee*, at eight P. M., (April 19th,) to find the *Merrimac* steam frigate disabled, the *Germantown*, *Raritan*, *Pennsylvania*, *Plymouth*, and other vessels either scuttled or given up to the flames. The *Cumberland* frigate alone, of all that fine fleet, was saved by the accidental presence of the *Yankee*, steam-tug, owned by William B. Astor, of New York, and sent out by him "to be of some service to Government somewhere." The buildings, timber, two thousand pieces of ordnance (of all sizes, from the heavy Columbiad and Dahlgren to the boat howitzer,) small-arms, stocks, shears, machinery—all were offered up, a holocaust to rebellion and James Buchanan's want of foresight and courage. Neither is the administration of Mr. Lincoln blameless, for it should have taken all the movable property away, under the guns of the very frigates which were committed to the flames and waves. Viewed in every aspect, it was a most wretched affair.

—At a second great Union meeting in Chicago, during the proceedings, at the suggestion of Judge Manniere, the entire audience raised their right hands and took the oath of allegiance to the United States Government—repeating the oath after the Judge.

—Orders were issued by the officers of the Western Union, and the New York, Albany and Buffalo Telegraphic Companies, that no messages be received ordering arms or munitions of war, unless for the use of the General Government.

April 20th. Governor Curtin, of Pennsylvania, convenes the Legislature of his State for the 30th of April, "to take into consideration and to adopt such measures as the present emergencies may demand."

—A letter was received at Philadelphia from Governor

Letcher, of Virginia, offering $30,000 to the patentee of the bullet-mould. The reply was, "No money can purchase it against the country."

—The Council of Wilmington, Del., appropriated $8,000 to defend the city, and passed resolutions approving of the President's proclamation. Also, asking the Governor to issue a proclamation for the same purpose. The Brandywine bridges and all on the road between Susquehanna and Philadelphia are guarded, and workmen have been sent to repair the bridges destroyed on the Northern Central road.

—The Missourians seized the United States arsenal, at Liberty, Mo., and garrisoned it with 100 men. In the arsenal were 1,300 stand of arms, ten or twelve pieces of cannon, and quite an amount of powder.

—Two thousand stand of arms were furnished the citizens of Leavenworth, from the arsenal at Fort Leavenworth, and the commander of that post accepted the services of 300 volunteers, to guard the arsenal, pending the arrival of troops from Fort Kearney.

—The Federal Government takes possession of the railway between Philadelphia and Baltimore.

—General Scott telegraphed to John J. Crittenden, of Kentucky, who had questioned him by telegraph as to the truth of the report that he had resolved to desert the Federal cause: "I have not changed; have no thought of change; always a Union man."

April 21st. The Mayor of Baltimore had an interview with the President, to try and persuade him not to order any more troops through Maryland.

—Arrival in New York of the Third battalion of Massachusetts rifles, Major Devens commanding.

—An immense mass meeting in Boston (it being Sunday) was held preparatory to raising a choice regiment for Fletcher Webster (son of Daniel Webster). It became a popular ovation before its close. A large number of the leading citizens addressed the crowd throughout the day.

—The First Rhode Island regiment passed through New

York, *en route* for Washington, by way of Annapolis. It sailed from New York this (Sunday) evening, in company with the New York Sixth, Twelfth, and Seventy-first regiments of militia. The crowd was dense in the streets, during the entire day, to witness the embarkation of the regiments on the transports. The incidents of this day in New York we advert to in a succeeding chapter.

—The North Carolinians seized the United States Branch Mint, at Charlotte, in that State.

—Great gatherings in all the churches throughout the North, to hear "Sermons on the Crisis." Some most remarkable demonstrations were witnessed. In Henry Ward Beecher's church, at Brooklyn, a communication was read from the Thirteenth regiment of New York militia, asking for help in uniforming and equipping them for service. Over $1,100 were forthwith contributed. In the city of New York patriotism was the theme of discourse. In the Broadway Tabernacle, the pastor, Rev. J. P. Thompson, D. D., preached a sermon in the evening on "God's Time of Threshing." The choir performed "The Marseillaise" to a hymn composed for the occasion by the pastor. A collection was taken for the Volunteers' Home Fund, amounting to $450—to which a member of the congregation afterwards added $100. Dr. Bethune's sermon was from the text: "In the name of our God we will set up our banners." In Dr. Bellows' church, the choir sang "The Star Spangled Banner," which was vigorously applauded by the whole house. At Grace Church, (Episcopal,) Dr. Taylor began by saying, "The Star Spangled Banner has been insulted." The gallant Major Anderson and his wife attended service at Trinity. At Dr. McLane's Presbyterian Church, Williamsburg, "The Star Spangled Banner" was sung. Dr. T. D. Wells (Old School Presbyterian) preached from the words: "He that hath no sword, let him buy one." Dr. Osgood's text was: "Lift up a standard to the people." The religious world certainly never before witnessed such an invasion of the pulpit. Great numbers of churches were organizing companies, and one pastor, Rev. Dr. Perry, of Brooklyn, assumed command of a regiment.

—The American flag was publicly buried at Memphis, Tenn., on this day, amid a great concourse of citizens. The funeral rites were read, and a volley fired over the grave.

April 22d. Great pressure brought to bear on the President to procure some countermand of the order for troops to march to Washington. One delegation of thirty, from five "Young Men's Christian Associations" of Baltimore, had a prolonged interview, but made no impression upon him. Governor Hicks approached him with a communication, again urging the withdrawal of troops from Maryland, a cessation of hostilities, and a reference of the National dispute to the arbitrament of Lord Lyons. To this the Secretary of State replied, that the troops were only called out to suppress insurrection, and *must* come through Baltimore, as that was the route chosen for them by the Commander-in-Chief, and that our troubles could not be "referred to *any* foreign arbitrament."

—Colonel Robert E. Lee, late of the U. S. Army, is named by the Governor of Virginia Commander-in-Chief of the forces of that State.

—The U. S. arsenal at Fayetteville, N. C., is seized by the orders of Governor Ellis. The Governor, at the same date, called out 30,000 troops, in addition to the organized militia, to be in readiness at a moment's notice.

—The N. Y. city Common Council appropriated one million of dollars for equipping and caring for the comfort of volunteers.

—The N. Y. Twenty-fifth militia regiment arrived in the city from Albany, *en route* for Washington.

—The N. Y. Seventh and Massachusetts Eighth regiments arrive, by transports from Philadelphia, at Annapolis, where they land and seize the railway to Washington. The troops of the Eighth seized the frigate *Constitution*—"Old Ironsides," which was in danger of capture by the Secessionists. General Butler, in his order congratulating the men on the safety of the old frigate, said: "The frigate *Constitution* has lain for a long time at this port substantially at the mercy of the armed mob which sometimes paralyzes the otherwise loyal State of Maryland. Deeds of daring, successful contests, and glorious victories, had rendered Old Ironsides so conspicuous in the naval history of the country, that she was fitly chosen as the school in which to train the future officers of the navy to like heroic acts. It was given to Massachusetts and Essex county first to man her; it was reserved to Massachusetts to have the honor to retain her for the service of the Union and the laws."

—The Secretary of War conveys to Major Anderson the approval of the Executive of his conduct in the defense of Fort Sumter, viz.:

"WAR DEPARTMENT, WASHINGTON,
April 23d, 1861.

"*Major Robert Anderson, late Commanding Officer at Fort Sumter:*

"MY DEAR SIR: I am directed by the President of the United States, to communicate to you, and through you to the officers and men under your command at Forts Moultrie and Sumter, the approbation of the Government of your and their judicious and gallant conduct there; and to tender to you and them the thanks of the Government for the same.

"I am, very respectfully,

"SIMON CAMERON, Secretary of War."

—Father Rafina, priest of the Montrose Avenue Catholic Church, Williamsburg, N. Y., with his own hands raised the American flag upon the top of his church. The ceremony was witnessed by at least two thousand people, who greeted the glorious emblem with cheer after cheer, as it waved majestically over the sacred edifice. The reverend father addressed the assemblage in a few appropriate remarks, which were received with marked enthusiasm.

—The Charleston *Mercury* flings defiance at the North—calling Lincoln a usurper, and saying: "he will deplore the 'higher-law' depravity which has governed his counsels. Seeking the sword, in spite of all moral or constitutional restraints and obligations, he may perish by the sword. He sleeps already with soldiers at his gate, and the grand reception-room of the White House is converted into quarters for troops from Kansas—border ruffians of Abolitionism."

—A fine Union meeting was held in Lexington, Kentucky. The Stars and Stripes were raised; the people generally expressed their determination to adhere to them to the last. Speeches were made by Messrs. Field, Crittenden, Codey, and others. The most unbounded enthusiasm prevailed, and the speakers were greeted with great applause.

April 23d. The feeling in the South at this date may be inferred from the call of the Governor of Louisiana for troops. He said: "The Government at Washington, maddened by defeat and the successful maintenance by our patriotic people of their rights and liberties against its mercenaries in the harbor of Charleston, and the determination of the Southern people forever to sever themselves from the Northern Government, has now thrown off the mask, and, sustained by the people of the non-slaveholding States, is actively engaged in levying war, by land and sea, to subvert your liberties, destroy your rights, and to shed your blood on your own soil. If you have the manhood to resist, rise, then, pride of Louisiana, in your might, in defense of your dearest rights, and drive back this insolent, barbaric force. Like your brave ancestry, resolve to conquer or perish in the effort; and the flag of usurpation will never fly over Southern soil. Rally, then, to the proclamation which I now make on the requisition of the Confederate Government." The enthusiasm in the South was represented as equal to that prevailing in the North. The contest was regarded as a war of sections, and the South seemed to entertain no other idea but that of the complete defeat of the North. The idea generally prevailed that a Southern soldier was equal to five Northern "hirelings." The terms used to characterize the Northern soldiers were very offensive, and the idea seemed to prevail that the army of Federal volunteers was composed of the very lowest scum of society. As Northern papers could not circulate in the South, the people really never knew better, until they learned at the bayonet's point.

—The Western Pennsylvania regiments pass through Philadelphia, *en route* for Washington, by way of Annapolis.

—The Eighth, Sixty-ninth, and Thirteenth regiments of New York militia start for Washington.

—Sherman's celebrated battery, consisting of ninety men and eight howitzers, passed through Philadelphia, Pa., on the route to Washington. The train containing the troops stopped in Market street, between Fifteenth and Sixteenth. Immediately the ladies of Benton street rushed out, and vied with each other in their attention to the weary soldiers. Bread, meat, pies, and cakes, were brought forward in goodly supplies, hundreds of girls running with hot dinners just from the ranges; bakers with baskets of bread and cakes; fruiterers with baskets of apples, oranges, etc., were quickly upon the ground. The men said that they were thirsty, and in a trice there were a dozen pretty girls handing up cups of water. After the battery had been thus refreshed, a collection was taken up, and the soldiers were supplied with enough cigars and tobacco to last for some days. The military cheered continually for the ladies of Philadelphia, and, as the train moved off, they gave nine hearty cheers for Philadelphia, the Union, the Constitution, and the success of the Federal arms in the South.

April 24th. The New York Twenty-fifth regiment of militia sailed for Washington.

—An immense Union meeting was held in Detroit, over which General Cass presided. His speech was brief, but strongly loyal. He called upon all citizens to stand by the Administration.

—The Faculty and students of the Brown High School, at Newburyport, Mass., raised the American flag near their school building, in presence of a large concourse of citizens. Patriotic speeches were made by Caleb Cushing, and others.

April 25th. General Harney, on his way to Washington, was arrested by the Virginia authorities, at Harper's Ferry. He left Wheeling, Virginia, for the purpose of reporting himself at head-quarters at Washington. Before the train reached Harper's Ferry it was stopped, and a number of troops mounted the platforms; while the train was moving slowly on, the troops passed through the cars, and the General being pointed out, he was immediately taken into custody.

—A deputation of twenty Indians, headed by White Cloud, in behalf of the Sioux and Chippewas, arrived in New York. They tender to the United States, in behalf of themselves and three hundred other warriors, their services against rebellion. Having heard that the Cherokees had sided with the rebels, they could not remain neutral, and, with a promptness worthy of imitation in high quarters, have come to offer their services in defense of the Government. They ask to be armed and led.

—A second detachment of Rhode Islanders arrived in New York, bound for Washington. The New York *Herald* said: "As a proof of the patriotic spirit which animates the citizens of Rhode Island, it may be mentioned that a man named William Dean, who lost one arm in the Mexican war, is now a volunteer in this corps, being willing to lose another limb in defense of the honor of his country. The noble fellow carries his musket slung behind his back, but it is said when the hour comes for bloodier action he can use it with as good effect and expertness as if in possession of his natural appendages. The regiment also carries a flag which was borne through all the terrors of the Revolution. The uniform of the regiment is light and comfortable; it consists of a blue flannel blouse, gray pants, and the army regulation hat. The volunteers bring along with them two very prepossessing young women, named Martha Francis and Katey Brownell, both of Providence, who propose to act as 'daughters of the regiment,' after the French plan."

—The N. Y. Seventh arrived at Washington to-day, and were welcomed with great demonstrations of joy. They were the first regiment to reach the Capital after the Massachusetts Sixth. The Massachusetts Eighth almost immediately followed the Seventh into the city. With these troops Washington was pronounced safe. From this date troops constantly poured into the Capital, by the Annapolis route. The route by Baltimore and the Northern Central railroad was not opened until May 13th.

—Virginia transferred to the Southern Confederacy, by treaty between the State Convention and Mr. Stephens, Vice-President of the Confederate States. By this transaction the people were literally "sold out of house and home."

April 26th. A correspondent of a Boston journal, writing from the West, over which he was travelling, said of the feeling prevailing in that section: "The enthusiasm of the people at the West, in rallying for the defense of the Union, far exceeds the expectations of the most sanguine. Throughout the entire North-west there is a perfect unanimity of sentiment. Ten days ago, men who now cry, down with the rebels, were apologizing for the South—justifying its action, and wishing it success. Every town in Illinois is mustering soldiers, and many of the towns of five or six thousand inhabitants, have two and three companies ready for action. Companies are also formed for drill, so that, in case of need, they will be prepared to march at any moment. Money is poured out freely as water, and ladies unite in making shirts, blankets, and even coats and pants for the soldiers. Arrangements have been made to take care of the families of the soldiers during their absence. All say, none shall fight the battles of their country at their own expense."

—The bridges over Gunpowder River, on the Philadelphia, Wilmington, and Baltimore Railroad, were burned by the rebels of Baltimore. The bridge over Bush River, on the same route, had been destroyed the evening previous. The mob still reigned in Baltimore, although the loyal press of the city represented that the "conservative" sentiment was growing.

—The Seventh regiment of New York took the oath to support the Constitution of the United States, at the War Department, in Washington, to-day. Not a man hesitated. The scene was most impressive.

—Many Southern men, still in the employ of the Departments, at Washington, refused to take the oath of allegiance. They all "resigned" and took their way South to give their services to the Slave States.

April 27th. Great numbers of Virginians whose loyalty to the Constitution forbade them to sustain the high-handed tyranny of the State Convention, are passing North to escape persecution. The outrages perpetrated on the Unionists of that State are daily becoming more atrocious. The State is in possession of the Confederate forces, and the Secession cut-throats have it all their own way. The mob everywhere appropriate to their own use whatever they may fancy; farmers are stopped on the road, their horses taken from them under the plea that they are for the defense of the South; granaries are searched, and everything convertible for food for either man or beast, carried off. This has been practiced to such an extent that, along the northern border of Virginia, a reaction is taking place, and instructions are being sent from Western Maryland, to the Delegates at Annapolis, that if they vote for secession the people will hang them on their return home. The news of the unanimous sentiment of the North, the prompt and decisive action on the part of the State Governments in enlisting men, has strengthened the Union men of Western Maryland and the border counties of Virginia.

—The "New York Ladies' Relief Union"—one of the organizations devised for centralizing the efforts of women in behalf of the Union cause—issue, to-day, their circular, setting forth the "importance of systematizing the earnest efforts now making by the women of New York for the supply of extra medical aid to the Federal army, through the present campaign."

—Mr. Lincoln issues his supplementary proclamation, including the coasts of Virginia and North Carolina in the order of blockade.

April 28th. The *Daylight*, the first steamer direct from New York, *via* Potomac, reached Washington at ten A. M. Many lights were out on the Virginia coast, and many buoys had been destroyed by the rebels. The *Daylight* came without convoy. She had no guns, except one howitzer, which Captain Viele obtained from the *Pocahontas*, at the mouth of the Potomac. Captain Viele and the one hundred and seventy two recruits for the New York Seventh regiment, have the honor of the first passage up the Potomac.

—The New York Fifth regiment of militia leaves to-day for Annapolis, in the British steam transport *Kedar*. This regiment, commanded by Colonel Schwartzwaelder, is composed almost entirely of Germans.

April 29th. B. F. Hallett, of Boston, a leading man in the opposition party of Massachusetts, comes out strongly for the war, at a meeting of the Suffolk bar.

—Great excitement in Tennessee, consequent on the seizure (April 26th) at Cairo, by the Federal forces, of the steamer *Hillman*, laden with munitions of war. Governor Harris orders $75,000 in Tennessee bonds, and $5,000 in coin—all in possession of the United States Collector at Nashville, to be seized as a reprisal.

—Grand military review in New Orleans, of troops prepared to march North. Thirty thousand people turned out to witness the pageant.

—Ellsworth's Fire Zouaves left New York for Annapolis. A grand demonstration was made by the New York city fire department in honor of their departure. One hundred thousand people were gathered in the route of their march to witness the proceedings.

April 30th. Persons from the South, residing in Washington, are warned to leave that city before its destruction by the Southern army.

—The School-teachers of the Boston, Mass., schools, relinquished a large portion of their salaries, to be applied, during the war, to patriotic purposes.

—The New York Yacht Club offer the Government the use of all their craft for any service for which they may be fitted.

—Governor Dennison, of Ohio, reports that, up to this date, 71,000 volunteers had offered to meet the President's requisition for thirteen regiments. All regiments furnished by the State, are picked men. The same may be said of the offers made in other States. It is now known that an army of three hundred thousand men could be made up of volunteers from New York, Pennsylvania and Ohio alone.

Every church and public building in New York, Philadelphia and Boston, is surmounted by the American flag. Public buildings generally throughout the North are thus decorated. The demand for bunting is so great, that the supply is exhausted, and flags are being made out of all kinds of materials of the proper color.

—The Twenty-eighth regiment of New York militia leaves Brooklyn for the seat of war. It is composed of the best class of German citizens—many men of wealth being in the ranks. It is commanded by Colonel Burnett. The streets were thronged to witness its departure.

—The Harvard University Medical School adopt a resolution, viz.: "That we, the members of the Harvard Medical School, do here and now resolve ourselves into a volunteer medical corps, and as such do hereby tender our services to the Governor of this Commonwealth, to act in behalf of this State or country, in whatever capacity we may be needed.

—The contributions of cities, individuals, Legislatures, banks, etc., up to this date, to the patriotic fund, are estimated to exceed twenty-eight millions of dollars. Government finds its soldiers literally made to order—taking the field armed and equipped, through the patronage and care of the localities from which the companies and regiments came.

This will end our Diary of Events, occurring in the brief space of fifteen days. What a record! The world never read its like. It will be read by our descendants with astonishment. Let us preserve the memory of these days to inspire our ardor, to strengthen our faith, to deepen our love for the Union, the Constitution and the Laws!

II.

THE NEW NATION.

MEN awakened on the morning of April 14th to enter upon the New Era of the Republic. The hour of trial had come. The people of the North were to say if the Union should survive or perish—if the "Great Democratic Experiment" should ignominiously fail, or should assert its true nobility by showing a consolidated front to revolution and disorganization. The guns which opened upon Sumter were aimed at the National heart, which the fortress typified in its silent grandeur as it lay away off in the waters, not to be awakened until assailed. Would the Nation protect its heart? It needed only such an assault to send the blood bounding through every loyal bosom; and the cry "TO ARMS!" which flew over the land, answered for the people. Rent into factions, divided in sentiment, antagonistic in personal interests, absorbed in schemes of gain, they had seemingly lived at open variance. As "Republicans," "Democrats," "Unionists," "Conservatives," "Abolitionists," "Pro-Slavery" and "Anti-Slavery" Extensionists, they had harbored bitter differences; but, these all melted away in that night when Major Anderson slept in his battered fortress, defeated in the defense of his assailed flag; and the people awoke on the morning of Sumter's evacuation to a new life—the New Nation was born. All partisan differences, all local antipathies, all personal dislikes, were buried, and over their grave arose the resurrected patriotism which had too long slumbered. Sumter lost but Freedom won when the madmen put the Union on its trial.

We cannot better convey an idea of the astonishing change

that came over the people than to recur to the utterances of the press chronicling the events of those hours, so potent with great results to the country.

The New York *Herald*, up to the hour of Sumter's bombardment, was inimical to the Administration, and strongly in favor of concessions to the South. After that event, its right hand of fellowship was withdrawn, and, with the common sentiment of the North, it declared for a vigorous policy against the revolutionists, saying: "Whatever opinions may have prevailed, and whatever views of expediency may have been advocated, hitherto, there is clearly no other course for Government to pursue now, than to 'retake the places and properties' that have been seized and occupied, in the Southern States. Upon this point, the people of the Northern and Western States will be nearly a unit. As a consequence, past organizations and platforms are virtually swept away, and none of the issues remain of present importance which recently agitated the public mind. * * The time for undue excitement has passed. The passing events of each hour are so solemn, that every pulse should beat equably, and every aspiration be for a speedy restoration of the Republic to peace, and its pristine unity and greatness. The utmost unanimity of feeling should prevail in sustaining the only policy which is any longer practicable; and every nerve should be strained to aid the Government in rendering its measures as efficient as possible."

The Boston *Post*, the organ of the Breckenridge Democracy, sent forth this clarion call: "The uprising is tremendous; and well would it be for each good citizen, South and North, to feel this invasion of the public order at Fort Sumter as his own personal concern. In reality it is so. There is left no choice but between a support of the Government and anarchy! The rising shows that this is the feeling. The Proclamation calls for seventy-five thousand men; and from one State alone, Pennsylvania, a hundred thousand are at the President's command at forty-eight hours' notice! Nor is this all. Capitalists stand ready to tender millions upon millions of money to sustain the grand Government of the Fathers. Thus the civilized world will see the mighty energy of a free people, supplying in full measure the sinews of war, men and money, out of loyalty to the supremacy of law. Patriotic citizen! choose you which you will serve, the world's best hope, our noble Republican Government, or that bottomless pit, social anarchy. Adjourn other issues until this self-preserving issue is settled."

The Philadelphia *Inquirer* (Opposition) spoke as well. It said: "'Take your places in line.' The American flag trails in the dust. There is from this hour no longer any middle or neutral ground to occupy. All party lines cease. Democrats, Whigs, Americans, Republicans and Union men, all merge into one or two parties—patriots or traitors. For ourselves, we are not prepared for either or any form of government which the imagination might suggest as possible or probable to follow in the wake of a republic. We are for the Government as handed down to us by our fathers. It was consecrated in blood, and given to us as a sacred legacy. It is ours to live by, and, by the blessing of God, it shall be ours to die by. We will have it and none other. We have no political feuds or animosities to avenge; we know no cause save to wipe an insult from our flag, and to defend and maintain an assailed Government and a violated Constitution. We care not who is President, or what political party is in power; so long as they support the honor and the flag of our country, we are with them; those who are not, are against us—against our flag—and against our Government. 'Take your places in line!'"

The New York *Times* correctly stated the facts and hopes of the hour in its issue of April 16th. It said: "The incidents of the last two days will live in history. Not for fifty years has such a spectacle been seen, as that glorious uprising of American loyalty which greeted the news that open war had been commenced upon the Constitution and Government of the United States. The great heart of the American people beat with one high pulsation of courage, and of fervid love and devotion to the great Republic. Party dissensions were instantly hushed; political differences disappeared, and were as thoroughly forgotten as if they had never existed; party bonds flashed into nothingness in the glowing flame of patriotism; men ceased to think of themselves or their parties—they thought only of their country and of the dangers which menaced its existence. Nothing for years has brought the hearts of all the people so close together, or so inspired them all with common hopes, and common fears, and a common aim, as the bombardment and surrender of an American fortress.

"We look upon this sublime outburst of public sentiment as the most perfect vindication of popular institutions—the most conclusive reply to the impugners of American loyalty, the country has ever seen. It has been quite common to say that such a Republic as ours could never be permanent, because it lacked the conditions of a profound and abiding loyalty. The Government could never inspire a patriotic instinct, fervid enough to melt the bonds of party, or powerful enough to override the selfishness which free institutions so rapidly develop. The hearts of our own people had begun to sink within them, at the apparent insensibility of the public, to the dangers which menaced the Government. The public mind seemed to have been demoralized—the public heart seemed insensible to perils which threatened utter extinction to our great Republic. The secession movement, infinitely the most formidable danger which has ever menaced our Government, was regarded with indifference, and treated as merely a novel form of our usual political contentions. The best among us began to despair of a country which seemed incompetent to understand its dangers, and indifferent to its own destruction.

"But all this is changed. The cannon which bombarded Sumter awoke strange echoes, and touched forgotten chords in the American heart. American Loyalty leaped into instant life, and stood radiant and ready for the fierce encounter. From one end of the land to the other—in the crowded streets of cities, and in the solitude of the country—wherever the splendor of the Stars and Stripes, the glittering emblems of our country's glory, meets the eye, come forth shouts of devotion and pledges of aid, which give sure guarantees for the perpetuity of American Freedom. War can inflict no scars on such a people. It can do them no damage which time cannot repair. It cannot shake the solid foundations of their material prosperity—while it will strengthen the manly and heroic virtues, which defy its fierce and frowning front.

"It is a mistake to suppose that war—even Civil War—is the greatest evil that can afflict a nation. The proudest and noblest nations on the earth have the oftenest felt its fury, and have risen the stronger, because the braver, from its overwhelming wrath. War is a far less evil than degradation—than the national and social paralysis which can neither feel a wound nor redress a wrong. When War becomes the only means of sustaining a nation's honor, and of vindicating its just and rightful supremacy, it ceases to be an evil, and becomes the source of actual and positive good. If we are doomed to assert the rightful supremacy of our Constitution by force of arms, against those who would overthrow and destroy it, we shall grow the stronger and the nobler by the very contest we are compelled to wage.

"We have reason to exult in the noble demonstration of American loyalty, which the events of the last few days have called forth from every quarter of the country. Millions of freemen rally with exulting hearts, around our country's standard. The great body of our people have but one heart and one purpose in this great crisis of our history. Whatever may be the character of the contest, we have no fears or misgivings as to the final issue."

Particularly referring to the unanimity of the political leaders in support of the Administration, the New York *Courier and Inquirer* of May 2d, said: "We have all witnessed the sudden transformation of the scene-painter's art—a whistle, a creak of a wheel, and in place of a cottage, a palace!—a sighing maiden is followed by an exultant conqueror; and seeing these delusions of the canvas, we have accustomed ourselves to look upon it as a trick of the drama, and never in our experience to be paralleled by the actual. We are to see all strange things in the nineteenth century, and of the very strangest is the sudden change of a Northern people from a race of quiet, patient, much-enduring, calm, 'consistent members of the Peace Society,' willing to compromise to the last possible interpolation of the Constitution, to a gathering of armed men, backing up courage by cash, and coming together with a union of the purse and the sword, which is to be one of the most remarkable chapters that history ever wrote.

"The Macaulay of American annals will record that in one brief, earnest, intense ten of days, the chain of party melted; the organization of party shivered; the leaders of opposing opinions were as brethren;—Seward, Douglas, Dix, even Caleb Cushing, wrote a full acquittance of past political strife, and declared that the life of their political doctrine was the preservation of the country's honor. Who shall ever despair of a nation after this? If from our quarrels, our pale compromises, our bondage to the exchange and to the warehouse, from all the indolence of prosperity, such a transformation to the camp of a brave and united soldiery, a close and compact counsel—the purse inverted over the soldier's needs—the struggle who shall quickest forget his party watch-word, and learn that of the line of battle—if this new life has thus sprung, the philosopher of history must learn of us new ideas of the power of a free people.

"The Revolution of 1776 witnessed no such union. More families left New York and her sister colonies, because they would not show steel to King George, (and that when New York had population only of thousands where it now has hundreds of thousands,) than have now suggested doubts of our right from all the vast numbers of the Northern States. We cannot even yet realize the change these ten days have wrought. We are like those who bring all their valuables to the fire of the furnace, and recast the compound. That process is now in our midst. Does any man suppose we are to be fused in just such party shape again? Differ we shall—but the gold has been tried, and the great fact established, that those dwelling in the Northern States have that devotion to the country at whose call the mother gives her son to the battle, the capitalist his treasure to the cause, and men blend as a *Nation*. Were we ever a Nation before?

"All lineages—the Mayflower man is in the front rank only to be met in line by those who look back to Delft Haven. I have found the warmest thought and act in those who but a month since were doubtful of the patriotism of those of us who could not see the merit of 'compromise.' The voice of Edward Everett rings out its call to arms—the men who have risked to offend the North by their ultra Southern views, have thrown all aside as the call for Union for the country's honor reached them."

Thus it was that the New Nation sprang into existence, to redeem the past and plant anew the tree of Liberty and Union, which the conspirators had so nearly torn up and shattered.

III.

THE MUSTERING.

Who shall tell the story of the gathering of those who flew to arms at the call? Every company of those first forward has its chapter of incidents honorable to its patriotic devotion and creditable to its intelligence. Every regiment has its record of patriotism and self-sacrifice, for in its ranks stood those whom no mercenary motive had impelled to arms. Doctors, lawyers, merchants, students, mechanics, were there—all deserting business and home to encounter the toils, privations, sufferings, and dangers of military service. The Massachusetts, New York, and Rhode Island militia regiments which were first ready, and, in a few days, were on the way to Washington, were composed almost entirely of citizens of the most respectable character—men, whose intelligence and social standing rendered them eminently fit to become the guardians of the Capital and pioneers of the immense host to follow. How their souls must have scorned the foe who called them "menials," "mercenaries," "hirelings," "Hessians!"* The press of the South almost generally resorted to such epithets, and sedulously sought to disseminate the idea that the Northern volunteers were drawn from the lowest classes. Thus the Mobile *Advertiser* characterized them, and welcomed them to Southern graves:

"These volunteers are men who prefer enlisting to starvation; scurvy fellows from the back slums of cities, whom Falstaff would not have marched through Coventry with; but these recruits are not soldiers—least of all the soldiers to meet the hot-blooded, thorough-bred, impetuous men of the South. Trencher soldiers, who enlisted to war upon their rations, not on men; they are such as marched through Baltimore—squalid, wretched, ragged, and half-naked—as the newspapers of that city report them. Fellows who do not know the breech of a musket from its muzzle, and had rather filch a handkerchief than fight an enemy in manly combat. White-slaves, peddling wretches, small-change knaves, and vagrants, the dregs and offscourings of the populace; these are the levied 'forces' whom Lincoln suddenly arrays as candidates for the honor of being slaughtered by gentlemen—such as Mobile sent to battle. Let them come South, and we will put our negroes to the dirty work of killing them. But they will not come South. Not a wretch of them will live on this side of the border, longer than it will take us to reach the ground and drive them off."

Under the chapter head "The Spirit of the South," we shall give further evidences of that *malignancy* of the Southern heart which was one of the prime causes of the Rebellion:—the above extract we introduce to show, at this point what a difference there was between the North and South, as exemplified in the relative spirit and character of their volunteers.

Adjutant-General Schouler, of Massachusetts, in his Report

* Private Moses Jenkins, of the Rhode Island First, was worth one million dollars. Others in the same regiment were worth their tens of thousands. Mr. Jenkins had arranged for a tour to Europe, and had purchased his ticket. At the call he tore up his ticket and followed his regiment.

for 1861, referred to some of the incidents illustrative of the alacrity with which the men came to the first call. He said: "The first call for troops was by a telegram from Senator Wilson, dated at Washington, April 15th, requesting twenty companies to be sent immediately to Washington, and there mustered into service. * * * This order was sent by mail and by special messengers to the Colonels, who severally resided at Lowell, Quincy, New Bedford, and Lynn. The companies were scattered through the cities and towns of Plymouth, Bristol, Norfolk, Essex, and Middlesex counties.

"*In obedience to orders, nearly every company in the above regiments arrived in Boston the next day.* The first were three infantry companies from Marblehead, under Captains Martin, Phillips, and Boardman. They arrived at the Eastern depot at nine o'clock A. M., and were welcomed by a large multitude of people, who cheered the gallant and devoted men as they marched to their quarters at Faneuil Hall, through rain and sleet, to the music of 'Yankee Doodle.' During the entire day the troops arrived at Boston by the different railroad trains.

"Captain Pratt, in command of the Worcester company, received his order to join the Sixth regiment late in the afternoon of the 16th, and he was in Boston with his full command early on the morning of the 17th. It was nine o'clock in the evening of the 16th before your Excellency decided to attach the commands of Captains Sampson and Dike to the Sixth regiment. A messenger was dispatched to Stoneham, with orders for Captain Dike. He reported to me at eight o'clock the next morning, that he found Captain Dike at his house in Stoneham, at two o'clock in the morning, and placed your Excellency's orders in his hands; that he read them, and said: 'Tell the Adjutant-General that I shall be at the State House with my full company by eleven o'clock to-day.' True to his word, he reported at the time, and that afternoon, attached to the Sixth, the company left for Washington. Two days afterward, on the 19th of April, during that gallant march through Baltimore, which is now a matter of history, Captain Dike was shot down while leading his company through the mob. Several of his command were killed and wounded, and he received a wound in the leg, which will render him a cripple for life."

The spirit of New York loyalty was betrayed in the eager attention given by all classes to the mustering and movements of the regiments. The New York Seventh, chiefly composed of the young men of wealthy families, volunteered to go on to Washington and remain there one month, or longer if necessary for the safety of the Capital. It left the city amidst the greatest excitement, April 19th. April 21st, it was followed by the New York Seventy-first, Twelfth, and Sixth regiments, all of the organized State militia, which volunteered as regiments, for the three months service. The Sixty-ninth, Eighth, and Thirteenth, started forward April 23d. It was thus the Empire State answered, with her choice troops, the first calls for aid. The departure of the regiments, by transports, April 21st, (Sunday,) was accompanied by such popular manifestations, as to be worthy of record. From the report prepared for the press we gather these paragraphs:

"The usual quiet of our city on the Sabbath-day was broken at an early hour, yesterday, with the note of preparation for the departure of the Sixth, Twelfth, and Seventy-first regiments, to whom orders had been issued on the day previous. The flags that had the day before been thrown to the breeze were generally still flying, and squads of recruits, with drum and fife, paraded the streets for an early airing. Officers in undress uniform may be seen, with an air of business, hurrying in different directions; and the chimes of Old Trinity mingled with the boom of cannon fired in the Park. By nine o'clock the multitudes began to swarm the streets, and Broadway bade fair to furnish a repetition of the patriotic scene of the day previous. The Sunday papers, in consequence of the surveillance under which the telegraph had passed, did not contain the gossiping dispatches which the public have so long been accustomed to find. In this respect there was a void.

"The Armories presented an animated scene. In front of

them the streets were filled with the patriotic masses, and the police experienced difficulty in keeping a passage open for the ingress and egress of those who were entitled to enter. None were allowed inside but members of the corps, their immediate friends, or those in some way connected with their movements, and the reporters. Inside all was business and bustle, not to any confusion. Here and there were mothers and sisters parting with sons and brothers, or with motherly and sisterly interest were engaged in assisting to arrange the blankets and pack the soldier's limited baggage, to which there was certain to be added some memento or other thing that relates to his comfort and welfare. Words of patriotic encouragement and tenderest affection were spoken at leave-takings. But these had generally been spoken at home, where we could not penetrate, though we might recite many a touching scene, where parents gave up their sons, and wives their husbands to serve their country.

"It was shortly after ten o'clock when the regiments began to form on Bond street, leading to Broadway. Hither the people had thronged in immense numbers, and what was among the noticeable things, was the presence in that vicinity and down Broadway, of some fifteen or twenty Fire Engines, and Hook and Ladder Companies, including two Steam Engines. It was appropriate, for hundreds of those about to leave have long served in the Department, or at least, in the expressive parlance of the day, have 'run with the machine' many a year. In the hour that elapsed, the crowd in Broadway swelled to the large proportions which we are accustomed to see only on great occasions. At the junction with Canal street, it was the largest, because the Sixth regiment would at this point leave Broadway, and proceed to the *Baltic*, at the foot of Canal street. While waiting for its appearance, 'The Star-Spangled Banner,' 'Hail Columbia,' 'Red, White and Blue,' and other similar airs, were sung by thousands of voices.

"It was about twelve o'clock when the Sixth regiment moved from their armory down Broadway. It was the signal for the wildest outburst. The shouts and cheers which rose from the multitude at the junction of these two streets, were caught up and prolonged almost the whole length of Broadway. At every step the soldiers were greeted with the wildest demonstrations, not only from the people that lined the streets, but from the windows and the roofs of buildings on the route. More than once a mother darted from the crowd, and in spite of police or other restraints, gave her son a parting kiss—only one—for the column moved on, and the boy was a soldier now, bound for the seat of war, and there was no such thing as stopping. Discipline could not restrain adieus between old friends, who *would* shake hands, and give and take hastily spoken but hearty good-byes. The Twelfth and Seventy-first regiments followed, when there was a repetition of the scenes of the previous half-hour.

"So great was the throng in Canal street that it was with the greatest difficulty that the police force could clear the way for the Sixth to pass. The crowd was entirely good-natured, but enthusiastic, and determined to extend its greetings to the soldiers from a position as close as they could assume. The Sixth was accompanied by several files of citizens as an escort, but the multitude mistook all in citizens' clothes for volunteers, and cheered them tremendously. At the foot of Canal street there were thousands of ladies congregated—the windows and roofs of the houses commanding a view of the pier teeming with crinoline and female apparel. Monahan's band, which headed the regiment, here struck up that favorite soldier's air, 'The Girl I left behind me,' which was received with tremendous cheering and waving of hats and handkerchiefs.

"Arriving on the covered pier, the regiment was marched on board the *Baltic*, taking position on the upper deck. Then came the order, 'All who are not going to fight, ashore;' the last farewell was hastily spoken; hands which might never be clasped again were clasped for a parting shake, and a stamp for the gang plank followed. But the vessel sailed not; and as the quarter-hours succeeded each other, the crowd on the piers, sheds and contiguous vessels, began to grow impatient. Gradually they began to depart, confident that some mismanagement would prevent the sailing of the *Baltic* for some hours. Still hundreds of people lingered, anxious to wave their hats after the departing regiment, but their patience was rapidly becoming exhausted when the announcement came that the Twelfth regiment was soon expected to arrive. This brought the multitude back in such numbers that for a time the efforts of the police to keep a passage clear were unavailing. The glitter of bayonets was soon seen in Canal street, and the Twelfth regiment, accompanied by a cheering throng, approached. Arriving at the gate leading to the pier at which the *Baltic* lay, the regiment halted for a quarter of an hour or more. This delay was improved by hundreds of persons to engage in conversation with departing friends, or to add the last item to their stock of comforts, not to mention luxuries. Cigars and tobacco were freely distributed among the recruits, most of whom appeared with no other uniform than knapsacks, belts, blankets, and muskets. One young man broke through the line of policemen, and forcibly seizing a young recruit, attempted to drag him away. The young soldier resisted, and the police interfered, when it appeared that the recruit was the only brother of the one who had seized him, and the latter contended that his brother was too young to become a soldier. The patriotic youth would not yield, however, and so, after a hasty and affectionate parting with his weeping brother, he resumed his place in the line, and marched onward.

"The Twelfth was eventually admitted on the pier, when the cause of the delay was made known. The mismanagement of some person in authority had got the two regiments most effectually mixed. It was intended that the Twelfth regiment should sail by the *Baltic*, and their baggage had accordingly been stowed in the hold of that vessel. The Sixth regiment received orders to march to the *Baltic*, and they complied immediately by taking possession of the ship. The consequence was, that the members of the Twelfth regiment were forced to dispose themselves as best they could among the bales of hay and other freight on the pier. Many of these soldiers were worn out with the fatigue of preparation, and had contemplated a good rest on shipboard, but in this they were mistaken. Added to the discomfort of their standing for hours on the pier, most of them had partaken of an early breakfast, and the pangs of hunger began to be seriously felt. From one o'clock to four they thus waited, with no place to rest and nothing to eat, surrounded by a curious and constantly moving crowd, when an attempt was made to comfort their inner individuals by a supply of food from the stores of the ship. Slices of bread and meat were brought, but the demand outrun the supply, and caused much scrambling among the recruits. Much disappointment was felt when it became known that the steamer *Ariel* would necessarily receive the Sixth regiment, and that consequently the soldiers would not leave until after dark. Still the crowd would not disperse. With short intervals for refreshments, they remained at their posts, and only dispersed when the steamers were fairly under weigh.

"The Seventy-first regiment, after marching down Broadway, turned toward the North River, and went through Albany street to Pier No. 12. The route was lined up to this place, where an immense crowd had gathered, which increased every moment. As the main part of the regiment were in the act of embarkation, the recruits which brought up the rear became the special object of attention from the crowd. Most of them had only muskets, some being old and rusty, and none of the recruits had yet put on the soldier's uniform. Some wore slouch hats, some 'plug' hats, some roundabouts, some peajackets, some had Sunday-go-to-meeting clothes, and some looked as if they had recently left the workshop. This impromtu appearance of the recruits, who numbered nearly half of the regiment, gave an aspect of earnestness to the cause. Enthusiasm burst forth in a continuous yell, which did not subside until the troops had left the streets. After this the crowd continued to look on until the *R. R. Cuyler* hauled out into the stream.

"The cheering on board the *Cuyler* was frequently responded to by a thousand Rhode Islanders on board the *Empire State.* The latter arrived in the harbor on Saturday night, and were anchored in the North River, off Jay street. Their red uniforms could be distinctly observed from the piers, where hundreds of people gathered as early as the day dawned. During the day, the Rhode Island Regimental Band from time to time played national airs, and at five o'clock the troops were transferred aboard the steamer *Coatzacoalcos*, which, until then, had been getting ready at the foot of Warren street."

What a Sabbath day's spectacle! Yet it was heightened by the stirring on the wharves and on the water of the transports loading for the South with the *materiel* of war, stores, &c. The press reported as follows of the steamers under orders on that day:

"West street witnessed such a scene as will not probably be often repeated within a century. In addition to the excitement caused by the departure of three regiments of New York troops, the presence of one regiment of Rhode Island troops, and the arrival in the evening of another regiment of Massachusetts troops, the usual quiet of Sunday was encroached upon by the occasional blowing and smoking of at least a dozen large ocean steamers, which had been quietly freighted, and were now gradually waking up their gigantic powers to depart hence in concert, on a most important mission. A stroll along West street was sufficient to find out that the following steamers (and there may have been more) were about to depart under Government orders:

"The *Ariel*, Pier No. 3, had steam up, and was making much noise. She had been taking on provisions and stores for some days. An inquisitive crowd gathered here at six o'clock in the morning, and continued throughout the day. In the afternoon a squad of Metropolitan Policemen were sent to the spot, to keep order on the arrival of troops from Massachusetts by the Fall River steamboat.

"At the next pier, No. 4, was the *Columbia*, the vessel, until recently, of the notorious traitor Captain Berry, who, it is said, is not an American, but an Englishman, and a Secessionist because he is unprincipled. She had steam up at 4 P. M. During Saturday night workmen were engaged on her all night. The *Marion* was at the same pier ready for departure, and had steam up at four o'clock.

"The *James Adger* was at the stern of the *Marion*, with steam up, some people aboard, and also ready for departure, as it appeared. Crowds of people were gathered along these steamers, and at some places on the decks and rigging of sailing craft in the docks and near by.

"The *R. R. Cuyler* which took the Seventy-first regiment on board, was at pier No. 12. She lay in the stream after three o'clock.

"Several of Mitchill's Line of Southern steamers, lying at pier No. 36, have also been chartered. The *Star of the South*, the *Alabama* and the *Augusta* are the ones. They did not have steam up yesterday, as they were not to depart until Monday or Tuesday.

"The *Coatzacoalcos* was at the foot of Warren street, and had steam up. She went out to the *Empire State* at 6 P. M. The *De Soto*, one of the New Orleans steamers, at the next pier south of the *Coatzacoalcos*, was steaming up with much noise as if about to sail, at 4 P. M.

"The propeller *Chesapeake*, of the Savannah line, got steam up yesterday afternoon, and went out into the stream, but soon after returned to her berth, where she remained until night. The propeller *Parkersburg*, of the same line and pier, had steam up at the same time.

"The propeller *Monticello*, of the Alexandria and Washington line, had steam up and was freighted with large quantities of war material, such as muskets, brass field pieces of improved manufacture, grape-shot for very large guns, and large piles of boxes and bundles, the contents of which were unknown.

"Adding considerably to the martial bustle, was the stated firing of guns from the several transport vessels having troops on board."

This was but the opening of the Crusade for the restoration of the Union which followed. It was a sublime prelude to a sublime tragedy—one at which the generation stood aghast, but one of those which, since the world began, has initiated all great political and social changes.

IV.

THE POETS.

No history of the Great Struggle will be complete that does not recur to the part which the poets of the land took in stirring the popular heart. City and country press teemed with lyrics and invocations, well calculated to awaken enthusiasm in the popular cause. The occasion called forth many fine compositions, well worthy of preservation—some of which will, indeed, find their way into our permanent literature. Patriotism found in the poet-heart a full and deep response; and the future will draw upon the poems of the spring of 1861 when it would refresh its love of country and its faith in the Right. We give such of the compositions as seem to us to possess a permanent interest.*

This Sonnet, from the pen of William H. Burleigh, gives admirable expression to the sense of relief felt by the nation at the end of the suspense regarding the course to be pursued in the crisis:

---

* Many of the finest contributions were lyrics devoted to special occasions, or themes whose interest was but local or temporary. A collection of the choicest Lyrics of the War could not fail to be well received, but it would require a good sized volume to contain them. Perhaps some "enterprizing publisher" may be found to place such a volume on his lists, even though it may not pay the profit of a popular novel. If issued, it should be compiled by an appreciative and fully competent and unbiassed mind—to find which it will be quite necessary to choose some other than one of the *standing* literary providers, who infest the publishing houses of the metropolis. That class rarely thinks of looking for merit outside the atmosphere of its own narrow associations, and warped sense of the beautiful.

APRIL 15TH, 1861.

THANK GOD! the Free North is awake at last!
When burning cannon-shot and bursting shell,
As, from the red mouth of some volcan's hell,
Rained on devoted Sumter thick and fast,
The sleep of ages from her eyelids past.
One bound—and lo! she stands erect and tall,
While Freedom's hosts come trooping to her call,
Like eager warriors to the trumpet's blast!
Wo! to the traitors and their robber-horde!
Wo! to the spoilers that pollute the land!
When a roused Nation, terrible and grand,
Grasps, in a holy cause, th' avenging sword,
And swears, from Treason's bloody clutch to save
The priceless heritage our fathers gave.

The "Alarum," by R. H. Stodderd, is a fine poem, brimming with that *terse* enthusiasm which characterizes all true war lyrics:

MEN of the North and West,
Wake in your might,
Prepare, as the Rebels have done,
For the fight;
You cannot shrink from the test,
Rise! Men of the North and West!

They have torn down your banner of stars;
They have trampled the laws;
They have stifled the freedom they hate,
For no cause!
Do you love it, or slavery best?
Speak! Men of the North and West!

They strike at the life of the State—
Shall the murder be done?
They cry, "We are two!" And you?
"*We are one!*"
You must meet them, then, breast to breast,
On! Men of the North and West!

Not with words—they laugh them to scorn,
And tears they despise;
But, with swords in your hands, and death
In your eyes,
Strike home! leave to God all the rest,
Strike! Men of the North and West!

"A Northern Rally," by John Clancy, is significant. Coming, as it did, from a leading Democratic Editor, of New York City, who had long supported the cause of the South, it happily illustrates the feeling which moved such men to action:

WE'VE borne too long this Southern wrong,
That ever sought to shame us;
The threat and boast, the braggart toast,
"That Southern men would tame us."
We've bent the knee to chivalry,
Have borne the lie and scorning;
But now, thank God, our Northern blood
Has roused itself from fawning.

The issue's made, our flag's displayed,
Let he who dare retard it;
No cowards here grow pale with fear,
For Northern swords now guard it.
The men that won at Lexington
A name and fame in story,
Were patriot sires, who lit the fires
To lead their sons to glory.

Like rushing tide down mountain side,
The Northern hosts are sweeping;
Each freeman's breast to meet the test
With patriot blood is leaping.
Now Southern sneer and bullies' leer,
Will find swift vengeance meted;
For never yet since foemen met
Have Northern men retreated.

United now, no more we'll bow,
Or supplicate, or reason;
'Twill be our shame and lasting blame
If we consent to treason.

Then in the fight our hearts unite,
One purpose move us ever;
No traitor hand divide our land,
No power our country sever.

Rev. John H. Hopkins gave utterance to this truly patriotic National Hymn,—before, we may say, the rush to arms in April. It was afterwards submitted to the Committee on National Hymns, in conjunction with music, (by C. Jerome Hopkins). It deserves to be embalmed in the Songs of the Nation.

GOD save our Fatherland from shore to shore;
God save our Fatherland, one evermore.
No hand shall peril it,
No strife shall sever it,
East, West, and North and South!
One evermore!
Chorus—God save our Fatherland! true home of Freedom!
God save our Fatherland, one evermore;
One in her hills and streams,
One in her glorious dreams,
One in Love's noblest themes—
One evermore!

Strong in the hearts of men, love is thy throne;
Union and Liberty crown thee alone;
Nations have sighed for thee;
Our sires have died for thee;
We'll all be true to thee—
All are thine own.
Chorus—God save our Fatherland, etc.

Ride on proud Ship of State, though tempests lower;
Ride on in majesty, glorious in power;
Though fierce the blast may be,
No wreck shall shatter thee—
Storms shall but bring to thee
Sunshine once more.
Chorus—God save our Fatherland, etc.

A well-known lady writer gave to our literature this nobly conceived and finely rhythmed "Invocation." It is one of these compositions called forth only by moments of great public excitement, and may be referred to as indicative of the strong undercurrent of devotion to country which possessed even the hearts of the women of the land:

Oh, mother of a matchless race!
  Columbia, hear our cry;
The children nursed in your embrace,
  For you will live and die.
We glory in our fathers' deeds,
  We love the soil they trod;
Our heritage we will defend
  And keep, so help us God!
Rise, rise! Oh Patriots, rise!
  Let waiting millions see!
What courage thrills, what faith inspires
  The Nation of the Free!

Hail! brothers in a common cause!
  True to your birthright stand!
The Constitution and the Laws
  Must know no Vandal hand.
Let foreign foes invidious gaze,
  To see our light expire;
They'll shrink in awe before the blaze
  Of Freedom's deathless fire.

Hark! how the hymns of glory swell
  Above our fathers' graves!
Th' unfaltering men of Seventy-six
  Begot no race of slaves.
The blood that bought our sacred right
  Still in their lineage runs;
No tribute gold, no traitor's might
  Shall wrest it from their sons.

Shade of heroic Washington!
  Still guard our Native Land!
Rebuke, rebuke each wavering one,
  Direct each ardent hand!
Oh, mother of a matchless race!
  Hear our united cry!
'Tis noble in your cause to live,
  And nobler still to die!

Charles G. Leland gave to the press the following resonant "Northerner's Call," set to the well-know German air, *Burschen heraus!*

Northmen, come out!
Forth unto battle with storm and shout!
Freedom calls you once again,
To flag and fort and tented plain;
Then come with drum and trump and song,
And raise the war-cry wild and strong:
Northmen, come out!

Northmen, come out!
The foe is waiting round about,
"With paixhan, mortar, and petard,
To tender us their Beau-regard;"
With shot and shrapnell, grape and shell
We'll give them back the fire of hell.
Northmen, come out;

Northmen, come out!
Give the pirates a roaring rout;
Out in your strength and let them know
How Working Men to Work can go.
Out in your might and let them feel
How Mudsills strike when edged with steel;
Northmen, come out!

Northmen, come out!
Come like your grandsires stern and stout;
Shough Cotton be of Kingly stock,
Yet royal heads may reach the block,
The Puritan taught it once in pain,
His sons shall teach it once again;
Northmen, come out!

Northmen, come out!
Forth into battle with storm and shout!
He who lives with victory's blest,
He who dies gains peaceful rest.
Living or dying, let us be
Still vowed to God and liberty!
Northmen, come out!

Oliver Wendall Holmes, after the burial of the Massachusetts dead, killed by the mob at Baltimore, penned this adjuration for the hour:

WEAVE no more silks, ye Lyons looms,
To deck our girls for gay delights!
The crimson flower of battle blooms,
And solemn marches fill the nights.

Weave but the flag whose bars to-day
Drooped heavy o'er our early dead,
And homely garments, coarse and grey,
For orphans that must earn their bread!

Keep back your tunes, ye viols sweet,
That pour delight from other lands!
Rouse there the dancer's restless feet—
The trumpet leads our warrior bands.

And ye that wage the war of words
With mystic fame and subtile power,
Go, chatter to the idle birds,
Or teach the lesson of the hour!

Ye Sibyl Arts, in one stern knot
Be all your offices combined!
Stand close, while Courage draws the lot,
The destiny of humankind!

And if that destiny could fail,
The sun should darken in the sky,
The eternal bloom of Nature pale,
And God, and Truth, and Freedom die!

One who had gone to the wars (Albert Bornitz), on his humble camp couch dreamed of her from whom his hands, not his soul, was torn. He penned her this passionate "Was it a Dream?"

I sat in her garden (or, was it a dream?)
At the quiet of night, in the middle of June:
Below, through the lawn, flowed a musical stream,
And above, in the cloudless expanse, hung the moon.

Around us the roses were blushing with red,
  And the air held the odor of blossom and bud;
On my breast (did I dream it ?) was pillowed her head,
  And the flame of the roses went into our blood !

The fire of the roses went into our veins,
  And the hue of the roses stole over her face!
And her sighs, faintly heard, were angelic refrains,
  As I folded her form in my ardent embrace.

Ah, golden-haired darling! proud hazel-eyed queen!
  Have I dreamed it? or was it not audibly sighed,
By a being whose presence was felt, though unseen,
  That our souls were forever and ever allied?

It may be that I dreamed it: but after the war,
  Should the Fates be propitious, the dream may prove true;
Should I perish in battle—then know that afar,
  In a land of romance, I am waiting for you.

There is in this fine poem an undertone of pathos, which makes it very touching in its sorrow:

I know the sun shines, and the lilacs are blowing,
  And Summer sends kisses by beautiful May—
Oh! to see all the treasures the Spring is bestowing,
  And think—my boy Willie enlisted to-day!

It seems but a day since at twilight, low humming,
  I rocked him to sleep with his cheek upon mine,
While Robby, the four-year old, watched for the coming
  Of father, adown the street's indistinct line.

It is many a year since my Harry departed,
  To come back no more in the twilight or dawn;
And Robby grew weary of watching, and started
  Alone, on the journey his father had gone.

It is many a year— and this afternoon, sitting
  At Robby's old window, I heard the band play,
And suddenly ceased dreaming over my knitting
  To recollect Willie is twenty to-day;

And that, standing beside him this soft May-day morning,
  The sun making gold of his wreathed cigar-smoke,
I saw in his sweet eyes and lips a faint warning,
  And choaked down the tears when he eagerly spoke.

"Dear mother, you know how those traitors are crowing,
They trample the folds of our flag in the dust;
The boys are all fire; and they wish I were going—"
He stopped, but his eyes said, "Oh say if I must!"

I smiled on the boy, though my heart it seemed breaking:
My eyes filled with tears, so I turned them away,
And answered him, "Willie, 'tis well you are waking—
Go, act as your father would bid you to-day!"

I sit in the window and see the flags flying,
And dreamily list to the roll of the drum,
And smother the pain in my heart that is lying,
And bid all the fears in my bosom be dumb.

I shall sit in the window when Summer is lying
Out over the fields, and the honey-bees hum
Lulls the rose at the porch from her tremulous sighing,
And watch for the face of my darling to come.

And if he should fall .... his young life he has given
For Freedom's sweet sake .... and for me, I will pray
Once more with my Harry and Robby in heaven
To meet the dear boy that enlisted to-day.

The spirit of scorn at treason and high resolve to strike and spare not, rings out in these stirring stanzas, by Franklin Lushington. It has in it the clang of the old Roman's steel.

No more words;
Try it with your swords!
Try it with the arms of your bravest and your best!
You are proud of your manhood, now put it to the test:
Not another word;
Try it by the sword!

No more NOTES:
Try it by the throats
Of the cannon that will roar till the earth and air be shaken;
For they speak what they mean, and they can not be mistaken;
No more doubt;
Come—fight it out.

8

No child's play!
Waste not a day;
Serve out the deadliest weapon you know;
Let them pitilessly hail in the faces of the foe;
No blind strife;
Waste not one life.

You that in the front
Bear the battle's brunt—
When the sun gleams at dawn on the bayonets abreast,
Remember 'tis for Government and Country you contest;
For love of all you guard,
Stand and strike hard.

You at home that stay,
From danger far away,
Leave not a jot to chance, while you rest in quiet ease;
Quick! forge the bolts of death; quick! ship them o'er the seas;
If war's feet are lame,
Yours will be the blame.

You, my lads, abroad,
"Steady!" be your word:
You, at home, be the anchor of your soldiers young and brave;
Spare not cost, none is lost, that may strengthen or may save;
Sloth were sin and shame;
Now play out the game.

Bayard Taylor thus charmingly worded the incident which it commemorates, of the old soldier of 1812 pleading with General Scott for a place in the ranks:

An old and crippled veteran to the War Department came,
He sought the Chief who led him, on many a field of fame—
The Chief who shouted "Forward!" where'er his banner rose,
And bore his stars in triumph behind the flying foes.

"Have you forgotten, General," the battered soldier cried,
"The days of eighteen hundred twelve, when I was at your side?
Have you forgotten Johnson, that fought at Lundy's Lane?
'Tis true I'm old, and pensioned, but I want to fight again."

"Have I forgotten?" said the Chief: "my brave old soldier, No!
And here's the hand I gave you then, and let it tell you so;
But you have done your share, my friend; you're crippled, old, and grey,
And we have need of younger arms and fresher blood to-day."

"But, General!" cried the veteran, a flush upon his brow;
"The very men who fought with us, they say, are traitors now;
They've torn the flag of Lundy's Lane, our old red, white, and blue,
And while a drop of blood is left, I'll show that drop is true.

"I'm not so weak but I can strike, and I've a good old gun
To get the range of traitors' hearts, and pick them, one by one.
Your Minie rifles and such arms it ain't worth while to try:
I couldn't get the hang o' them, but I'll keep my powder dry!"

"God bless you, comrade!" said the Chief—"God bless your loyal heart!
But younger men are in the field, and claim to have their part.
They'll plant our sacred banner in each rebellious town,
And woe, henceforth to any hand, that dares to pull it down!"

"But, General!"—still persisting, the weeping veteran cried;
"I'm young enough to follow, so long as you're my guide:
And some, you know, must bite the dust, and that, at least, can I;
So, give the young ones place to fight, but me a place to die!

"If they should fire on Pickens, let the Colonel in command
Put me upon the rampart, with the flag-staff in my hand;
No odds how hot the cannon-smoke, or how the shells may fly,
I'll hold the Stars and Stripes aloft, and hold them till I die!

"I'm ready, General, so you let a post to me be given,
Where Washington can see me, as he looks from highest Heaven,
And say to Putnam at his side, or, may be, General Wayne;
'There stands old Billy Johnson, that fought at Lundy's Lane!'

"And when the fight is hottest, before the traitors fly;
When shell and ball are screeching, and bursting in the sky,
If any shot should hit me, and lay me on my face,
My soul would go to Washington's, and not to Arnold's place!"

It was chronicled among the incidents illustrative of the spirit which prevailed at the South, that "a company of Confederate Horse Guards, at Memphis, lately took a United States flag and buried it in a grave in the earth, with appropriate funeral ceremonies." Some poet adverted to the act in this poem, which strongly reminds the reader of Mrs. Browning's numbers:

So you've buried the flag at Memphis?
How many fathoms deep?
What seal did you set on the Stars and Stripes?
And who that grave shall keep?

Alas for the dead at Memphis!
Mere dust to dust you bear;
No vision of Life all glorified,
Of Love grown heavenly fair—

No radiant dream, with a Christly sign,
Of the Victor's living palm;
Of the odorous golden joy that dares
Join Seraphs in their psalm!

You never read, in a rich man's cave
The Life of the world lay, slain!
And the mourning women went to watch,
But found—where he *had* lain.

Come, guess—who roll'd from his cave the rock?
Who broke great Pilate's seal?
"*While the soldiers sleep, and the women weep,*
Base hands the Body steal."

Vain guess for knowledge! Children dear,
Not Death lay in that cave,
But Living Love! While the world above
Went wailing—"*Died to save!*"

Well—judge if Freedom's sacred sign
Can molder under ground,
With the march of a million men o'erhead,
Their banners eagle-crowned?

From Plymouth Rock to the Golden Gate
A shout goes right and left;
The aliens' dreamful watch is done—
The sepulcher is cleft.

Weak hands! Heap clay on the Stars of God!
They never shone before!
They rend the shroud, and they pierce the cloud,
All hail, then, Thirty-Four!

Nor should we omit the humor and satire which also flowed from the pens of those who scorned the traitors' and plunderers' part. *Punch* came forward, from over the sea, with this terribly bitter—but who shall say inappropriate?—"National Hymn of the Confederate States":

When first the South, to fury fanned,
  Arose and broke the Union's chain,
This was the Charter, the Charter of the land,
  And Mr. Davis sang the strain :
Rule Slaveownia, Slaveownia rules, and raves—
"Christians ever, ever, ever have had slaves."

The Northerns, not so blest as thee,
  At Aby Lincoln's foot may fall,
While thou shalt flourish, shalt flourish fierce and free
  The whip, that makes the Nigger bawl.
Rule Slaveownia, Slaveownia rules, and raves—
"Christians ever, ever, ever should have slaves."

Thou, dully savage, shalt despise
  Each freeman's argument, or joke ;
Each law that Congress, that Congress thought so wise,
  Serves but to light thy pipes for smoke.
Rule Slaveownia, Slaveownia rules, and raves—
"Christians ever, ever, ever must have slaves."

And Trade, that knows no God but gold,
  Shall to thy pirate ports repair ;
Blest land, where flesh—where human flesh is sold,
  And manly arms may flog that *air*.
Rule Slaveownia, Slaveownia rules, and raves—
"Christians ever, ever, ever should have slaves."

Jefferson Davis, in his Message at the opening of the extra session of the Confederate Congress, 1861, said among other remarkable things, that all the South wished was *to be let alone.* Some appreciative person, through the Hartford (Conn.) *Courant*, embodied the Secessionist's wishes in this effusion :

As vonce I valked by a dismal swamp,
There sot an Old Cove in the dark and damp,
And at everybody that passed that road
A stick or a stone this Old Cove throwed.
And venever he flung his stick or his stone,
He'd set up a song of "Let me alone."

"Let me alone, for I loves to shy
These bits of things at the passers by—
Let me alone, for I've got your tin
And lots of other traps snugly in—
Let me alone, I'm riggin' a boat
To grab votever you've got afloat—
In a veek or so I expect to come
And turn you out of your 'ouse and 'ome—
I'm a quiet Old Cove, says he, with a groan:
All I axes is—Let me alone."

Just then came along, on the self same way,
Another Old Cove, and began for to say—
"Let you alone! That 's comin' it strong!—
You've been let alone—a darned sight too long—
Of all the sarce that ever I heerd!
Put down that stick! (You may well look skeered!)
Let go that stone! If you once show fight,
I'll knock you higher than any kite.
You must have a lesson to stop your tricks,
And cure you of shying them stones and sticks,
And I'll have my hardware back, and my cash,
And knock your scow into tarnal smash.
And if ever I catches you 'round *my* ranch,
I'll string you up to the nearest branch.
The best *you* can do is to go to bed,
And keep a decent tongue in your head;
For I reckon before you and I are done,
You'll wish you had let honest folks alone."

The Old Cove stopped, and the t'other Old Cove,
He sot quite still in his cypress grove,
And he looked at his stick, revolvin' slow,
Vether 'twere safe to shy it or no—
And he grumbled on, in an injured tone,
"All that I axed vos, *let me alone*."

To the ever-living Yankee Doodle the world owes much of its best humor. Southern dislike of "the Yankees" did not serve to render the term any the less popular among the loyalists. Hence we find a large number of songs to the good old "tune" which were re-echoed among the hills of much of the "sacred soil" by the Northern troops—so little respect had they for the prejudices of their enemies! Early in the campaign against rebellion, the following "Suggestions" were made by G. W. Westbrook:

Yankee Doodle's come again
  Among the sons of Gotham—
Not to see the gods and shows,
  But to see the facts, and quote 'em.

He heard of South Carolina's boast
  That Jonathan was craven—
That Cotton was the king of earth,
  And nothing else could save 'em.

But, Yankee Doodle says: "Dear sirs,
  You know not what's the matter—
You see through glasses darkly smoked
  With error and tobacker!

"Your darkies plough, and hoe, and dig,
  To raise your rice and cotton,
And sugar, too, and cornstalks big,
  And many things forgotten.

"You orter know that Yankees make
  Your cotton into muslin,
And thread, and tape, and hosiery,
  And ladies' wear quite puzzlin'.

"Besides, they make the canvas sheets
  That forms the wings of commerce,
To take your schooners and your fleets
  To every harbor on earth.

"They also make the canvas bags,
  And send them to the prairies
Of Indiana, Illinois,
  As the soil and climate varies.

"To hold potatoes, corn, and oats,
And wheat, and rye, and barley,
And sometimes coal, and ice in boats,
And coverings for the darkey.

"They also take your rice in ships
Built by the Yankee nation—
From Charleston's docks and New York slips
All over the creation.

"Your sugar, too, the Yankees take—
Although they tap the maple,
That produces matter saccharine,
And forms a Yankee staple.

"Tobacker, too, the Yankees chew,
And smoke and snuff in plenty—
The ladies, too, if you only knew,
Send to you by the twenty

"For early fruits and early flowers,
Before the North can raise 'em,
To decorate their lovely bowers,
Their sweethearts to amaze 'em.

"Then why this strife? like man and wife
In a domestic quarrel—
That after all must end with life,
With no unfading laurel?

"Jonathan's advice, therefore,
Is, peacefully be living,
And kind and true to every one,
Forbearing and forgiving.

"If you refuse to take this hint
Intended for your favor,
We'll show you how the cap and flint
Will cause you much more labor."

Edward S. Ellis, a popular writer in the fields of romance, came out of the regions of fiction to discourse facts in this humorous strain:

Clergymen are mustering
  Members of their flocks,
Satisfied they 're able
  To inflict some Knocks:
    Editors are gathering,
      And the walls of Fame
    Soon will show their "devil"
      What *is* in a name.
Every inland steamer,
  Every train of cars,
Bring their eager thousands
  Going to the wars.

Tailors, clerks, mechanics,
  Shoemakers *to boot;*
Teachers tell their "ideas"
  Now's the time to shoot!
    Bronzed and honest farmers
      Say, "We're bound to jine,"
    As the hardy fellows
      Hasten "into line."
Students, doctors, lawyers,
  Make a sight sublime,
With the shoulder-hitters
  "Coming up to time."

Officers and seamen,
  Salts and jolly tars,
All are now enlisting—
  Going to the wars.
    Timid, tender maiden
      Softly gasps "My gracious!"
    As her gallant lover
      Swears he'll shoot Jeff Davis.
Proud and doating father,
  When he says "My son!"
Hears his martial progeny
  Answer—"*of a gun.*"

Gallant-looking firemen,
  In their flannel shirts,
"Reckon they can handle
  Them 'ere Southern squirts."

Armies from the mountains—
Armies from the hills—
Armies from the workshops—
Armies from the mills.
Hosts of *freemen* rushing
Round the STRIPES AND STARS!
Verily the Southerns
Will get their full of wars!

This may suffice for our half hour with the Poets. That it will prove a pleasant treat for the reader, we are assured. We have quoted such poems as were available. Many fine things are necessarily omitted if we would not absorb too much of our book with rhymes. The contributions of Mrs. Howe, Mrs. Whitman, Rose Terry, Miss Proctor, Oliver Wendall Holmes, R. H. Stoddard, George H. Boker, T. B. Read, Lowell, A. J. H. Duganne, Alice Cary, Bayard Taylor, Whittier, John Neal, Park Benjamin, were very noticeable for their spirit and strength.*

* We can but hope that some competent hand will gather and publish them in a volume fitted for popular circulation. A large number of the finest poems went without an author's name. These it should be the duty of the editor to carefully gather, and, if possible, to ascertain and make known their authorship.

V.

EARLY INCIDENTS.

WHEN one of the New York city regiments was marching to the steamer, a young man, who had risen from a sick bed to go with his company, fainted in the street. A sturdy fellow stepped from the crowd on the sidewalk, saying, "Give me his musket and cartridge-box." They were given to him, and without another word he marched on in the place of the sick man.

In one of the Massachusetts regiments was a young citizen of Maine. He had come from that State to Massachusetts to visit his mother, whom he had not seen for five years, and had been with her only an hour, when he was asked if he did not wish to volunteer. He said his grandfather went to Bunker Hill on short notice, and he would go now; so he bade his mother good by, and was gone.

One of the captains of the Massachusetts Sixth regiment stated that four hundred were refused admittance to the ranks. "It went agin me," said he, "to leave one fellow behind. When we told him he could not go—'I've walked fourteen miles,' exclaimed he, 'and given up a situation of a dollar and a quarter a day just to go, and I think you might take me.' When I had to refuse," said the Captain, "he sat down and cried."

A Southern merchant wrote to a large firm in New York, requesting a list of the names of those who supported and sympathized with the "movement against the South." The New Yorker replied by sending through Adams & Co.'s Express, a copy of the "City Directory!"

A wealthy Quaker merchant in New York, had in his employ a stout, healthy, able-bodied young man, without family. He thought the fellow could serve his country to advantage, and he accordingly addressed him thus: "William, if it is thy desire to become a soldier, thou art at liberty to do so, and thy salary shall be continued during thy absence as if thou wert here; but if thou dost *not* desire to become a soldier and serve thy country, I no longer require thy services here." The young man enlisted.

"My son," said a solid merchant to his heir and namesake, "I would rather give $1,000 than have you go to Washington soldiering." "Father," was the kindly but decided response, "if you could make it $100,000 it would be of no use; for where the Seventh regiment goes, I go."

Before the sailing of the *Columbia*, transport from New York, a demand was made in the name of the regiment that the emblematic Palmetto trees on the bow, paddle-boxes, and stern, should be painted black. The ceremony of obliteration was performed amid the most unbounded applause of the regiment, and the citizens on the wharf.

The Harmony Society, of Beaver County, Pa., deposited five thousand dollars in the bank at New Brighton, to the order of Daniel Agnew, Chairman of the Committee of Safety, for such general purposes as the war movements might require. This society consists of men of advanced age and peaceful pursuits, too old for active defense; but they were patriotic, and determined to do all that loyal citizens could do for the Government.

A lady of known patriotism who had done good service in sewing and contributing for the volunteers, visited her country place in Byberry, near Philadelphia, when the farmer, in honor of her arrival, run up a flag upon the barn. Said flag had been made some years ago for the children, and, to economise material and stitches, contained but three stripes and a short dozen of stars. Some of the neighbors beheld the tri-striped colors and at once gave the alarm. In a short time an excited crowd from all the country around approached the place, brandishing weapons of every description, threatening to burn down the buildings. They took the strange flag to mean secession. It was promptly removed, and the crowd invited to an *extempore* collation.

Among other incidents worthy of mention is that of Roderick W. Cameron, a worthy Scotchman, one of the leading citizens of New York, who was offered a place on the staff of the brigade in which the Seventy-ninth (Scotch) regiment was to serve. In answer to the offer he said :

"MY DEAR COLONEL : I am rejoiced to see the prompt action of the gallant Seventy-ninth.

"Scotchmen are invariably true to their allegiance. Although as a subject of Great Britain, I could not accept the flattering offer tendered to me by your good self, of a staff appointment ; still, there is no reason why a good subject of Great Britain should not be an acceptable volunteer to defend the laws and the flag of this great country. I therefore heartily tender myself to serve in the ranks of the Seventy-ninth Highlanders, and share the dangers of those who wear the tartan of my clan. I cannot promise to be constantly with the regiment, but if danger threatens, I will endeavor to be present at the moment when the first shot is fired.

"All loyal Britons must feel as I do, that it is for the honor and safety of Great Britain to support their cousins of the United States, and to maintain the Stars and Stripes as an emblem of true freedom on this continent."

It was this gallant Seventy-ninth which Colonel Cameron (a brother of the then Secretary of War) led to battle, (Bull Run,) and, in leading them, perished.

The Cincinnati *Times* related a good story of an old fifer employed at the Military Institute near Frankfort, Kentucky. The old fellow had served in the North-west in the second war with Great Britain, and took part in the battle of the Thames and other fights. During the late Secession tornado over Kentucky, the cadets, affected with the fever, talked pretty severely against those devoted to the Stars and Stripes. The old veteran listened, but said nothing. One evening he went into the room of our informant, and seemed to be in something of a passion. He paced backward and forward, saying nothing, and refusing to answer all questions. At last he pulled out his fife, and, sitting down, sent forth "Yankee Doodle" with its shrillest strains. Then he played "Hail Columbia," and then "The Star-Spangled Banner," while the tears rolled down his aged and weather-beaten cheeks. Concluding that, he jumped to his feet, and exclaimed: *"Now, d—n 'em, I guess they know which side I'm on!"*

Five sons of one mother volunteered at the first call for troops. The mother was absent from home at the time, and was informed by letter of the step taken by her sons. Her reply deserves to be embalmed in the casket of the Roman mother's jewels. It read:

"MY DEAR HUSBAND: Your letter came to hand last evening. I must confess I was startled by the news referring to our boys, and for the moment I felt as though a ball had pierced my own heart. For the first time I was obliged to look things full in the face. But although I have always loved my children with a love that none but a mother can know, yet, when I look at the state of my country, I cannot withhold them; and in the name of their God, and their mother's God, and their country's God, I bid them go. If I had ten sons, instead of five, I would give them all sooner than have our country rent in fragments. The Constitution must be sustained at any cost. We have a part to act and a duty to perform, and may God, our father, strengthen us, and nerve us to the task, and enable us to say, Whatever Thou requirest that will I cheerfully give and do. May He bless and protect our dear children, and bring them home to us in safety. I hope you will provide them each with a Bible, and give them their mother's love and blessing, and tell them our prayers will accompany them, and ascend on their behalf night and day."

Colonel Hazard, the great powder manufacturer, wrote to Colonel Colt as follows:

"I am informed that the regiment you are so generously and patriotically arming and fitting out is nearly full. May I be permitted, through you, and in behalf of my company, to furnish them with powder sufficient for fifty thousand cartridges, or as much as you may require for target practice, which they and you will please accept from your friend."

Colonel Colt fitted out and fully armed with his choicest weapons a complete regiment. As early as January, 1861, it is said, the Colonel gave orders that no arms should be sold to the South. It has been stated that arms were supplied to all orders up to the breaking out of hostilities, though it is certain that Colonel Colt was thoroughly loyal.

A letter from Philadelphia, dated April 21st, gave this picture of affairs in that city: "Pennsylvania has for once eclipsed New York! In this contest for the prize of self-sacrificing patriotism which now prevails among the States, you can generously afford to listen and acknowledge the fact. Pennsylvania passed the first thoroughgoing war bill, authorizing the Governor to call out any number of men, and giving $500,000. New York followed with $3,000,000 and thirty thousand men. This was worthy of the great heart of New York. It electrified and staggered us—we were fairly outdone. But when Sumter was assailed we recovered our equilibrium, and our Legislature, by unanimous vote—the whole Democracy fusing with us—pledged the State of Pennsylvania 'to any amount, and to every extent,' to sustain the Government and put down treason. There it stands upon the record, wholly unsurpassed, overtopping even glorious New York. Do what others may, can any devotion to the Union exceed this? Now this is not bravado. Our whole population is ablaze with eagerness to see it realized. Our city banks immediately offered all the money Pennsylvania might want. Private citizens tendered money in amounts never before offered, and I do believe that if Government were to offer $100,000,000 of Treasury notes in Pennsylvania, small enough for general circulation, they would be absorbed in less than thirty days. Our confidence in the Government is firmer than it ever was, and every new development of its vigorous policy serves to strengthen it. Two such communities as New York and Pennsylvania moving shoulder to shoulder, seeking to outdo each other in the race of devotion to a common country, present a spectacle at which the world may not only wonder, but exult, and before which treason will, ere yet, call upon the mountains to cover it.

"On Friday last it was discovered that ten thousand uniforms for our volunteers must be supplied by the State, and orders were at once issued for making them. The empty Girard House was rented, an army of cutters employed, cloth furnished by merchants at mere nominal prices, and our women, taking fire at the call, came by thousands to offer their help to make up. No such sight was ever seen. The large building is now filled with ladies, wives of our best citizens, with their daughters, working all day on coats and blankets, aided by an army of sewing-machines. At least three thousand persons, mostly ladies, are now at work, aided by one hundred cutters. Ladies come from all parts, town and country, volunteering to take home work, and Chesnut street is fairly blocked up with these patriotic women seeking to do something for the cause. The work thus goes bravely on. Another incident of the times is the organization of a body of some three hundred women as nurses, experienced hands, who intend going with the troops to take care of the sick and wounded. Most of these are young women in robust health This same anxiety to aid the cause appears in all the neighboring towns. In short, the spectacle of a people so united has probably never been seen."

The same letter added these incidents of the hour: "The general enthusiasm breaks forth in a multitude of novel shapes. Boys are peddling Union flags mounted on sticks in all our thoroughfares, and from their hands they find their way into all the neighboring towns, where they hang from window and doorpost. Men walk our streets under umbrellas made of material printed with the Stars and Stripes. The first who showed himself under such a banner was greeted with cheers as he moved along. Union parasols of printed silks are coming out for the ladies. Four hundred girls in one of our pub lic schools have each contributed stitches in a huge flag, and raised it on the school-house amid tremendous cheering. The women are working laboriously for the volunteers and their families, whom they leave behind them. One lady has smuggled herself in as a volunteer alongside her husband, dressed in a suit of his clothes, and passing as his brother. Others, unmarried, have offered themselves as vivandiers, to accompany the troops. The owners of many small houses occupied by departing volunteers have notified them that they shall charge no rent while they are absent at the wars, and others are imitating the example thus set. A vast array of names—some forty thousand—has been signed to the pledge of faithfulness to the Government, drawn up and headed by Horace Binney. Captain Archambault, an old officer under Napoleon, has called out the French citizens to swell the ranks of the Garde Lafayette under his command, and they respond heartily. The utmost rivalry prevails among the companies now forming as to which shall be first filled. Drilling goes on nightly in at least fifty places. I saw some six hundred volunteers marching in one body behind the recruiting officer, through as drenching a rain as ever fell. The Stock Brokers, as a body, have unanimously pledged themselves to sustain the Government. The Drug Exchange people have done the same thing. Factory hands are every where giving combined expression to similar sentiments. Men over sixty years old are presenting themselves as volunteers, and insisting on being accepted. Merchants and business men, exempt by age from military duty, have organized a home guard of ten thousand for city defense. Arms are in great demand, and our manufactures are as busy as bees. There is a complete cessation of shipments of all kinds of merchandise to the rebel States, money in hand not tempting our citizens to either feeding or clothing them. I hear a rumor of a force of five thousand blacks being organized. They offer to raise that number of men provided a pledge is given them that they will be marched directly down among the rebels. Such a body could be raised here, and in this neighborhood."

It may be said, in reference to this last sentence regarding the blacks, that great numbers of those residing in the Northern States—large numbers of whom were well-to-do people—were anxious to serve their country; but, in no instance during the war were they called into field service. Numbers of "contrabands" were employed in camp, hospital and laborer service; but, throughout all the war the loyal blacks were not permitted to take up arms. The reason, doubtless, was, that a great hue and cry would have been raised by the enemies of this Government, here and in Europe, that the negroes were being let loose to "commit atrocities" upon the South. As if negroes could rival in atrocity the savages who made drinking cups of the skulls of the "Fire Zouaves," and who brutally scourged, starved, robbed and hung the defenseless Unionists of Tennessee! When Parson Brownlow, at an early day of the rebellion, said: "If it shall so happen, in the progress of affairs, that the authorities of the land shall give us our choice, and submit the same to us as an *ultimatum*, either to go to h— or take refuge in the Southern Confederacy, we will claim a week to consider of the matter, and to make up our mind, as between the two evils"—he simply showed that he appreciated the spirit of malice and evil upon which the whole movement was founded.

The following is a specimen of the *news* dealt out to the Southern people. It is from a New Orleans journal: "All the Massachusetts troops now in Washington are negroes, with the exception of two or three drummer-boys. General Butler, in command, is a native of Liberia. Our readers may recollect old Ben, the barber, who kept a shop in

Poydras street, and emigrated to Liberia with a small competence. General Butler is his son." As General Butler and some Massachusetts troops had the *pleasure* of taking possession of New Orleans, the people of that city had an opportunity of testing his "quality."

When General Butler, in command of the Massachusetts regiments, landed at Annapolis, Md., some of the authorities protested against the passage of Massachusetts troops over Maryland soil; to which he replied: "Sir, we came here not as citizens of Massachusetts, but as citizens of and soldiers of the United States, with no intention to invade any State, but to protect the Capital of our common country from invasion. We shall give no cause of offense; but there must be no fugitive shots or stray bricks on the way."

Butler's troops soon became noted for their general efficiency. Probably no regiment was called to the field, embodying more ingenious men than the Massachusetts Eighth. When sailors were wanted to take the *Constitution* ("Old Ironsides") out of danger in Annapolis harbor, fifty-four men stepped from the ranks. When the railway to the Annapolis junction with the Washington railway was seized for the transport service of the Government, the only engine was found crippled and useless. Butler's call for machinists was answered by eight excellent workmen—one of whom had helped to construct that identical engine. The machine was in running order in two hours' time. The railway track had been torn up, culverts destroyed, bridges burned: the men were there to place all in order.

The Sixth Massachusetts regiment—the regiment assailed by the mob in Baltimore—was chiefly drawn from the county of Middlesex, which embraces the battle-fields of Bunker's Hill, Concord and Lexington, and many of the men were lineal descendants of those who fought on those fields.

In the Fifth Massachusetts was the Concord company, four

members of which were named Buttrick, sons of one man, a direct descendant from the Colonel Buttrick who gave the command at Concord bridge: "Fire, fellow soldiers! for God's sake, *fire!*"

How it sounded, to Northern ears at least, to hear its volun teers characterised as the lowest scum of society. The Raleigh *Banner* said, in urging the attack on Washington City: "The army of the South will be composed of the best material that ever yet made up an army; whilst that of Lincoln will be gathered from the sewers of the cities—the degraded, beastly offscourings of all quarters of the world, who will serve for pay, and run away as soon as they can when danger threatens them." The Charleston *Mercury* characterised our troops as "invading swine." And so of almost innumerable papers. The opinion was so sedulously disseminated that the Northern volunteers were a beggarly set of cowards, (see page 40,) that the only wonder is, Southern "gentlemen" could consent to take the field against them. The Mobile *Advertiser* enlightened us in this fashion: "*Our* volunteer soldiery is not the soldiery of necessity—men worth their hundreds of thousands carry the musket in the ranks. Plenty reigns in our dwellings, and is gladly abandoned for the privations of the camp. Such is the *materiel* with which we meet a mercenary pauper soldiery. Who would doubt the issue when it is man to man? The creatures of one side, sordid and indifferent, fight for so much per diem as the alternative of starvation. The men on the other side fight for rights and liberties, filled with ardor by the noblest impulses. Let these foes meet in pitched battle, and the sons of the South will triumph, were the enemy five to one." Alas! how their dream dissolved in mist—*how their tune changed* before a twelvemonth!

Let us append, as a comment on the above, the following pleasing incident from the New York *Sun*:—"A tall, splendid-looking man, dressed in the uniform of the Allen Greys, Vermont, stood conversing with a friend on Broadway. He was entirely unconscious that his superior height was attracting universal attention, until a splendid barouche drove up to the sidewalk, and a young man sprang from it and grasped his hand, saying, 'You are the most splendid specimen of humanity I ever saw. I am a Southerner, but my heart is with the Union; if it were not, such noble-looking fellows as yourself would enlist me in the cause.' The subject of the remark, although surprised, was perfectly self-possessed, and answered the cordial greeting of the young Southerner with warm enthusiasm. He was several inches above six feet, and his noble, open countenance, beamed with the ancient patriotism of the Green Mountain Boys, of which he was so fine a specimen. He had walked fifteen miles from the village of Chittenden to enlist, and was the only representative of that village; but he was a host in himself. Long may he live to honor our Stars and Stripes."

In the same company of one of the Ohio regiments, were *sixteen* brothers by the name of Finch, all from Dayton, in that State, though born in Germany. This remarkable circumstance—sixteen members of one family in one military company—has not its parallel, we believe, in the annals of war.

The Newport Artillery (company F of the First Rhode Island regiment) has a most notable history, which was thus narrated by a good authority: "It is one of the oldest military organizations in the country. It is an independent company, and was chartered by the British Crown in 1741. With but three exceptions since that time (during the Revolutionary war, when Newport was in possession of English and Hessian troops) the company has held annual meetings under the charter and elected officers, who consist of a Colonel and others connected with a regiment. The names of Generals Greene and Vaughan, of Revolutionary fame, Commodore Perry, and other distinguished personages, are among the enrolled members of the company, which number between two and three thousand since its organization. In their armory, at Newport, they have an autograph letter from General George Washington, written in 1792, thanking them for an invitation to be with them at their annual celebration on the 22d of February of that year, which is handsomely framed. Of the fifty-two active members, forty-seven volunteered their services for the defense of the National Capital, when Governor Sprague telegraphed to inquire the number of men they could furnish, and in a few hours the number was increased to one hundred and thirty-five by recruits.

VI.

THE HUMOR OF THE HOUR.

One of the Ohio regiments chose for its chaplain Rev. Granville Moody, a well-known Methodist minister. He refused to serve except the regiment properly equipped him with a full *fighting* costume, "for," said he, "in our persuasion we do not believe in faith without works." A good thing is also told of another "member of the cloth," in Ohio—Rev. Mr. Beattie, of Cleveland. Presenting a revolver to a member of the Seventh (Ohio) regiment, he said: "If you get in a tight spot, and *have* to use it, ask God's blessing if you have time, but be sure and not let your enemy get the start of you. *You can say 'Amen!' after you shoot!*"

Corporal Tyler, of the Massachusetts Sixth regiment, when describing his experience in Baltimore, says he saw a man with three stones under his arm and one in his hand, pelting away at the troops, when he fired at him, and—to use Mr. Tyler's own language—"*The man dropped the bricks, and laid down.*"

Southern Illinois was named "Egypt," because of the multitude of Southern men who had brought, as residents, ignorance, and its concomitant, insolence, along with them. During the excitement following upon the President's call for troops, the Southern spirit manifested itself pretty plainly in the lower section of the Prairie State. The occupation of Cairo by the Federal forces effectually "squelched" this secession spirit. An old farmer one day said to the Chicago Light Artillery, whose guns made Cairo a terror to Secessionists along the two rivers: "I tell you what it is, boys, them *brass missionaries* has converted a heap of folks hereabouts that was on the anxious seat, and scared some others *right into kingdom come!*"

A deputation of sixteen Virginians and eight Marylanders visited the President on the 21st of April, and demanded a cessation of hostilities until after the session of Congress! Mr. Lincoln, of course, declined the proposition. One of the deputation said, that 75,000 Marylanders would contest the passage of troops over her soil; to which the President replied, that he presumed there was room enough on her soil to bury 75,000 men. This is grim humor, but a fine instance of dignified retaliation to threat.

The Charleston *Mercury* relagated its readers with these tales of the Fire Zouaves—a regiment which struck more real terror to the Southern heart than any other brought into the service during the entire war.

"The first inquiry made by the Fire Zouaves on landing at Washington, was, with grave-faced earnestness, "Can you tell us where Jefferson Davis is? we're lookin' for him." "Yes," said another, "we're bound to hang his scalp in the White House before we go back." Another one, whose massive underjaw and breadth of neck indicated him 'some in a plug muss,' remarked, that they had expected to have arrived by way of Baltimore. "We would have come through Baltimore like a dose of salts," he added, with an air of disappointment. One of them beckoned a citizen, confidentially, to his side, and inquired, "Is there any secession flags about here?" He was assured that secession bunting was an article that did not prevail there. He nodded, and added, "I only wanted to know."

"On coming down the Avenue, the Franklin Fire Company reel passed them at a sharp run, on its way to a fire; and the familiar apparatus was saluted with such a yell of recognition along the entire line, as must have fairly astonished the staid old reel.

"Somebody remarked to one of the b'hoys, that his hair was cut *rayther* short. "Oh, yes," was the reply, "we all had our heads *filed* before we left New York." They all look like fighting boys; but one company seems to have a special prestige that way. "If there's any mischief done, lay it onto Company 68," seemed to be a pet phrase amongst the b'hoys,

"Some of the Zouaves, in emerging from their quarters (Columbian Market building) this morning, disdaining the tedious, common-place mode of exit by the stairway, let themselves down to the street from the third story by a rope, like so many monkeys."

"One blank cartridge, hereafter, Captain, will be sufficient; that being given, you can fire with ball; ammunition is just now rather expensive," said General Lyon to one of his captains, after four blank shots had been fired to bring about a steamboat that was passing the arsenal at St. Louis, without answering the summons of the river guard.

This, from "Secessia," will bear repeating. The New Orleans authorities seized a ship called *American Union*. The telegraph operators were somewhat confounded when the captain (Lincoln) called on them to send a dispatch of this nature:

"W. V. O. Moses, Bath—*American Union* in the hands of the enemy.

(Signed) "A LINCOLN, Master."

The *Crescent* says the operator would not let it go. "Why not?" says the red-haired captain. Operator replies, "The Governor must countersign it." The captain inquires, "Where is the Governor?" "On Canal street, at his office," replies the operator. Off goes the captain to Governor Moore, presents the dispatch, who was taken all aback, and so much amused, that the *American Union*, Captain Lincoln, "was in the hands of the enemy," that he permitted the dispatch to go, saying, with a smile, to the Captain, that it *would be* so by-and-by.

Nobody *persecuted* the South more than George D. Prentice, editor of the Louisville (Kentucky) *Journal.* His words of satire, daggers of derision, lightnings of lampoon, and withering storms of wit, did more outrage upon the feelings of the rebels than a dozen battles lost to them. In the earlier stages of rebellion, his paper fairly scintillated with the flashes of its keen-cutting, though invisible, weapons. We here quote a few paragraphs by way of illustration:

It will be a hard fight, and perhaps about an even one between the. United States and the Confederate States. The former has twice as many men and five times as much money as the latter, but the latter has Colonel Blanton Duncan. The thing is about even, we guess.

The Mobile *Register* recommends the Secessionists to sell their watches. They might as well—have been behind the time, for a long while, by several centuries. If they wait a little, however, the United States will furnish them with "regulators."

Some people kick a little at the Morrill tariff. This is small business, just now, when the rebels and their abettors are kicking over the *moral* tariff, in the face of all Christendom.

Something the enemy will not be likely to do—Go Scott-free.

A Northern editor calls Virginia "the seat of war and the seat of honor." He is making a butt of her.

A man upwards of fifty years of age has sent us a communication, insisting upon Kentucky's plunging into the war. We can understand why these old codgers are so anxious for hostilities. They know that their age would protect them from service, whilst we young fellows would have to do all the fighting.

The North Carolina *Sentinel* says that a military company,

just organized in its town, has "elected Mr. Wing, Captain, and Mr. Head, First Lieutenant." That company is like a sleeping hen—it has its Head under its Wing.

The prevalence of patriotism at the North, in its entire ignoring of partizanship and politics, suggests the coining of a new word for its proper expression, viz. :—UNIONIMITY.

Who wants a better "National Him" than General Scott?

UNIVERSITY OF VIRGINIA, May 17th, 1861.

PRENTICE—Stop my paper. I can't afford to read abbolition journals these times—the atmosphere of old Virginia will not admit of such a filthy sheet as yours has grown to be.

Yours, etc., GEORGE LAKE.

To Editors of Louisville *Journal.*

LAKE!—I think it a great pity that a young man should go to a University to graduate a traitor and a blackguard—and so ignorant as to spell abolition with two "b's." G. D. P.

The Charleston *Mercury* calls the Yankee troops, now threatening the South, "tin peddlers." It is true that the Yankees have, generally, in their visits South, peddled tin, but we guess they mean to peddle lead this time.

The man who, to make a show of chivalry, would wantonly provoke a war, the horrors of which must fall upon his wife and children, is unworthy to have wife and children.

If any man scratched a name from our noble ticket on Saturday, we hope that his wife (if any woman has the hard luck to be his wife) scratched his face when he went to tea.

Some fellows are getting to call every man who is for the Union, an *Abolitionist.* We have only to say that any man who applies that term to us is a base liar. We mean this for any "chivalrous" son of the South who wishes to make his words good.

Mr. Yancey has not been publicly received by the British Ministry, yet he seems to have succeeded in getting its private-ear—(*privateer.*)

Humphreys county, Tennessee, is a fighting district. A Nashville paper would have us believe that seven hundred recruits came from it to join the Secession army, and when the last company left, *they had to tie the old men to keep them from going;* and that the women in that county, even, are ready now to volunteer in the service of the Confederate States. This is the first time we ever heard of a Tennessee woman offering to serve in a bad cause.

Some wretch proposes, as a great peace measure, that all the lawyers in the country go off to the war.

Why is the Union like a crab-apple? Because to be worth anything, it must be preserved.

A Norfolk paper says: "While the ladies of this city were recently gathered in cutting out drawers for the soldiers, it appeared that after their labor was concluded, cloth was left for just one leg of the same. The question being raised as to what should be done with this, one of the number promptly responded, 'Oh, that will do for use, after they get back.'" All very good—*as far as it goes.* But as the Yankees don't mean to leave any legs on the Southern soldiers who get in their way, the ladies of Norfolk will have to keep that one leg of a drawer to remind them of what *was.* It will be their *only* leg-i-see.

The Confederates propose to remove their capital to Richmond. As this consists of stocks, bonds and treasury notes, the Montgomery people will be a little poorer and the Richmond people little the richer by this removal of the deposits.

The only letters the Secessionists will have after the 31st instant, are their letters of marque—which are likely to prove dead letters to those who take them out.

It is said that the gambling saloons in Washington are languishing for want of business. The patriotic excitement in the city has been the ruin of faro, and "the board of green cloth" has adjourned sine DIE. All it has to do is to go after its friends and emigrate to—Richmond!

The following rather remarkable story will do to go with that mentioned above, of sixteen brothers enlisting in one company. Though sounding somewhat fabulous, we are assured of its truth. The New York *Evening Post* related: "Before the departure of the Fourteenth New York regiment, a man who carried on a blacksmith shop in connection with two of his sons, went to the head-quarters and concluded to enlist. He said that he could leave the blacksmith business in the hands of the boys—'he couldn't stand it any longer, and go he must.' He was enlisted.

"Next day down comes the oldest of the boys. The blacksmith's business 'wasn't very drivin', and he guessed John could take care of it.' 'Well,' said the old man, 'Go it.' And the oldest son went it. But the following day John made his appearance. He felt lonesome, and had shut up the shop. The father remonstrated, but the boy would enlist, and enlist he did. Now the old gentleman had two more sons who 'worked the farm' near Flushing, Long Island. The military fever seems to have run in the family, for no sooner had the father and two elder brothers enlisted, than the younger sons came in for a like purpose. The *pater-familias* was a man of few words, but he said that he 'wouldn't stand this anyhow.' The blacksmith business might go to — some other place, but the farm must be looked after. So the boys were sent home. Presently one of them reappeared. They had concluded that one could manage the farm, and had tossed up who should go with the Fourteenth, and he had won the chance.

"This arrangement was finally agreed to. But on the day of departure the last boy of the family was on hand to join and on foot for marching. The old man was somewhat puzzled to know what arrangement could have been made which would allow all of the family to go, but the explanation of the boy solved the difficulty: 'Father,' said he, with a confidential chuckle in the old man's ear: '*I've let the farm on shares!*' The whole family—father and four sons—went with the regiment."

At Bangor, Me., a young man offered himself as a recruit at one of the offices in that city, who, evidently being a minor, was asked if he had his father's permission to volunteer. He replied that he had no father; but admitted that his mother was not willing. "Then you must get your mother's consent," said the officer. The young man retired, and returned with the following brief but noble letter:—"*He is my all, but I freely give him to my country!*"

An Indiana man, with hair whitened by age, applied for admission to the ranks. He was rejected, owing to his evident age. Repairing to a barber's he had his hair and beard colored black, and again applied. The metamorphosis was so complete that he "passed." When asked his age he replied: "rising of thirty-five."

VII.

THE SPIRIT OF THE SOUTH.

A BRIEF section will not be uninteresting which will show to the reader the spirit moving the Southern heart in the conflict with the North. It is by knowing the hidden springs of a man's actions that we are best able to judge him: so of a state, or a country:—by knowing the *animus* of its people we are all the better prepared to consider the justice or injustice of its cause.

The rebellion sprung from a spirit of dishonor. It originated in no "wrongs" committed by the North; the North, as the dominant section, had rather sacrificed its own feelings and self-respect to assist the South to place and prosperity. From the date of the first purchases of territory to add to the area of Slavery and its political power, the South had experienced only a constant succession of benefits from the General Government. The great, oft repeated complaints of the non-enforcement of the Fugitive Slave law, was shown, over and over again, to be most trifling.* The election of a "sectional" President was entirely and solely owing to the fact that the Southern malcontents ran Breckenridge against Douglas. The united vote for these two Democrats would have defeated Mr. Lincoln by over *three hundred and fifty thousand* votes! And, all they (the Democrats) had to do to elect their man, was to run but one candidate at the next election. Besides this, they first set the example of electing a purely "sectional" ticket—Jackson and Calhoun as President and Vice President on the ticket of 1831, being both Southern men. The asseveration of the existence of an inimical feeling at the North against the South, was shown to be unfounded in fact; the combined Democratic and Bell-Everett tickets polled within one hundred thousand as many votes, in the *Free* States alone, as were given (in the same States) to the Lincoln ticket.

What, then, was the cause of the secession rebellion? It originated in what the Western men call a spirit of "pure cussedness"—in the ambition of a few daring, resolute men to found a new government, in which they should be the master spirits—to engraft the idea of property in man upon the organic law of such Government† and thus nationalize Slavery. If other causes existed they were such as only would serve to strengthen the judgment of mankind, that it was one of the most wicked attempts against a good government that the world ever saw.

The spirit fostered by the conspirators was one of Evil. Their game depended for its success upon the complete alienation of the South from the North, and, in the place of respect, to plant the seeds of dislike. The press—that great engine for evil or for good—in the Cotton States was suborned, bullied, bought or cajoled into a support of the schemes for a new confederacy; and, once on the side of the conspiracy, it lent

* See the speeches of Mr. Douglas and of George E. Pugh, United States Senator from Ohio, (a Breckenridge Democrat,) in the U. S. Senate, Dec. 11, '60.

† See the Exposition of the Southern Constitution made by the Vice-President of the Confederate States at Savannah, March 23d, 1861.

its energies to a dissemination of the most shocking falsehoods which human depravity could conceive. By these falsehoods the masses of the South were led astray, and kept ignorant of the most vital facts. They were excited into a violent *hate* of everything appertaining to the North; and, when the hour came for the shock of battle, the leaders found themselves at the head of a people swayed by passions whose malignancy were only excelled by their baseness. Does this seem a strong statement of the case? Alas! that the page of history is darkened by a record which proves all we have asserted and more than we care to assert.

[A leading journalist—a Democrat—who had candor enough to express his sentiments on the relations so long existing between his party and the aristocrats of the South, wrote (May 15th): "Southern people misunderstand us, and in fact despise us, in so vital a particular that we are not fit to live together until both are forced to mutual respect. They actually look upon us, in regard to courage, as little better than so many Chinamen or Sepoys, and the secret of this whole rebellion is, not any new endangerment of Slavery, but the revolt of a set of barons, who for thirty years have encouraged themselves to believe they are of a superior race, and fancied they had hit upon a proper period to withdraw and prove it. Though essentially aristocratical in all their sentiments and institutions, they had maintained an alliance with the Democratic party, because they had certain commercial principles in common, but they promptly sacrificed that party as soon as their mistaken pride had culminated, and left it captive in the hands of the Republicans. It was some time before the Democracy could understand the philosophy of this action by its aristocratic ally; but the depth of the desertion broke upon it in the acknowledgments of such men as Yancey, Keitt and Rhett, while the recently-developed predictions of statesmen like Calhoun, enabled it to realize the uses to which it had been put. The result is that the indignant Democratic party now stands foremost in this war, and seeks a fresh ascendancy by new devotion to the nation. It will not be hasty to form new alliances with a party which acknowledges that all its tendencies are aristocratical, and whose main maxim, as uttered by one of its leading statesmen, is, that 'all labor is dangerous.'"

This statement of the case is so eminently just that we are impelled to give it place.

The first essay of the leaders was to rob and steal from the Government all that it was possible to appropriate. In Mr. Buchanan's cabinet one of the conspirators was placed at the head of the Treasury Department. He took the keys to find a treasury so over full as to render it burdensome; he left it utterly depleted and the country's credit almost ruined "on change." His part of the enterprise appears to have been so far to bankrupt the Government finances as to render the incoming Administration powerless to punish treason or to stay the revolution. Another conspirator was Secretary of War. His office in the enterprise was to fill all the arsenals in the South with arms and munitions, to stock all the forts with ordnance and supplies, and to send away all their garrisons and guards. How well he performed his part is apparent in the sobriquet by which he is now known—"Floyd, the Prince of thieves."

When the moment came to "spring the trap," these worthies withdrew from their dishonored places to receive the acclaims of their fellow-conspirators. A general "seizure" followed of everything which a confiding Government had permitted to remain in the rebellious sections—arms, munitions, money, military property, buildings, &c. These "seizures" honorable men termed thefts or highway robberies: the Secessionists called them "captures" or "appropriations." The moral turpitude of the acts only indicated the baseness of "the cause," and the baseness of the cause only reflected the degeneracy of the people who approved of the secession revolution.

A general repudiation of debts due to Northern creditors followed. The North, with astonishing liberality, had trusted the South for goods, for machinery, for provisions—had built Southern railways and canals—had stocked their marts with capital ready for any want of the planter or real estate operator. As a consequence the South became an enormous debtor—owing over sixty millions of dollars to New York city alone, which came due in the year 1861. To repudiate was an easy way, with dishonorable men, to discharge an honorable obligation; and that Legislatures forbade the collection of debts due to the North through the State Courts, was only another crime to add to the category of sins which are now scheduled under the name of *secession.*

It was so natural to abuse those whom they had injured, that we are not surprised to find the Cotton States, in 1861, fairly slippery with falsehood and misrepresentation. With a few honorable exceptions—exceptions which stand like green spots out of that Dismal Swamp of demoralization—the press adopted a system of paragraphing, whose first and last principle was to misinform their readers—to overrate their own importance and strength and to underrate that of "their enemy"—to deceive and betray. A first impulse of men base enough to act the part performed by the Secessionists would be to contemn, and affect to despise, those whose favors they had fattened upon. Such paragraphs as that quoted on page 40 followed fast in the van of events, as if to pilot the South in the way it should not go. A few more extracts will suffice to convince the most incredulous, of the base part played by the press in exciting the baser passions of Southern human nature.

A gentleman of Richmond, Va., was in New York. The scenes which he witnessed in the streets reminded him of the descriptions of the Reign of Terror in Paris. Nothing was wanting but the bloody guillotine to make the two pictures identical. The violent and diabolical temper everywhere conspicuous, showing but too clearly whither all things are tending in the commercial metropolis. A spirit is evoked which can only be laid in blood. The desperadoes of that great city are now in the ascendant.—*Richmond Whig.*

The tremendous outburst of ferocity that we witness in the Northern States, is simply the repetition of one of the most common traits of their national character. It is the fashion of the day, the humbug of the hour, and it will cease as suddenly as it has commenced. Like straw on fire, the periodical sensations of the North make a great flame, but to sink to the ashes and the dust of indifference as swiftly as they sprang.—*Richmond Examiner.*

When the Commonwealth of Rome was subverted, the people were compelled to worship the image of the despots whom the brute force of the mercenary soldiery had elevated to brief authority. So it seems the Black Republican mobs of the Northern cities compel the people to worship striped rags as evidence of their obeisance to the Abolition despots who now desecrate the seats of power in the Federal city.—*Charleston News.*

The Richmond *Whig* says that the last reliable intelligence represents that Old Abe had been beastly intoxicated for the previous thirty-six consecutive hours, and that eighty Border Ruffians, from Kansas, under the command of Lane, occupied the East Room to guard His Majesty's slumbers. It is broadly hinted in a Washington paper, that his guard exerts a despotic control over the Presidential inmate—that all his decrees are of its inspiration. The paper (*The States and Union*) then proceeds to shed a becoming quantity of tears over this "sad subject for contemplation."—*N. O. Sunday Delta.*

General Scott, it seems, has taken position against his native State. It is a sight to see the drivelling old fop, with his skinny hands and bony fingers, undo, at one dash, the labors of a long and active life. With the red-hot pencil of infamy, he has written upon his wrinkled brow the terrible, damning word, "Traitor."—*Abingdon (Va.) Democrat.*

It was, no doubt, the profound policy of Lincoln and his faction to throw the operatives of the North out of employ, to secure the recruits for the army of coercion. Starvation produces a certain sort of valor, and a hungry belly may stimulate patriotism to a kind of courage which, on a good feed, will risk the encounter with a bullet. It appears that the Lincoln recruits from Massachusetts, at Baltimore, were in large proportion cobblers. The revolution seems to have affected their craft more than any other, according to some of the accounts; their vocation gave them admirable facilities in the fight, especially in running; they used their *footing* expeditiously, and took a free flight with their *soles* (souls)—not one of them apparently being anxious, under the fire of Baltimore brickbats, to see his *last.*—*Charleston Mercury.*

Massachusetts, the telegraph so reports, is all alive with the war spirit. Those who know these Puritan fanatics will never believe that they intend to take the field against Southern men. They may muster into service to garrison posts comparatively free from attack, and when they can be sheltered within impregnable walls, but the hereafter will have little to tell of their deeds in the tented field, or the "imminent deadly breach."—*New Orleans Bulletin.*

VIII.

THE FIRST AND THE SECOND TRAGEDY.

THE movement forward, early in the morning of May 24th, 1861, of the Union army, was the first definite step toward meeting the enemy. General Scott's plans were only known to the President and Cabinet, whose confidence he had, in an eminent degree. A journal well versed in matters, said, (May 15th): "General Scott is about to remodel the United States army upon the French system, so as to give it more efficiency and perfection. The old hero works with astonishing zeal, and his mind operates as actively as many a man at fifty-five. It is undoubted that he contemplates a long campaign, that Washington is to be the base of operations, that a large force will be kept permanently stationed here, and that all demonstrations in support of the loyal men in the South, and in furtherance of the determination to retake stolen property, will move from this point. Some complaints are made because an expedition has not already been sent into Virginia, for the purpose of capturing Richmond; but I am disposed to repose my trust entirely upon the experience and patriotism of General Scott. He is heartily sustained by the President and Messrs. Chase, Cameron, Seward, and the rest of the Cabinet, although it is not doubted that Postmaster-General Judge Blair favors a more extreme and aggressive policy."

The gathering of troops at the Capital argued something more than its defense. With approaches all open and commanding positions unoccupied by Federal forces, the mere retention of the city would have been to insure its destruction for the enemy's artillery on Arlington Heights would have laid the Capital itself in ruins. The safety of the city depended on an advance. But, more than the protective policy it was evident was required. The fact became daily clearer that, if the Union was sustained it must be done *vi et armis;* if rebellion would be crushed and treason punished, it would be done only by a campaign in the heart of the rebellious region; if the Southern madmen were stayed in their designs, it would be necessary to meet them, on land and sea, with the fullest terrors of the outraged Government. No one comprehended this more fully than the President and the venerable General-in-Chief; and we find their plans well developed, by May 20th, for an active prosecution of the war.

It became evident at Washington, on the 23d of May, that some important movement was contemplated—that, in fact, Virginia was to be "invaded." The note of preparation was sounded throughout the camps on the afternoon of that day, though the officers were ignorant of the extent of the service to be performed. At midnight, the District Militia, six companies, moved forward as scouts and pickets, over the Long Bridge. They were first on the "sacred soil." The New York Seventh was detailed as the reserve, and, forming line near the bridge, saw the whole forces, under General Mansfield, pass over, before it brought up the rear. The New York Twelfth and Twenty-fifth, the First Michigan, and the First, Second, Third and Fourth New Jersey, passed over Long Bridge between two and four o'clock A. M.—the Seventh crossing at daybreak. Above, at the Chain Bridge, McDowell's forces passed over, at the same time, comprised of the New York Sixty-ninth and Twenty-eighth, with Drummond's cavalry and a battery. This detachment took possession of Arlington Heights, and immediately commenced the work of constructing defences. The New York Fire Zouaves (Colonel Ellsworth) moved down by transports to Alexandria, landing, at five o'clock, under the guns of the *Pawnee.* The First Michigan, (Colonel Wilcox) moved down from the Long Bridge to co-operate with the Zouaves in the occupancy of Alexandria.

The New York Twelfth took position about half-way between the two points. The Twenty-fifth advanced toward Falls Church. The Seventh held Long Bridge. The morning of the 24th found Virginia in possession of the "hireling mob," who had thus made their first step toward the work of "coercion."

No enemy opposed the invasion—contrary to all expectation. General Scott, in person, was at the bridge to be prepared for any emergency which might arise, but was not called to the field. Generals Mansfield and McDowell only found pickets far in advance of their lines in the morning.

This step excited the country greatly, for the moment. The Confederates fairly shrieked in their imprecations; and their vows of a summary revenge were neither few nor made in the most civilized spirit of modern warfare. We quote from the *Enquirer* of Richmond, as a specimen of the rhetoric excited by the Federal act:

"We congratulate the people of Virginia that the last flimsy pretext of the Rump Government at Washington, of regard for constitutional laws, has been thrown aside. The sovereign State of Virginia has been invaded by the Federal hirelings, without authority of Congress, which alone has the war-making power. Heretofore, the pretense that it was the duty of the Federal Government to repossess itself of the forts and arsenals in the Seceded States, has been put forward to justify the aggressive movements of Federal troops. But in the present case there is no such pretense; no forts, or arsenals, or other Federal property have been seized at Alexandria. The 'bloody and brutal' purposes of the Abolitionists, to subjugate and exterminate the Southern people, stands confessed by this flagrant outrage upon Virginia soil.

"Virginians, arise in your strength and welcome the invader with 'bloody hands to hospitable graves.' The sacred soil of Virginia, in which repose the ashes of so many of the illustrious patriots who gave independence to their country, has been desecrated by the hostile tread of an armed enemy, who proclaims his malignant hatred of Virginia because she will not bow her proud neck to the humiliating yoke of Yankee rule. Meet the invader at the threshold. Welcome him with bayonet and bullet. Swear eternal hatred of a treacherous foe, whose only hope of safety is in your defeat and subjection."

But the occupation was not bloodless. Our country lost one of its most promising officers. Colonel Elmer Ellsworth, of the New York Fire Zouaves, fell by the hand of an assassin while in the performance of his duty at Alexandria.

Colonel Ellsworth was, in many respects, a remarkable person. His regiment of Zouaves were remarkable men. Both officers and men had been counted upon for extraordinary service from the known ability of the commander and the known courage and endurance of the entire regiment. A New York city journal said of him:

"It is about a month since a young man of soldierly bearing, of an unusually fine physique, of frank and attractive manners, and of great intelligence, called on us on the day of his arrival from Washington, to state his wishes and purposes, in relation to raising a regiment among the New York firemen. A fortnight later we saw him on his way to embark for Washington at the head of his men, and escorted by the most imposing procession this city has ever witnessed. This man was Colonel Ellsworth of the Firemen Zouaves. 'I want,' he said, 'the New York firemen, for there are no more effective men in the country, and none with whom I can do so much. They are sleeping on a volcano at Washington,' he added, 'and I want men who can go into a fight *now.*' The impression he made upon us was that of a fearless, gallant and energetic man, one of those possessed of the qualities that distinguish those who have them as soldiers, and of powers that especially fit them to be leaders among men. In him we think the country has lost a very valuable life."

The Zouaves gathered at his call with alacrity; two regiments could have been made up immediately from the firemen of New York city, had they been wanted. A short time sufficed to place the commander at the head of his men. In *twenty* days from the date of his first appearance in New York he was in Washington (May 2d) with one thousand of as brave and reckless men as ever walked the field. They only required to be ruled with a firm hand and led by a fearless heart to perform great service. In Ellsworth they at once had a leader whom they idolized and a ruler whom they obeyed with alacrity, for out of their wild natures he promised to coin heroes whom the country would love to honor.

The regiment was chosen for the first forward movement in expectation of hard work. Theirs were spirits too eager for action, too accustomed to excitement, to bear the dead life of a camp. "Onward to Richmond!" became their cry. The troops broke up camp at two o'clock A. M., and passed down to Alexandria by transports. So utterly unexpected had the movements been conducted, that the Virginia people were completely taken by surprise, and no opposition was offered at any point. Had the design of General Scott been betrayed, it is probable the rebels would have stubbornly opposed the descent and occupation. The Zouaves landed at Alexandria unopposed. The tragedy of Ellsworth's death soon followed. One who was present and witnessed the assassination, thus detailed its circumstances:

"The Colonel gave some rapid directions for the interruption of the railway course, by displacing a few rails near the depot, and then turned toward the centre of the town, to destroy the means of communication southward by the telegraph; a measure which he appeared to regard as very seriously important. He was accompanied by Mr. H. J. Winser, Military Secretary to the regiment; the Chaplain, the Rev. E. W. Dodge; and myself. At first he summoned no guard to follow him, but afterwards turned and called forward a single squad, with a sergeant from the first company. We passed quickly through the streets, meeting a few bewildered travellers issuing from the principal hotel, which seemed to be slowly coming to its daily senses, and were about to turn toward the telegraph office, when the Colonel, first of all, caught sight of the secession flag, which has so long swung insolently in full view of the President's House. He immediately sent back the sergeant, with an order for the advance of the entire first company, and, leaving the matter of the telegraph office for a while, pushed on to the hotel, which proved to be the 'Marshall House,' a second-class inn. On entering the open door the Colonel met a man in his shirt and trowsers, of whom he demanded what sort of flag it was that hung above the roof. The stranger, who seemed greatly alarmed, declared he knew nothing of it, that he was only a boarder there. Without questioning him further the Colonel sprang up stairs, and we all followed to the topmost story, whence, by means of a ladder, he clambered to the roof, cut down the flag with Winser's knife, and brought it from its staff. We at once turned to descend, private Brownell leading the way, and Colonel Ellsworth immediately following him with the flag. As Brownell reached the first landing-place, or entry, after a descent of a dozen steps, a man jumped from a dark passage, and hardly noticing the private, levelled a double-barrelled gun square at the Colonel's breast. Brownell made a quick pass to turn the weapon aside, but the fellow's hand was firm, and he discharged one barrel straight to its aim, the slugs or buckshot with which it was loaded entering the Colonel's heart, and killing him at the instant. He was on the second or third step from the landing, and dropped forward with that heavy, horrible, headlong weight which always comes of sudden death inflicted in this manner. His assailant turned like a flash to give the contents of the other barrel to Brownell, but either he could not command his aim or the Zouave was too quick with him, for the slugs went over his head, and passed through the panels and wainscot of a door. Simultaneously with this second shot, and sounding like the echo of the first, Brownell's rifle was heard and the assassin staggered backward. He was hit exactly in the middle of the face, and the wound, as I afterward saw it, was the most frightful I ever witnessed. Brownell did not know how fatal his shot had been, and so before the man dropped, he thrust his sabre bayonet through and through the body, the force of the blow sending the dead man violently down the upper section of the second flight of stairs, at the foot of which he lay with his face to the floor. Winser ran from above crying, 'Who is hit?' but as he glanced downward by our feet, he needed no answer.

"Bewildered for an instant by the suddenness of this attack, and not knowing what more might be in store, we forbore to proceed, and gathered together defensively. There were but seven of us altogether, and one was without a weapon of any kind. Brownell instantly reloaded, and while doing so perceived the door through which the assailant's shot had passed, beginning to open. He brought his rifle to the shoulder, and menaced the occupants, two travellers, with immediate death if they stirred. The three other privates guarded the passages, of which there were quite a number converging to the point where we stood, while the Chaplain and Winser looked to the staircase by which we had descended, and the adjoining chambers. I ran down stairs to see if any thing was threatened from the story below, but it soon appeared there was no danger from that quarter. The first thing to be done was to look to our dead friend and leader. He had fallen on his face, and the streams of blood that flowed from his wound had literally flooded the way. The Chaplain turned him gently over, and I stooped and called his name aloud, at which I thought then he murmured inarticulately. I presume I was mistaken, and I am not sure that he spoke a word after being struck. Winser and I lifted the body with all care and laid it upon a bed in a room near by. The rebel flag, stained with his blood, we laid about his feet. Before the first company, ordered up by the Colonel, as before stated, arrived, we had removed some of the unsightly stains from the Colonel's features, and composed his limbs. His expression in death was beautifully natural. The Colonel was a singularly handsome man, and, excepting the pallor, there was nothing different in his countenance now from what all his friends had so lately been accustomed to gladly recognize. The detachment was heard approaching at last, a reenforcement was easily called up, and the surgeon was sent for. His arrival, not long after, of course sealed our own unhappy belief. A terrible scene was enacting on the floor below. A woman had run from a lower room to the stairway where the body of the defender of the secession flag lay, and recognizing it, cried aloud with an agony so heart-rending that no person could witness it without emotion. She flung her arms in the air, struck her brow madly, and seemed in every way utterly abandoned to desolation and frenzy. She offered no reproaches—appeared indeed almost regardless of our presence, and yielded only to her own frantic despair. It was her husband that had been shot. He was the proprietor of the hotel. His name was James T. Jackson. Winser was confident it was the same man who met us at the door when we entered, and told us he was a boarder. His wife, as I said, was wild almost to insanity. Yet she listened when spoken to, although no consolation could be offered her.

"It is not from any wish to fasten obloquy upon the slayer of Colonel Ellsworth, but simply because it struck me as a frightful fact, that I say the face of the dead man wore the most revolting expression of rage and hatred that I ever saw. Perhaps the nature of his wound added to this effect, and the wound was something so appalling that I shall not attempt to describe it, as it impressed me. It is probable that such a result from a bullet-wound could not ensue once in a thousand times. Either of Brownell's onslaughts would have been instantaneously fatal. The saber-wound was not less effective than that of the ball. The gun which Jackson had fired lay beneath him, clasped in his arms, and as we did not at first all know that both barrels had been discharged, it was thought necessary to remove it, lest it should be suddenly seized and made use of from below. In doing this, his countenance was revealed.

"As the morning advanced, the townspeople began to gather in the vicinity, and a guard was fixed, preventing ingress and egress. This was done to keep all parties from knowing what had occurred, for the Zouaves were so devoted to their Colonel that it was feared if they all were made acquainted with the real fact, they would sack the house. On the other hand, it was not thought wise to let the Alexandrians know thus early the fate of their townsman. The Zouaves were the only regiment that had arrived, and their head and soul was gone. Besides, the duties which the Colonel had hurriedly assigned before leaving them had scattered some companies in various quarters of the town. Several persons sought admission to the Marshall House, among them a sister of the dead man, who had heard the rumor, but who was not allowed to know the true state of the case. It was painful to hear her remark, as she went away, that 'of course they wouldn't shoot a man dead in his own house about a bit of old bunting.' Many of the lodgers were anxious to go forth, but they were detained until after I had left. All sorts of arguments and persuasions were employed, but the Zouave guards were inexorable.

"At about seven o'clock, a mounted officer rode up, and informed us that the Michigan First had arrived, and had captured a troop of rebels, who had at first demanded time for reflection, but who afterward concluded to yield at discretion. Not long after this, the surgeon made arrangements for the conveyance of Colonel Ellsworth's body to Washington. It was properly veiled from sight, and, with great tenderness, taken by a detachment of the Zouaves and the Seventy-first New York regiment (a small number of whom, I neglected to state, embarked in the morning at the Navy-yard, and came down with us) to the steamboat, by which it was brought to the Navy-yard and given over to the tender care of Captain Dahlgren."

The excitement which followed this assassination was great. The Secessionists of course gloated over it. The press of the South was jubilant, and the ruffian who did the act was placed in their Pantheon of heroes. The press of the North mourned the death of one so chivalrous, so young, so early lost to his country. The President was shocked at the calamity, for his personal attachment to Ellsworth was sincere. A gentleman who happened to call at the White House to see the President, on the morning of the sad day, thus narrated the incident:

"I called at the White House with Senator Wilson of Massachusetts, to see the President on a pressing matter of business, and as we entered we remarked the President standing before a window, looking out across the Potomac. He did not move till we approached very closely, when he turned round abruptly and advanced towards us, extending his hand. 'Excuse me,' he said, 'but I cannot talk.' The President burst into tears, and concealed his face in his handkerchief. He walked up and down the room for some moments, and we stepped aside in silence, not a little moved at such an unusual spectacle, in such a man, in such a place. After composing himself somewhat, the President took his seat and desired us to approach. 'I will make no apology, gentlemen,' said the President, 'for my weakness; but I knew poor Ellsworth well, and held him in great regard. Just as you entered the room, Captain Fox left me, after giving me the painful details of Ellsworth's unfortunate death. The event was so unexpected, and the recital so touching, that it quite unmanned me.'

"The President here made a violent effort to restrain his emotions, and after a pause he proceeded, with a tremulous voice, to give us the incidents of the tragedy that had occurred. 'Poor fellow,' repeated the President, as he closed his relation, 'it was undoubtedly an act of rashness, but it only shows the heroic spirit that animates our soldiers, from high to low, in this righteous cause of ours. Yet who can restrain their grief to see them fall in such a way as this, not by the fortunes of war, but by the hand of an assassin?' Towards the close of his remarks, he added: 'There is one fact which has reached me, which is a great consolation to my heart, and quite a relief after this melancholy affair. I learn from several persons, that when the Stars and Stripes were raised again in Alexandria, many of the people of the town actually wept for joy, and manifested the liveliest gratification at seeing this familiar and loved emblem once more floating above them. This is another proof that all the South is not Secessionist; and it is my earnest hope that as we advance we shall find as many friends as foes.'"

The remains were removed to the White House on the morning of the 25th, under escort of the New York Seventy-first, as a guard of honor, accompanied by a detachment of Zouaves, including Brownell, the slayer of the assassin. From the White House, where it lay in state, until three o'clock, P. M., the body was taken to the house of his parents, at Mechanicsville, New York, for burial. Vast and imposing demonstrations were made over the remains in New York and Albany; and at Mechanicsville he was buried amid the tears of a large concourse of people and in the presence of the local military and the guard of honor.

This act of assassination was in perfect keeping with the spirit of Secession. A community where the use of pistol and knife were almost every day occurrences—where all indignities were wiped out in blood, was not likely to foster a feeling of loyalty to a Government, where just men aimed to suppress all violations of the peace. Jackson was a violent Secessionist. He flouted his odious flag from his house as expressive of defiance; and, though Southern gentlemen did not make him their equal as an associate, they did not disdain to applaud his act and to accord him the place of a martyr in the cause of the South.

IX.

ELLSWORTH.

THE death of Ellsworth served to arouse the inimical feelings of the North, even more than could have been anticipated. The fall of the officer in battle would have been mourned as a calamity, but would, nevertheless, have been ascribed to the inevitable necessities of war. His fall, by an assassin shot, gave no palliation to grief, but rather added to its intensity, and did not fail to reawaken animosities, which had somewhat subsided since the assault upon the Massachusetts men in the streets of Baltimore. Flags were placed at half-mast in all places; men met on the streets to discuss the circumstances of the tragedy; committees and town authorities continued to pass resolutions of respect; everywhere was enlisted a feeling at once suggestive of respect for the memory of the deceased, and of undying hostility to the cause which the assassin represented and typified.

Ellsworth was a pure embodiment, in his tastes, experiences, and character, of the true American. It has been said by a supercilious foreign flunky—and his words are still repeated by the race of flunkies generally: "What is an American? Composed of English, Irish, German, French, Spanish, with an admixture of all other civilized nations, to say nothing of the uncivilized and barbarian, it is difficult to realise what an American is. Will some one tell us?" There is a fair presumption that the person who penned the above might trace his own origin to the race of asses. Had the question been—"Tell us the characteristics which typify the true American it would have been answered as readily as the question: "What is the characteristic of an Englishman—a Frenchman—a German—a Moor—an Indian."

In the record of Ellsworth's life we have the life-history of many thousands of American youth, who have grown up under the same peculiar circumstances—the same incentives to exertion—the same sole dependence on personal merit for success; while in his energy, quickness of intellect, shrewdness, rapidity of performance of duty, his truth and manliness, we have the results of his *American* training and American incentives to development. From a humble printer boy he became a distinguished man, as thousands of humble apprentice boys have done before him, and as thousands will continue to do in a land where no law of *caste* lives down human energies, where no discriminations against choice of occupation prevails, where the *dignity* of labor is recognized.

Ephraim Elmer Ellsworth, we are informed, was born at Mechanicsville, in New York State, April 23d, in the year 1836—being a little less than twenty-five years of age at the moment of his assassination. His parents (still living) were then well-to-do people, of the village; but, owing to great reverses, did not command the means necessary to educate their son as became his evident, and early manifested talents. His education was obtained in the schools of his native place. The taste for military art and action soon became a leading mental inclination; and his reading of books relating to war, campaigns and military service, soon embraced every volume within his reach.

His habits of industry and thirst for a wider experience with men and books, led him into a printing office. Having acquired a knowledge of type-setting, he struck out for New York, to carve his way "to fortune and to fame." His experiences in the great Metropolis were severe and sad, and were scarcely less so after a year's experience in Boston. In 1857 he found his way to Chicago, where, in company with Arthur F. Devereux (afterwards the most gallant Captain of the Salem Zouaves, Eighth Massachusetts regiment) he started in business—an agency for securing patents to inventors. All promised fairly for the two energetic men, when the rascality of an agent hopelessly shipwrecked their little enterprise. This so dashed the hopes of Devereux that he returned to Massachusetts, but Ellsworth remained. A biographical sketch in the *Atlantic Monthly* for July, 1861, said:

"The next year of Ellsworth's life was a miracle of endurance and uncomplaining fortitude. He read law with great assiduity, and supported himself by copying, in the hours that should have been devoted to recreation. He had no pastimes and very few friends. Not a soul besides himself and the baker who gave him his daily loaf, knew how he was living. During all that time he never slept in a bed—never ate with friends at a social board. So acute was his sense of honor, so delicate his ideas of propriety, that, although the most generous of men, he never would accept from acquaintances the slightest favors or courtesies which he might be unable to return. He told me once of a severe struggle between inclination and a sense of honor. At a period of extreme hunger, he met a friend in the street who was just starting from the city. He accompanied his friend into a restaurant, wishing to converse with him, but declined to take any refreshment. He represented the savory fragrance of his friend's dinner as almost maddening to his famished senses, while he sat there pleasantly chatting, depreeating his friend's entreaties to join him in the repast, on the plea that he had just dined."

The same writer, evidently thoroughly familiar with the man, thus further wrote of his mental, physical and moral nature:

"What would have killed an ordinary man did not injure Ellsworth. His iron frame seemed incapable of dissolution or waste. Circumstance had no power to conquer his spirit. His hearty good-humor never gave way. His sense of honor, which was sometimes even fantastic in its delicacy, freed him from the very temptation to wrong. He knew there was a better time coming for him. Conscious of great mental and bodily strength, with that bright lookout that industry and honor always give a man, he was perfectly secure of ultimate success. His plans mingled in a singular manner the bright enthusiasm of the youthful dreamer and the eminent practicality of the man of affairs. At one time, his mind was fixed on Mexico—not with the licentious dreams that excited the ragged *Condottieri* who followed the fated footsteps of the 'grey-eyed man of Destiny,' in the wild hope of plunder and power—nor with the vague reverie in which fanatical theorists construct impossible Utopias on the absurd framework of Icarias or Phalansteries. His clear, bold, and thoroughly executive mind planned a magnificent scheme of commercial enterprise, which, having its centre of operations at Guaymas, should ramify through the golden waters that stretch in silence and solitude along the tortuous banks of the Rio San Jose. This was to be the beginning and the ostensible end of the enterprise. Then he dreamed of the influence of American arts and American energy penetrating into the twilight of that decaying nationality, and saw the natural course of events leading on, first, Emigration, then Protection, and at last Annexation. Yet there was no thought of conquest or rapine. The idea was essentially American and Northern. He never wholly lost that dream. One day last winter, when some one was discussing the propriety of an amputation of the States that seemed thoroughly diseased, Ellsworth swept his hand energetically over the map of Mexico that hung upon the wall, and exclaimed—'*There* is an unanswerable argument against the recognition of the Southern Confederacy.'

"But the central idea of Ellsworth's short life was the thorough reorganization of the militia of the United States. He was convinced that there was much of well-directed effort yet lacking to its entire efficiency. In fact, as he expressed it, a well-disciplined body of five thousand troops could land anywhere on our coast and ravage two or three States before an adequate force could get into the field to oppose them. To reform this defective organization, he resolved to devote whatever of talent or energy was his. This was a very large undertaking for a boy, whose majority and moustache were still of the substance of things hoped for. But nothing that he could propose to himself ever seemed absurd. He attacked his work with his usual promptness and decision.

"The conception of a great idea is no proof of a great mind; a man's calibre is shown by the way in which he attempts to realize his idea. A great design, planted in a little mind, frequently bursts it, and nothing is more pitiable than the spectacle of a man staggering into insanity under a thought too large for him. Ellsworth chose to begin his work simply and practically. He did not write a memorial to the President, to be sent to the Secretary of War, to be referred to the Chief Clerk, to be handed over to File-Clerk No. 99, to be glanced at, and quietly thrust into a pigeon-hole labelled 'Crazy and trashy.' He did not haunt the ante-room of Congressman Somebody, who would promise to bring his plan before the House, and then, bowing him out, give general orders to his footman, 'Not at home, hereafter, to that man.' He did not float, as some theorists do, ghastly and seedy, around the *Adyta* of popular editors, begging for space and countenance. He wisely determined to keep his theories to himself until he could illustrate them by living examples. He first put himself in thorough training. He practised the manual of arms in his own room, until his dexterous precision was something akin to the sleight of a juggler. He investigated the theory of every movement in an anatomical view, and made several most valuable improvements on Hardee. He rëarranged the manual, so that every movement formed the logical groundwork of the succeeding one. He studied the science of fence, so that he could hold a rapier with De Villiers, the most dashing of the Algerine swordsmen. He always had a hand as true as steel, and an eye like a gerfalcon. He used to amuse himself by shooting ventilation-holes through his window-panes. Standing ten paces from the window, he could fire the seven shots from his revolver, and not shiver the glass beyond the circumference of a half-dollar. I have seen a photograph of his arm taken at this time. The knotted coil of thews and sinews looks like the magnificent exaggerations of antique sculpture.

"His person was strikingly prepossessing. His form, though slight—exactly the Napoleonic size—was very compact and commanding; the head statuesquely poised, and crowned with a luxuriance of curling black hair; a hazel eye, bright, though serene, the eye of a gentleman as well as a soldier; a nose such as you see on Roman medals; a light moustache just shading the lips, that were continually curving into the sunniest smiles. His voice, deep and musical, instantly attracted attention; and his address, though not without soldierly brusqueness, was sincere and courteous. There was one thing his backwoods detractors could never forgive: he always dressed well; and, sometimes, wore the military insignia presented to him by different organizations. One of these, a gold circle, inscribed with the legend 'NON NOBIS, SED PRO PATRIA,' was driven into his heart by the slug of the Virginian assassin.

"He had great tact and executive talent, was a good mathematician, possessed a fine artistic eye, sketched well and rapidly, and, in short, bore a deft and skilful hand in all gentlemanly exercise.

" No one ever possessed greater power of enforcing the respect and fastening the affections of men. Strangers soon recognized and acknowledged this power; while to his friends he always seemed like a Paladin or Cavalier of the dead days of romance and beauty. He was so generous and loyal, so stainless and brave, that Bayard himself would have been proud of him. The grand bead-roll of the virtues of the Flower of Kings contains the principles that guided his life; he used to read with exquisite appreciation these lines:

> 'To reverence the King as if he were
> Their conscience, and their conscience as their King,—
> To break the heathen and uphold the Christ,—
> To ride abroad redressing human wrongs,—
> To speak no slander, no, nor listen to it,—
> To lead sweet lives in purest chastity,—
> To love one maiden only, cleave to her,
> And worship her by years of noble deeds,
> Until they won her';

and the rest,—

> 'high thoughts, and amiable words,
> And courtliness, and the desire of fame,
> And love of truth, and all that makes a man.'

"Such, in person and character, was Ellsworth, when he organized, on the 4th day of May, 1859, the United States Zouave Cadets, of Chicago.

" This company was the machine upon which he was to experiment. Disregarding all extant works upon tactics, he drew up a simpler system for the use of his men. Throwing aside the old ideas of soldierly bearing, he taught them to use vigor, promptness, and ease. Discarding the stiff buckram strut of martial tradition, he educated them to move with the loafing *insouciance* of the Indian, or the graceful ease of the panther. He tore off their choking collars and binding coats, and invented a uniform which, though too flashy and conspicuous for actual service, was very bright and dashing for holiday occasions, and left the wearer perfectly free to fight, strike, kick, jump, or run.

"He drilled these young men for about a year, at short intervals. His discipline was very severe and rigid. Added to the punctilio of the martinet was the rigor of the moralist. The slightest exhibition of intemperance or licentiousness was punished by instant degradation and expulsion. He struck from the rolls at one time twelve of his best men, for breaking the rule of total abstinence. His moral power over them was perfect and absolute. I believe any one of them would have died for him.

"In two or three principal towns of Illinois and Wisconsin, he drilled other companies: in Springfield, where he made the friends who best appreciated what was best in him; and in Rockford, where he formed an attachment which imparted a coloring of tender romance to all the days of his busy life that remained. This tragedy would not have been perfect without the plaintive minor strain of Love in Death.

"His company took the Premium Colors at the United States Agricultural Fair, and Ellsworth thought it was time to show to the people some fruit of his drill. They issued their soldierly *defi* and started on their *Marche de Triomphe.* It is useless to recall to those who read newspapers, the clustering glories of that bloodless campaign. Hardly had they left the suburbs of Chicago, when the murmur of applause began. New York, secure in the championship of half a century, listened with quiet metropolitan scorn to the noise of the shouting provinces; but when the crimson phantasms marched out of the Park, on the evening of the 15th of July, New York, with metropolitan magnanimity, confessed herself utterly vanquished by the good thing that had come out of Nazareth. There was no resisting the Zouaves. As the erring Knight of the Round Table said:

'men went down before his spear at a touch,
But knowing he was Launcelot; his great name conquered.'"

A New York journal thus chronicled their advent to the Metropolis, and their successes: "On their arrival in this city they were received with appropriate honors, and on the day of their arrival, after having journeyed over one thousand miles, they gave an exhibition drill in the Park before the Mayor and Common Council, a large number of military men, and at least eight thousand spectators. Their evolutions were pronounced unexcelled. At that time the Zouave drill was new to most of us. The unique and jaunty dress of the Chicagoians, their quick and strange evolutions, their masterly precision and unanimity of drill, attracted general admiration from the public and won golden opinions for Colonel Ellsworth. All the colonels of our crack regiments attended their drills, (of which they gave a series in this city and Brooklyn,) and studied Colonel Ellsworth's manœuvres. At the urgent solicitation of many of our leading civilians and military men—among the latter was the lamented Colonel Vosburgh—they gave an exhibition at the Academy of Music, and notwithstanding it was midsummer and the heat very oppressive, that colossal edifice was filled from parquette to ampitheatre by the *elite* of the city. On the departure of the Chicago Zouaves from this city they were magnificently entertained by the Second company National Guard, at the St. Nicholas Hotel. In reply to a sentiment, complimenting his corps, Colonel Ellsworth replied, 'that it was from witnessing the proficiency of the National Guard, of New York, in military movements, that induced him to take command of his comrades, and take them as his model.' After visiting Boston, Colonel Ellsworth and his command returned to this city, and were escorted hence to West Point, where they gave an exhibition drill in the presence of Governor Banks, Jeff. Davis and Colonel Hardee. At Boston, Philadelphia, Washington and the other cities visited, Colonel Ellsworth and his command were received with marked favor. Indeed, there is not an instance in our military history where a military company were so hospitably received. Colonel Ellsworth's name will go down to posterity as the founder, in this country, of the popular Zouave drill. At this time there are several thousand Zouave organizations in this section and the West, all dating their organization since the tour of the Chicagoians."

This military *escapade* of course had seriously interrupted his legal studies. After the return from the East, of the Zouaves, Ellsworth entered the law office of Abraham Lincoln, at Springfield, Illinois. But, the excitement of a warmly contested political campaign, in which he took an active and very popular part, sorely interfered with the prosecution of his studies of the law. An enthusiastic devotion to military science with special reference to an elaboration of his plan for a State and National Military organization, left little thought of legal lore in his mind. Conceiving the election of Mr. Lincoln to be assured, he gave such detailed consistency to his plan as to have drawn up his schedule of organization. It embraced —as quoted by the writer in the *Atlantic Monthly* from Ellsworth's own exquisitely neat memorandum—the following sections:

"*First:* The gradual concentration of all business pertaining to the militia now conducted by the several bureaus of this Department.

"*Second:* The collection and systematizing of accurate information of the number, arm, and condition of the militia of all classes of the several States, and the compilation of yearly reports of the same, for the information of this Department.

"*Third:* The compilation of a report of the actual condition of the militia, and the working of the present systems of the General Government and the various States.

"*Fourth:* The publication and distribution of such information as is important to the militia, and the conduct of all correspondence relating to militia affairs.

"*Fifth:* The compilation of a system of instruction for light troops, for distribution to the several States, including everything pertaining to the instruction of the militia in the school of the soldier—company and battalion, skirmishing, bayonet, and gymnastic drill, adapted for self-instruction.

"*Sixth:* The arrangement of a system of organization, with

a view to the establishment of a uniform system of drill, discipline, equipment, and dress, throughout the United States."

Mr. Lincoln became strongly attached to Ellsworth—as the incident already related (page 100) will prove. When the journey to Washington was arranged, he became one of the chosen few to form the *cortege* of the President-elect. On that journey he was the life and spirit of the party. He seemed to entertain hopes of a realization of his dreams: why should he not have been happy? How little the novice in intrigue knew of the humiliation, mortification, self-abasement, sacrifices of personal independence necessary to secure "an office"! How his soul must have shrunk from contact with the countless horde of "seekers" who infested Washington in March, 1861! If his pen had been asked to portray the impression which that scramble for office made on his mind, what a loathing picture it would have been!

With the President's endorsement he applied formally for the position of First Clerk in the War Department—hoping, ultimately, to obtain a bureau organization devoted to his scheme of reconstruction of the military department. The First Clerkship, he ascertained to his astonishment and mortification, had long been bestowed upon another. Inquiry showed him that almost all other responsible places in the War Department had been allotted to political favorites. He withdrew, in disgust, from the scene of such bargain and sale of place, and would have returned immediately to the West, to work out his schemes unaided, had not the President interposed, by commissioning him Second Lieutenant in the regular army, with the promise of detailing him to a special service. This opened the way for military activity, and gave promise of the golden opportunity for initiating his reforms. But here the jealousy of the "regulars" came to mortify and annoy him. The appointment to the army of a "civilian" was bad enough; but when this same "outsider" came with schemes of *reform*—bah! he was not to be endured! And so the young aspirant was put "in Coventry," and a fever followed.

The bugle note of alarm came sounding up from the South

to catch his ear. The crisis so long threatened had come, and it found him prepared. His sick couch was deserted. The President's commission was quietly returned to the War Department, and Ellsworth was soon on his way to New York to enlist a regiment of men whom he knew would follow him to the death. The pages of this work attest how well he succeeded in his original design. In twenty days' time he returned to the Capital with a regiment, eleven hundred strong—turbulent spirits, many of them, but all brave and heroic to the last degree. The writer in the *Atlantic* said:

"He divided his regiment, according to his own original idea, into groups of four comrades each, for the campaign. He exercised a personal supervision over the most important and the most trivial minutiæ of the regimental business. The quick sympathy of the public still followed him. He became the idol of the Bowery and the pet of the Avenue. Yet not one instant did he waste in recreation or lionizing. Indulgent to all others, he was merciless to himself. He worked day and night, like an incarnation of energy. When he arrived with his men in Washington, he was thin, hoarse, flushed, but entirely contented and happy, because busy and useful.

"Of the bright enthusiasm and the quenchless industry of the next few weeks, what need to speak? Every day, by his unceasing toil and care, by his vigor, alertness, activity, by his generosity, and by his relentless rigor when duty commanded, he grew into the hearts of his robust and manly followers, until every man in the regiment feared him as a Colonel should be feared, and loved him as a brother should be loved.

"On the night of the twenty-third of May, he called his men together, and made a brief, stirring speech to them, announcing their orders to advance on Alexandria. 'Now, boys, go to bed, and wake up at two o'clock for a sail and a skirmish.' When the camp was silent, he began to work. He wrote many hours, arranging the business of the regiment. He finished his labor as the midnight stars were crossing the zenith. As he sat in his tent by the shore, it seems as if the mystical gales from the near eternity must have breathed for a moment over his soul, freighted with the odor of amaranths and asphodels. For he wrote two strange letters: one to her who mourns him faithful in death; one to his parents. There is nothing braver or more pathetic. With the prophetic instinct of love, he assumed the office of consoler for the stroke that impended."

The letter to his beloved, no eyes have seen but hers for whom they were written—eyes that never more were to look upon their ideal until the portals of Heaven open to reveal him as transfigured in the light of a world where all is peace. The letter to his parents, so touching and so true in its divided devotion, we may quote as a fitting close to this record of one of the sixty thousand lives sacrificed in the struggle with conspiracy and treason:

"HEAD-QUARTERS FIRST ZOUAVES, CAMP LINCOLN,
WASHINGTON, D. C., May 23d, 1861.

"MY DEAR FATHER AND MOTHER: The regiment is ordered to move across the river to-night. We have no means of knowing what reception we are to meet with. I am inclined to the opinion that our entrance to the city of Alexandria will be hotly contested, as I am just informed a large force have arrived there to-day. Should this happen, my dear parents, it may be my lot to be injured in some manner. Whatever may happen, cherish the consolation that I was engaged in the performance of a sacred duty; and to-night, thinking over the probabilities of to-morrow, and the occurrences of the past, I am perfectly content to accept whatever my fortune may be, confident that He who noteth even the fall of a sparrow, will have some purpose even in the fate of one like me.

"My darling and ever-loved parents, good-bye. God bless, protect and care for you. ELMER."

X.

THE FIRST CAPTURE OF THE FLAG.

THE tragedy of Ellsworth gave a sad interest to the flag which had floated from the roof of the "Marshall House," in Alexandria. That flag had floated there in defiance, in full view of the Capital, and its insolent proprietor had sworn it never should come down as long as he was alive.

Before the occupation of the place, on the morning of the 24th of May, by the Federal forces, an attempt to seize and bear away the detested emblem of rebellion and defiance had been made by the daring of a single man. The incident so happily illustrates the *nerve* of the true "Yankee," and is, withal, so full of exciting interest, that we give the story at length.

Two brothers were seen in Alexandria on the evening of Tuesday, May 21st. They entered their names on the "Marshall House" register, as Charles E. Fuller, of Boston, and W. J. A. Fuller, of New York. Of course both became "spotted" characters from that moment. They extended their observations to all parts of the place, where sentinels did not bar the way. After a thorough exploration of the city, they dined at the hotel, with about fifty officers of the Secession army, and the elder brother took the last stage for Washington, which he reached that night without any striking adventure. The younger brother, Charles, had tarried, to accomplish his purpose of seizing the flag which covered the house, and which Jackson, its proprietor, insolently told Mr. Fuller, 'no d—d *Yankee* ever would see come down!" As Mr. Fuller hailed from Boston, the taunt had made him resolved that a Yankee would not only see it down, but that he himself would be the very person to take it down. So it was arranged by the brothers that Charles should stay at the hotel all night, while W. J. went to Washington, and then pulled down the river to the sloop of war, *Pawnee*, which lay off Alexandria, with guns shotted and men ready for any emergency. With the officers of the *Pawnee* he concerted to answer his brother's signals, and to offer his aid when he should plunge into the river, after seizing the flag.

The hotel, a large four-story building, was filled with Secession officers and men. Mr. Fuller had a room assigned him in the main building, from the roof of which the flag-staff ran up through an open scuttle. After tea he groped his way toward the roof, and found the upper doors locked. He then climbed the nearest window, eight or ten feet above the stairway, and found it nailed down. He bought a hammer at a hardware store, went back, and drew the nails. Being a perfect gymnast, and active as a cat, he expected to climb to the roof by the spout, but this proved rotten as paper, and compelled him to abandon the attempt. He next searched about the city and found a locksmith, whom he told that he wanted a bunch of keys to open a closet. The man offered to go with him and fit the lock, but Mr. Fuller "did not see it" in that light. He said he would not trouble him to go, but would take a bunch of keys, and leave five dollars deposit for their return.

Armed with ten keys, he returned to the hotel, watched like a cat for his opportunity, and, when the coast was clear, ascended to the upper story, and tried his keys. Six of them were tried unsuccessfully, and the seventh had turned the lock, when he was nearly surprised by a party of soldiers who came up the stairs. He rushed into a sort of dark closet adjoining, secreted himself under a mattress, and waited with breathless anxiety until they passed into the next room, where they soon became absorbed in a lively game of "poker," at five cents "ante;" he then went back, unlocked the door, felt his way in the dark to the flag-staff, tried the signal halyards, found that everything worked beautifully, and that he was sure, at least, of hauling down the flag. He mounted to the roof, and took a general survey of the premises. This was about eight o'clock in the evening; the streets were full of citizens and troopers, and the full moon shone bright as day. He was again alarmed by a party of soldiers mounting the stairs, and feared that the slight lowering and raising of the flag, made when he was trying the halyards, had been observed from the streets. He stood behind the door, determined to jump by the first comers, and over the heads of those coming after, and make a run for the dock, some four or five blocks off, jump in and swim to the *Pawnee.* Happily the troops went into another room. He then went toward the river to alter the moorings of a small vessel, so that her change of position might signify to his brother, that a boat could approach within hail; but was turned back by sentinels at every street approaching the river; the whole shore was guarded. He then determined to go back to the hotel, haul down the flag, and trust to the chapter of accidents. After a careful reconnoissance, at about ten o'clock, when everybody's attention was engaged by the passing of three cavalry companies, he hauled down the flag, cut the halyards and made them fast to the cleet, that they might not be observed swinging loosely. To his horror he discovered that he had caught an "elephant." The flag was over thirty feet long, and about fifteen feet wide. He took off his coat, vest, and pants, and commenced winding the flag about his body. To use his own expression, he thought he never should get it all coiled away. He succeeded, however, by making a sort of Daniel Lambert of himself. Tying around him his pants and coat with a cord, he effectually hid the piratical emblem. Marching boldly down stairs, he got out of the house without exciting suspicion, and started on his travels. Critical as was his position, with the river bank lined with sentries, and the picket guards extended to Long Bridge, where he knew the draw was raised, it soon became perilous in the extreme, by a general alarm, which was given in consequence of the flag having been missed. Patrolmen rushed in every direction to "cut off retreat" from the house, yet the fleet-footed Yankee only laughed at their pains, for he was safely beyond the square. An old shed offered a retreat from the excited street. Into it he crept, proposing to lie concealed until the moon should be obscured by passing clouds, when he determined to push for the back country, make a circuit above the town, and swim across to Ellsworth's Zouave camp, whose fires he could plainly see. He saw his brother's boat (with a detachment of twelve men from the Massachusetts Fifth) lying off in the middle of the river, but dared not hail her, for fear of causing his certain arrest. He managed to push from picket to picket, by wary advances, at one time lying flat on his back for half-an-hour, while the guard was smoking within a few feet of him, until he broke cover in the open country, beyond the suburbs, when the moon shown out brightly, and he found himself suddenly confronted by two sentries. He made a rush to pass them, when both of them seized him. He grasped one by the breast and threw him to the ground with such violence that he wrenched off one of the Virginian army buttons, which he afterward wore on his watch-guard as a trophy. The other sentry dropped his gun and fled; but a third soldier, a powerful man, clinched him from behind, and, after a brief but fierce struggle, he was hopelessly a prisoner. He retained his presence of mind, and by ready wit and fertility of invention saved himself from personal violence.

His captor proved to be Jackson, who, at first indignant at the theft, was so pleased with the *nonchalance* of the Yankee as to be disarmed of his anger; and he marched the prisoner back to the hotel in perfect good humor. Fuller was permited to retire to his room on his parole not to escape. Jackson remarked that he was "too smart and decent for a miserable Yankee." Fuller tried the power of money, but the rank rebel replied that "it could not be bought for $10,000"—that "old Lincoln had threatened to take it down, and he wanted to see him do it."

After a night of anxious unrest, Mr. Fuller came down to breakfast, and found that everybody was observing him and pointing him out as the "d—d Yankee" who had hauled down the flag. He sauntered through the city, made small purchases of tobacco, &c., in the deserted stores, and went to a secession meeting at night. One of the speakers alluded very feelingly to the imperishable glory which covered the Stars and Stripes, and related with thrilling pathos how his father, a veteran of eighty years, still clung to them. At this point Fuller's patriotic feeling overcame his prudence; he clapped his hands loudly in applause, when the whole meeting, electrified by the speaker, applauded to the echo. But the excitability of "the Yankee" caused the crowd to glower at him so ferociously that he concluded "to beat a retreat rather than be borne down in front or outflanked."

The detention of Charles caused great apprehensions for his safety. Arranging with the officers of the *Pawnee* for the co-operation of its guns and marines in event of his (W. J.'s) detention, he pushed down to Alexandria from the Long Bridge, Wednesday morning. After much negotiation, and the menacing position assumed by the sloop-of-war, Charles was released on Thursday and given over to Commander Rowan, of the *Pawnee*. Arrangements had been thoroughly made to assault and burn the city, had the Fullers been detained. Several companies of the Massachusetts Fifth took a solemn vow that they would take the city, "orders or no orders," and Ellsworth's "boys" were "in the ring." But the orders would have been given. On the night of Thursday, Mr. Fuller, sure of co-operation by water, again tried to take the flag; but it was guarded by two soldiers, sleeping in the attic, and watched incessantly by sentinels outside. So he contented himself with taking the flag which hung up in the hall. This he wound round his person, and succeeded in bringing away with him.

The elder brother had arranged a "seizure" of his own—thus to anticipate Charles and snatch the trophy from him, or at least to insure its certain capture as well as the capture of Alexandria itself! The story runs: W. J. Fuller, in command of a detachment of twelve sailors from Captain Wardwell's company, under Lieutenants Stoddard and Williams, determined to go round the *Pawnee*, and then pull straight to shore, answering any hail with—"boat from the *Pawnee*."

He *knew* the fears of the city, troops and all, that her guns could level the place in thirty minutes. He intended to take half his men, seize the sentries, march openly to the hotel, demand the flag, his brother, and the unconditional surrender of the troops and the city. But this pretty scheme was vetoed by the Commander. It was, of course, not in the Commander-in-Chief's programme of operations; but was, nevertheless, a characteristic *Yankee invention.*

In conceiving this assault, Mr. Fuller was but embodying the ideas which he enunciated at the great demonstration in New York city, May 20th—on which occasion he was one of the chosen speakers. He said, among other stirring things:

"Let the Government forever discard its 'do little and drift along' policy, and give the people action, action—prompt, vigorous, energetic, crushing, bloody and decisive. Let it quit searching musty law tomes for precedents. Make precedents. The idea of the Government being harnessed down by the iron bands of formula and delay when dealing with revolutionists, traitors and rebels, is criminal and absurd. *Inter arma leges silent.* When General Jackson threatened to hang Calhoun, he was told by his Attorney-General that there was no law for it. His reply was, 'If you can't find law for me, I will appoint an Attorney-General who can.' If the Government will adopt a vigorous policy, the law for everything it does will be found in the hearts of the people. The eyes of the people are upon the Government. They cannot wait its tardy action. They will reward energy, and will hold it to a strict accountability for imbecility."

XI.

A NORTHERN BREEZE FROM THE SOUTH.

THE Great Rebellion called forth many splendid efforts of oratory. It is probable that no people on the face of the globe are more constantly associated with the sublime elements of country, which are supposed to influence the minds of men to sublime expression, than Americans; yet, it has frequently been remarked by ourselves, as well as by foreigners, that no country produces so few truly eloquent orators. The experience of the past few months proves that the talent for eloquent expression is wide-spread, and that only the occasion is wanting to call it forth. The Congress of 1860–61 gave birth to many supurb declamations:—indeed, the entire session was one succession of speeches and argumentative efforts, which alone, would immortalize the occasion. We may point to them, in confidence, as a living evidence of the extraordinary mental resources of the American people, as the war which followed was an evidence of their tremendous physical resources.

Our volume of "Incidents and Anecdotes" scarcely permits the reproduction of these oratorical efforts; yet, some of them were made under such peculiar circumstances as to become incidents of the struggle. Such were the impassioned speeches made in the Virginia Convention and General Assembly by the Union men; in Tennessee, by the fearless men of the hills; in Kentucky, by the worthy sons of "Old Kentuck" sires. Few of these, however, were reported, much to the loss of our patriotic literature; only sketches were placed on record, to outline what was, at the moment, a splendid creation.

One made by Mr. Rosseau—afterwards a brilliant General in the Union army—in the Kentucky Senate, May 21st, 1861, was reported. It came at a critical moment in the destiny of his State, when she hung in the meshes of the miserable "neutrality," which was nothing more nor less than an attitude of defiance of the General Government, by refusing to honor its call for troops, and arming the State to resist any occupation of its soil by Federal troops, prosecuting the war for the Union. Against this attitude the Senator protested, and finally came out, with his splendid declamation, against the revolution and in behalf of a hearty support of the General Government in its contest with treason. Our young men will find in the Kentuckian's words and thoughts incentives to patriotism and honor, and to them we sincerely commend the extracts which we may feel at liberty to give:

"Mr. Speaker: Permit me to tell you, sir, what I think of this whole atrocious scheme of Secession. I speak for myself only, and am alone responsible for what I say; and I thank God that I may still speak what I think on Kentucky soil. Yes, sir, good, brave old Kentucky, my mother, 'my own native land,' is still free. There is no reign of terror here. We still have free speech, a free press, and, as yet, we are free men. Kentucky is true and loyal to the Government. She still rests her head in peace and security upon the fond breast of her mother—the Union; and there may she rest forever! She has called upon her gallant sons to rally around her, and beat off the Vandals who would tear her away from her earliest and holiest associations, and bear her to certain destruction.

"Kentucky is in a false position. I felt it from the first. Yet, she having assumed a neutral attitude, I felt it to be my duty to stand by her, and I have faithfully done so. I am willing still to stand by the position of Kentucky, if we can do so in peace and security. But the position is an awkward one, and may be more awkward yet before our difficulties are ended. The Union is threatened; the Government is threatened by those who have not one well-grounded complaint to make against it—by those who have controlled its destinies for years. I denounce the effort, and those who make it. I say it is wrong—infamous! and, if successful, it must entail ruin upon us and ours. We see the work of mischief going on, and quietly sit by with folded arms while it is done.

"Kentucky has as much interest in the Union as any other State. She loves it as devotedly, and shares its benefits and blessings in common with her sister States. She owes it her allegiance, and her aid. Her people work for the Union; they talk for it; they pray for its preservation; yet they stand idly by, and let others, who have no more interest in it than themselves, defend it, and save it if they can. It is in a death struggle for existence, yet we have not a hand to raise in its defence. You say that it is the best Government that ever existed on earth—it has ever protected and never oppressed you. But we are told that this is a fratricidal war—a *wicked* war! Well, who began it? Who caused it? Who attempted to break up the Government? Who set the will of the people at defiance, and overturn the "best Government on earth?" Let recently passed events, and those which are daily being enacted, answer.

* * * "The truth is, our duty at first was to stand by our Government, and protect and defend it. If fit to live under, it was entitled to our respect and confidence and allegiance. If unfit, it should have been abandoned at once, and another formed more perfect. But while we owe our allegiance to it, let us acknowledge it like true men, and not turn our backs upon its greatest peril. We should not do this if we desire its preservation. We should stand by it like men, or pull it down at once. But we should not stand by and see others pull it down over our heads against our will to the destruction of our liberties, and say:

"'We oppose you. We love the Government. It is the Government of our fathers; bought with their blood, and bequeathed to us. It is the best Government on earth, and in its destruction we see ruin to us and ours; but as you and we live in Slave States, go on and do as you please. We will not resist you. Ruin us if you will.'

"And so never lift a hand to save us and our children the

blessings of liberty. In my heart I do not approve of this course, and what I do not approve, no power on earth shall make me say. I am for the old Constitution of Washington and his compeers. For the old flag, the Stars and Stripes. God bless them; and I am against all factions that would take them from me. It matters not who they are or whence they come. Whether they come from England, France, Massachusetts or South Carolina. If they would destroy the Government of our fathers, I am against them. No matter what may be the pretext. No, sir, I am for the Union, and I am willing to defend it by any and all proper means.

"Our Government is the best in the world. It has answered well all the ends for which governments are made. We all know this. It has oppressed no man, nor has it burdened us a feather's weight. It has brought us nothing but blessings. Under it we have been happy, prosperous and free. What more can we ask? All that Government can do, our Government has done for us. We have been free, as no nation was ever free before; we have prospered as no nation ever prospered before, and we have rested in peace and security. Yet all this would not do. Mr. Lincoln was elected, and corrupt politicians lost their places. They had controlled the Government in their own way for years. When they lost their power, they declared that the Government was corrupt and oppressive, and that they would destroy it. They robbed it of its arms and munitions of war, sending them South; they involved the Government in a debt of nearly a hundred millions of dollars; robbed the treasury; and thus leaving the Government impoverished and distracted, they commenced the atrocious business of secession. They had lost the offices, and they thought it necessary to create new ones for the benefit of the defunct politicians, and they did it. This is the grand secret of the whole affair. Had they retained their grip upon the offices, you had never heard of secession. All our losses, all our troubles and suffering, are the legitimate results of secession. We must bear all, we must submit to all this in silence, that those disappointed politicians may be presidents, ministers, and high officials. Their day was ended by the election of Lincoln. They knew this, and seceded—made new offices and filled them!

"Behold the results of secession! Distress and ruin stare men in the face. Strong men, honest and industrious men, cannot get bread for their wives and children. The widow and the orphan, helpless and destitute, are starving. In all the large cities the suffering is intense; work is not to be obtained; and those who live by their labor get no money. Property of every description has depreciated until it is almost worthless. In the Seceded States, Union men are driven penniless from their homes, or hanged; and all this, that 'peaceable secession' may go on, and that politicians may fill offices! And, after you gentlemen bring all these calamities upon us, you falsely say that 'Lincoln did it,' and that we Union men are Abolitionists, and aid him! I tell you that Lincoln has *not* done it. He was elected President by *your* help. You ran a candidate for the Presidency, that the Democratic party might be divided, and Lincoln elected. That was your *purpose*, and you accomplished it; and now you have elected Lincoln thus, you must break up the Government because he is elected! This is your programme—deny it who can!

"South Carolina was irritated at the presence of Major Anderson and fifty-five men at Fort Sumter; so irritated that she could not bear it. She tried to starve him to death; she tried to knock his head off, and burn him up; she bombarded the people's fort; shot into the flag of our Government, and drove our soldiers from the place. It was not Mr. Lincoln's fort; not his flag, nor his soldiers, but ours. Yet after all these outrages and atrocities, South Carolina comes with embraces for us, saying: 'Well, we tried; we intended to kill that brother Kentuckian of yours; tried to storm him, knock his brains out, and burn him up. Don't you love us for it? Won't you fight with us, and for us, and help us overthrow your Government?' Was ever a request so outrageously unnatural; so degrading to our patriotism? And yet, Mr.

Speaker, there were those among us who rejoiced of the result, and termed the assault upon their own fort and the capture of their own flag and their own soldiers, a *heroic victory!*

"Mr. Speaker, I am sick and tired of all this gabble about irritation over the exercise by others of their undoubted right; and I say once for all to you secession gentlemen, that we Union men know our rights; intend to maintain them. If you get irritated about it, why—get irritated! Snuff and snort yourselves into a rage; go into spasms if you will; die if you want to, and can't stand it—who cares? What right have you to get irritated because we claim equal rights and equality with you? We are for peace; we desire no war, and deprecate collision. All we ask is peace. We don't intend you any harm. We don't want to hurt you, and don't intend you shall injure us if we can help it. We beg of you to let us live in peace under the good old Government of our fathers. We only ask that. Why keep us ever on the alert watching you, to prevent you from enslaving us by a destruction of that Government?

* * * "Kentucky is an armed neutral, it is said. I submit, with others, to that position. I hope that circumstances may not drive us from it. I hope that our secession friends will be, in fact, neutral. If we remain so, it is said we shall have peace. I hope so; but the neutrality that fights all on one side I do not understand. Troops leave Kentucky in broad daylight, and our Governor sees them going to fight against our own Government, yet nothing is said or done to prevent them. Is this to be our neutrality? If it is, I am utterly opposed to it. If we assume a neutral position, let us be neutral in fact. It is as little as we can do.

"Our Government, constitutionally administered, is entitled to our support, no matter who administers it. If we will not support it, and yet enjoy its blessings, in Heaven's name let us not war against it, nor allow our people to do so. Let us be true to our position, whatever it may be. We are nullifying at any rate. Our Government has not objected to it. But who can look an honest man in the face, while professing neutrality, refusing to help his Government to preserve its existence, yet secretly and traitorously warring against it? For one, sir, I'll none of it. Away with it. Let us be men—honest men, or pretend to be nothing but vagabonds.

"I hear it said that Kentucky will go out of the Union; that if she goes anywhere, she will go South, &c., &c. Mr. Speaker, let me tell you, sir, Kentucky will not 'go out.' She will not stampede. That has been tried. Secessionists must invent something new in the way of secession appliances before they can either frighten or 'drag' Kentucky out of the Union. I tell you sensation gentlemen that your exciting events have ceased to effect us. Try something else. Get up a fight at Cairo, that you may get us to side with you. That is your game, and you will play it whenever you think you can succeed at it. You tried to scare us, but you failed in your purpose. And if you illegally and against right assault Cairo, I hope every man of you will get his head knocked or be taken prisoner, and that the Cairo folks will never permit you to come to Kentucky again. That's what I wish, and what I believe would happen in such an event.

"But we won't 'go out'—have not the least notion of it in the world. You must take us out according to law and right, or take us dead. Believe this, and act accordingly. It would be better for all of us. We shall be but too happy to keep peace, but we cannot leave the Union of our fathers.

"When Kentucky goes down, it will be in blood. Let that be understood. She will not go as other States have gone. Let the responsibility rest on you, where it belongs. It is all your work, and whatever happens will be your work. We have more right to defend our Government than you have to overturn it. Many of us are sworn to support it. Let our good Union brethren of the South stand their ground. I know that many patriotic hearts in the Seceded States still beat warmly for the old Union—the old flag. The time will come when we shall all be together again. The politicians are having their day. The *people* will yet have theirs. I have an abiding confidence in the *right*, and I know that this secession movement is all wrong. There is, in fact, not a single substantial reason for it. If there is, I should be glad to hear it; our Government has never oppressed us with a feather's weight. The direst oppression alone could justify what has brought all our present suffering upon us. May God, in his mercy, save our glorious Republic!"

There is in this noble address the impassioned eloquence of the patriot and the incorruptible citizen. In reading it the vision of Patrick Henry rises up before us as he appeared to the Virginia House of Delegates when he uttered his ever-memorable anathema against King George. It was such declarations as those which fell from Rosseau's lips—as those which fell from the pen of the incorruptible Joseph Holt—as those which the sage and patriot John J. Crittenden eventually avowed—that saved Kentucky to the Union and preserved her hills and vallies from becoming the battle-fields of the horrid struggle to achieve the independence of a Slave Dominion.

XII.

GENERAL SCOTT.

"So long as that man is true, the nation is safe," Joseph Holt said to a friend during the "dark days" of April. None knew the weight of responsibility resting upon the veteran's shoulders better than the ex-Secretary of War, and none better knew than he Scott's ability to discharge his trust. Like Mr. Holt, the North reposed the utmost confidence in the General-in-Chief, though his rapidly growing feebleness of body gave great anxiety lest his strength should fail ere his great work was done.

At an early stage of the rebellion, Scott was cautiously approached by the emissaries of the rebellion—many of whom were his life-long friends and coadjutors. His sturdy loyalty was his protection against open proposals to desert his flag; yet the enemy's anxiety to obtain either his acquiescence to the right of secession and his resignation from the Federal service, or his active co-operation in the Southern scheme for a Confederacy of Slave States, led them to hope, to the last, that he would not conduct the campaign against them. How fallacious that hope was events soon determined. From the incipient stages of the treason the old general—comprehending its true character, and having a clearer knowledge of it than the majority of men—had arranged, so far as lay in his power, to meet the coming storm; and the call for troops in April, found him at his post in Washington, ready to assume their command.

The country will hardly realise the peculiar position in which Scott was placed. His extreme age and bodily infirmities would have excused his retirement from service. His Virginia parentage, and relationship by near, and life-long association with leading Southern families, were powerful instruments to impel him to retire from a contest with these friends. His close personal intimacy with officers who had become directing military leaders in the rebel cause, made a campaign against them one of extreme painfulness, and might very naturally have impelled his soul to shrink from the ordeal of crushing those men and bringing their necks to the scaffold.

But, as all true greatness ever rises above adverse circumstances and personal considerations, so Scott's soul arose to the claims of his country. The very magnitude of the crisis was the leading motive which, undoubtedly, impelled him to retain his leadership—fearing that, in that hour of great peril, no other hand could do so well as his own. Forgetful of all social ties, of life-long associations, of the distasteful nature of the imprecations which would be heaped upon his head, of his bodily feebleness and need of rest, he assumed the trust wil-lingly, and essayed the herculean task of creating a vast army, and of placing it in the field ready for duty. Mind, body, heart, and soul were enlisted in the work: his personal comfort, happiness, fame—all were cast aside in that hour of duty. It is a sublime spectacle to contemplate: and, in the future, when the story of the rebellion is written from the stand-point of history, the conduct of the man will command the admiration of all discriminate and dispassionate minds.

April 19th (1861) it was announced by telegraph, to the South from Washington, that General Scott had resigned his position in the army of the United States and had tendered his sword to his native State, Virginia. Immense rejoicing followed. In Mobile, for instance, one hundred guns were fired in honor of his defection to the Union cause! So generally was the report credited throughout the Southern States, that John J. Crittenden, of Kentucky, telegraphed to the General to know the truth. The reply was:

"*I have not changed—have no thought of changing—always a Union man!*"

This set at rest the calumny hatched to bolster up the Southern cause, and to "fire the Southern heart." When it was thus announced, by authority, that he was true to his flag and his oath, the Southern press opened its vile batteries of abuse and defamation of the incorruptible patriot, whom they had but the day before "exalted to the seventh Heaven" by their praise. As an evidence at once of the depravity of the Southern press and of the malignity of the spirit which animated the breasts of the rebels, we may quote a few of the notices made of Scott by the Secessionist journals.

The Richmond *Examiner*, edited by John M. Daniel—Mr. Buchanan's *Chargé* to one of the leading cities of Southern Europe—thus spoke:

"The infamy of this man constitutes no small portion of the crushing load of shame under which Virginia is now struggling. She gave birth to this unnatural monster. She has heaped honors and rewards upon this war mandarin of the Abolitionists. That Scott was born in Virginia is a misfortune which cannot be remedied; but there are means by which the State may brand him with the marks of her indignant scorn. The treason of Arnold swallowed up and effaced all recollection of his long deeds of valor and patriotism, and this name was blotted from the list of our Revolutionary Generals. The Legislature of Virginia should expunge from their journals every resolution expressive of Virginia's confidence, respect, and admiration for this man. We should offer to pay him a pecuniary consideration fifty times their value, if necessary, for the medals and swords which we gave him, when he was esteemed a worthy and grateful son of the Old Dominion, and the now dishonored name of Scott should no longer be borne by one of our counties.

How fortunate for the old General's fame and honor that he did not act so as to win the applaudits of such a man as the writer of the above!

The following, from the Richmond *Whig*, if more dignified, is yet indicative of the disappointment and hate which rankled in its editor's breast:

The ancients had a saying, that no man was happy till his death. The hero of Chippewa and Lundy's Lane is a living illustration of this antique apothegm. When all the noble and chivalrous spirits of the Federal service were abandoning the flag which had become the badge of despotism, and, flying to the rescue of Liberty and their native States, he, oblivious of every sense of duty to his "dear old mother," remained with her enemies, to organize armies for her invasion and desolation. It is not worth while to inquire whether he was prompted by vanity, avarice, or ambition. He has chosen his part. He must be a parricide, or he must betray the cause which he has now espoused. He can never again put foot upon the soil that gave him birth, except as an invader or a traitor, with a rope around his neck. To any feeling mind would not death be a thousand times preferable to such a fate?

The New Orleans *Delta* was quite exercised in its peculiar way that any Southern man should adhere to the Stripes and Stars. It said:

The three greatest villains and traitors which the present war has produced are, beyond all doubt, Governor Hicks, of Maryland, and Generals Scott and Harney. We place them in the order of their infamy. Hicks ranks his confederates by long odds. Scott and Harney have some palliation in the fact of their being *mercenaries*, and in their carnal weakness, etc., etc.

And more of the same sort. It afterwards became evident that the *Delta's* patriotism was of a kind the goat on the house-top betrayed to the lion on the street below—impudent, because of its own distance from danger. When General Butler took possession of New Orleans, the "leading journal" hastened to write to the Union General's acceptance. It had neither the spirit to close its rooms, nor the courage to sauce the lion then on the house-top.

As a choice specimen of Southern use of the Billingsgate dictionary, we may give the following extract from the Florida *Sentinel*, of Tallahassee—the leading journal of the Alligator State:

Our indignation, contempt, and abhorrence of this plebeian demagogue [Lincoln] are only equalled by what we feel for his friend and adviser, the traitor to the home of his birth, "the jackass in politics, and Jupiter in vanity," Lieutenant-General Winfield Scott. If there be not "some chosen curse, some hidden thunder in the store of heaven," to blast this wretch who causes his country's ruin, the curse of unborn millions will damn him to the lowest depths of human degradation.

It is a relief to turn from these disgusting expressions of malice and baseness to contemplate the old general at his labors to avert the threatened dangers to his country. A correspondent, who was at the Capital early in June, wrote:

"We must advert to a scene, now a daily one, in one of the lofty apartments of the War Office, where General Scott passes many hours of the day and night, at a time of life when most men naturally court ease, but which the old hero is now devoting to the greatest achievement of his eventful and honorable career, the demonstration of the strength and power of a republican form of government.

"Enfeebled in body, but clear-minded and vigorous in intellect as ever, General Scott is now cheerfully undergoing labors that would overtax the strength of many far his juniors in life and in service. An early hour of the day finds him surrounded by aids and advisers, and not until a late hour of the night does the work cease. The bustle and din of the city and camp are hushed at nightfall, but not for many hours later does the headquarters of the Lieutenant-General lose its features of activity.

"The scene on the day in question was one on which the pencil of a Leutze would dwell lovingly to the production of a painting that should be vivid history. General Scott, suffering more than usual by an attack of gout, lay half reclining upon a lounge drawn into the centre of the large apartment, his feet resting upon pillows. About the old chieftain, whose massive frame seemed more impressive from the contrast, were gathered men in uniform of army and navy, eminent citizens in the plain black civilian's dress, with here and there one whose dress and features told of rough service on some errand, whose results were now to be reported to the modification or comprehensive plans of the War Department.

"On the wall opposite the lounge, occupied by General Scott were suspended two large military maps of Virginia and Maryland, with all their careful details, closely representing the country, its features, accesses, fastnesses and approaches. It was noticeable that about Harper's Ferry, Richmond, and Norfolk, were drawn large circles, within which the details became more minute, with symbols and signs abundant, of significance to military men, the key to which belongs to the War Office.

"By General Scott's side lay a long, light reed, which he made use of in pointing to different localities on these maps. Aids, amanuenses, advisers, were all busy, quietly, and all without stir or confusion. In that room, and on such scenes and consultations hang safely the fate of this war, in the speedy and condign punishment of traitors. Probably no one but the hungrier of the Washington correspondents, will regret, or fail to applaud the wisdom of the War Department, or, indeed, of the Government as a whole, in only sparingly admitting to confidence the newspapers and the general public. It is enough to know that the Government is thoroughly at work in all its departments for the crushing out of treason, and that General Scott is indeed a close and voluntary 'prisoner' to duties whose execution will make the setting sun of the old hero illustrious in all time."

The gratification felt by all classes at the General's devotion to duty was expressed in the address of leading citizens of Philadelphia—including a number of those who had opposed the coercion of the South up to a late hour. This document, so honorable to both recipient and the signers, read:

"PHILADELPHIA, April 30th, 1861.

"*To Lieutenant-General Winfield Scott, General-in-Chief of the Army of the United States:*

"SIR: The shock of a civil war in our beloved country, whose history, for more than half a century, has been illustrated, not less by your wisdom and patriotism than the splendor of your achievements in arms, will, we trust, justify this letter to you, even though it be a departure from usage.

"We are your fellow-citizens of the United States. We are devotedly attached to our country. Her renown is precious to us. It is our richest inheritance; and we had fondly hoped to transmit it to our children untarnished, as it came to us from our fathers.

"In the civil strife which has just lighted up our land with an unnatural and deadly glare, we do not stop to inquire into the soundness of conflicting opinions as to the origin of the deplorable controversy. It is enough for us to know that the beloved and glorious flag of our Federal Union has been assailed, and we ask no further questions. In such a crisis, we are for sustaining, to any and every extent, the constituted authorities of the Union, believing, in the language of Mr. Jefferson, that '*the preservation of the General Government, in its whole constitutional vigor, is the sheet-anchor of our peace at home and safety abroad.*' While the Government stands by the flag, we stand by the Government. In this determination we obliterate, for the time being, all traces of party difference by which many of us have been heretofore widely separated.

"The citizens of Philadelphia—a city which, we are sure, must be endeared to your recollections, as it is to ours, by some of the proudest memories of the era of Independence—

where the Declaration was signed—where the Constitution was signed, and from whence our illustrious founder issued to his countrymen his immortal farewell address — we adopt this mode of testifying our admiration, and offering you our deep-felt thanks for your great services to your country, in this hour of her extremest peril—services which will rival in immortality, and, we trust, in their triumphant results, your early and subsequent renown in the second and third great wars of the United States.

"At a time like this, when Americans, distinguished by the favor of their country, intrenched in power, and otherwise high in influence and station, civil and military, are renouncing their allegiance to the flag they have sworn to support, it is an inexpressible source of consolation and pride to us to know that the General-in-chief of the army remains like an impregnable fortress at the post of duty and glory, and that he will continue to the last to uphold that flag, and defend it, if necessary, with his sword, even if his native State should assail it.

"That your career of rare distinction may be prolonged for many years of continued usefulness to your country, and happiness to yourself, and that you may live to see that great country once more in the enjoyment of the prosperity and renown among nations, to which your wisdom in council and your sword in battle have so largely contributed, is the anxious, earnest hope of those who here unite in tendering to you, not only the assurances of their profound respect, but what we believe you will value as highly, the spontaneous tribute of loyal American hearts."

This admirable address was prepared by the eminent counsellor, Horace Binney. It was signed by more than two hundred names of those whose endorsement it was an honor to win. The address was only one of several offered to the old hero.

A sketch of the life of the "hero of an hundred battles" will find admiring readers; and we here append one prepared by a leading journalist immediately after his retirement from the service, November 1st, when all was well for the Union cause.

Lieutenant-General Winfield Scott is a native of Virginia, having been born in Petersburg on the 13th of June, 1786. He is of Scottish descent, and it would appear, from the records of his family, that his great military abilities were inherited, the name being a celebrated one in the military annals of Scotland. At the battle of Culloden, in 1746, so disastrous to the last hopes of the Stuarts, his grandfather played a conspicuous part, and his grand uncle was left among the slain in that sanguinary struggle for the British crown. It may, however, be safely stated that none of his family ever rose to such distinction in the pursuit of arms. His ancestors having been ardent supporters of the unfortunate Stuarts, the defeat of the Pretender at the battle of Culloden led to their involuntary exile, as well as that of their royal leader.

The Scott family, on their arrival in the then British colonies, settled down in Virginia, where, as we have already stated, the future general of the American Republic was born. His preparatory education having been completed, he entered William and Mary College, where he devoted a couple of years to the study of the higher branches. On leaving college he entered the profession of the law, and at the age of twenty was admitted to the bar. As Charleston, South Carolina, appeared to the mind of the young lawyer to present a more fruitful field for the successful practice of his profession, he proceeded to that city in the autumn of 1807. Here, however, he was not as successful as he desired, and, having satisfied himself that fortune and fame were slow to reward him in this pursuit, he determined to leave Charleston and return to the North. It may, in fact, well be doubted, from his subsequent career, whether the inclinations of young Scott qualified him for the peculiar duties and labors of the legal profession. His mind was naturally adapted to a more active and vigorous life—a life made up of the dangers and perils of the battle-field—a life in camp and field—in which only the sterner qualities of the soldier could hope to achieve success.

Accordingly he entered the army, and, although his first experience of military life was rather discouraging, still he was determined to persevere in the new career which he had chosen. It appears that in 1809 the conduct of his superior officer—General Wilkinson—led him to indulge in some expressions which, though just, betrayed a want of discretion, which, viewed with leniency, might be regarded as pardonable in one who had just entered the army. The rigidity of military discipline is a stranger to the milder virtue of clemency, and after a trial by court martial, sentence of suspension from pay and service for twelve months was pronounced upon the offender. To a man not wedded to the profession of arms this would have proved a discouragement too great to be borne; but Scott had made his final resolution, and was determined to persevere despite of all obstacles.

The twelve months for which he was suspended were devoted to unremitting study of military service, so that on the proclamation of war in 1812, between the United States and Great Britain, there was none better qualified to lead his countrymen against the enemy. He was at this time promoted to the position of Lieutenant-Colonel of artillery, and he acquired the reputation of being one of the best officers in that important department of the army.

At the battle of Queenstown Heights his intrepidity and skill as a commanding officer were for the first time brought out in a most conspicuous and creditable manner. The engagement was one of the most desperate recorded in the annals of American warfare, and, although it ended in the defeat of the American forces, the victory of the enemy was dearly purchased. Scott, with his surviving comrades, was captured and sent to Quebec; but he was soon afterwards liberated, by an exchange of prisoners. In this battle his personal daring and lofty stature rendered him a prominent mark for the Indian sharpshooters, who, as in the instance recorded in the life of Washington, exerted their skill to the utmost, but without success, to bring him down. Failing in open, manly conflict to destroy their fearless and intrepid foe, they had recourse to Indian cunning and treachery to carry out their fell design. Gaining access to his prison, two of them rushed upon him, but were foiled by the superior agility and strength of Scott, as well as by the fortunate interposition of Captain Coffin, of the British army, to whose timely presence in the hour of danger his escape from his savage enemies was partly attributable.

The bravery of Scott was recognized in a substantial manner, after his release, by his promotion to the position of Adjutant-General and chief of the staff under General Dearborn, who at that time was commanding on the Northern frontier. The justice of this promotion was made manifest by his conduct on the capture of Fort George, at which he was severely wounded by a splinter, after performing prodigies of valor. At the battle of Chippewa, the credit of which the commanding officer generously acknowledged was due to Scott, he added another brilliant page to the history of his country, and another leaf to the chaplet which was one day to adorn his brow. We would not be doing justice to his gallant conduct did we fail to notice an incident which occurred during that battle, and which affords a happy illustration of the indomitable character of the man. As the two armies approached to close quarters, Scott called aloud to McNeil's battalion, "The enemy say we are good at long shot, but cannot stand the cold iron. I call upon the Eleventh instantly to give the lie to that slander. Charge!" And, responding with an exultant hurra, they did charge, and with a vengeance. Sweeping upon the enemy with the force of a mountain torrent swollen by autumn floods, they drove them from the field, and that, too, with their own favorite weapon, before which it had been the boast of the British, no foe was ever able to stand. These, too, were a portion of that world-renowned army of veterans with which British generals had expelled the French from Spain, and who, it was vauntingly said, would drive the American forces from one end of the country to the other. The victory was accomplished before the American commander, General Brown, could engage the enemy with his division. In his report he spoke as follows of the heroism of the youthful General:

"Brigadier-General Scott is entitled to the highest praise our country can bestow. His brigade covered itself with glory."

But it was at Niagara, July 28th, 1814, that he even surpassed himself. Here he was twice wounded, once by a bullet through the shoulder, and the second time by a spent ball. Placing himself at the head of his men, he cheered them on to the attack, and although the British had the advantage in the strength of their position, they gave way before the terrible charge of the Americans and fled in confusion, leaving Scott, who was the first man to enter, in possession of the fort. The victorious commander hauled down the British colors with his own hands and amid the cheers of his brave troops.

These constant successes attracted to him the eyes of the whole country, who regarded with the most enthusiastic admiration the brilliant career of the young officer—for he had not yet quite attained his twenty-seventh year. On the 9th of March, 1814, he was promoted to the rank of Brigadier-General, with the hearty approval of all classes of his countrymen. For his services at Chippewa and Niagara—commonly called Lundy's Lane—he received the rank of Major-General. This was not all. The gratitude of the country could not be easily exhausted, in view of the great services which he had rendered, and the glory he had reflected on the flag. November 3d, 1814, the National Legislature passed a resolution awarding him a gold medal "in testimony of the high sense entertained by Congress of his distinguished services in the successive conflicts of Chippewa and Niagara, and of his uniform gallantry and good conduct in sustaining the high reputation of the arms of the United States."

When peace was proclaimed the position of Secretary of War was tendered General Scott, in the Cabinet of President Madison, but the offer was declined, as the General was still suffering from his wounds. He visited Europe soon after for the restoration of his health, having also been entrusted with an important diplomatic mission by the Government, which was so successfully discharged as to elicit a letter of thanks from the Secretary of State in the name of the President.

In his career thus far we have seen him only as the brave and successful General; but we are now to view him in another aspect—one in which the finer qualities of his nature were brought out, if possible, in a still stronger light. The truly brave are always humane; and never was bravery so blended with humanity as in the conduct of Scott while on his way with his forces to put down Black Hawk and his savage tribes. On his passage from Buffalo to Chicago, with about a thousand troops, in the summer of 1832, the cholera broke out among his men with such terrible violence that on one vessel, on board of which there were two hundred and twenty, no less than one hundred and thirty cases of cholera and fifty-one deaths occurred in six days. On his arrival at the Mississippi river from Chicago, the same fearful pestilence made its appearance, making dreadful ravages among the troops. Nothing could exceed the kindness and delicate care with which he attended to the poor sufferers, fearlessly exposing himself to the contagion in his all-absorbing desire to alleviate the misery and suffering by which he was surrounded.

The Black Hawk war having been successfully terminated, General Scott and Governor Reynolds were appointed Commissioners to treat with the Northwestern Indians, in reference to all pending difficulties. It is sufficient to say that this task, which displayed the qualities of a statesman in no ordinary degree, was as successfully discharged as the others with which he had been entrusted. The Indians ceded the title to more than ten millions of acres, forming the greater part of the present States of Iowa and Michigan. In the same year (1832), by his prudence and firmness in South Carolina, which then threatened the country with all the evils of civil war, by her nullification principles, he saved the country from rebellion and its attendant horrors.

Next followed the Florida war, where he added new laurels to his already historic fame; his successful mission to the Canadian frontier, which was greatly excited by the burning of the *Caroline;* the removal of the Cherokees, which displayed his energy and humanity in a remarkable degree. In 1839, by his judicious course on the Northeastern boundary difficulty, he avoided a war with England, which at the time was regarded as inevitable.

But the crowning success of all these glorious achievements was his campaign in Mexico, which, in the brilliancy of its successes, the rapidity of its marches, and its results, will bear comparison with those of any other campaign of ancient or modern times. On the 10th of March, 1847, he arrived before Vera Cruz, and, on the 14th of September of the same year, having stormed the "impregnable castle" of San Juan d'Ulloa, and fought the battles of Cerro Gordo, Contreras, San Antonio, Cherubusco, Molino del Rey, Chepultepec, besides lesser battles, and taken several cities, he entered the City of Mexico at the head of six thousand men.

Had his advice and directions been followed, before the unfortunate battle of Bull Run—which the veteran rightly styled a Congressional battle—the backbone of the Southern rebellion would have been broken ere this. But, unfortunately, the cry of "On to Richmond" drowned the prudent advice of the General, whose counsel would have saved the nation from a humiliating defeat.

As a commander, Scott had but few equals among his contemporaries, and even his enemies bear willing testimony to his great military genius. One of the British Generals who was opposed to him in 1812, speaking of his qualities in the freedom of conversation, expressed the most unqualified admiration of his genius and skill as a commander. In the opinion of many he was not second to Wellington himself, and there is certainly no campaign in the career of that great General which can be said to surpass, if it equals, Scott's campaign in Mexico. He was the only American General, with the exception of Washington, who received the title of Lieutenant-General, and this was conferred upon him as the highest testimonial which could be bestowed by a grateful country.

His retirement from the high position which he has occupied so many years, with honor and distinction to himself and advantage to the interests of the nation, was an event well calculated to arrest attention at home and abroad, for it may be said with truth, that the principal events in the last fifty years of his life would, to a great extent, embrace the most prominent and important facts in the history of the country. Although he has never been honored with the highest office in the gift of the people, no man has occupied a more distinguished and exalted position, and none of his contemporaries will fill a larger space in the future annals of the Great Republic. His withdrawal from the active duties of official life, and his generous resignation of his command into the hands of a General so much his junior, indicate a self-abnegation which proves the truth of the time-honored adage, that he only who can command himself is truly qualified to govern others.

XIII.

McCLELLAN'S FIRST CAMPAIGN.

THE appointment of Captain McClellan to the responsible position of Major-General of the Volunteers of the State of Ohio (April 24th, 1861), was soon followed by the General Government's creation of the "Department of the West," over which he was placed in superior command. It comprised the States of Ohio, Indiana, Illinois, Western Pennsylvania, and Western Virginia.

The proposed assemblage (June 14th) of the Wheeling Convention, for re-organizing the State of Virginia as a State of the Union, rendered it necessary to arrange a campaign in Western Virginia, both to expel the rebel armies from that section, and to give stability to the new State Government.

The promulgation by McClellan (May 26th) of the following proclamation announced the movements on foot:

"HEAD-QUARTERS, DEPARTMENT OF OHIO,
CINCINNATI, May 26th, 1861.

"*To the Union Men of Western Virginia:*

"VIRGINIANS:—The General Government has long enough endured the machinations of a few factious rebels in your midst. Armed traitors have in vain endeavored to deter you from expressing your loyalty at the polls. Having failed in this infamous attempt to deprive you of the exercise of your dearest rights, they now seek to inaugurate a reign of terror, and thus force you to yield to their schemes, and submit to the yoke of the traitorous conspiracy, dignified by the name of the Southern Confederacy. They are destroying the property of citizens of your State, and ruining your magnificent railways. The General Government has heretofore carefully abstained from sending troops across the Ohio, or even from posting them along its banks, although frequently urged by many of your prominent citizens to do so.

"It determined to await the result of the State election, desirous that no one might be able to say, that the slightest effort had been made from this side to influence the free expression of your opinions, although the many agencies brought to bear upon you by the rebels were well known. You have now shown, under the most adverse circumstances, that the great mass of the people of Western Virginia are true and loyal to that beneficent Government under which we and our fathers have lived so long. As soon as the result of the election was known, the traitors commenced their work of destruction. The General Government can not close its ears to the demand you have made for assistance. I have ordered troops to cross the river. They come as your friends and brothers; as enemies only to armed rebels who are preying upon you. Your homes, your families, and your property are safe under our protection. All your rights shall be religiously respected.

"Notwithstanding all that has been said by the traitors to induce you to believe our advent among you will be signalized by an interference with your slaves, understand one thing clearly: Not only will we abstain from all such interference, but we will, on the contrary, with an iron hand, crush any attempt at insurrection on their part.

"Now that we are in your midst, I call upon you to fly to arms and support the General Government; sever the connection that binds you to traitors; proclaim to the world that the faith and loyalty so long boasted by the Old Dominion are still preserved in Western Virginia, and that you remain true to the Stars and Stripes.

"G. B. McCLELLAN, Major-General Commanding."

This document gave the proper reasons for the contemplated movement. To his troops, then cantoned in Eastern Ohio, he addressed a stirring address, well calculated to win the confidence of the people among whom they were to move. It read:

"SOLDIERS:—You are ordered to cross the frontier, and to enter on the soil of Virginia. Your mission is to restore peace and confidence; to protect the majesty of the law, and to secure our brethren from the grasp of armed traitors. I place under the safeguard of your honor the persons and property of the Virginians. I know you will respect their feelings and all their rights, and will preserve the strictest discipline.

"Remember, that each one of you holds in his keeping the honor of Ohio and the Union. If you are called to overcome armed opposition, I know your courage is equal to the task. Remember that your only *foes* are *armed traitors*. Show mercy even to them, when in your power, for many of them are misguided.

"When, under your protection, the loyal men of Western Virginia have been enabled to organize and form until they can protect themselves, you can return to your homes, with the proud satisfaction of having preserved a gallant people from destruction."

Prior to the issue of these documents, everything had been arranged for the advance. Colonel Kelly, in command at Camp Carlisle, in Ohio, opposite Wheeling, gave the word of command for the onward movement, Sunday evening, (May 26th), by reading the Proclamation and Address.

The announcement was received with wild huzzas by the troops, the First Virginia Volunteers. Monday morning they poured over into Virginia eleven hundred strong, and, at seven o'clock, were *en route* for Grafton, a place of some strategic importance, lying at the junction of the Baltimore and Ohio and the Northwestern Virginia railways. The First Virginia was followed immediately by the Sixteenth Ohio Volunteers, Colonel Irvine. The Fourteenth Ohio, Colonel Steadman, crossed the river at Marietta, and occupied Parkersburg, the western terminus of the Northwestern railroad.

The rebels, then in possession of Grafton, designed a descent on Wheeling; but, hastily evacuated on the night of Monday, having previously destroyed railway bridges at various points to the west of Grafton. The Federal forces did not fully occupy the place until Thursday morning, when the two regiments, with all their baggage and trains, took possession. The rebels withdrew to Phillippi, where they resolved to make a stand. The Federal advance was soon joined by the Fifteenth Ohio, and the Sixth Indiana, Colonel Crittenden, regiments, the Seventh Indiana, Colonel Dumont, while the forces landed at Parkersburg had pushed up the railroad to a conjunction. The attack on Phillippi was not delayed—McClellan having ordered the enemy to be surprised by a forced march. On the night of June 2d, the Federal forces (four regiments) started for the point of attack by two routes—one division by way of Webster, under command of Colonel Dumont, consisted of eight companies of the Seventh Indiana; four companies of the Fourth Ohio, Colonel Steadman, with his artillery, under command of Lieutenant-Colonel Sturgis, assisted and directed by Colonel Lander; four companies of the Sixth Indiana, Colonel Crittenden. The other division consisted of the First Virginia, and companies from the Sixteenth Ohio and Seventh Indiana regiments, under command of Colonel Kelly, which moved east, by way of Thornton, thence south to Phillippi (twenty-two miles) by a forced march. The darkness was intense, the mud deep, and the storm of wind and rain unceasing. The division of Kelly did not reach the enemy's position at four o'clock—the time indicated for the conjunction and combined attack—owing to the dreadful fatigues of the march. His forces were to strike the enemy's rear, and while Colonels Dumont and Lander pressed the front, to cut off the retreat, and thus "bag" the entire rebel force. Dumont arrived at the appointed time, and disposed his forces for battle. It soon became evident that the rebels had discovered the movements of their foe, and were preparing to run. Lander not deeming it prudent longer to await Colonel Kelly's appearance, ordered the artillery to open. The Associate Press account of the fight read:

Simultaneously with the roar of the first gun, Colonel Kelly, at the head of his command, came in sight across the river below the camp, and, comprehending the position of affairs, he rushed forward in the direction of the camp. Meanwhile the battery, having got accurate range, played upon the camp with marked effect, tearing through the tents and houses at a fearful rate. This the chivalry could not stand, and they scattered like rats from a burning barn, after firing at random a volley which did no damage.

Colonel Kelly's command was close after them, and, at the same time, Colonel Lander's force came rushing down the hill yelling like Indians. After chasing them a few miles, the already exhausted men returned to the evacuated camp, to learn the painful fact that their victory, though complete, was dearly bought. Colonel Kelly, who, with bravery amounting to rashness, was foremost from first to last, was rallying his men in the upper part of the town, the enemy having all apparently fled, when he fell by a shot from a concealed foe. The assassin was an Assistant-Quartermaster in the Confederate force, named Sims. He was immediately seized.

A correspondent who was present thus referred to Colonel Lander's ride down the hill on which the artillery was posted, and his subsequent achievement:

"The hill on which the artillery was planted is both high and steep, and it would be dangerous for an inexperienced rider to walk a horse down the slope toward the pike. Seeing Dumont's right rushing for the bridge, closely followed by the Ohio Fourteenth, (Colonel Steadman,) and supposing the passage of the bridge would be disputed, he grasped a revolver in each hand, plunged spurs into the flanks of his horse, and dashed down the hill, over fences, and stumps, and stones, and dead timber, through a wheat field, to the pike, and swept past the column like the wind, looking (as one who saw him says) more like a demon than a man. Colonel Steadman, in the excitement of the moment, had advanced some three hundred yards ahead of his command as Lander passed. 'Go back, Colonel Steadman—go back to your column,' said he, 'or you will be cut off!' forgetting that he was exposed to the same danger.

"By this time Colonel Kelly had arrived and attacked the rear of the rebels. Colonel Lander now rode alone across the town to join Kelly, but just after he had passed Kelly, a rebel brought Kelly down by a shot through the lungs. Lander at once charged among the enemy and chased the rebel into an angle of a fence, where he guarded him until the infantry came up. An unsuccessful charge was made by a few of the rebels to rescue the prisoner. On Kelly's men arriving they were determined to bayonet the prisoner, but were prevented by Colonel Lander, against their urgent remonstrances. The Quartermaster of the Virginia regiment took charge of him, becoming responsible for his safety. Colonel Lander maintained that the man had thrown down his arms and yielded himself to him as a prisoner of war; that if he had killed Kelly he would have done it in actual fight, and after our troops had commenced the engagement, and that he should protect him with his life."

The enemy retreated, with a loss of all his baggage, tents, &c., to Beverly, finally taking up position on Laurel Hill, which he proceeded to fortify. The campaign which followed was thus chronicled by one who participated in it:

"The rebel forces, after the battle of Philippi, lay at Laurel Hill, near Beverly, in a strong position, which commanded our road to the southern portion of the State, and in which they had fortified themselves with great labor and care. From this point they had repeatedly threatened us with attack, and our officers felt very eager to repeat the action by which the campaign had been so successfully opened at Philippi. A plan was formed, therefore, to move down from our head-quarters at Grafton and capture or destroy the enemy. The fortifications at Laurel Hill had, however, greatly strengthened a position of the most advantageous kind, and the attack was not to be lightly undertaken.

"On the side of the Laurel Mountain lies a fine, broad and cleared plateau, which afforded ample room for an encampment and a parade-ground in the rear. The slopes in front down to the valley were fortified with a more extended system of intrenchments, which our men are now engaged in destroying, and which were so complete as almost to defy a direct attack by any force at our command. It was resolved, therefore, to combine with the direct assault a movement in the enemy's rear, for which the shape of the country afforded peculiar facilities. Stretching away, north-east and south-west, lay the western range of the Alleghanies, impassable without great difficulty for an army, and even then passable only at certain points. At the foot of the mountain was the main road, which gives access to Southern Virginia on this western slope of the range. By this route alone could the enemy receive reenforcements or supplies, and this fact determined the scheme of operations. To occupy his attention by a direct attack in front, while another body of our forces should go around into his rear, and cut off communication with his base, would place him at our mercy, and enable us to assail him in his intrenchments with an overpowering force, and in both directions at once, or else to starve him out, should it be deemed best not to conclude the affair by a direct engagement.

"The plan thus formed was executed by the two divisions of General McClellan's army. The main body of ten thousand, led by himself, went round by Clarksburg and Buckhannon, on the west of the enemy; while the other and smaller division of four thousand, under General Morris, made the direct attack, which was to hold the rebels in check on the north, and occupy them while the former force should be getting into their rear.

"General McClellan, after a sharp skirmish at Buckhannon, approached the rear of the enemy, which, however, he found strongly fortified at Rich Mountain, and defended by a force of some two or three thousand under Colonel Pegram. Sending General Rosecrans with a force of some three thousand to assail them in the rear, while he was himself to attack them in front, he hoped to capture the enemy entirely; but some want of co-operation took place, which interfered with the completeness of the result. General Rosecrans reached the rear of the mountains, which was held by some three hundred rebels, but did not succeed in communicating to General McClellan the information that he was ready to attack, and the command of McClellan lay inactive for many hours, waiting for this intelligence. Hence, though the attack of Rosecrans was entirely successful upon the small force before him, Colonel Pegram took the alarm, and silently moved off with his main body to join Garnett at Laurel Hill. He found it impossible, however, to do so, and after lying in the woods for two days, utterly destitute of provisions, was obliged to surrender with all those of his troops who had not succeeded in getting away. This successful move captured or killed about one thousand or perhaps twelve hundred rebels.

"Meanwhile, the division of General Morris was cautiously making its way down upon the enemy from Grafton and Philippi. The command of the advance brigade was given by General Morris to his chief engineer officer, Captain Benham, of the United States Topographical Engineers, an officer of great experience and skill, whose judgment had before been tested by the conduct of several difficult operations. Captain Benham had thoroughly explored and mapped the country, and his accurate delineations of the topography had given essential aid in the planning of the expedition. When General McClellan's order was received to march upon Laurel Hill, Captain Benham arranged the plan of the march, and started at two A. M. on the 7th of July. By skillfully availing himself of the peculiarities of the country, he avoided the necessity of thrice fording a stream, as had been supposed necessary by the commanding General, in order to avoid defiles where effective resistance might be offered; and thus brought the army to its designated position some two hours earlier than would have been possible otherwise, to the complete surprise of the enemy. Here a position was chosen at Beelington, on the opposite side of the valley from Laurel Hill, and within rifle-shot of the enemy's intrenchments; and, notwithstanding repeated attacks and skirmishes with the enemy, it was successfully fortified and held till the approach of the other column.

"Upon the overthrow of Colonel Pegram at Rich Mountain, General Garnett, the rebel commander, began to understand the extent of his danger, and made haste to extricate himself from a position in which he could no longer fight with advantage, nor even retreat with success. He left his intrenchments, and moved at once south toward Beverly, hoping, by great expedition, to reach that place before General McClellan should arrive. But by the time he had got within a few miles of it the fugitives from Pegram's corps informed him that the effort was hopeless. Beverly was occupied in force by the Union troops. His only remaining resource was to turn upon his steps, and retrace his path to Leedsville, where another turnpike road branched off to the north-east, on the other side of Laurel Mountain. Pursuing this route with all speed, he passed Leedsville the same afternoon, and pressed on along the base of the mountains down the Cheat River, hoping to find some practicable path across the mountains into the valley of Virginia. Throwing away, therefore, all superfluous baggage, he fled rapidly, and soon turned off from the main road into a narrow path along the mountains, in which pursuit might be more easily obstructed. Here he closed the narrow path after him, and filled every defile through which he passed, by felling the largest trees into and across it.

"His flight, however, which took place on Thursday evening, was ascertained on Friday morning by some of our men at Laurel Hill; and, on word being sent to General Morris, he gave immediate orders for pursuit, though his force was greatly inferior to that of the enemy. Following with the somewhat larger portion himself, he sent Captain Benham forward with the advance division, giving him orders to press forward after the rebels as far as Leedsville, secure the ford at that place, and await his arrival. Captain Benham set out instantly, at first with caution, for it might be only a feint to draw us on into an attack; but, on reaching the intrenchments, they were found entirely deserted, and the Captain had the pleasure to be the first officer within the abandoned works. The command pressed on to Leedsville and there halted, according to orders. This order to halt was unfortunate; had Captain

Benham been authorized to advance further, a more effectual pursuit might have been made; but, held back by positive directions, he was compelled to wait—his men under arms and ready to resume the pursuit—till General Morris arrived at ten P. M. It was then too late to move till morning; the men must have some rest; and they were allowed a brief slumber of three hours, from eleven in the evening till two A. M., when the pursuit was eagerly resumed.

"The pursuit was a memorable one. Captain Benham led, with one thousand eight hundred men, composed of Ohio and Indiana troops. General Morris followed with the rear. Up and down the mountains, through defiles, and over rugged ridges, everywhere impeded by the obstructions thrown in the way by the flying enemy—the pursuit was pressed with an ardor which was not to be repressed. Many men fell behind, exhausted with hunger and exertion.

"At length, after crossing one of the branches of Cheat River, we saw before us the provision-train of the rebels at rest; but a foolish boy firing his musket set it in motion again in full retreat, and brought out two heavy regiments to protect it, before our first regiment could reach the ford. This caused a further pursuit of three or four miles, when the train was again overtaken half across the stream; and here General Garnett made a vigorous stand for its defense.

"The locality afforded a fine position to repel our assault. Cheat River, in one of its numerous bends, winds here round a bluff of fifty or sixty feet high, the lower portion of which is covered with a dense growth of laurel, through which it is almost impossible to penetrate. On the top of this bluff he placed his cannon, which swept our approach to the ford; while his troops were drawn up in line—some two thousand in number—on either side of their guns, in a line some four hundred feet in length, with the remainder of his force within a mile. They were well protected from our fire by a fence, which showed only their heads above it, and by numerous trees which afforded them cover.

"On coming up, Colonel Dumont's men, the Seventh Indiana regiment, pressed into the stream, crossed it, and attempted to scale the bluff in front, in face of the enemy's fire of musketry and artillery, but the steepness of the ascent rendered it impossible. When Captain Benham came up he found the men climbing the steep ascent almost on their faces; and, seeing the difficulty of success, he ordered them down again into the stream. On our right was a depression in the bluff, just where a ravine came down to the river, and he directed them to try the ascent there. They did so, but found the way so steep, and so obstructed by the dense cedar roots, that they soon found this, too, impossible. Captain Benham then ordered the regiment to cross the stream, and, keeping in its bed, immediately under the bluff, to pass down it to our left, where they could gain the road. This happy manœuvre was immediately executed. The men passed down the whole front of the enemy, protected so effectually by the steepness of the bank from his fire, that they emerged on the right of the rebels without losing a man; and, as the head of the column showed itself on their flank, the rebels fled, leaving one of their guns, and a number of killed, wounded, and prisoners in our hands.

"About a quarter of a mile in advance, the river makes another turn, and here the enemy again attempted a stand. General Garnett himself bravely stood, and tried to gather his men around him, but in vain. He then begged for thirty skirmishers to go back with him and pick off our officers—as we were informed by our prisoners subsequently. A few did return with him to the bank of the stream; but, as we came up, they fired a volley and again fled, and left him with only a single companion. Our men ran forward to the bank of the stream, where a group of three cedars gave them a slight cover, and fired upon the fugitives. General Garnett was standing with his back to us, trying in vain to rally his men, when he received a Minie ball just on the left of the spine. It made a terrible wound, piercing the heart and coming out at the right nipple, and the poor General threw up his arms, and with his single companion fell dead. Our men passed over, and finding by the straps on his shoulder that he was an officer of rank, sent word back immediately to the commanding officer. Captain Benham was still at the bluff, caring for the wounded and directing the removal of the cannon, but, on receiving the news, he at once rode forward to the spot, and himself first identified the body as that of General Garnett, late Major Garnett, U. S. A.

"The body, which had remained undisturbed, was carried, by Captain Benham's order, into a small log-house, where the General's money was taken from his pockets and counted, and, with his watch and sword, preserved for his family; his field-telescope, an elegant opera-glass, a large map of Virginia, and some small sketches of our own positions near Grafton, became the legitimate trophies of the conqueror."

The enemy was utterly broken—hopelessly defeated. Not more than two thousand of the five thousand with which Garnett had commenced his flight, escaped; and these were in such a disorganized condition as to be unavailable. Parties of them kept coming in to the Union camps for several days. They were well received and humanely cared for—hungry and almost naked, as they were in most instances. After recruiting them, the lenient policy was adopted of administering the oath of allegiance, or of a release on parole. Of course, men base enough to take up arms against their country scorned oaths and paroles; and those scoundrels, almost without exception, were soon in the ranks of the Confederates. The Union Generals were long in discovering that the best way to serve a rebel was to place him where his honor or oath were not to be called into requisition.

This infamous disregard of oaths and honor was happily illustrated in the sarcasm of a Captain in one of the Ohio regiments. A rattlesnake was caught alive on the mountains and brought into camp. After tiring of its presence, its captor asked the Captain what he should do with the reptile. "Oh, swear him and let him go!" was the curt reply.

With the destruction of Garnett's army Western Virginia was left to pursue its course of reorganization. The Wheeling Convention labored zealously and patriotically, heartily endorsed in their efforts by the vast majority of people in the thirty counties west of the Blue Ridge Mountains. The new State soon came up like a Phœnix, and with Governor Pierrepont at its head, became the recognized State of Virginia. Such were the fruits of McClellan's first campaign.

XIV.

THE FIRST DISASTER.

THE first real disaster which fell upon the Union arms occurred at Big Bethel, on York Peninsula, on Monday, June 10th. Butler, in his report, stated the reasons for the advance ordered, as follows:

"Having learned that the enemy had established an outpost of some strength at a place called Little Bethel, a small church, about eight miles from Newport News, and the same distance from Hampton, from whence they were accustomed nightly to advance both on Newport News and the picket guards of Hampton to annoy them, and also from whence they had come down in small squads of cavalry and taken a number of Union men, some of whom had the safeguard and protection of the troops of the United States, and forced them into the rebel ranks, and that they were also gathering up the slaves of citizens who had moved away and left their farms in charge of their negroes, carrying them to work in intrenchments at Williamsburg and Yorktown, I had determined to send up a force to drive them back and destroy their camp, the head-quarters of which was this small church. I had also learned that at a short distance further on, on the road to Yorktown, was an outwork of the rebels, on the Hampton side of a place called Big Bethel, a large church, near the head of the north branch of Back River, and that here was a very considerable rendezvous, with works of more or less strength in process of erection, and from this point the whole country was laid under contribution."

He accordingly ordered Brigadier-General Pierce "to send Duryea's regiment of Zouaves to be ferried over Hampton creek at one o'clock on the morning of the 10th, and to march by the road up to Newmarket bridge, then crossing the bridge, to go by a by-road, and thus put the regiment in the rear of the enemy, and between Big Bethel and Little Bethel, in part for the purpose of cutting him off, and then to make an attack upon Little Bethel." This regiment was to be supported by Colonel Townsend's regiment (Third New York volunteers) at Hampton, which was to take up its line of march at two o'clock. Colonel Phelps, at Newport News, was ordered to send forward "such companies of the regiments under his command as he thought best, under command of Lieutenant-Colonel Washburne, in time to make a demonstration upon Little Bethel in front, and to have him supported by Colonel Bendix's regiment, with two field pieces." Bendix and Townsend were to form a junction at the forks of the roads leading from Hampton and Newport News, about a mile and a half from Little Bethel.

These movements were so arranged that the attack upon Little Bethel was to be made at daybreak; when, the enemy being repulsed, Duryea's Zouaves and one of the Newport News regiments were to "follow upon the heels of the flying rebels and attack the battery on the road to Big Bethel, while covered by the fugitives, or, if it was thought expedient by General Pierce, failing to surprise the camp at Little Bethel, they should attempt to take the work at Big Bethel. To prevent the possibility of mistake in the darkness, Butler directed that no attack should be made until the watchword was shouted by the attacking regiment; and, in case that, by any mistake in the march, the regiments to make the junction should unexpectedly meet and be unknown to each other, it was directed that the members of Colonel Townsend's regiment should be known, if in daylight, by something white worn on the arm."

These orders were explicit, it will be seen, and exonorate Butler from blame for the disaster which attended the expedition, since, had they been carried out, the objects of the expedition would have been accomplished.

The troops were all put in motion as ordered. The beautiful night, clear with the light of stars, rendered every movement easy. The regiments had passed to their several designated positions—Duryea's in the advance and Lieutenant Colonel Washburne with the Newport News troops close at hand. Townsend's regiment was coming up, and when within a few yards of the rendezvous, suddenly a furious fire was poured in upon his ranks, of small arms and cannon. This fire was supposed to proceed from an ambuscade of the enemy, and was returned, while the assailed regiment left the road and took the cover of a ridge in the rear. Not until several rounds had been discharged and two of Townsend's men killed and eight wounded did the assailants (who proved to be a portion of Colonel Bendix's regiment of German riflemen, together with a few companies of Massachusetts and Vermont men) discover their grievous mistake.

In the meanwhile, Colonel Duryea and Lieutenant-Colonel Washburne, hearing the firing, supposed the attack to proceed from the enemy; and, fearing that their communications might be cut off, fell back. The enemy's pickets had been reached by Duryea, and five of them were captured ; but, the alarm being given, and the advance retarded, the rebels had ample time to evacuate their position at Little Bethel, and to make good their retreat to Big Bethel, where they had, as it afterwards appeared, excellent defensive works, held by a North Carolina regiment, and strong batteries manned by Magruder's own choice men.

A conference was held by the several officers in command, when it was determined to push forward and assail Big Bethel—Duryea still on the advance. A messenger was dispatched to Butler giving an account of affairs, and suggesting that a regiment be sent forward as a reserve. Colonel Allen was, thereupon, thrown forward upon Hampton. No opposition was offered, save from one house, from which a shot was fired, wounding one man. The house was in flames in a few moments. The vicinity of Big Bethel was reached by half-past nine A. M. The position was thus described:

"On the right of the road as the troops advanced was a wood; in the centre lay the road, and, on their left, a large open field. The enemy's batteries were placed so as not only to command the field, which was directly in front of them, but also the road and the centre woods on its left. A private house and some outbuildings stood in the plain, so that the Secessionists were placed on a hill, backed and concealed by woods; in their entire front a stream, on the further side of that stream a large plain, with no shelter but that of one or two insignificant houses, and to the right, but commanded by their guns, a wood, through which ran the road."

The enemy opened his cannonade at the first appearance of the Federal troops. Duryea, covered by two howitzers and a brass six-pounder, took the centre; Townsend the left, near the plain, with two guns; Bendix the right, in the woods, with Lieutenant Greble serving his single piece of artillery, in front, openly. The fight was, from the first, extremely unequal. The enemy, lurking behind intrenchments, and with guns commanding the entire approach, was also further guarded by a narrow, but deep stream, passing along their entire front, and covering their flank from approach. Thus secure, the contest was alarmingly unequal. Pierce, seeing how unexpectedly warm was to be his reception, dispatched a second messenger to Butler for reenforcements, when Colonel Carr's regiment, then advanced as far as Newmarket bridge, moved to the scene of conflict—only reaching it, however, to participate in the retreat.

The fortunes of the day only needed a master-hand to direct them, to have turned in favor of the Union troops. General Pierce refrained from much command—each regiment seeming to act entirely on its own responsibility. Several most gallant advances were made by the Zouaves, up to the enemy's very face, to pick off the men lurking behind their guns. Colonel Bendix prepared for a final assault, but found no orders given for a support. Townsend's men behaved with great gallantry, and were only brought away from the murderous fire of the artillery by the personal leadership of the Colonel, who, on his horse, rode between the fires, and compelled his troops to retire. Lieutenant-Colonel Washburne had, also, arranged for a flank movement which, with a combined attack from the front, must have ended the struggle; but the order for retreat was given before the movement could be executed. One who was present as an observer, wrote:

"The raw troops, recruits not yet two months enlisted, and many of them not having received two weeks drill, stood fire well. They were almost utterly unable to defend themselves, from the nature of things, but never flinched. Some were less disciplined than others, and their efforts less available, but no lack of the most difficult sort of courage, that which consists in enduring without the excitement of performing, was manifested. The cannonading of the enemy was incessant. Shrapnell, canister, and rifled balls came at the rate of three a minute; the only intervals being those necessary to allow their guns to cool. Our own guns, although of comparatively little use, were not idle, until the artillery ammunition was entirely exhausted. Almost all of the cartridge rounds of the Zouaves were also fired.

"At about one o'clock, Colonel Allen's regiment, the First New York, came up as a reenforcement, and, at about the same time, Colonel Carr's, of the Troy Volunteers; these also received several discharges of artillery; but did not move upon the open field, with the exception of two hundred of the Troy Rifles. Their approach, however, seemed to the commanding General to give no hope that he would be able, without more artillery, to take or silence the batteries, and, at about twenty minutes past one, he gave the order to withdraw."

The Federal loss was fourteen killed, forty-nine wounded, and five missing. Among the killed were two of the most gallant and noble men in the service—Major Theodore Winthrop, Secretary and Aid to General Butler, and First-Lieutenant John T. Greble, of the United States regular Artillery, Second regiment. The enemy pronounced his loss to have been but one killed and four wounded. The retreat was accomplished in good order—the enemy not pursuing. A troop of cavalry sallied over the bridge, and fell upon the wagons collecting the wounded—disregarding the flag of truce borne by the Chaplain in command, but no attack was made on the lines. Colonel Phelps had dispatched two hundred and fifty men, under Colonel Hawkins, to the scene of combat; but these troops only met the retreat.

This contest excited the public mind greatly. Upon General Pierce the censure of defeat fell, with merciless severity. He was charged with inefficiency, ignorance of field manœuvres, want of pluck, etc., etc. It is questionable if the charges were wholly true. The first error was in dispatching so large a force without equivalent artillery. Had there been a dozen good field pieces, the enemy would have been driven from his position in half-an-hour. As it was, Greble's single gun did memorable service, and, had Bendix and Duryea been allowed to charge, as they wished, at a moment when it was evident that Greble and the sharpshooters had silenced over half of the enemy's guns, it is more than probable that the day would have been won. General Pierce lacked confidence in himself. It was his first experience on the battle field; he seemed confused by its responsibilities. Conceded to be a brave officer and a good disciplinarian, he still lacked the experiences of a general field command. Had he wisely conferred that command upon Duryea, or, indeed, upon any one of his Colonels, that army never would have retreated, especially after the arrival of Colonel Carr's fine troops, with their two effective pieces of artillery.

In the enemy's account of the fight, as given by the Richmond *Dispatch*, the fact was made known that Magruder commanded in person. The infantry present consisted of the First North Carolina regiment, Colonel Hill. Their guns consisted of a superb howitzer battery (seven guns), embracing one fine Parrot field-piece. The battery was worked by one hundred chosen men, under Major Randolph. The account stated, among other things:

"About nine o'clock, the glittering bayonets of the enemy appeared on the hill opposite, and above them waved the Star Spangled Banner. The moment the head of the column advanced far enough to show one or two companies, the Parrot gun of the howitzer battery opened on them, throwing a shell right into their midst. Their ranks broke in confusion, and the column, or as much of it as we could see, retreated behind two small farm-houses. From their position a fire was opened on us, which was replied to by our battery, which commanded the route of their approach. Our firing was excellent, and the shells scattered in all directions when they burst. They could hardly approach the guns which they were firing for the shells which came from our battery. Within our encampment fell a perfect hailstorm of canister-shot, bullets, and balls. Remarkable to say, not one of our men was killed, inside of our encampment. Several horses were slain by the shells and bullets.

"Finding that bombardment would not answer, the enemy, about eleven o'clock, tried to carry the position by assault, but met a terrible repulse at the hands of the infantry, as he tried to scale the breastworks, The men disregarded sometimes the defenses erected for them, and, leaping on the embankment, stood and fired at the Yankees, cutting them down as they came up. One company of the New York Seventh regiment, under Captain Winthrop, attempted to take the redoubt on the left. The marsh they crossed was strewn with their bodies. Thoir Captain, a finc-looking man, reached the fence, and, leaning on a log, waved his sword, crying, 'Come on, boys, one charge, and the day is ours.' The words were his last, for a Carolina rifle ended his life the next moment, and his men fled in terror back. At the redoubt on the right, a company of about three hundred New York Zouaves charged one of our guns, but could not stand the fire of the infantry, and retreated precipitately.

"During these charges, the main body of the enemy on the hill were attempting to concentrate for a general assault, but the shells from the howitzer battery prevented them. As one regiment would give up the effort, another would be marched to the position, but with no better success, for a shell would scatter them like chaff. The men did not seem able to stand fire at all.

"About one o'clock their guns were silenced, and a few moments after, their infantry retreated precipitately down the road to Hampton."

The Raleigh *State Journal* published the following in an extra:

"YORKTOWN, Va., June 11th, 1861.

"*Hon. J. W. Ellis, Governor of North Carolina:*

"SIR: I have the honor to report that eight hundred men of my regiment and three hundred and sixty Virginians were engaged for five and a half hours with four and a half regiments of the enemy, at Bethel Church, nine miles from Hampton.

"The enemy made three distinct and well-sustained charges, but were repulsed with heavy loss. Our cavalry pursued them for six miles, when their retreat became a total route. Fearing that heavy reenforcements would be sent up from Fortress Monroe, we fell back at nightfall upon our works at Yorktown. I regret to report the loss of one man killed, private Henry L. Wyatt, Edgecomb Guards, and seven wounded.

"The loss of the enemy, by their own confession, was one hundred and fifty, but it may be safely estimated at two hundred and fifty.

"Our regiment behaved most gallantly. Not a man shrunk from his post or showed symptoms of fear. When more at leisure, I will give you a detailed report of the operations.

"Our Heavenly Father has most wonderfully interposed to shield our hearts in the day of battle; unto His great name be all the praise for our success.

"With much respect, D. H. HILL,

"Colonel First Regiment N. C. Volunteers."

XV.

MAJOR WINTHROP.

MAJOR Theodore Winthrop was one of those luminaries whose worth was not fully estimated until it had departed forever. His brief career—his heroic death—gave to the newspaper paragraphist a theme for a brief record; but to those who valued those qualities in man which render him adorable, the life of Major Winthrop was a theme of abiding interest, and his death the source of an abiding sorrow.

If the young Ellsworth was the embodiment of the spirit of American energy and vitality, the young Winthrop was none the less a representative of American nobility of nature. His scarcely opened life had but just begun to display its purity and grace ere it was closed again—to become a tender memory. Over Ellsworth's tomb hangs a halo of the glory which bursts and burns from the brow of the resistless man. Over the tomb of Winthrop beams the halo of glory which radiates and glows from the brow of the adorable man. It is well to enshrine the story of such lives in the history of the cause in which they were offered as sacrifices.

The *Atlantic Monthly* for August, 1861, contained a paper on Winthrop, which so fully revealed the man, that we adopt it as the estimate which we desire to attach to his memory. It was understood to emanate from the pen of George Henry Curtis, Esquire, an intimate associate of the deceased officer, and one familiar with that *inner* life of Winthrop which rendered him the type of man, whom it should be the study of our young men to emulate. We extract from that paper such portions of it as are material to a clear comprehension of the life and character of our subject:

"He was born in New Haven on the 23d of September, 1828, and was a grave, delicate, rather precocious child. He was at school only in New Haven, and entered Yale College just as he was sixteen. The pure, manly morality which was the substance of his character, and his brilliant exploits of scholarship, made him the idol of his college friends, who saw in him the promise of the splendid career which the fond faith of students allots to the favorite classmate. He studied for the Clark scholarship, and gained it; and his name, in the order of time, is first upon the roll of that foundation. He won the Townsend prize for the best composition on history. For the Berkeleian scholarship he and another were judged equal, and, drawing lots, the other gained the scholarship; but they divided the honor.

"In college his favorite studies were Greek and mental philosophy. He never lost the scholarly taste and habit. A wide reader, he retained knowledge with little effort, and often surprised his friends by the variety of his information. Yet it was not strange, for he was born a scholar. His mother was the great grand-daughter of old President Edwards; and, among his ancestors upon the maternal side, Winthrop counted seven College Presidents. Perhaps, also, in this learned descent we may find the secret of his early seriousness. Thoughtful and self-criticizing, he was peculiarly sensible to religious influences, under which his criticism easily became self-accusation, and his sensitive seriousness grew sometimes morbid. He would have studied for the ministry or a professorship, upon leaving college, except for his failing health.

"In the latter days, when I knew him, the feverish ardor of the first religious impulse was past. It had given place to a faith much too deep and sacred to talk about, yet holding him always with serene, steady poise in the purest region of life and feeling. There was no franker or more sympathetic companion for young men of his own age than he; but his conversation fell from his lips as unsullied as his soul.

"He graduated in 1848, when he was twenty years old; and, for the sake of his health, which was seriously shattered—an ill-health that colored all his life—he set out upon his travels. He went first to England, spending much time at Oxford, where he made pleasant acquaintances, and walking through Scotland. He then crossed over to France and Germany, exploring Switzerland very thoroughly upon foot—once or twice escaping great dangers among the mountains—and pushed on to Italy and Greece, still walking much of the way. In Italy he made the acquaintance of Mr. W. H. Aspinwall, of New York, and, upon his return, became tutor to Mr. Aspinwall's son. He presently accompanied his pupil and a nephew of Mr. Aspinwall, who were going to a school in Switzerland; and, after a second short tour of six months in Europe, he returned to New York, and entered Mr. Aspinwall's counting-house. In the employ of the Pacific Steamship Company he went to Panama, and resided for about two years, traveling, and often ill of the fevers of the country. Before his return he traveled through California and Oregon—went to Vancouver's Island, Puget Sound, and the Hudson Bay Company's station there. At the Dalles he was smitten with the small-pox, and lay ill for six weeks. He often spoke with the warmest gratitude of the kind care that was taken of him there. But when only partially recovered, he plunged off again into the wilderness. At another time, he fell very ill upon the Plains, and lay down, as he supposed, to die; but, after some time, struggled up and on again.

"He returned to the counting-room, but, unsated with adventure, joined the disastrous expedition of Lieutenant Strain, during which his health was still more weakened, and he came home again in 1845. In the following year he studied law, and was admitted to the bar. In 1856 he entered heartily into the Fremont campaign, and from the strongest conviction. He went into some of the dark districts of Pennsylvania, and spoke incessantly. The roving life and its picturesque episodes, with the earnest conviction which inspired him, made the summer and autumn exciting and pleasant. The following year he went to St. Louis to practice law. The climate was unkind to him, and he returned and began the practice in New York. But he could not be a lawyer. His health was too uncertain, and his tastes and ambition allured him elsewhere. His mind was brimming with the results of observation. His fancy was alert and inventive, and he wrote tales and novels. At the same time he delighted to haunt the studio of his friend Church, the painter, and watch day by day the progress of his picture, the Heart of the Andes. It so fired his imagination that he wrote a description of it, in which, as if rivalling the tropical and tangled richness of the picture, he threw together such heaps and masses of gorgeous words, that the reader was dazzled and bewildered.

"The wild, campaigning life, was always a secret passion with him. His stories of travel were so graphic and warm, that I remember one evening, after we had been tracing upon the map a route he had taken, and he had touched the whole region into life with his description, my younger brother, who had sat by and listened with wide eyes all the evening, exclaimed, with a sigh of regretful satisfaction, as the door closed upon our story-teller, 'It's as good as Robinson Crusoe!' Yet, with all his fondness and fitness for that kind of life, or, indeed, any active administrative function, his literary ambition seemed to be the deepest and strongest.

"He had always been writing. In college and upon his travels he kept diaries; and he has left behind him several novels, tales, sketches of travel, and journals. The first published writing of his which is well known, is his description of the March of the Seventh Regiment of New York to Washington. It was charming by its graceful, sparkling, crisp, off-hand dash and ease. But it is only the practised hand that can "dash off" the story of a day, or a week, in the life of the regiment, and he will see that the writer did that little thing well, because he had done large things carefully. Yet, amid all the hurry and brilliant bustle of the articles, the author is, as he was in the most bustling moment of life they described, a spectator, an artist. He looks on at himself, and the scene of which he is part—he is willing to merge his individuality; but he does not merge it, for he could not,

"So, wandering, hoping, trying, waiting, thirty-two years of his life went by, and they left him true, sympathetic, patient. The sharp private griefs that sting the heart so deeply, and leave a little poison behind, did not spare him. But he bore everything so bravely, so silently —often silent for a whole evening in the midst of pleasant talkers, but not impertinently sad, nor even sullen—that we all loved him a little more at such times. The ill-health from which he always suffered, and a flower-like delicacy of temperament, the yearning desire to be of some service in the world, coupled with the curious, critical introspection which marks every sensitive and refined nature and paralyzes action, overcast his life and manner to the common eye with pensiveness and even sternness. He wrote verses in which his heart seems to exhale in a sigh of sadness. But he was not in the least a sentimentalist. The womanly grace of temperament merely enhanced the unusual manliness of his character and impression. It was like a delicate carnation upon the cheek of a robust man; for his humor was exuberant. He seldom laughed loud, but his smile was sweet and appreciative. Then the range of his sympathies was so large, that he enjoyed every kind of life and person, and was everywhere at home. In walking and riding, in skating and running, in games out of doors and in, no one of us all in the neighborhood was so expert, so agile as he. For, above all things, he had what we Yankees call faculty—the knack of doing everything. If he rode with a neighbor who was a good horseman, Theodore, who was a Centaur, when he mounted, would put any horse at any gate or fence; for it did not occur to him that he could not do whatever was to be done. Often, after writing for a few hours in the morning, he stepped out of doors, and, from pure love of the fun, leaped and turned summersaults on the grass, before going up to town. In walking about the island, he constantly stopped by the roadside fences, and, grasping the highest rail, swung himself swiftly and neatly over and back again, resuming the walk and the talk without delay.

"I do not wish to make him too much of a hero. 'Death,' says

Bacon, 'openeth the gate to good fame.' When a neighbor dies, his form and quality appear clearly, as if he had been dead a thousand years. Then we see what we only felt before. Heroes in history seem to us poetic because they are there. But if we should tell the simple truth of some of our neighbors, it would sound like poetry. Winthrop was one of the men who represent the manly and poetic qualities that always exist around us—not great genius, which is ever salient, but the fine fibre of manhood that makes the worth of the race.

"Closely engaged with his literary employments, and more quiet than ever, he took less active part in the last election. But when the menace of treason became an aggressive act, he saw very clearly the inevitable necessity of arms. We all talked of it constantly—watching the news—chafing at the sad necessity of delay, which was sure to confuse foreign opinion and alienate sympathy, as has proved to be the case. As matters advanced and the war-cloud rolled up thicker and blacker, he looked at it with the secret satisfaction that war for such a cause opened his career both as thinker and actor. The admirable coolness, the promptness, the cheerful patience, the heroic ardor, the intelligence, the tough experience of campaigning, the profound conviction that the cause was in truth 'the good old cause,' which was now to come to the death-grapple with its old enemy, Justice against Injustice, Order against Anarchy—all these should now have their turn, and the wanderer and waiter 'settle himself' at last.

"We took a long walk together on the Sunday that brought the news of the capture of Fort Sumter. He was thoroughly alive with a bright, earnest forecast of his part in the coming work. Returning home with me, he sat until late in the evening talking with an unwonted spirit, saying playfully, I remember, that, if his friends would only give him a horse, he would ride straight to victory. Especially he wished that some competent person would keep a careful record of events as they passed; 'for we are making our history,' he said, 'hand over hand.' He sat quietly in the great chair while he spoke, and at last rose to go. We went together to the door, and stood for a little while upon the piazza, where we had sat peacefully through so many golden summer-hours. The last hour for us had come, but we did not know it. We shook hands, and he left me, passing rapidly along the brook-side under the trees, and so in the soft spring starlight vanished from my sight forever.

"The next morning came the President's proclamation. Winthrop went immediately to town and enrolled himself in the artillery corps of the Seventh regiment. During the two or three following days he was very busy and very happy. On Friday afternoon, the 19th of April, I stood at the corner of Courtland street and saw the regiment as it marched away. Two days before, I had seen the Massachusetts troops going down the same street. During the day the news had come that they were already engaged, that some were already dead in Baltimore. And the Seventh, as they went, blessed and wept over by a great city, went, as we all believed, to terrible battle. The setting sun in a clear April sky shone full up the street. Mothers' eyes glistened at the windows upon the glistening bayonets of their boys below. I knew that Winthrop and other dear friends were there, but I did not see them. I saw only a thousand men marching like one hero. The music beat and rang and clashed in the air. Marching to death or victory or defeat, it mattered not. They marched for Justice, and God was their Captain.

"From that moment he has told his own story in these pages* until he went to Fortress Monroe, and was made acting military secretary and aid by General Butler. Before he went, he wrote the most copious and gayest letters from the camp. He was thoroughly aroused, and all his powers happily at play. In a letter to me soon after his arrival in Washington, he says:

"'I see no present end of this business. We must conquer the South. Afterward we must be prepared to do its police in its own behalf, and in behalf of its black population, whom this war must, without precipitation, emancipate. We must hold the South as the metropolitan police holds New York. All this is inevitable. Now I wish to enroll myself at once in the *Police of the Nation*, and for life, if the nation will take me. I do not see that I can put myself—experience and character—to any more useful use. . . . . My experience in this short campaign with the Seventh assures me that volunteers are for one purpose and regular soldiers entirely another. We want regular soldiers for the cause of order in these anarchial countries, and we want men in command who, though they may be valuable as temporary satraps or proconsuls to make liberty possible where it is now impossible, will never under any circumstances be disloyal to *Liberty*, will always oppose any scheme of any one to constitute a military government, and will be ready, when the time comes, to imitate Washington. We must think of these things, and prepare for them.'

"The last days of his life at Fortress Monroe were doubtless also the happiest. His energy and enthusiasm, and kind, winning ways, and the deep satisfaction of feeling that all his gifts could now be used as he would have them, showed him and his friends that his day had at length dawned. He was especially interested in the condition and fate of the slaves who escaped from the neighboring region and sought

* Referring to articles contributed to the *Atlantic Monthly*.

refuge at the fort. He had never for an instant forgotten the secret root of the treason which was desolating the land with war; and in his view there would be no peace until that root was destroyed. In his letters written from the fort he suggests plans of relief and comfort for the refugees; and one of his last requests was to a lady in New York, for clothes for these poor pensioners. They were promptly sent, but reached the fort too late.

"As I look over these last letters, which gush and throb with the fullness of his activity, and are so tenderly streaked with touches of constant affection and remembrance, yet are so calm and duly mindful of every detail, I do not think with an elder friend, in whom the wisdom of years has only deepened sympathy for all generous youthful impulse, of Virgil's Marcellus, '*Heu, miserande puer!*' but I recall, rather, still haunted by Philip Sidney, what he wrote, just before his death, to his father-in-law, Walsingham—'I think a wise and constant man ought never to grieve while he doth play, as a man may say his own part truly.'

"The disastrous day of the 10th of June, at Great Bethel, need not be described. It is already written with tears and vain regrets in our history. It is useless to prolong the debate as to where the blame of defeat, if blame there were, should rest. But there is an impression somewhat prevalent that Winthrop planned the expedition, which is incorrect. As military secretary of the commanding general, he made a memorandum of the outline of the plan as it had been finally settled. Precisely what that memorandum (which has been published) was, he explains in the last letter he wrote, a few hours before leaving the fort. He says: 'If I come back safe, I will send you my notes of the plan of attack, part made up from the General's hints, part my own fancies.' This defines exactly his responsibility. His position as aid and military secretary, his admirable qualities as adviser under the circumstances, and his personal friendship for the General, brought him intimately into the council of war. He embarked in the plan all the interest of a brave soldier contemplating his first battle. He probably made suggestions some of which were adopted. The expedition was the first move from Fort Monroe, to which the country had been long looking in expectation. These were the reasons why he felt so peculiar a responsibility for its success; and after the melancholy events of the earlier part of the day, he saw that its fortunes could be retrieved only by a dash of heroic enthusiasm. Fired himself, he sought to kindle others. For one moment that brave, inspiring form is plainly visible to his whole country, rapt and calm, standing upon the log nearest the enemy's battery, the mark of their sharpshooters, the admiration of their leaders, waving his sword, cheering his fellow-soldiers with his bugle voice of victory—young, brave, beautiful, for one moment erect and glowing in the wild whirl of battle, the next falling forward toward the foe, dead, but triumphant.

"On the 19th of April he left the armory-door of the Seventh, with his hand upon a howitzer; on the 21st of June his body lay upon the same howitzer at the same door, wrapped in the flag for which he gladly died, as the symbol of human freedom. And so, drawn by the hands of young men lately strangers to him, but of whose bravery and loyalty he had been the laureate, and who fitly mourned him who had honored them, with long, pealing dirges and muffled drums, he moved forward."

XVI.

THE SECOND DISASTER.

THE defeat of the Federal army of invasion at Bull Run Sunday, July 21st, 1861, was one of the most remarkable and mysterious affairs recorded in the annals of modern warfare. A magnificent army, having fought, against great odds, a battle of an unusually sanguinary nature, at a moment when victory was about to rest upon its standard, broke up in a panic, retreated in disorder to their fartherest defenses, abandoned vast stores, artillery and equippage, forsook positions which a few brave men could have held securely, and collected in camp a disorganized and dispirited mass—all from no perceptible good reason and without being able to fasten the first fault upon any particular corps or regiment.

That the battle was virtually won by the Federal forces the rebel leaders themselves confess. Beauregard, at a dinner given him in Richmond, stated, with minuteness, the circumstances of his peril and his defeat—that he had just given the order to his aid for the grand retreat to Manassas, but retained the aid to await the solution of a single movement: a banner was seen in the distance, to the west, advancing at the head of a division—if that of the Federals all was lost—if that of one of his own divisions it would steady the movements about to be ordered, or possibly turn the tide of defeat. He depicted the intensity of his emotions at that moment, and how his heart leaped for joy upon distinguishing, with his glass, that the flag was that of the Confederacy. The order for retreat was not issued, and soon the General-in-Chief learned that the long looked-for reenforcements from Johnson's army had arrived. This timely arrival of fourteen thousand comparatively fresh men saved Beauregard's overwhelming defeat and gave him the vantage ground. The Union troops, however, fought the way on—were pushing the enemy slowly but surely backward when, without just cause, a stampede commenced, which no power of officers, or of eminent civilians present, could prevent. The regiments of most undoubted bravery, those whose ranks were deplorably thinned by service fled in dismay before an imaginary pursuit. Artillery of the most costly and efficient character was abandoned—the gunners taking to the horses for escape. Wagons loaded with immense quantities of stores were abandoned, while the teamsters or the flying infantry seized the horses and mules to hasten in advance of the disordered mass. Officers came on without commands, wild with frenzy at the course of their troops, but perfectly powerless to stay the disgraceful scamper. A few regiments moved on in comparatively good order, but their course was Washington-ward, and no efforts to stand were made. Blenker's fine division—held as a reserve at Centerville, covered the rout in good order, but did no service as no enemy pursued. It was a causeless, senseless, disgraceful panic—one which ever will stand as one of the inexplicable phenomena of the modern battle-field.

No battle ever was fought where so many and such various opinions were expressed by those present. Many newspapers were represented by able and vigilant correspondents; numbers of Congressmen were there; eminent civilians came out to view the conflict, which was heralded by the skirmishing of three previous days;—most all of whom published statements and narratives of the disaster, many of which disagreed in important, specific and general particulars. The statements of officers only added to the confusion, while official reports failed to throw any light upon the actual cause or the extent of the disaster.

A letter from an officer of the regular service present at the battle, gave the following general narrative of the events of the day:

"The march from our bivouac, near Centreville, was taken up at 2½ A.M. on Sunday. Among officers and men the impression prevailed that the action would occur at Bull's Run, the scene of General Tyler's repulse a day or two previously. In this they were disappointed. Tyler's brigade posted themselves at the bridge over Bull's Run, where they were ordered to feign an attack as soon as General Hunter's division were known to be in position. This order was partially obeyed. Hunter's division, composed of Burnside's brigade and Porter's brigade, after proceeding a mile beyond Centreville, made a detour to the right, and proceeded over a wood road, well covered from observation, to the left flank of the enemy at Manassas, a distance of about eight miles. At six o'clock firing was heard on the heights at Bull's Run, from a battery in Tyler's brigade, which was promptly answered by the enemy's batteries. Their position thus revealed, the advance division (Hunter's) ascended a hill at double quick, and almost immediately the Rhode Island battery and Griffin's West Point battery were in brisk action. The former was supported by the First regiment Rhode Island volunteers, who maintained their ground nobly for a half hour. At this moment Porter's brigade, composed of the Fourteenth, Seventh and Twenty-seventh New York, with a battalion of United States marines, under Major Reynolds, and a battalion of United States Third, Second and Eighth infantry, under Major Sykes, took their position in line of battle upon a hill, within range of the enemy's fire. Burnside's battery being sorely pressed, the enemy having charged closely upon it, the gallant Colonel galloped to Major Sykes and implored him to come to his assistance. Major Sykes brought up his men at a run, and, with a deafening shout, they charged upon the enemy's skirmishers, who fled before them several hundred yards. Forming in column of divisions, Sykes' battalion advanced a considerable distance, until they drew upon themselves an intensely hot fire of musketry and artillery. This was a trying moment. The volunteers expected much of the regulars, and gazed upon them as they stood in unbroken line, receiving the fire, and returning it with fatal precision. Impressions and resolutions are formed on the battle-field in an instant. The impression at this moment was a happy one, and Heintzelman's brigade coming up into line, our forces steadily advanced upon the retreating rebels. The batteries, which had been meanwhile recruited with men and horses, renewed their fire with increased effect, and our supremacy upon the field was apparent. The enemy's fire was now terrific. Shell, round-shot and grape from their batteries covered the field with clouds of dust, and many a gallant fellow fell in that brief time. At this juncture the volunteers, who hitherto had behaved nobly, seeing their ranks thinned out, many losing their field and company officers, lost confidence, and in a panic fell back. Three fresh regiments coming on the field at this time, would have formed a nucleus upon which a general rally could have been effected, but while the enemy had reenforcements pouring in upon them momentarily, our entire force was in the field and badly cut up. Thus was our action maintained for hours. The panic was momentarily increasing. Regiments were observed to march up in good order, discharge one volley, and then fall back in confusion. But there was no lack of gallantry, generally speaking, and not a great many manifestations of cowardice. Our artillery, which made sad havoc upon the rebels, had spent their ammunition or been otherwise disabled by this time, and in the absence of reenforcements, a retreat was inevitable. The time for the last attack had now come. Nearly all of the rebel batteries were in place, though silent. There was a calm—an indescribable calm. Every man on the field felt it. I doubt if any one could describe it. General McDowell was near the front of our lines, mounted on his gray charger. And here let me say, emphatically, that, whatever may be the criticisms upon his conduct by the military or the abominable stay-at-home newspaper scribblers and politicians, no braver man trod that turf at Manassas than General McDowell. Major Sykes' battalion of eight companies, five of Third infantry, two of the Second, and one of the Eighth, were marched several hundred yards to the right, and formed the right flank of the line. Several volunteer regiments were deployed as skirmishers on the centre and left. Thus they advanced to the crest of the hill. The enemy met them with batteries and musketry in front, and two batteries and a thousand cavalry on the right. The fire was terrific. We maintained our position for a half hour. Then it was discovered that the rebel cavalry were attempting to outflank our right. We had no force to resist them, and the bugle of the regulars sounded the march in retreat. This, so far as we were concerned, was conducted in good order. On Major Sykes was imposed the responsible duty of covering the retreat of the army. In this he was assisted on part of the route by the United States cavalry, under Major Palmer. The enemy followed us with their artillery and cavalry, shelling us constantly, until we reached Centreville. Here we bivouacked for an hour, and then again took up the line of march."

This speaks for the regulars, but does meager justice to those many gallant regiments that bore the brunt of the fight; while it omits the most material incidents of the retreat. Blenker's troops (four regiments from Mills' division) covered the retreat —being specially detailed as the reserve and to hold the heights of Centreville.

From another more detailed account we glean such items as will, taken in connection with the above, give a consistent idea of the character of the contest.

"On a line, right and left with Fairfax, the entire column halted and bivouacked during the night of Wednesday the 17th. Beyond a false alarm caused by the discharge of a sentinel's musket, which aroused the entire camp, and placed the division under arms, nothing of any account occurred. Eleven rebel soldiers belonging to the Sixth Alabama regiment, and two citizens, were captured by the Fire Zouaves and brought to Colonel Blenker, who commanded them to the lock-up under a strong guard. At eight o'clock A. M., on the 18th, we broke camp and proceeded to Centreville, where the Fifth division arrived in advance of all others. Our march to this spot was difficult and dangerous. The pioneers worked like beavers; the roads were barricaded to such an extent, that we had to cut our way inch by inch. The road being straight through heavy pine woods, we were compelled to throw out skirmishers on our right and left, to guard against a surprise attack.

" At Centreville, we remained from Thursday morning until Sunday the 21st, the day of the memorable battle of Bull's Run. While the Fifth division was encamped in the valley, about half-a-mile from Centreville, the right flank of the grand column arrived, and a portion of it, in command of General Tyler, was sent in advance towards Bull's Run Creek, to reconnoitre the enemy's position and detect his batteries.

"On Friday morning the Secretary of War, accompanied by

Colonel Scott and Mr. Moore, his private secretary, arrived at the encampments, to note the position and condition of the troops. It was soon rumored that General Scott was at Centreville, and great enthusiasm was manifested by the soldiers when they were told that the veteran Commander-in-Chief was among them. The statement, however, was false, for the hero of a hundred battles was not there *pro. personæ.* In the evening, the commanding officers were invited to a council of war at the quarters of General McDowell.

"The orders of General Tyler, it is understood, were specific not to give the enemy battle; but the skirmishers of the Twelfth New York volunteers were scarcely one mile and a half from Centreville, before a masked battery opened upon them, killing and wounding a number of the men. The First Massachusetts, Second Wisconsin, and First Minnesota regiments suffered badly. The Twelfth regiment retreated in disorder. The Sixty-ninth, Colonel Corcoran, and the Seventy-ninth, Colonel Cameron, both New York State militia, came up to reenforce our troops, but arrived too late to render any effectual service. In fact they did not even have an opportunity to participate in this fight, all the troops having been ordered back to Centreville first. The Twelfth New York volunteers and the First Massachusetts volunteers suffered most; their loss in killed, wounded, and missing could not have been less than from one hundred to one hundred and fifty. In the evening, however, those regiments, besides the Connecticut volunteers, were moved forward, and camped upon the late battle-field, the enemy having retreated from their position. With the exception of driving in our pickets, the capture of a rebel named Wingfield, by Captain Forstner, of the Eighth regiment New York volunteers, and the surrender of an orderly sergeant, named Leadbeater, of the Virginia Ninth, our camps remained quiet until Sunday morning.

"Early Sunday morning the divisions began to move. The Warrington road was taken by the centre column; and General McDowell directed Colonel Heintzelman to march with his division in that direction. Sherman's battery, Lieutenant Haynes' thirty-pound rifled siege gun, Parrott's patent, and Carlisle's battery accompanied this division. Further to the right, was Colonel Hunter's, Franklin's, Keyes' and Porter's divisions. Each of them were supported by artillery. At six o'clock, Lieutenant Haynes opened the ball by sending a shot from his battery, which he repeated alternately for upwards of an hour, without receiving any reply from the enemy. Finally, the rebels responded with some grape and canister, which was duly appreciated and returned with interest. The rebels seemingly had the proper range of their guns.

"The firing then became general, and the enemy slowly retreated, followed closely by our troops. An assault was contemplated; and the Sixty-ninth, Seventy-ninth, and Fire Zouaves were ordered to storm the battery. These valiant soldiers steadily advanced under a galling fire, and were almost in possession of the guns, when a tremendous volley raked their front, and they were compelled to fall back. The reason of the repulse was obvious. The field officers made a great mistake in attempting to carry a battery from the front, and neglected to deploy on the flanks. From this instant the fight became more general. The entire column on the right now pressed forward, and the Fire Zouaves, the Sixty-ninth, and Seventy-ninth regiments had actually captured three masked batteries, when an immense troop of cavalry advanced, and commenced cutting the gallant men to pieces. The Zouaves lay flat on their faces to load, and their fire was so steady and accurate, that whoever was hit by them was seen to bite the dust.

"Colonel Cameron, of the Highlanders, gallantly led on his men to the charge. The brave Scotchmen were so eager for the fight, that some of them actually stripped off their shoes and coats and rushed upon the enemy. The colonel of this fine regiment did not live long enough to see the valiant deeds of those whom he commanded, for, after discharging his revolver twice, and while in the act of shooting the third time, a ball from a musket penetrated his left breast, and he fell from his horse upon the field. Instead of becoming disheartened by this event, the gallant Highlanders pushed on, encouraged by the brave Major McClelland (Lieutenant-Colonel Elliott not being on the ground) in their charge on the enemy. The Sixty-ninth regiment, Colonel Corcoran, also evinced the most unflinching courage, and the only charge that in any way approaches that of the rebel cavalry, was the famous charge at Balaklava; and it has yet to be proved whether it was so gallantly resisted as the charge was by these three New York regiments. The Rhode Island, Maine, Connecticut, Wisconsin, Massachusetts, and the rest of the New York regiments all fought furiously, regardless of danger. The New York Seventy-first and Eighth regiments also signalized themselves, and clearly demonstrated that their military training was not altogether confined to parading on Broadway in full dress uniform. These men, although their term of service was about to expire, did not flinch a hair from the duty they owed to their country, and sprang forward to the charge, although their ranks were thinned.

"The Rhode Island battery did good service, the enemy at one time took the guns, but the gallant boys recaptured them with considerable slaughter. Thus the fight raged for nine consecutive hours without interruption. When our troops in the first place came upon the battle-field, on double-quick time, they were exhausted to such an extent on reaching the ground, that their tongues actually hung out of their mouths. The poor soldiers suffered terribly for the want of drinking water, and whenever a rill or a moist place was discovered, the half-famished men threw themselves upon the ground, licking the moisture. According to instructions, General Patterson was to have come to the reenforcement of our division, and was expected at Centreville at twelve o'clock noon. Had he arrived, our weary troops would have been relieved and given time to rest, while the attack would have been followed up. Everything went on gloriously until about three o'clock in the afternoon, and although a goodly number of our men were killed, still the spirit of those remaining was unbroken, but physically they were unable to maintain their position much longer.

"Captain Ayres' battery and a portion of Rickett's battery fell into the hands of the enemy, but were retaken after an immense sacrifice of life. A regiment of Black cavalry made a circuitous dash at our right and left flanks, which was observed by the Zouaves. They immediately fell to the ground, and each marked his man. Some picked off two and three, and in less than half an hour from their first appearance the black cavalry horses were seen dashing back riderless. Only a few of this troop returned, out of about eight hundred men.

"About half-past four o'clock in the afternoon a terrible dash of cavalry and a fierce charge of artillery was made at our exhausted troops. This charge did the most devastating damage, mowing down everything in its furious career. The agonized shrieks of the wounded, the terrible roar of artillery, snorting of frightened animals, tended to strike terror into the hearts of the soldiers. In this charge, Griffin's, Ricket's and the Rhode Island batteries were taken. Those in citizen's dress became alarmed and took to their heels, taking whatever conveyance they could lay their hands upon. From them the teamsters, some five hundred, who had driven their wagons further in advance than was any necessity for, took fright. The road being very narrow, in fact a gorge, the ponderous vehicles could not be turned, and in many cases the cowardly drivers cut the traces, mounted their steeds and rode off, leaving the valuables which were entrusted to their care by the Government to take care of itself. Thus thousands of dollars worth of provisions were left behind. The army wagons dashing down the road, spread the panic among the citizens, who made all possible haste to leave so hot a neighborhood.

"Colonel Miles in the meantime had received instructions to move his reserve forward, and the German brigade, under Colonel Blenker, following Green's, Hunt's and Tidball's batteries, started on a double-quick to the scene of battle. The brigade, however, had scarcely advanced three miles from Centreville before the entire army came along, every man looking out for himself. Through the firmness of Colonel Blenker, a short stand was made at Centreville, and the flying troops somewhat reassured. All the threats, promises and denunciations were of no avail, and the only course to be pursued was to cover the retreat as much as possible in case of a pursuit. The troops reached Fairfax in safety, and those regiments that were sent into Virginia on Sunday were ordered back, and joined the column of the retreating forces. Between Washington and Alexandria all travelling communication was cut off by the Government, so as not to allow the panic-stricken soldiers to push into the Capital."

As might be expected, the most intense feeling pervaded all classes. The defeat, at the very moment of victory, was mortifying, but the rout and demoralization was mortifying in the extreme. The public in its eager desire to find some palliation for the disaster, sought victims for its blame; and the Secretary of War—the "On to Richmond!" press—the Congressmen who had goaded General Scott by their displays of temper at his deliberate way of pressing the campaign—all suffered at the hands of the indignant people. But, as the excitement of the moment cleared away, and matters came to be understood, attention was directed to the reenforcements received by Beauregard—Johnson's entire army from Winchester: why were they allowed to escape Patterson's heavy columns sent specifically to engage the rebel, at every hazard, and thus to keep him away from Manassas? That failure to engage resulted, as Scott foreknew it must, in overpowering McDowell's thirty-two thousand men. Had Patterson detained Johnson, as ordered, all would have been well, and "On to Richmond!" would have been, in all probability, a fulfilled command.

How inscrutable are the ways of Providence! Had the rebels been defeated at Bull Run and forced from Manassas, an armistice might have followed—doubtless would have followed; when a "settlement" would have replaced the rebels in power as in the past, to domineer over, to browbeat and insult, to cast a stigma upon, the North and its Free State sentiment, and have only postponed the day of final decision of the great principles of Government involved. That defeat called forth the yet but half-aroused sentiment of the North, convincing the people of the true nature of the struggle, and commanding those mighty resources which alone were capable of finally crushing out the rebellion to the last degree, leaving the great principle of the supremacy of the Central Government no longer questioned, and the right of the majority to rule a fixed fact.

XVII.

INCIDENTS OF THE BATTLE OF BULL RUN.

A VOLUME would scarcely suffice to contain all the stories related of haps and mishaps, personal achievements and adventures, incidents and anecdotes of the field of Bull Run. We can devote but a section to them, showing such as seem to illustrate, in an indirect way, the fortunes and circumstances of the struggle.

The battle consisted of a succession of fires from masked batteries, which opened in every direction, (when one was silenced, its place was supplied by two,) and in the daring charges of our infantry in unmasking them. The Second Ohio and Second New York militia were marched by flank through the woods by a new-made road, within a mile of the main road, when they came on a battery of eight guns, with four regiments flanked in the rear. Our men were immediately ordered to lie down on either side of the road, in order to allow two pieces of artillery to pass through and attack the work, when this battery opened upon us, and killed, on the third round, Lieutenant Dempsey, of company G, New York Second, and William Maxwell, a drummer, and seriously wounding several others. Our troops were kept for fifteen or twenty minutes under a galling fire, they not being able to exchange shots with the enemy, although within a stone's throw of their batteries. They succeeded in retiring in regular order, and with their battery.

The most gallant charge of the day was made by the New York Sixty-ninth, Seventy-ninth, and Thirteenth, who rushed up upon one of the batteries, firing as they proceeded, with perfect *eclat*, and attacking it with the bayonet's point. The yell of triumph seemed to carry all before it. They found that the rebels had abandoned the battery, and only taken one gun, but this success was acquired only after a severe loss of life, in which the Sixty-ninth most severely suffered. The Zouaves also distinguished themselves by their spirited assaults on the batteries, at the point of the bayonet.

Colonel Cameron seemed to have a presentiment of his death. In a conversation with him at his tent, on the evening prior to the battle, he said that he had accepted the command of the gallant Highlanders because he admired them, and inasmuch as he had only a short time to live, he might as well devote it to his country. He asked a correspondent whether he was going to the battle-field. Receiving an affirmative answer, he said: "Good bye, God bless you. We may meet again, but I am afraid not in this world." Some sixteen hours afterwards the gallant Colonel was shot from his horse and killed.

A member of the Sixty-ninth thus wrote of the services of that splendid regiment (composed wholly of Irish, drawn from the City of New York, and commanded by Colonel Corcoran):

"About ten o'clock we discovered two batteries, and drove the enemy out. The Sixty-ninth advanced. We went off at a run, but could not overtake the enemy, as they scattered in every direction through the woods. We kept up the run, turned to the right, waded through streams, climbed steep hills, left our battery behind us, and out-flanked the enemy, and came on them when we were not expected. The Louisiana

Zouaves were doing big damage when we came on them. We gave a yell that could be heard far above the roar of the cannon. We fired into them, and charged them with the bayonet. They were panic-striken and fled. We covered the field with their dead. Haggarty rushed forward to take a prisoner, and lost his life. The man turned and shot him through the heart. We drove the enemy before us for some distance, then got into line and had them surrounded. General McDowell came up just then, took off his hat, and said, 'You have gained the victory.' Our next fly was at a South Carolina regiment. We killed about three hundred of them. After fighting hard for some time, we cleared the field of all the enemy. The enemy again rallying, the real fight then commenced. We were drawn up in line, and saw the other regiments trying to take the masked batteries. They were cut to pieces and scattered. We were then ordered forward to attack the batteries. We fought desperately, but we were cut down. We lost our flag, but took it back again with the assistance of a few of the Firemen Zouaves, who fought like devils. We charged a second time, but were mowed down by the grape and rifle of the enemy. We came together again, to make another charge, but we could not get together over two hundred men. We formed into a hollow square, when we saw the enemy turn out their cavalry, about a mile in length, and the hills all about covered with them, trying to surround us. All the regiments on our side were scattered and in disorder, except what were left of the Sixty-ninth. The Fire Zouaves had to retreat, leaving a number of wounded on the field. What we could gather together of our regiment marched back to Fort Corcoran during the night."

Governor Sprague, of Rhode Island, had two horses killed under him during the action. After the first one was killed, by his head being shot away by a cannon-ball, his men came around him and insisted upon his going to the rear. This he positively refused to do, and continued throughout the engagement at the head of his brigade, gallantly leading them on and encouraging their efforts.

Colonel Cowdin, of the First Massachusetts regiment, was leaning his back against a tree in a very exposed position, when a friend expostulated with him for his recklessness. The Colonel said the bullet was not moulded that would shoot him that day. In a few seconds after, another personal friend came up, and putting out his hand to the Colonel, the latter stooped a little to grasp it, when a conical cannon-ball struck on the spot where an instant before was the head of Colonel Cowdin, shattering the tree into splinters. The Colonel turned about calmly and remarked, "that he was certain that the ball that would kill him was not yet cast;" and proceeded to issue his commands.

The brave conduct of Colonel Hunter, commanding the Second division, deserves special notice. He was shot in the throat, while directing in person the Second Rhode Island regiment, in its gallant assault upon a battery. Just before being wounded, he had given an order to one of his aids for a distant regiment. The aid was about galloping off, when he saw the Colonel fall from his horse. He immediately came to his assistance, but the Colonel motioned him off, telling him "deliver your order, and never mind me—I will take care of myself."

Lieutenant-Colonel Boone, of Mississippi, one of the few prisoners taken by our troops, states that had the Union troops held their ground on the other side of Bull Run for half-an-hour longer, the entire rebel army would have given way.

A Mississippi soldier was taken prisoner by Hasbrouck, of the Wisconsin Second regiment. He turned out to be Brigadier-Quartermaster Pryor. He was captured, with his horse, as he by accident rode into our lines. He discovered himself by remarking to Hasbrouck, "We are getting badly cut to pieces." "What regiment do you belong to?" asked Hasbrouck. "The Nineteenth Mississippi," was the answer. "Then, you are my prisoner," said Hasbrouck.

The Fire Zouaves received the special attention of the "Black Horse Cavalry"—the pride of the Southern army, who had sworn to *wipe out* the "red devils" from New York. The story of their assault was thus told :

"They came upon the Zouave regiment at a gallop, and were received by the brave firemen upon their poised bayonets, followed instantly by a volley, from which they broke and fled, though several of the Zouaves were cut down in the assault. They quickly returned, with their forces doubled—perhaps six or seven hundred—and again they dashed with fearful yells upon the excited Zouaves. This time they bore an American flag, and a part of the Zouaves supposed for an instant that they were friends, whom they had originally mistaken. The flag was quickly thrown down, however, the horses dashed upon the regiment, the *ruse* was discovered, and the slaughter commenced. No quarter, no halting, no flinching now, marked the rapid and death-dealing blows of our men, as they closed in upon the foe, in their madness and desperation. Our brave fellows fell, the ranks filled up, the sabers, bowie-knives and bayonets glistened in the sunlight, horse after horse went down, platoon after platoon disappeared—the rattle of musketry, the screams of the rebels, the shout of 'Remember Ellsworth !' from the lungs of the Zouaves, and the yells of the wounded and crushed belligerents filled the air, and a terrible carnage succeeded. The gallant Zouaves fought to the death, and were sadly cut up ; but of those hundreds of Black Horse Guards, not many left that bloody recounter !"

When the Fire Zouaves stormed the masked battery at Bull Run, and were forced to fall back by the grapeshot and cavalry charge, one of them was stunned by a blow from a saber, and fell almost under one of the enemy's guns. The Secessionists swarmed around him like bees, but feigning death, in the excitement he was unnoticed, and when a sally was made, managed to crawl back into the thicket inside the Confederate lines. Here he waited some time for an opportunity to escape, but finding none, concluded he would make the best of a bad bargain, and if he was lost, would have a little revenge beforehand. Hastily stripping the body of a Confederate near by, he donned his uniform, and seizing a rifle, made his way to the intrenchments, where he joined the Secessionists, and, watching his opportunities, succeeded in picking off several of their most prominent officers whenever they advanced out upon the troops. Here he remained some time, until, thinking it best to leave before his disguise should be discovered, he joined a party who were about to charge upon our forces, and was, to his gratification, again captured, but this time by his own men.

A remarkable incident was related of a private of the New York Twenty-eighth regiment of volunteers: He had been wounded in the groin, and was hobbling off the field, when he was pursued and overtaken by three rebels. As the foremost one came up he laid his hand heavily upon his shoulder. The soldier stumbled forward, and as he fell he drew his bayonet the only weapon he had—from its scabbard, with which he run the rebel through the body, and, at the same time, seized upon his captor's revolver, drew it from the belt, and shot the other two. He then made good his escape, and arrived safely at Washington.

An Ohio paper correspondent adverted to the services of some of the regiments from that State in glowing strains. He said:

"The Ohio regiments were in the thickest of the fight, but fortunately lost but few men. The First regiment, under Colonel McCook, has covered itself with glory. They were detailed at an early hour in the day to hunt up batteries, and they seemed to understand that work to perfection. The Grays were sent out as skirmishers early in the morning, and drove in the pickets of the rebels, and commenced the fight. These two Ohio regiments have been trained by Colonel McCook, and were frequently brought right into the very range and front of the enemy's most terrible and formidable guns; but no sooner would they see the flash than every man was prostrate upon his face, and the balls and grape would pass harmlessly over them; then they would up and at them with a vengeance in double-quick time."

Colonel McCook's younger brother—but seventeen years old—was a member of the Second Ohio regiment, and was left as a guard to the hospital. One of the enemy's cavalry dashed upon him and ordered him to surrender; the brave youth, with fixed bayonet, steady nerve, and cool bearing, replied, "I never surrender!" The father, Judge McCook, who had all the day been arduously engaged in assisting and taking care of the wounded, bringing them in from the field, and that, too, at the imminent peril of his own life, was in the hospital tent and heard the order to his son, and saw others of the enemy's cavalry near by, and rushed out, and speaking in a loud tone, "Charley, surrender, for God's sake, or you are lost." Charley turned to his father, and with all the lion in his countenance, replied, "Father, I will never surrender to a rebel." In a moment a ball pierced his spine, but he instantly discharged his musket at the rebel horseman, and laid him low in death, and then fell himself. The rebels then undertook to drag him off, but his father rushed in and released him, and he died Monday morning. His body was brought away by his father, and was sent to Ohio for burial. The Colonel McCook above alluded to was afterwards the well known General McCook in Halleck's army.

Colonel W. R. Montgomery, for thirty years an efficient officer of the United States Army, who had seen service where-ever during that time it was to be seen, was in command of the First New Jersey regiment. In the midst of the torrent of the retreat, he stemmed its tide, forced his regiment in good order through its surge of men and horses and wagons, which carried back with them his associate regiment, the Second New Jersey, Colonel McLean, but had no effect on him. With exhortations, remonstrances and bayonets, he checked, but could not stop the disastrous flight. Abandoned by Colonel McLean and the Second, he pressed on alone, and alone his regiment reached the field, and took the post which his orders indicated, formed in square to receive the enemy's cavalry, and *staid five hours on the battle-field waiting for orders.*

With regard to this flight, much was, at the time, written as to the bad effects of the civilians present. It was stated and believed that their scampering away from danger first alarmed the teamsters, and thus produced the panic. It would appear that a few men here and there in citizens' dress, could have very little to do in creating a panic, even if they did run. But testimony is abundant that these non-professional soldiers really acted a noble part—that they, in reality, greatly aided in restraining the headlong flight of brave regiments from the battle-field. An eye-witness wrote to the *National Intelligencer:* "Whatever credit there was in stopping that rout, is due wholly to Senators Wade and Chandler; Representatives Blake, Riddle and Morris; Mr. Brown, Sergeant-at-Arms of the Senate; Mr. Eaton of Detroit, and Thomas Brown of Cleveland. These gentlemen, armed with Maynard rifles and navy revolvers, sprang suddenly from their carriages some three miles this side of Centreville, and, presenting their weapons, in loud voices commanded the fugitives to halt and turn back. Their bold and determined manner brought most at that point to a stand-still. Many on horseback attempted to dash by them, and had their horses seized by the bits. Some of the fugitives were armed, and menaced these gentlemen; and one, a powerful man, supposed to be a teamster, shot Mr. Eaton through the wrist, as he held his horse by the bridle-rein. None, however, were permitted to pass, except an army courier, who exhibited his dispatches. Mr. Wade and his party held the crowd until the arrival of the First New Jersey regiment, then on its way toward the battle-ground, the Colonel of which turned back the flying soldiers and teamsters. Two or three officers were stopped and turned back." We are glad to record this, to so well-known men, simple justice. Congressman Ely, of New York, was taken prisoner in his efforts to keep the men up to the assault.

General McDowell was so overcome by fatigue, that while writing a short dispatch in the telegraph office, at Fairfax, he fell asleep three times. He had been busy all the night preceding in making preliminary arrangements, and had been in the saddle from two o'clock in the morning until ten at night. At nine and a half o'clock his dispatch was received at Washington, announcing his retreat, and his purpose to make a stand at Centreville. At one and a half A. M. it was announced that he would fall back to Fairfax. It was left to his own judgment whether to retire to the Potomac line or not.

Regarding the barbarity of the rebels, the stories told almost defied belief. The New York *Herald* correspondent wrote: "The barbarity practiced by the rebels towards wounded men in this encounter, throws to the winds the boasted chivalry of the South, and their assumption of Samaritan tenderness. They trampled the wounded and dying victims of their powder and lead to the ground—fired upon nurses engaged in carrying away the mortally wounded—threw hot shot into buildings used as hospitals, setting fire to them. The rebels engaged with our forces at Bull's Run committed all those diabolical deeds, which have, as yet, only been equalled by the East India Sepoys and the Tartars of old. They commenced these acts on Thursday, this side of Bull's Run, on the wounded of the First Massachusetts and Twelfth New York volunteer regiments, and continued it on Sunday."

The Boston *Post* wrote :

"But where shall we find words, in this enlightened age, to reprobate the infamy of their conduct, after their success, toward our noble soldiers! Are soldiers turned butchers? Is their boasted chivalry a mockery? Who can read without a thrill of horror the loathsome reports of their brutality. The wounded are fired into while mangled lying on the field—the bleeding soldiers are tied to trees and bayoneted—the weapons of the fallen soldier are taken from him and plunged into him, dead or dying. A Union soldier takes up the wounded rebel, ministers to him a cup of cold water, and the dastard dispatches his benefactor while in the act! To what depths of barbarism have American soldiers stooped in their treatment of their fellow-citizens! The blood of the wronged and the outraged cries aloud for vengeance."

The incident of soldiers sending home Zouave skulls as trophies—of Zouaves having their heads cut off and put upon poles—confirmed by repeated proofs—will ever remain on record to add to the weight of infamy which attaches to the Southern cause.

XVIII.

GENERAL McCLELLAN.

THE reverse at Bull Run so disorganized—if not demoralized—our army of the Potomac, as to render an *acting* General-in-Chief necessary. All eyes turned, instinctively, to General McClellan, whose Western Virginia Campaign had just closed, to crown him with the laurels of a great commander. His energy, his knowledge of his profession, his physical strength, the prestige of his name, all combined to render him qualified for the responsible trust of bringing order out of that chaos at and around Washington; and he was called immediately (July 22d) to the General command of the field—a position he assumed August 1st, 1861.

The position since filled so eminently by this General, has rendered his reputation world-wide, and renders a sketch of his life eminently proper, if we would answer the interest now felt in his life; we therefore compile from such sources as are available, the following:

George B. McClellan, the son of an eminent physician at Philadelphia, was born in that city, December 3d, 1826. At the age of sixteen, or in 1842, he entered the West Point

Academy, and graduated in 1846, at the age of twenty, at the head of his class. On the 1st of July of that year, his title was Brevet Second Lieutenant of Engineers.

This was the period of the Mexican war, and McClellan, about the age of Alexander Hamilton when he began to show extraordinary ability, was called into active service. Congress (May 15th, 1846) had passed an act, adding a company of sappers, miners, and pontoniers to the corps of engineers, and McClellan was made Second Lieutenant in this company. Colonel Totten names with warm approbation his great exertions, with two others, in organizing and drilling this corps. As the recruits assembled at West Point, they were at once put into a course of active drill as infantry, and of practical instruction in making the different materials used in sieges, running saps, and forming pontoons; and, through the exertions of three officers only, when they sailed from West Point (September 24th) seventy-one strong, the Colonel says they were "in admirable discipline." This company was first ordered to report to General Taylor, and went to Camargo, but were then ordered to countermarch to Matamoras, and move with the column of Patterson. Here Captain Swift and nineteen men were left in the hospital, and from that time until a few days before the landing at Vera Cruz, the company was under Lieutenant Smith (Gustavus W. Smith, now a Major-General in the rebel army), who had but one other officer, Lieutenant McClellan. "During the march," Colonel Totten says, "to Vitoria from Matamoras, the company, then reduced to forty-five effectives, executed a great amount of work upon the roads, fords, etc., as it did in proceeding thence to Tampico, when it formed, with one company of the Third and one of the Seventh infantry, a pioneer party, under Captain Henry of the Third infantry. The detailed reports of these labors exhibit the greatest efficiency and excellent discipline under severe and trying circumstances, Lieutenant Smith having then but one officer, Lieutenant McClellan, under his command."

Colonel Totten at Vera Cruz, saw this company, now rejoined by its captain, land with the first line on the beach under General Worth, and its service here. "During the siege of Vera Cruz," Colonel Totten says, "I was witness to the great exertions and service of this company, animated by and emulating the zeal and devotion of its excellent officers, Lieutenants Smith, McClellan, and Foster." Until the surrender of the Castle, Lieutenant McClellan was engaged in the most severe and trying duties, in opening paths and roads to facilitate the investment, in covering reconnoisances, and in the unceasing toil and hardship of the trenches. "The total of the company," Colonel Totten writes, "was so small, and demands for its aid so incessant, that every man may be said to have been constantly on duty, with scarcely a moment for rest or refreshment." Captain Swift was still too ill for such labors, and died soon afterwards; but, Colonel Totten remarks, the other officers directed "the operations of the siege with unsurpassed intelligence and zeal."

Such is the record of the experience, at the age of twenty, of the soldier called to the command of the Army of the Potomac. Let the next be related in the official words of Colonel Totten:

"Severe labors followed the surrender of Vera Cruz and its castle, and accompanied the march to the battle of Cerro Gordo, in which the company displayed, in various parts of the field, its gallantry and efficiency. It entered the city of Jalapa with the advance of Twiggs' division, and Puebla with the advance of Worth's. During the pause at the latter place, the instruction of the company in its appropriate studies and exercises was resumed by its persevering and zealous officers, and assistance was given by all in the repairs of the defenses. Marching from Puebla with General Twiggs' division, the company was joined to General Worth at Chalon, and arrived in front of San Antonio on the 18th of August, having greatly assisted in clearing the road of obstructions placed by the enemy."

The company, on the 19th, was ordered to take the head of General Pillow's column, at St. Augustine. The service of the company was notable, and is specified all along in the official reports. Before the day of Contreras, General Twiggs, on discovering his enemy in a naturally strong position, with breastworks that commanded approach in every direction, dispatched two engineers to reconnoitre, one of whom was Lieutenant McClellan. They were stopped by the Mexican pickets, had their horses shot under them, and were compelled to return. The action soon commenced—the battle of Contreras in which Lieutenant McClellan was with Magruder's battery, which rendered splendid service. In his official report, General Twiggs thus writes:

"Lieutenant George B. McClellan, after Lieutenant Calendar was wounded, took charge of and managed the howitzer battery (Lieutenant Reno being detached with the rockets) with judgment and success, until it became so disabled as to require shelter. For Lieutenant McClellan's efficiency and gallantry in this affair, I present his name for the favorable consideration of the General-in-Chief."

After a night of exposure to a pitiless storm, the army fought the next day, August 20th, the battle of Cherubusco; and that fine soldier, General Persifer F. Smith, thus completes the record of McClellan:

"Lieutenant G. W. Smith, in command of the engineer company, and Lieutenant McClellan, his subaltern, distinguished themselves throughout the whole of the three actions. Nothing seemed to them too bold to be undertaken, or too difficult to be executed, and their services as engineers were as valuable as those they rendered in battle, at the head of their gallant men."

For his conduct on that day McClellan was breveted First Lieutenant.

Lieutenant McClellan was breveted Captain for gallant and meritorious conduct in the next battle, El Molino del Rey; but declining, he was still Lieutenant on the great day of Chepultepec, and the General-in-Chief, naming him with four others, uses these words: "Those five lieutenants of engineers won the admiration of all about them." His name appears in the official reports in connection with varied and most arduous service. On the night of the 11th of September, Captain Lee and Lieutenants Tower, Smith, and McClellan, with a company of sappers, were employed in establishing batteries against Chepultepec, which were actively served during the next day (12th), which was the day before the assault.

Lieutenant McClellan, long before daybreak of the 13th, was in the field, and Major Smith, of the Engineer Corps, thus says of his morning's work: "At three o'clock a party of the sappers moved to the large convent in advance, and found it unoccupied. Lieutenant McClellan advanced with a party into the Alamada, and reported, at daylight, that no enemy was to be seen. The sappers then moved forward, and had reached two squares beyond the Alamada, when they were recalled. This company was under senior Lieutenant Smith, and was engaged during the day in street fighting, until three o'clock in the afternoon, and particularly in breaking into houses with crowbars and axes. Major Smith says: "Lieutenant McClellan had command of a company for a time in the afternoon, while Lieutenant Smith was searching for powder to be used in blowing up houses from which our troops had been fired upon contrary to the usages of war. During this time, while advancing in company, he reached a strong position, but found himself opposed to a large force of the enemy. He had a conflict with this force, which lasted some time; but the advantage afforded by his position enabled him at length to drive it off, after having killed more than twenty of its number."

Such is the official record of McClellan, so far as brilliant special service is concerned. This, however, can convey no just idea of the labor and skill that are required, in order that lasting honor may be conferred on the country. It is the every day life of the officer that is keenly watched by the men; and what is said of McClellan is, that it was so marked by thoroughness as to command confidence, and so filled with sympathy as to win esteem. Chief-Engineer Totten thus gives in general his term of service: "Lieutenant McClellan, on duty with the engineer company from its organization at West Point; in the siege of Vera Cruz, and in all the battles of General Scott's march to the city of Mexico." The company left that city May 23d, 1848, marched to Vera Cruz, and arrived at West Point on the 22d of June.

Lieutenant McClellan was breveted captain for gallant and

meritorious conduct in battle at Chepultepec, and the following year (1848) saw him commander of this great company of sappers and miners and pontoniers. He continued here until 1851, but the military routine was not enough for him. During this period he translated from the French, a manual, which has become the text book of the service, and introduced the bayonet exercise into the army.*

Captain McClellan's next service was to superintend the construction of Fort Delaware, in the fall of 1851; in the spring of 1852 he was assigned to duty under Major Marcy in the expedition that explored the Red River; and then ordered as senior engineer to Texas, on the staff of General P. F. Smith, with whom he was engaged in surveying the rivers and harbors of that State.

Captain McClellan, in the next year, was one of the engineers who were ordered to make explorations and surveys to ascertain the most practicable route for a railroad from the Mississippi River to the Pacific Ocean; and among other duties, he made the reconnoissance of the Vakima Pass, among the Rocky Mountains, and the most direct route to Puget Sound. He was associated in the exploration of the forty-seventh and forty-ninth parallels of north latitude with Governor Stevens, of Oregon.† The Secretary of War, Jefferson Davis, in his official report to Congress, says of McClellan's services :

"The examination of the approaches and passes of the Cascade Mountains, made by Captain McClellan, of the corps of

---

* See Victor's Life of McClellan—Dime Biographical Series, No. 12, page 25.

† The results of these laborious surveys on the northern route, formed Vol. I. of the twelve large quartos published by Congress. The other volumes were devoted to the exploration of various other routes and sections—the entire series forming a very exhaustive examination of the vast wilds between the valley of the Mississippi and the western declivity of the continent. The West Point education of the explorers proved in an eminent degree satisfactory. The surveys demonstrated that its graduates were qualified for almost any duty.

engineers, presents a reconnoissance of great value, and, though performed under adverse circumstances, exhibits all the information necessary to determine the practicability of this portion of the route, and reflects the highest credit on the capacity and resources of that officer." Nor was this the whole service of this indomitable public servant. In this report, its closing words, Secretary Davis says: "Captain McClellan, of the corps of engineers, after the completion of his field operations, was directed to visit various railroads, and to collect information and facts established in the construction and working of existing roads, to serve as data in determining the practicability of constructing and working roads over the several routes explored. The results of his inquiries will be found in a very valuable memoir herewith submitted."

This allusion to McClellan's labors, succeeding the survey, deserves further mention. He was chosen to investigate the railway system of the United States, with a view to obtain all the data on construction, equipping and running, necessary to give the Pacific Railway the benefit of all recent experience and discoveries in its construction and operation. This duty occupied the summer of 1854. McClellan not only visited the chief railways in the Northern States, and inspected them thoroughly, but he called to his aid the knowledge and assistance of several of the best engineers and machinists in the country. He thus was enabled to report in a very complete manner—his report, in truth, being a treatise on railways which possessed value as such to the railway interests of the country. The report was rendered early in November, 1854, and gave to the Department entire satisfaction. Its completeness proved to railroad managers and directors of so much interest, that when, a few years later, McClellan resigned his commission in the army, railway men sought and obtained his services in the management of two of the largest enterprises in the country.

To this engineering service succeeded, for three years, other duties which largely raised the reputation of Captain McClellan. After executing a secret service in the West Indies, and receiving a commission in the United States cavalry, he was appointed, April 2d, 1855, one of a military commission of three officers, to proceed to the Crimea and Northern Russia for observation on the then existing war; and his report "On the Organization of European Armies and the Operation of the War," evinced so much grasp of the subject, as to add to the reputation of a brave and efficient officer in the field, that of a large comprehension of the science of war.

The record of this tour in Europe is one of exceeding interest even to the general reader. The three officers composing it were Major Delafield, Major Mordecai and Captain McClellan—who were constituted a commission to proceed to Europe and the seat of War in the Crimea to inspect forts, armories, foundries, &c.; to examine into military systems and organizations; to study the conduct of a campaign on the field; to inquire into the special forms of rifled arms and ordnance then being introduced; to study harbor and coast defenses, &c., &c. That the duty was ably performed, the country is proud to bear witness. The three separate reports made by the officers, viz.: On ordnance, gunnery, construction, armories, &c., by Major Mordecai; on army organization, defenses, field service, &c., by Major Delafield; on cavalry, infantry, discipline, barracks, &c., by McClellan, whose report also contained a fine disquisition on operations before Sebastopol, which proved how critically he studied and apprehended the whole art of war. McClellan's report was the first of the three submitted—appearing under date of February 25th, 1857. The character of the volume will better appear from a citation of its contents, viz.:

"Report on the operations in the Crimea, with an historical sketch of the campaign, and strictures on its conduct.

"Report upon the European troops, embracing a *resume* of the systems of the Russians, Prussians, Austrians, French and English.

"Report upon the French, Austrian, Prussian and Sardinian infantry, with a digest of their composition, regulations, &c.

"Report upon the Russian army, comprising 1st, organization, uniform, recruiting stations, etc.; 2d, the instruction and tactics of cavalry;

3d, the equipments, arms, stables, horses, etc., of cavalry; 4th, the Russian Infantry

"Report on the Prussian cavalry.
"Report on the Austrian cavalry.
"Report on the French cavalry.
"Report on the English and Sardinian cavalry.
"Report on the United States cavalry."

This was also followed (in the same volume) by "*The Regulations and Instructions for the Field Service of Cavalry, in time of war, for the United States Army.*"

The several reports were very full expositions of the several systems in use in the best armies, and serve to show how intimately acquainted Captain McClellan was with the subject in all its features. His final report, devoted to the United States cavalry, was an embodiment of his suggestions in regard to its reorganization, so as to adapt it to the improved condition of that arm of service as perfected by the European nations. The last section of the volume, as stated, was devoted to a manual of instruction and regulations for the United States army cavalry. In the preface modestly announcing his work the author said:

"I have translated from the original Russian, and have endeavored to adapt them (the regulations, etc.) to our own organization, preserving the original arrangement, and adding merely a few minor details suggested by the recollections of former readings and of service in the field. It is more than probable that they will be found to fill usefully an important want in our military literature: while they undoubtedly are based upon true military principles."

This adverts to the fact of the writer's acquaintance with the Russian language. While in Russia the Captain was an arduous student of that uncouth and severe idiom of the descendants of the Tartars; and so readily mastered its lingual and idiomatic structure as to be able to converse without difficulty with the native Russ. Already a thorough French scholar from his West Point education, with a good command of Spanish, and a reading knowledge of German, the acquisition of Russian served to elevate the Captain into the category of linguistic scholars.

The "regulations" have since been republished in convenient 12mo form for use as a text-book in the service, which it has become—making the second manual from his hand.

And now, as there was no call by his country for service in the field, he resigned (1857) his position in the army, but still kept, as it were, in the line of his profession of engineer, for he became Vice-President and Engineer of the Illinois Central Railroad. Having served here three years, so much valued were his services that he was chosen General Superintendent of the Ohio and Mississippi Railroad, in which capacity he was acting when the rebellion broke out. He was tendered the Major-Generalship of the Ohio State forces, and, a little later, Governor Curtin, of Pennsylvania, also endeavored to secure his services in organizing the volunteers of that State. He accepted, however, the earliest offer of Ohio, and very promptly organized the militia of that State in a manner so original and efficient as to elicit the warmest encomiums. No State in the Union has a citizen soldiery truer to the duties of both citizen and soldier than Ohio under the system inaugurated by McLellan.

As stated by us, in a former section of this work, on the 14th day of May, 1861, he was assigned to the command of the Department of the West. From that date the record of his life up to the date (Aug. 1st) when he assumed command of the army of the Potomac, is written in the sketch already given of the Campaign of Western Virginia.

In private circles the General is known as an amiable man and a gentleman of the true kind. He is married—his wife being the daughter of General Marcy, U. S. A. She is a lady of many virtues of head and heart. The General is, we believe, a communicant in the Presbyterian (Old School) denomination.

XIX.

THE THIRD DISASTER.

THE Ball Bluff defeat, October 21st, 1861, was a melancholy affair resulting not only in disaster to our arms but in great loss of life, owing to a deficiency of transportation. Men were pressed by superior numbers back upon the river, (the Potomac,) there to find no adequate provision made for their safe passage over. Many were, therefore, killed in making a last desperate stand at the river's bank, many plunged into the river only to be swept down by the current, many were taken prisoners—disasters which came after the battle was closed by defeat. The ranks of the regiments came forth from the conflict literally riddled, and their gallant leader, Colonel Baker, was among the slain. It was not a Bull's Run stampede; but a fearful sacrifice of men whose devotion and courage rendered their loss all the more keenly deplored.

For several days prior to the 21st, the brigades on the right bank of the Potomac, above the Chain Bridge and the Falls of the Potomac, had been pushed up in the direction of Leesburg. These brigades, however, commanded by General McCall, did not advance further than Drainesville, twelve miles south-east of Leesburg, although their scouts were pushed forward to Goose Creek, four miles from that place. On Saturday and Sunday General McCall made two reconnoissances towards Leesburg, and could find no trace of the enemy. The country people declared that the rebels had abandoned that place some days before.

It was believed at Washington that Leesburg had been evacuated by the rebels, that they had retired from that place to Aldie, ten miles south-west, where they were fortifying. Aldie is a stronger position than Leesburg, for there the rebels could place Goose Creek between themselves and the advancing Union troops. Goose Creek is about the size of Bull's Run, but has high and steep banks, and cannot be crossed by artillery, except by bridges. On the right bank of the creek are some high hills admirably calculated for defense, and these, it was understood, the rebels were fortifying. These facts, or rather, these reports, were current in the army and in Washington.

General Stone, upon his own responsibility, it would appear, determined upon a demonstration toward Leesburg, looking to its occupation.

McCall's movement upon Drainesville had excited the attention of the enemy, it appeared; for a regiment soon appeared near Edwards' Ferry, evidently to watch the movements of Stone. This regiment took position on a hill about one mile and a half from the ferry. It afterwards proved that the regiment was only "a blind"—that General Evans' forces, five thousand strong, had not evacuated Leesburg, but had *feinted* the evacuation to draw on the Federal forces.

Stone having completed his arrangements, October 20th, proceeded, at one P. M., to Edwards' Ferry, from Poolsville, with Gorman's brigade, the Seventh Michigan volunteers, two troops of the Van Alen cavalry, and the Putnam Rangers, sending at the same time to Harrison's Island and vicinity four companies of the Fifteenth Massachusetts volunteers, under Colonel Devens, (who had already one company on the island,) and Colonel Lee with a battalion of the Twentieth Massachusetts. And to Conrad's Ferry, a section of Vaughn's Rhode Island battery and the Tammany regiment, under Colonel Cogswell. A section of Bunting's New York State militia battery, under Lieutenant Bramhall, was at the time on duty at Conrad's Ferry, and Rickett's battery, already posted at Edwards' Ferry, under Colonel Woodruff. Orders were also sent to Colonel Devens, at Harrison's Island, some four miles up the river, to detach Captain Philbrick and twenty men to cross from the island and explore by a path through woods little used, in the direction of Leesburg, to see if he could find anything concerning the enemy's position in that direction; but to retire and report on discovering any of the enemy.

General Gorman was ordered to deploy his forces in view of the enemy, and in so doing, no movement of the enemy was excited. Three flat-boats were ordered, and at the same time shell and spherical case shot was thrown into the place of the enemy's concealment. This was done to produce an impression that a crossing was to be made. The shelling of Edwards' Ferry, and launching of the boats, induced the quick retirement of the enemy's force seen there, and three boat-loads, of thirty-five men each, from the First Minnesota, under cover of the shelling, crossed and recrossed the river, the boats consuming in crossing from three to seven minutes. The spirit displayed by officers and men at the thought of crossing the river was cheering, and satisfied the General that they could be depended on for gallant service.

As darkness came on, General Stone ordered Gorman's brigade and the Seventh Michigan to fall back to their respective camps, but retained the Tammany regiment, the companies of the Fifteenth Massachusetts and artillery near Conrad's Ferry, in their position, waiting the result of Captain Philbrick's scout, he (Stone) remaining with his Staff at Edwards' Ferry. About four P. M., Lieutenant Howe, Quartermaster of the Fifteenth Massachusetts, reported to General Stone that Captain Philbrick had returned to the island after proceeding, unmolested, to within a mile and a half of Leesburg, and that he had there discovered, in the edge of a wood, an encampment of about thirty tents, which he approached to within twenty-five rods without being challenged, the camp having no pickets out any distance in the direction of the river.

General Stone at once sent orders to Colonel Devens to cross four companies of his regiment to the Virginia shore, and march silently, under the cover of night, to the position of the camp referred to, to attack and destroy it at daybreak, pursue the enemy lodged there as far as would be prudent with the small force, and return rapidly to the island; his return to be covered by the Massachusetts Twentieth, which was directed to be posted on a bluff directly over the landing place. Colonel Devens was ordered to use this opportunity to observe the approaches to Leesburgh, and the position and force of the enemy in the vicinity, and in case he found no enemy, or found him only weak and in a position where he could observe well and be secure until his party could be strengthened sufficiently to make a valuable reconnoissance, which should safely ascertain the position and force of the enemy, to hold on and report. Orders were dispatched to Colonel Baker, to send the First California regiment to Conrad's Ferry, to arrive there at sunrise, and to have the remainder of his brigade in a state of readiness to move after an early breakfast. Also to Lieutenant-Colonel Ward, of the Fifteenth Massachusetts, to move with a battalion of a regiment to the river bank opposite Harrison's Island, to arrive there by daybreak. Two mounted howitzers, from Rickett's battery, were detailed to the tow-path opposite Harrison's Island.

In order to distract attention from Colonel Devens' movement, and at the same time to effect reconnoissance in the direction of Leesburgh from Edwards' Ferry, General Stone ordered General Gorman to throw across the river at that point, two companies of First Minnesota, under cover of fire from Rickett's battery, and sent a party of thirty-one Van Alen cavalry, under command of Major Mix, accompanied by Captain Charles Stewart, Assistant Adjutant-General; Captain Murphy, Lieutenants Pierce and Gouraud, with orders to advance along Leesburgh road until they should come to the vicinity of the battery, which was known to be on that road, and then turn to the left, and examine the heights between that and Goose Creek; see if any of the enemy were posted in that vicinity, ascertain as near as possible their number and disposition, examine the country with reference to the passage of troops to the Leesburgh and Georgetown turnpike, and return rapidly to cover behind the skirmishers of the First Minnesota.

This reconnoissance was most gallantly made by all in the party, which proceeded along the Leesburgh road nearly three miles from the ferry, and when near the position of a hidden battery, came suddenly on a Mississippi regiment about thirty-five yards distant, received its fire and returned it with their pistols. The fire of the enemy killed one horse, but Lieutenant Gouraud, the gallant Adjutant of the cavalry battalion, seized the dismounted man, and drawing him on his horse behind him carried him safely from the field. One private of the Fourth Virginia cavalry was brought off by the party, and as he was well mounted and armed, his mount replaced the one lost by the fire of the enemy.

Meantime Colonel Devens on the right, having in pursuance of his orders arrived at the position indicated by the scouts as the site of the enemy's camp, found that they had been deceived by the uncertain light, and had mistaken the openings in the trees for a row of tents. He found however, wood, in which he concealed his force from view, and proceeded to examine the space between that and Leesburgh, sending back word to General Stone, that thus far he could see no enemy. Immediately on receipt of this intelligence, which was carried by Lieutenant Howe, Quartermaster of the Fifteenth Massachusett, General Stone ordered a non-commissioned officer and ten cavalry to join Colonel Devens, for the purpose of scouring the country near him, while he continued his reconnoissance, and to give him due notice of the approach of any enemy, and that Lieutenant-Colonel Ward, with his battalion of the Fifteenth Massachusetts, should move on to Smart's Mill, half-a-mile to the right of the crossing-place of Colonels Devens and Lee, where, in strong position, he could watch and protect the flank of Colonel Devens on his return, and secure a second crossing-place more favorable than the first, and connected by a good road with Leesburgh.

Captain Candy, Assistant Adjutant-General, and General Lander, accompanied the cavalry, to serve with it.

The battalion under Colonel Ward was detained on the bluff in the rear of Colonel Deven, instead of being directed to the right.

Stone said in his official report: "For some reason never explained to me, neither of these orders were carried out. The cavalry were transferred to the Virginia shore, but were sent back without having left the shore to go inland, and thus Colonel Devens was deprived of the means of obtaining warning of any approach of the enemy." The report then went on to state the orders given to Colonel Baker, under which he acted, viz.:

"Colonel Baker having arrived at Conrad's Ferry, with the First California regiment at an early hour, proceeded to Edwards' Ferry, and reported to me in person, stating that his regiment was at the former place, and the three other regiments of his brigade ready to march. I directed him to Harrison's Island to assume command, and in a full conversation explained to him the position as it then stood. I told him that General McCall had advanced his troops to Drainsville, and that I was extremely desirous of ascertaining the exact position and force of the enemy in our front, and exploring, as far as it was safe, on the right towards Leesburgh, and on the left towards the Leesburgh and Gum Spring road. I also informed Colonel Baker that General Gorman, opposite Edwards' Ferry, should be reenforced, and that I would make every effort to push Gorman's troops carefully forward, to discover the best line from that Ferry to the Leesburgh and Gum Spring road, already mentioned, and the position of the breastworks and hidden batteries, which prevented the movement of troops directly from left to right, were also pointed out to him.

"The means of transportation across, of the sufficiency of which he (Baker) was to be the judge, was detailed, and authority given him to make use of the guns of a section each of Vaughan's and Bunting's batteries, together with French's mountain howitzers (of Rickett' battery), all the troops of his brigade and the Tammany regiment, beside the Nineteenth and part of the Twentieth regiments of Massachusetts volunteers. I left it to his discretion, after viewing the ground, to retire from the Virginia shore under the cover of his guns and the fire of the large infantry force, or to pass our reenforcements in case he found it practicable, and the position on the other side favorable. I stated that I wished no advance made unless the enemy were of inferior force, and under no circumstance to pass beyond Leesburgh, or a strong position between it and Goose Creek, on the Gum Spring, *i. e.*, the Manasses road. Colonel Baker was cautioned in reference to passing artillery across the river, and I begged, if he did so, to see it well supported by good infantry. The General pointed out to him the position of some bluffs on this side of the river, from which artillery could act with effect on the other, and, leaving the matter of crossing more troops or retiring what were already over, to his discretion, gave him entire control of operations on the right. This gallant and energetic officer left me about nine A. M. or half-past nine, and galloped of quickly to his command."

This statement is precise, and if Colonel Baker was caught without transports for a retreat, was surprised by an overwhelming force which cut off his retreat, in part, it was not General Stone's fault, if the orders explicitly detailed above were given and were understood. Baker's friends as explicitly state that he undertook the enterprize, conscious that he should be overwhelmed, and that he so expressed himself to General Stone, urging the practical impossibility, with the transports at his disposal, of throwing over the river the force which he deemed safe—but was ordered forward. From an examination of all the evidence produced, we credit the General's statement, and feel that the censures heaped upon him were really unmerited.

Reenforcements were rapidly thrown to the Virginia side by General Gorman, at Edwards' Ferry, and his skirmishers and cavalry scouts advanced cautiously and steadily to the front and right, while the infantry lines were formed in such position as to act rapidly and in concert, in case of an advance of the enemy, and shells were thrown by Lieutenant Woodruff's Parrott guns, especial care being taken to annoy the enemy by the battery on the right.

Messengers from Harrison's Island informed General Stone, soon after the arrival of Colonel Baker opposite the island, that he was crossing his whole force as rapidly as possible, and that he had caused an additional flat-boat to be lifted from the canal into the river, and had provided a line, by which to cross the boats more rapidly.

During the morning a sharp skirmish took place, between two of the advance companies of the Fifteenth Massachusetts and a body of about one hundred strong of Mississippi riflemen, during which a body of the enemy's cavalry appeared, causing Colonel Devens to fall back in good order on Colonel Lee's position, after which he again advanced, his officers and men behaving admirably, fighting, retiring, and advancing in perfect order, and exhibiting every proof of high courage and good discipline. Had he, at this time, had the cavalry scouting party which was sent him in the morning, but which, most unfortunately, had been turned back without his knowledge, he could, doubtless, have had timely warning of the approach of the superior force, which afterwards overwhelmed his regiment and their brave commander and comrades. To that surprise was owing the disaster.

General Stone, evidently thinking that Colonel Baker might be able to use more artillery, dispatched to him two additional pieces of Vaughan's battery, supported by two companies of infantry, with directions to its officer to come into position below the place of crossing, and report to Colonel Baker. Later in the day, and but a short time prior to the arrival of the guns, Colonel Baker suggested the same movement to General Stone, thus justifying the General's opinion.

A correspondent of the New York *Times* said, in reference to the transports and their apparent want of capacity:

"After Colonel Devens' second advance, Colonel Baker seems to have gone to the field in person, but he has left no record of what officers and men he charged with the care of the boats, and insuring the regular passage of the troops. If any one was charged with this duty, it was not performed, for it appears that the reenforcements, as they arrived, found no system enforced, and the boats were delayed most unnecessarily in transporting back, a few at a time, the wounded that happened to arrive with attendants. Had an efficient officer been in charge at each landing, with one company guarding the boats, their full capacity would have been made serviceable, and sufficient men would have passed on to secure the success of his operation. The forwarding of artillery (necessarily a slow process) before its supporting force of infantry, also impeded the rapid assembling of an imposing force on the Virginia shore. The infantry which was waiting with impatience should have been first transported, and this alone would have made a difference in the infantry line at the time of attack of at least one thousand men—enough to have turned the scale in our favor."

It was about one o'clock P. M., when the enemy appeared in force, in front of Colonel Devens. A sharp skirmish then ensued, which was maintained for some time by the Massachusetts Fifteenth. Unsupported, and finding himself about to be outflanked, Colonel Devens retired a short distance in good order, and took up a position in the edge of the wood, about half-a-mile in front of Colonel Lee's position, where he remained until two P. M., when he again retired with the approach of Colonel Baker, and took his place in line with those portions of the Twentieth Massachusetts and First California regiments which had arrived.

Colonel Baker at once formed his line, awaiting the attack of the enemy, which came upon him with great vigor about three P. M., and was met with admirable spirit by our troops, who, though evidently struggling against largely superior numbers, nearly if not quite three to one, maintained their ground and a most destructive fire upon the enemy.

Colonel Cogswell, with a small portion of his regiment, succeeded in reaching the field in the midst of the heaviest fire, and they went gallantly into action with a yell, which wavered the enemy's line.

Lieutenant Bramhall, of Bunting's battery, had succeeded, after exertions of labor, in bringing up a piece of the Rhode Island battery, and Lieutenant French, First artillery, his two mountain howitzers; but while for a short time these maintained a well-directed fire, both officers and nearly all the men were soon borne away wounded, and the pieces were handed to the rear to prevent their falling into the hands of the enemy.

At about four o'clock P. M., Colonel Baker, pierced by a number of balls, fell at the head of his command, while cheering on his men, and by his own example maintaining the obstinate resistance they were making. In full uniform, with a "regulation" hat and feather, and mounted on his horse, he was a conspicuous mark for the bloodthirsty traitors. He was one of the finest appearing men in full uniform and mounted that I have seen in the service. Entirely regardless of personal safety, he led and cheered on his men. He remarked to those around him, "A rascal up in that tree has fired at me five or six times;" and the rascal in the tree was speedily brought down by a well-directed ball. Shortly after this Colonel Baker was surrounded by a body of rebel cavalry and taken prisoner; but the right wing of the battalion charged with the bayonet, routed the cavalry, killed numbers of them, and recaptured their Colonel.

But a few minutes had elapsed, however, before a tall, ferocious Virginian, with red hair and whiskers, came rushing from behind a tree, with a huge revolver in his hand, and, placing the weapon almost against the Colonel's head, inflicted a mortal wound. Not satisfied with his deadly work, he fired the second ball, while simultaneously the body was pierced with four bullets from the tops of trees, and the brave Colonel fell lifeless from his horse.

Captain Louis Berial, of New York city, commanding Company G., California regiment, seeing the assassination of Colonel Baker, rushed upon the ruffian, seized him by the throat, and shot him dead on the spot with his revolver.

Colonel Lee then took command, and prepared to commence throwing our forces to the rear, but Colonel Cogswell, of the Tammany regiment, being found to be senior in rank, assumed command, and ordered dispositions to be made immediately for marching to the left, and cutting a way through to Edwards' Ferry.

Unfortunately, just as the first dispositions were being made, an officer of the enemy rode rapidly in front of the Tammany regiment and beckoned them towards the enemy.

Whether the Tammany understood this as an order from one of our officers, or an invitation to close work, is not known; but the men responded to the gesture with a yell, and charged forward, carrying with them in their advance the rest of the line, which soon received a murderous fire from the enemy at close distance. Our officers rapidly recalled the men, but in the position they had now placed themselves, it was impracticable to make the movement designed, and Colonel Cogswell reluctantly gave the order to retire. The enemy pursued our troops to the edge of the bluff over the landing-place, and thence poured in a heavy fire on the men who were endeavoring to cross to the island.

Rapid as the retreat necessarily was, there was no neglect of orders. The men formed near the river, deploying as skirmishers, and maintained for twenty minutes or more the unequal and hopeless contest rather than surrender.

The smaller boats had disappeared, no one knew whither. The largest boat, rapidly and too heavily laden, swamped some fifteen feet from the shore, and nothing was left to the gallant soldiers but to swim, surrender or die.

With a devotion worthy of the cause they are serving, officers and men, while quarter was being offered to such as would lay down their arms, stripped themselves of their swords and muskets and hurled them out into the river to prevent their falling into the hands of the foe, and saved themselves as they could by swimming, floating on logs, and concealing themselves in bushes and forests to make their way up and down the river, back to a place of crossing.

The *Times* correspondent, already quoted from, and who appears to have been in the confidence of General Stone, said:

"While these scenes were being enacted on the right, General Stone was preparing for a rapid push forward to the road by which the enemy would retreat if driven, and entirely unsuspicious of the perilous condition of the troops on the right. The additional artillery had already been sent in anticipation, and General Stone was told by a messenger from Baker's position, that the Colonel could, without doubt, hold his own in case he did not advance. Half an hour later—say at half-past three P. M.—a similar statement was made by another messenger from Colonel Baker, and it was the expectation of General Stone that an advance on the right would be made, so that he could push forward General Gorman. It was, as had been explained to Colonel Baker, impracticable to throw Gorman's brigade directly to the right, by reason of the battery in the wood, between which we had never been able to reconnoitre."

Presuming that all was progressing favorably, Stone telegraphed to General Banks requesting him to send a brigade of his division, intending it to occupy the ground on the Maryland side of the river, near to Harrison's Island, which could be abandoned in case of a rapid advance.

Captain Candy arrived at head-quarters from the field of Colonel Baker about five P. M., and announced to General Stone the news of Colonel Baker's death, but giving no news of further disaster, though he stated that reenforcements were slow. General Stone telegraphed this fact to General Banks, and the fact of Colonel Baker's death, and instantly rode to the right to assume command. Before he reached the point opposite the island, evidences of disaster began to be met, in men who had crossed the river by swimming, and on reaching the landing the fact was asserted in a manner leaving no possible doubt. It was reported to General Stone that the enemy's force was ten thousand—an evident exaggeration. He gave orders to hold the island for the removal of the wounded, and established a patrol on the tow-path from opposite the island to the line of pickets near Monocacy, and then returned to the left, to secure the troops there from disaster, preparing means of removing them as rapidly as possible.

Orders arrived from head-quarters of the army of the Potomac to hold the island and Virginia shore at Edwards' Ferry at all hazards, and promising reenforcements, and General Stone forwarded additional intrenching tools to General Gorman, with instructions to intrench and hold out against any force that might appear. That evening General Stone learned by telegraph that General Banks was on the way to reenforce him, and at about three A. M., he arrived and assumed command.

XX.

INCIDENTS OF THE BALL'S BLUFF DISASTER.

THE instances of personal gallantry of the highest order were so many, that it would be unjust now to detail particular cases. Officers displayed for their men, and men for their officers, that beautiful devotion which is only to be found among true soldiers. Regiment after regiment of fresh rebel troops came rushing upon them down the hill, yelling like fiends, and pouring in deadly volleys, while the trees still swarmed with riflemen, who made the air black with bullets aimed at our devoted little band. At times the contending parties were within four or five feet of each other; still our men stood steadily, returning their fire, or plunging at them with the bayonet. So near were they at one time that our men actually caught a lieutenant, by seizing him as he stood in the enemy's ranks. He was taken over the river safely by his captors.

During the fiercest portion of the struggle, an officer, mounted on a fine horse, rushed forward from the woods, exclaiming to the Federal force behind him: "Rally on me, boys!" Knowing that other Union regiments were to cross another ferry, some of our men were deceived and followed the horseman; but they were led as sheep to the slaughter, for they had proceeded but a few rods when a deadly volley was poured into them, killing many and hastily dispersing the rest. In a few minutes the same man appeared again, to try the same game. Colonel Baker chanced to see him and exclaimed,

"Good heaven! there is Johnson, what is he doing there?" It was not the rebel General, however, but some other, equally bold and unscrupulous.

The apparent desertion of Leesburg was only a ruse on the part of the enemy, who had drawn their forces out of the town, and were posted in strength in such positions between Leesburg and the river, that they could enfilade our advancing columns, and attack them not only in front and in the flanks, but in the rear also. Skirmishers were thrown out as the column advanced, but no signs of an enemy were seen, until the brigade had advanced fully half-way to their destination. The first intimation of the presence of the enemy was the simultaneous discharge of about a hundred rifles, from a thicket on the top of an eminence. The fire was received by the right wing of the Fifteenth Massachusetts, who were in the advance. A lieutenant and six or eight men were killed, and eighteen severely wounded. Three companies, however, immediately dashed up the slope, in the direction of the fire, and, on reaching the spot, found themselves confronted with a regiment of Mississippi riflemen, who, reserving their fire till our brave fellows were within thirty yards, poured into them another volley. A captain, a lieutenant, and twelve or thirteen men were killed by this discharge. Our men, however, nothing daunted, delivered their fire with good effect, and then charged with the bayonet. The enemy did not wait for the latter, but cut and ran towards Leesburg in disorder. Colonel Devens then pushed on, but soon found that even that apparent flight was a ruse to draw him on. He was soon so surrounded as to have but little hope of the escape of a single person in his ranks. It is stated that the conduct of Colonel Baker, in his effort to rescue the Massachusetts and other men, under fire, was heroic beyond description.

Just prior to the fall of Colonel Baker, the enemy made a flank movement to turn the latter's line. Colonel Baker, perceiving this, immediately wrote an order to be conveyed to the Tammany companies, which had just arrived, and while the right was facing his command, to meet the flank movement, and when about giving orders to charge, he was killed, falling ten feet in advance of his column.

One of the bravest of the brave was Lieutenant Bramhall, of the New York Ninth. He was in command of two pieces of artillery, one of which was left on the island when the advance was made. During the fight he was wounded by a spent ball in his back, and had two other bullets pass through him, through his side. He was carried to the island. When the rout took place, he asked Rev. Mr. Scanlan what he should do with his battery, where he should place it to cover the retreat. Then, as the thought flashed into his mind, said, "I will place it to cover Conrad's Ferry." And though thus wounded, he called two soldiers to his aid, who carried him in their arms round the island, and sustained him while he placed his battery in position! He was about 23 years of age. Besides these wounds, he had six bullets pass through his clothes and hat. One struck the scabbard of his sword. It was only till he had got every thing right about his guns that he would allow himself to be brought from the island.

A German sergeant, on seeing his captain fall, toward the close of the fight, collected four or five files of his company, about a dozen men altogether, and crying, "Boys, we can only die once; we'll avenge the captain's death." led them fighting into the very heart of the enemy's position. He immediately disappeared, and nothing was afterward seen of him or any of his band.

The officers and men behaved with the most extraordinary courage. They were pressed by an overpowering force, but stood firm until their whole supply of ammunition was exhausted, and then retreated to the river, and threw their guns and swords into it to prevent the enemy getting possession of them. Colonel Raymond Lee and staff were furnished with a skiff to make their escape. The Colonel gallantly refused, and gave orders to use it for conveying the wounded across the river. It was filled with wounded, who reached the Maryland shore in safety, and the humane and gallant officer was taken prisoner.

Many of the survivors of the fight escaped by swimming. Captain Crowninsheld, long known in Harvard as the stroke-oar of the boat club, swam to Harrison's Island, without clothing, and saving nothing but his watch, which he carried in his mouth. Being greatly fatigued, he turned in beneath the most convenient hay-rick, and slept till morning, when, in the hurry of departure, and the especial anxiety of procuring clothes, he departed without giving a thought to the watch which he had taken such pains to keep possession of the night before, and which he had tucked away beside him before going to sleep.

A story was related of an Irishman in company D, of the Massachusetts Fifteenth, which is very funny. When the retreat was ordered, he threw off his coat and pants and plunged into the icy current of the Potomac. He swam boldly across the river, and had just gained the Maryland shore, when he remembered that he had left $13 25 in the pocket of his coat. "Be jabers, Billy," said he, "thim thirteen dollars is in me coat, and the bloody ribels will git 'em, and besides, I can't consint to part with the amount, so I'll jist go for them," and in he plunged again. He got safely over, found his coat, secured his money, and recrossed the river. I saw him in camp this afternoon, and congratulated him on his pluck, endurance and success, to which he replied, "Oh, yis sir, 'twas all I'd saved from my three months' sarvice, and I'm very fond of me pipe."

A most exciting scene transpired at the sinking of the launch, in which were some sixty wounded men, and twenty or thirty members of the California First. The launch had been safely taken half way across the river, when, to their utter consternation, it was discovered that it was leaking, and the water gradually, but surely, gaining upon them. The wounded were lying on the bottom of the launch—some shot in the head, others mangled by the tramp of cavalry, and others suffering intolerably from their various dislocations, wounds and injuries, and all soaking in water, which, at the very start, was fully four inches deep. As the water grew deeper and rose above the prostrate forms of the wounded, their comrades lifted them into sitting postures, that they might not be strangled by the fast-rising stream. Despite all that could be done, the fate of the launch, and all that were in , with the exception of a few expert swimmers, was sealed; suddenly, and like a flash of lightning, the rotten craft sank, carrying with it at least fifty dying, mangled, groaning sufferers, and some twenty or thirty others, who had trusted their lives to its treacherous hold.

After all was finished, and the fragments of the regiments were brought together at the water's edge, it was determined to push upward along the shore, with the uncertain hope of finding some means of recrossing to the Maryland side. In the event of meeting the enemy, however, it was determined to surrender at once, since any contest under the circumstances would be a useless sacrifice of life. After progressing a mile or so, the officers (Captains Bartlett and Tremlett, and Lieutenants Whittier and Abbott) discovered a mill, surrounded by cottages, about which numbers of persons were seen moving. Here it seemed that they must yield. The officers ordered a halt, and directed the men to cast all their arms into the river, so that the enemy should gain as little as possible by the surrender. Lieutenant Whittier walked on in advance with a white handkerchief tied on his sword, to be used when occasion should demand. The first person met was an old negro, who, though greatly terrified, contrived to reveal that an old boat was stored near the mill, which might be bailed out and used to convey the fugitives across the river. A gift of five dollars insured his services, and the boat was in due time launched and ready for use. It was small, and only a few could pass at each trip. Until dawn it passed back and forth, until all were transferred in safety. One officer went over in the third boat, to keep the men well together on the Maryland side; the others waited till the last. For that service the old negro was afterwards dreadfully whipped, and only escaped more tortures by "passing over Jordan"—crossing the Potomac and making his way to Pennsylvania.

Before starting upon the expedition on Monday morning, the men had left their knapsacks and blankets upon Harrison's Island. In the retreat it was impossible for more than a few to gather them up again. A Lieutenant volunteered on Wednesday, after the island had been visited by the rebel scouts, to go over with five and collect what remained. He did so, and returned with more than a hundred knapsacks and blankets, to the great comfort of many of the men who had suffered from the icy weather. While there, the men scoured nearly the whole island, but could not be persuaded to enter the building which had been used as a hospital, in which so many corpses of their former comrades lay.

The loss of the Federals in this affair never was accurately stated. About seventy were killed; as many were drowned and shot in the water; over one hundred and fifty were wounded; and about four hundred were taken prisoners. The rebel General in command, Evans, in his report of the affair, stated his forces to have been twenty-five hundred, and his loss to have been three hundred killed and wounded. The Federal force, all told, was seventeen hundred and fifty.

As to the responsibility of the movement made, and of the surprise, the following orders will afford due light; they were found in the Colonel's hat, underneath the lining. Both were deeply stained with Colonel Baker's blood, and one of the bullets, which went through his head, carried away a corner of the first:

EDWARDS' FERRY, October 21st, 1861.

Colonel E. D. Baker, Commander of Brigade :

COLONEL: In case of heavy firing in front of Harrison's Island, you will advance the California regiment of your brigade, or retire the regiments under Colonels Lee and Devens, now on the [almost rendered illegible by blood] Virginia side of the river, at your discretion—assuming command on arrival.

Very respectfully, Colonel, your most obedient servant,

CHARLES P. STONE,
Brigadier-General Commanding.

The second order, which follows, was delivered on the battle-field by Colonel Cogswell, who said to Colonel Baker, in reply to a question what it meant, "All right, go ahead." Thereupon, Colonel Baker put it in his hat without reading. An hour afterward he fell.

HEAD-QUARTERS CORPS OF OBSERVATION,
EDWARDS' FERRY, October 22d—11:50.

E. D. BAKER, COMMANDING BRIGADE—COLONEL: I am informed that the force of the enemy is about four thousand, all told. If you can push them, you may do so as far as to have a strong position near Leesburg, if you can keep them before you, avoiding their batteries. If they pass Leesburg and take the Gum Springs Road, you will not follow far, but seize the first good position to cover that road.

Their desire is to draw us on, if they are obliged to retreat, as far as Goose Creek, where they can be reenforced from Manassas, and have a strong position.

Report frequently, so that, when they are pushed, Gorman can come up on their flank.

Yours, respectfully and truly,
CHARLES P. STONE,
Brigadier-General Commanding.

This little error of the Colonel—in not reading the last dispatch—was the cause of the surprise. Colonel Coggswell's remark—"All right, go ahead!" doubtless served to answer, in Baker's mind, for the contents of the envelop, and therefore it was not broken open. It serves at least to relieve General Stone from the inattention and ignorance of the enemy's force which were freely charged upon him at one time. The movement over the river was Stone's conception, and that remains open for stricture.

XXI.

COLONEL BAKER.

THE loss of this officer created a profound sensation, in all circles. He was well known personally by an immense number of persons in the East and West and on the Pacific coast; while his reputation as the United States Senator from Oregon was such as to have made his name one familiar to the public ear. His splendid talents as a speaker and debater gave him a prominent position in the Senate, from which he withdrew to raise regiments in New York city and Philadelphia, to be known as the California brigade. His loss was a cause for national regret; and the notices bestowed upon his career, his character and talents evinced the depth of the feeling all felt at his fate.

Edward Dickinson Baker was born in London, England, February 24th, 1811. His parents were both persons of refinement, honorably connected and of fair repute. The parents emigrated to America in 1815, residing in Philadelphia for ten years. "Early in the spring of 1825," says a writer in Harper's *Magazine*, (December, 1861,) "the elder Baker, impelled by that spirit of restless adventure and enterprise that seems the heritage of all the race, gathered up his household gods and turned his face once more to the sunset. Over the trackless mountains, along the strange rivers, through the still wilderness where life was bursting into beauty and bloom, he journeyed until, tired of wandering, he rested in the rich valley of the Wabash. Only a little while though; for in a year or so we find him at the pleasant old town of Belleville, in the county of St. Clair, the earliest settled of all Central Illinois, filled with a population more wealthy and refined than that which settled in the Southern peninsula between the Mississippi and the Ohio, or that which fought and traded along the Illinois and Rock Rivers. Most of the educational and social advantages of the State clustered at that early day around the villages facing the trading station that Laclede had built and called St. Louis, and those that nestled cozily in the winding valley of Kaskaskia. In later years these towns have lost their ancient prosperity, and all that reminds the visitor of what has been is the dignified idleness of the men and the still, proud beauty of the women.

"Finding in the good county of St. Clair a congenial social atmosphere, the elder Baker pitched there his tent, and opened an academy for boys, which he continued with great success for many years, conducting it upon a system of instruction then called the Lancasterian plan. His son, Edward, then a handsome lad of fifteen, by the grace and dignity of his bearing, by his personal beauty, and by the astonishing charm of conversation which even at that early day distinguished him, became a general favorite in the best society there. He was always received with kindness in the family of Governor Edwards, a magnificent old gentlemen in fair top-boots and ruffled wristbands, who added to a character of great generosity and executive ability the *grand Seigneur* airs of the Old School. Young Baker availed himself with avidity of the treasures of the Governor's library, the best in the State. He was always a ravenous reader. He had one of those rare memories—wax to receive, and marble to retain. He was indebted to its trustiness and quickness for much of his success as a debater. He was rarely mistaken, and never at fault for a fact or an allusion. Thus reading and remembering, dreaming and growing, he passed the pleasant days in pleasant Belleville, in congenial study and edifying society. He took much interest in the political contests that convulsed the State upon the old and always mischievous question of Slavery—in which, singularly enough, Northern and Eastern men favored the introduction of Slavery, while the Governor and his Kentucky associates opposed it. By their untiring efforts Slavery was prohibited, and Illinois remained a Free State.

"From Belleville young Baker went to Carrollton, in Greene county, a town of less social culture, though filled with a wealthy and sterling population. Here he studied law in the office of Judge Caverly, and practiced for some time with indifferent success. He married here a lady of high character and position, who still survives him, in desolation and sorrow, on the far shore of the Pacific Ocean.

"He removed to Springfield, afterward the capital city of the State, in 1835. In 1837, when Dan Stone—the member who joined Abraham Lincoln in what his opponents styled the 'Abolition protest'—resigned his seat in the Legislature to secure a place on the Supreme Bench, Baker was elected to fill the vacancy thus created, and re-elected soon thereafter. He paid little attention to Legislative business; was often out of his seat, and more pleasantly employed. He was, however, always called on when an obnoxious measure was to be defeated or an opponent demolished. He mastered details with great ease when he cared, but he did not often care. He was State Senator from 1840 to 1844, defeating in the canvass John Calhoun, who afterward became memorable on accout of an election manœuvre in Kansas not wholly unconnected with candle-boxes.

"All this time he was applying himself assiduously to the practice of law. His infallible memory, his quickness of perception, and his ardent eloquence, were powerful agencies in the management of juries, and were usually successful against the most determined energy and labor. His *bonhommie* and impetuosity of delivery were irresistible to Western men; and his Kentucky admirers delighted to liken him to the great lights of the South-western bar, Barry and Grundy. He was fortunate in being associated with men of industry and learning, such as Judge Logan, the Nestor of the profession in Illinois; M. Hay; and, for a while, Albert T. Bledsoe, lately Assistant Secretary of War in the Southern Confederacy."

The writer of the article above quoted from—understood to be Mr. John Hay, Second Private Secretary to President Lincoln—adverted with some pride to the coterie of really notable men who, at that day, controlled the sentiment of Illinois. He said: "It would be hard to find in any backwoods town, at the period of which I have been speaking, a coterie of equal ability and equal possibilities with those who plead, and wrangled, and electioneered together in Springfield. Logan, one of the finest examples of the purely legal mind that the West has ever produced; M'Dougal, who afterward sought El Dorado; Bissell, and Shields, and Baker, brothers in arms and in council, the flower of the Western chivalry, and the brightest examples of Western oratory; Trumbull, then as now, with a mind pre-eminently cool, crystalline, sagacious; Douglas, heart of oak and brain of fire, of energy and undaunted courage unparalleled, ambition insatiate and aspiration unsleeping; Lincoln, then as afterward, thoughtful, and honest, and brave, conscious of great capabilities and quietly sure of the future, before all his peers in a broad humanity, and in that prophetic lift of spirit that saw the triumph of principles then dimly discovered in the contest that was to come."

In 1844, Baker was sent to represent the Sangammon District, Illinois, in Congress, and was found in his seat at the moment of the Mexican war. He opposed the war strenuously; yet the restless fire in his heart impelled him to the field. Mr. Hay rather humorously observed: "There was something in his veins that would not let him be quiet when there was fighting going on. He had had some little experience of soldiering in the Black Hawk war. Lincoln was a Captain then; Robert Anderson and Jefferson Davis were together in an expedition up the Mississippi, and Abraham Lincoln and Jefferson Davis probably bivouacked together in the Iowa forests, and dreamed of battles by the dying fire." Very few Western men of distinction of the elder generation, who have not had early experience in the use of arms in defense of their firesides.

Baker left the Halls of Congress, and proceeded to recruit the Fourth Illinois regiment in Springfield. With them he embarked for Metamoras. From thence he returned to Washington upon important business and as bearer of special dispatches. He resumed his seat in Congress long enough to make a powerful speech in behalf of the volunteers. Then, resigning his membership, he returned to the seat of war, to find his regiment at the siege of Vera Cruz. Assuming the active command, he passed with the army into the interior by the National Road. At Cerro Gordo heights, the first engagement after leaving Vera Cruz, Shields—to whose brigade the Fourth Illinois was attached—was shot through the body, and, as was then supposed, was mortally wounded. Baker, as senior Colonel, assumed the brigade command, instantly, and bore out the responsible duty entrusted to the battalions of Shields. He led the flank charge upon the Mexican rear battery, which crossed and enfiladed the road, and thus secured their way open for a retreat. The charge was a most gallant affair, capturing the battery and cutting off the Mexicans from escape.

He served out the war, returning home with the reputation of being a competent, courageous, and spirited officer.

Baker was succeeded in Congress by Abraham Lincoln. He did not settle again in Springfield, but at Galena. A few months residence there served to give him such a popular ascendancy that he was again elected to Congress—this time in a district which had for years been Democratic. Baker was a Whig, as was Abraham Lincoln—a devoted admirer and follower of the principles of Henry Clay; and his election from that Democratic District, where the influence of Douglas then was measurably felt, proves the strength of his personal popularity.

It was on the floor of the House of Representatives in Washington, in 1850, that he pronounced his eulogy on General Taylor—his old leader-in-arms, and his personal friend. That effort has been pronounced one of the most splendid efforts of oratory ever listened to within those walls, and will remain a monument to his memory if eloquence and extraordinary power over human passions constitute a claim to remembrance.

His term expiring with the session of 1850, Baker, finding his professional business in Illinois seriously interrupted by four years absence in Mexico and at Washington, and finding it necessary to take some active measures for the comfort of his growing family, effected a contract with the newly-organized Panama Railroad Company, in pursuance of which he collected and conveyed to Panama four hundred laborers, with whom he rendered most important aid to that great enterprise. In surveying and cutting out the track through those deep, dark morasses, frequently passing the whole day in slimy swamps, teeming with venomous insects and reptiles, his health gave way, and, senseless and apparently dying from a severe attack of Panama fever, he was carried on board a vessel and removed to New York. He escaped with his life, but shattered in constitution, and ten years older in appearance.

In 1852, having measurably recovered, Colonel Baker removed with his family to San Francisco, where he practised law with distinction and success; and as a forensic and political orator, was without a rival in that young State, whose Bar, culled as it is, from all the States of the Union, is so rich in ability. If Colonel Baker had stopped when he returned from Mexico, we should all have said he was a remarkable man to distinguish himself in so many and such diverse pursuits—in the Court Room, and in the forum, on the stump and halls of legislation. But he did not stop; he went to California with his family in 1852, and there he became as active and prominent as he had been in Illinois; perhaps more successful as a public speaker. We have heard Californians represent the effects of his speaking in San Francisco, where ten thousand people assembled to hear him at once; and from the days that Demosthenes harangued the Greeks, no orator has been more successful than he in the Golden State. It made no difference what the occasion, the call was for Baker. Were they to consecrate a cemetery, he was the orator; were they to bury in that cemetery some martyr to freedom, he pronounced the funeral oration. In politics, he led the van of the Republican forces; he stumped the State, and would have been elected to Congress, if some hundreds of votes more than his party commanded, could have done it. In law, he was retained to do the most important pleading, as Choate was in his time in Massachusetts.

Mr. Hay says: "When a man went to talk for Fremont among the squatters of Mariposa, or inveigh against slavery among the refuse ruffianism of the Gulf, that haunted Yuba and Sonoma, or expound a hated doctrine to the desperadoes of Tuolumne, he took his life in his hand, and considered his pistols and knife as necessary companions as his pamphlets and papers. And who was so qualified as Baker for a strife like this? His geniality beguiled as much as his courage impressed. Because he was always known to be ready for a fight, it was never necessary. He won the hearts of the rough people who cursed his doctrine, and his name became coupled in the mouths of the mountaineers with every expletive of profane admiration. He was utterly at home on the hustings. Those who are acquainted only with his grave senatorial efforts can form no adequate idea of the ready, sparkling, ebullient wit—the glancing and playful satire, mirthful while merciless—the keen syllogisms—and the sharp sophisms, whose falacies, though undiscoverable, were perplexing—and the sudden splendors of eloquence that formed the wonderful charm of his backwoods harangues. His fame became co-extensive with the coast; and the people, in allusion to 'the good gray head which all men knew,' used to call him the 'Gray Eagle.'

"Years passed on, and Baker made money and friends in California. At last the great party of the North became divided on the interminably vexing question of slavery in the Territories. Broderick—one of the truest diamonds that ever existed in the rough—after battling with unavailing pluck for what he deemed truth and justice in the Senate, came back to rally his clansmen for conflict with a haughty and implacable organization. Here was a conflict that at once enlisted all the soul of Baker. It was not so forlorn in prospect as his former one, and a glimmer of hope is very inspiriting in politics. A coalition was effected between the Republicans and the Douglas Democrats, by which Baker and M'Kibbin became the candidates for Congress against the distinctive pro-slavery men. The story of that well-fought campaign was not a particularly pleasant one. It was like all sudden insurrections of free thought and manhood against powerful and disciplined tyranny. The Broderick ticket was defeated, and the baffled Senator was bullied into a criminal folly that his better judgment condemned, and was slain. His last words were, 'They have killed me because I was opposed to the extension of slavery and a corrupt Administration.'

"The words and the event fell heavily on the heart of the nation. Far more crushingly they rested on the saddened spirits of his friends. The dull heaviness of their grief forbade parade, and made ceremony mockery. The American mind runs naturally to committees when great men fall. But there was that within the hearts of Broderick's friends, like the anguish of the royal Dane, 'passing show.' By common consent Baker was the funeral orator. With none of the ordinary accessories of solemn burials, the dead Senator lay in the great square of the city, and the saddened people flocked silently to the scene. From all the streets of the crowded town they gathered in the hush of the autumnal noon, till the square was filled with the mourning multitudes, whispering with lowered voices of the virtues of the departed, and striving to come near enough to gaze upon the calm features of the murdered tribune, turned stonily to the brightness of the skies. Aloft the church bells were jangling mournfully, and their wild lament, floating down to earth, deepened the emotion of the hour. As their ringing vibrated into silence the voice of the orator stole out upon the air, tremulous with tender feeling and musical with the memories of dead friendship. The mind of the mighty multitude, softened by the excitement of their sorrow, lay plastic to his hand, and for an hour the homage of tears and sobs was paid to Baker's genius and Broderick's memory, until he ended in those grandly pathetic words, whose touching music breathes alike the abandon of sorrow and the joy of ultimate fame :

"'The last word must be spoken, and the imperious mandate of death must be fulfilled. Thus, O brave heart! we bear thee to thy rest. Thus, surrounded by tens of thousands, we leave thee to the equal grave. As in life, no other voice among us so rang its trumpet blast upon the ear of freemen, so in death its echoes will reverberate amidst our mountains and our valleys until truth and valor cease to appeal to the human heart.

"'Good friend! true hero! hail and farewell!'

"It is worth while to die if one could be mourned so gloriously."

The murder of Broderick by Judge Terry—then serving on the bench—and the shocking perversion of justice by which the murderer was allowed his liberty, after a mockery of a trial in a court composed of his political friends—so oppressed Baker's spirits as to make him resolve to abandon California. The anti-Administration men of Oregon wanted a leader—one who could rally all the elements of the Opposition to the one point of defeating the Gwin-Lane Democracy. Baker was solicited, and accepted that leadership. He removed at once to Oregon, and entered upon the canvass with a spirit which proved how much his heart was in the work of defeating the enemies of law, order and human rights—for such he deemed the Breckenridge-Lane party in Oregon. He gave his entire time up to the work, vainly hoping that, even in the face of the overwhelming majority of south-side Democrats, he might succeed in sending Daniel Segar to Congress. Segar was an Illinois man, of fine character, and talents of a high order, chosen for his excellence to contest the supremacy of the Breckenridge Democracy; but, so immensely was the majority against him that, in spite of Baker's and his own almost incredible exertions, he was defeated—ballot-box fraud being resorted to in many "hard" localities, to serve a hard end, as was the case in Kansas. Segar was defeated; but the Legislature chosen was so strongly anti-Administration as to elect

Baker to represent Oregon in the United States Senate—an honor he had long coveted, and one for which he was eminently fitted. No abler man could have been selected to attend to the interests of his section, and of the country, in the stirring crisis at hand.

Baker's services in the Senate were brief, but brilliant. He arrayed himself upon the side of the Administration; "the Union at all hazards," became his motto at an early moment of the Congressional struggle with Secession. His first effort was his memorable reply to Benjamin, of Louisiana—delivered in the Senate, Wednesday, January 2d. His fame as an orator drew to the Senate Hall one of the most brilliant audiences ever assembled within those sounding walls. The orator fully answered public expectation. Two afternoon sessions were consumed in its delivery. It was so exhaustive as an argument against Secession and of the demands of those whom Benjamin represented, and so clear in its exposition of the Union policy, as to give great satisfaction to the loyal public.

Mr. Hay says: "He was especially great upon great occasions. He was a man whom the subtle magnetism of events always inspired. Those who heard will surely never forget the magnificent burst of red-hot rhetoric with which he electrified the crowding thousands that filled Union Square last April. It was a mighty assemblage—great in numbers—tremendous in earnestness—awful in aroused enthusiasm. We saw that day how hard it was for common men to address that crowd. Some simply raved, mastered by emotion. Some, wishing to be solemn, prosed. There were few who could ride on that whirlwind, and direct that storm. Baker was one. From the instant when his graceful form was discovered on the stand—his handsome face, pale but quiet; his eye fierce in its brilliancy; his white hair crowning the splendid head like a halo; and the tones of his clear, firm voice, rang out on the air in the words: 'The majesty of the people is here to-day to sustain the majesty of the Constitution'—to the moment when he closed in a gust of passionate plaudits, he held the audience fettered and still. A visible thrill ran through the dense mass when, in closing, he consecrated himself anew to the service of his country in these words of exquisite melody:

"'And if from the far Pacific a voice, feebler than the feeblest murmur upon its shore, may be heard to give you courage and hope in the contest, that voice is yours to-day; and if a man whose hair is gray, who is well-nigh worn out in the battle and toil of life, may pledge himself on such an occasion and in such an audience, let me say—as my last word—that, as when, amidst sheeted fire and flame, I saw and led the hosts of New York as they charged in contest upon a foreign soil, for the honor of your flag; so again, if Providence shall will it, this feeble hand shall draw a sword never yet dishonored, not to fight for distant honor in a foreign land, but to fight for country, for home, for law, for Government, for Constitution, for right, for freedom, for humanity, and in the hope that the banner of my country may advance, and wheresoever that banner waves, there glory may pursue and freedom be established!'

"This was no idle trick of rhetoric. Before the echoes of his words had died, he was hard at work recruiting the California regiment. It filled rapidly. Men came from a distance to join in squads or singly. Many came from Philadelphia and its outlying country. He liked to receive those. 'There must be a fighting streak somewhere about us Quakers,' he used to say. There was an inspiration in this man's words and presence that made men love to fight under him. His regiment soon was over-full. The President appointed him a Brigadier-General. He declined it. The same friendly hand desired to place upon his shoulder-straps the double star of a Major-General. He quietly refused it, and kept the eagles to which his regiment entitled him. As for honors, he had enough of them in another field. He went into this war for use, not fame."

The end was rapidly approaching. Baker flitted in and out of Washington like a spirit—a restless, eager, devoted servant of his country, of his troops, of his friends. One day he would be in his seat in the Senate Chamber to dash in a few strokes of eloquent appeal or stirring sarcasm—the next, out on the field, manœuvering his regiment, to make it, in drill and soldierly accomplishments, worthy of the first place he hoped to acquire by its service. His reply, in August, to Breckenridge, in the United States Senate, was his last effort. Colonel Forney said:

"Breckenridge was delivering a set disunion harangue, as ingenious and able as any heard on behalf of Secession. Baker, whose camp was a mile or two from the Capitol, entered the Senate Chamber hastily from the duties of a drill, while Breckenridge was speaking. He was presently called into the lobby by a message from Mr. Holt, of Kentucky, who begged him to reply to Breckenridge, as no one else would probably be ready to do so. He did so off-hand, when Breckenridge sat down, and made one of the most thrilling speeches which had been heard for years in the chamber. It squelched Mr. Breckenridge. Who would not rather now be Baker dead than Breckenridge living."

A settled conviction of his early death pressed upon him. To a friend he remarked, in August, that he had made his last appearance in the Senate Chamber, saying: "I am certain I shall not live through this war, and if my troops should show any want of resolution, I shall fall in the first battle. I cannot afford, after my career in Mexico, and as a Senator of the United States, to turn my face from the enemy." There was no gloom or depression in his manner, ; it was characterized by a temperate earnestness which carried conviction to the mind of his friend of its fatal truth. Mr. Hay relates, in affecting terms, Baker's last visit to Washington and to the President's mansion, where he ever was a welcome guest. He says: "Why that solemn farewell to his parents, penned by the dauntless Ellsworth, as live a man as ever breathed, in the dead of the last midnight that he ever watched? Why the strange reckless bewilderment of the brave Lyon on that disastrous day, when his gallant heart was breaking under the double conviction that death had marked him, and the Government had forgotten him? Colonel Baker for several days was oppressed by this overhanging consciousness. He became as restless as an eagle, in his camp. He came down to Washington and settled all his affairs. He went to say farewell to the family of the President. A lady—who in her high position is still gracefully mindful of early friendships—gave him a bouquet of late flowers. 'Very beautiful,' he said, quietly, 'these flowers and my memory will wither together.' At night he hastily reviewed his papers. He indicated upon each its proper disposition 'in case I should not return.' He pressed with quiet earnestness upon his friend Colonel Webb, who deprecated such ghostly instructions, the measures which might become necessary in regard to the resting-place of his mortal remains. All this without any ostentation. He performed all these offices with the quiet coolness of a soldier and a man of affairs, then mounted his horse and rode gayly away to his death."

The rest of the tragedy is related in the story of the Ball Bluff disaster. It is a painful chapter to peruse, but one which ever comes out of the horrid drama of war. Oh, how many tragedies will blot and blur the page of Christian history when the story of the rebellion is all written! The land is filled with mourning. Everywhere are the weeds of wo. At almost every fireside sits a spectre—the spirit of one gone forever. Men haunt the streets bereft of limbs, or scarred fearfully, or wasted by suffering and disease. The graveyards are filled with long rows of mounds, beneath each of which sleeps one around whose life so many hopes, so much affection clustered. Every grave is the stanza of a National requiem. A sorrow lays, night and day, by threshholds where peace and happiness once were ceaseless visitants. Little children look up in tears to tell us of him whose loss no human agency can replace. Widows, and orphans, and the childless walk in our midst, separated from us by a sorrow which no human sympathy can bridge over or obliterate.

This is the fruit of treason.

XXII.

JOSEPH HOLT AND THE KENTUCKY SOLDIERS.

No firmer patriot graced the trying times of 61–62 than Joseph Holt of Kentucky. In the cabinet of Mr. Buchanan, at a late day—when it would seem as if a dissolution of the Union was not only to be accomplished, but the country to be thoroughly humiliated—he had the *nerve* to face the crisis and the ability to cope with it. In conjunction with General Dix, Attorney-General Stanton and General Scott, he labored with almost superhuman energy to stay the terrible tide of treason then sweeping everything before it; and he succeeded so admirably that, when Mr. Lincoln came into power, the country hoped to see Mr. Holt continued in the Cabinet. He did not remain, however, in the Cabinet, though he continued to give all his time and abilities to his country's service. Kentucky balanced in the throes of revolution, and he hastened to the aid of those sustaining the cause of the Union, speaking, writing and talking for the Federal Government, sustaining the Administration in its attitude of offense against the rebellion, and opposing the "neutrality" which Kentucky Legislators had prescribed as their duty. His labors added so much to the strength of the *actively* loyal element that he soon had the satisfaction of finding Kentucky's quota of troops for National service rapidly gathering in the field, under tried and true Kentucky leaders.

The Kentucky troops gathered at "Camp Jo Holt," in Indiana—where General Rousseau was in command—before to taking the field in their own State against the Confederates then preparing for the subjugation of Kentucky. These troops he visited prior to the day named for their departure, and addressed them (July 31st) on the crisis and their duty as citizens and soldiers. That address is worthy of repetition, for the nobility of its sentiments, the strength of its lessons and the moral of its teachings. We take pleasure and pride in reproducing such portions of it as our space and plan permit. He said:

"It is not my purpose to occupy you with any political discussion. The gleaming banner, the glistening bayonets, and the martial music, and, indeed, all that meets the eye or the ear upon this tented field, admonish me that with you at least the argument is exhausted, and that you have no longer doubts to solve or hesitating convictions to confirm. Your resolution is taken, and you openly proclaim that, let others do as they will, as for yourselves, unchilled by the arctic airs of neutrality, you are determined to love your country, and, unawed by traitors, to fight its battles, and, if need be, to lay down your lives for its preservation. It is indeed transporting to the patriot's heart to look upon the faces of men thus sublimely resolved; and there is to me a positive enchantment in the very atmosphere whose pulsations have been stirred by the breathings of their heroic spirits. Now that the booming of the cannon of treason and the cry of men stricken unto death for fidelity to our flag, are borne to us on almost every breeze, it is harrowing to the soul to be dragged into companionship with those who still vacillate, who are still timidly balancing chances and coldly calculating losses and gains; who still persist in treating this agonized struggle for national existence as a petty question of commerce, and deliberately take out their scales and weigh in our presence the beggarly jewels of trade against the life of our country.

"Soldiers: next to the worship of the Father of us all, the deepest and grandest of human emotions is the love of the land that gave us birth. It is an enlargement and exaltation of all the tenderest and strongest sympathies of kindred and of home. In all centuries and climes it has lived and defied chains and dungeons and racks to crush it. It has strewed the earth with its monuments, and has shed undying lustre on a thousand fields on which it has battled. Through the night of ages, Thermopylæ glows like some mountain peak on which the morning sun has risen, because twenty-three hundred years ago, this hallowing passion touched its mural precipices and its crowning crags. It is easy, however, to be patriotic in piping times of peace, and in the sunny hour of prosperity. It is national sorrow, it is war, with its attendant perils and horrors, that tests this passion, and winnows from the masses those who, with all their love of life, still love their country more. While your present position is a most vivid and impressive illustration of patriotism, it has a glory peculiar and altogether its own. The mercenary armies which have swept victoriously over the world and have gathered so many of the laurels that history has embalmed, were but machines drafted into the service of ambitious spirits whom they obeyed, and little understood or appreciated the problems their blood was poured out to solve. But while you have all the dauntless physical courage which they displayed, you add to it a thorough knowledge of the argument on which this mighty movement proceeds, and a moral heroism which, breaking away from the entanglements of kindred, and friends, and State policy, enables you to follow your convictions of duty, even though they should lead you up to the cannon's mouth. It must, however, be added that with elevation of position come corresponding responsibilities. Soldiers as you are by conviction, the country looks not to your officers, chivalric and skilful as they may be, but to you and to each of you, for the safety of those vast national interests committed to the fortunes of this war. Your camp life will expose you to many temptations; you should resist them as you would the advancing squadrons of the enemy. In every hour of peril or incitement to excess, you will say to yourselves, "Our country sees us," and so act as to stand forth soldiers, not only without fear, but also without reproach. Each moment not absorbed by the toils and duties of your military life, should, as far as practicable, be devoted to that mental and moral training without which the noblest of volunteers must sink to a level with an army of mercenaries. Alike in the inaction of the camp and amid the fatigues of the march, and the charge and shouts of battle, you will remember that you have in your keeping not only your own personal reputation, but the honor of your native State, and, what is infinitely more inspiring, the honor of that blood-bought and beneficent Republic whose children you are. Any irregularity on your part would sadden the land that loves you; any faltering in the presence of the foe would cover it with immeasurable humiliation. You will soon mingle in the ranks with the gallant volunteers from the North and the West, and with me you will admire their moderation, their admirable discipline, and that deep determination, whose earnestness with them has no language of menace, or bluster, or passion. When the men from Bunker Hill and the men from the 'dark and bloody ground,' unestranged from each other by the low arts of politicians, shall stand side by side on the same national battle-field, the heart of freedom will be glad.

"The Government has been like a strong swimmer suddenly precipitated into the sea, and like that swimmer it has unhesitatingly and most justifiably seized upon any and every instrumentality with which it could subdue the treacherous currents and waves by which it has found itself surrounded. All that was irregular or illegal in the action of the President has been fully approbated by the country, and will no doubt be approbated by Congress, on the broad and incontestable principle that laws and usages of administration designed to preserve the existence of the nation should not be suffered to become the instruments of its death. So, for the future I do not hesitate to say that any and every measure required to save the Republic from the perils that beset it not only may, but ought to be, taken by the Administration, promptly and fearlessly. Within so brief a period no such gigantic power has ever been placed at the disposal of any government as that which has rallied to the support of this within the last few months, through those volunteer who have poured alike from hill and valley, city and village, throughout the loyal States. All classes and all pursuits have been animated by the same lofty and quenchless enthusiasm.

"While, however, I would make no invidious distinctions, where all have so nobly done their duty, I cannot refrain from remarking how conspicuous the hard-handed tillers of the soil of the North and West have made themselves in swelling the ranks of our army. We honor commerce with its busy marts, and the workshop with its patient toil and exhaustless ingenuity, but still we would be unfaithful to the truth of history did we not confess that the most heroic champions of human freedom and the most illustrious apostles of its principles have come from the broad fields of agriculture. There seems to be something in the scenes of nature, in her wild and beautiful landscapes, in her cascades, and cataracts, and waving woodlands, and in the pure and exhilarating airs of her hills and mountains, that unbraces the fetters which man would rivet upon the spirit of his fellow-man. It was at the handles of the plough and amid the breathing odors of its newly-opened furrows that the character of Cincinnatus was formed, expanded and matured. It was not in the city full, but in the deep gorges and upon the snow-clad summits of the Alps, amid the eagles and the thunders, that William Tell laid the foundations of those altars to human liberty, against which the surging tides of European despotism have beaten for centuries, but, thank God, have beaten in vain. It was amid the primeval forests and mountains, the lakes and leaping streams of our own land; amid fields of waving grain; amid the songs of the reaper and the tinkling of the shepherd's bell that were nurtured those rare virtues which clustered star-like in the character of Washington, and lifted him in moral stature a head and shoulders above even the demi-gods of ancient story.

"There is one most striking and distinctive feature of your mission that should never be lost sight of. You are not about to invade the territory of a foreign enemy, nor is your purpose that of conquest or spoliation. Should you occupy the South, you will do so as friends and protectors, and your aim will be not to subjugate that betrayed and distracted country, but to deliver it from the remorseless military despotism by which it is trodden down. Union men, who are your brethren, throng in those States, and will listen for the coming footsteps of your army, as the Scottish maiden of Lucknow listened for the airs of her native land. It is true, that amid the terrors and darkness which prevail there, they are silenced and are now unseen, but be assured that by the light of the stars you carry upon your banner you will find them all.

"It has been constantly asserted by the conspirators throughout the South that this is a war of subjugation on the part of the Government of the United States, waged for the extermination of Southern institutions, and by vandals and miscreants, who, in the fury of their passions, spare neither age, nor sex, nor property. Even one of the Confederate generals has so far steeped himself in infamy as to publish, in choice Billingsgate, this base calumny, through an official proclamation. In view of what Congress has recently so solemnly resolved, and in view of the continuous and consistent action of the Administration upon the subject, those who, through the press and public speeches, persist in repeating the wretched slander, are giving utterance to what everybody, themselves included, knows to be absolutely and infamously false. It will be the first and the highest duty of the American army as it advances South, by its moderation and humanity, by its exemption from every excess and irregularity, and by its scrupulous observance of the rights of all, to show how foully both it and the Government it represents have been traduced.

"When, therefore, you enter the South, press lightly upon her gardens and fields; guard sacredly her homes; protect, if need be, at the point of your bayonets, her institutions and her constitutional rights, for you will thereby not only respond fully to the spirit and objects of this war, but you will exert over alike the oppressed and the infatuated portion of her people, a power to which the most brilliant of your military successes might not attain. But, when you meet in battle array those atrocious conspirators who, at the head of armies, and through woes unutterable, are seeking the ruin of our common country, remember that since the sword flamed over the portals of Paradise until now, it has been drawn in no holier cause than that in which you are engaged. Remember, too, the millions whose hearts are breaking under the anguish of this terrible crime, and then strike boldly, strike in the power of truth and duty, strike with a bound and a shout, well assured that your blows will fall upon ingrates, and traitors, and parricides, whose lust for power would make of this bright land one vast Golgotha, rather than be balked of their guilty aims—and may the God of your fathers give you the victory.

"Soldiers: when Napoleon was about to spur on his legions to combat on the sands of an African desert, pointing them to the Egyptian pyramids that loomed up against the far-off horizon, he exclaimed, 'From yonder summits forty centuries look down upon you.' The thought was sublime and electric; but you have even more than this. When you shall confront those infuriated hosts, whose battle-cry is, 'Down with the Government of the United States,' let your answering shout be, 'The Government as our fathers made it;' and when you strike, remember that not only do the good and the great of the past look down upon you from heights infinitely above those of Egyptian pyramids, but that uncounted generations yet to come are looking up to you, and claiming at your hands the unimpaired transmission to them of that priceless heritage which has been committed to our keeping. I say its unimpaired transmission—in all the amplitude of its outlines, in all the symmetry of its matchless proportions, in all the palpitating fullness of its blessings; not a miserably shrivelled and shattered thing, charred by the fires and torn by the tempests of revolution, and all over polluted and scarred by the bloody poinards of traitors.

"Soldiers: you have come up to your present exalted position over many obstacles and through many chilling discouragements. You now proclaim to the world that the battles which are about to be fought in defense of our common country, its institutions and its homes, are your battles, and that you are determined to share with your fellow-citizens of other States alike their dangers and their laurels; and sure I am that this determination has been in nothing shaken by the recent sad reverse of arms whose shadow is still resting upon our spirits. The country has indeed lost a battle, but it has not lost its honor, nor its courage, nor its hopes, nor its resolution to conquer. One of those chances to which the fortunes of war are ever subject, and against which the most consummate generalship cannot at all times provide, has given a momentary advantage to the forces of the rebellion. Grouchy did not pursue the column of Bulow, and thus Waterloo was won for Wellington at the very moment that victory, with her laurelled wreath, seemed stooping over the head of Napoleon. So Patterson did not pursue Johnston, and the overwhelming concentration of rebel troops that in consequence ensued was probably the true cause why the army of the United States was driven back, excellent as was its discipline, and self-sacrificing as had been its feats of valor. Panics, from slight and seemingly insignificant causes, have occurred in the best drilled and bravest of armies, and they prove neither the want of discipline nor of courage on the part of the soldiers. This check has taught us invaluable lessons, which we could not have learned from victory, while the dauntless daring displayed by our volunteers, is full of promise for the future. Not to mention the intrepid bearing of other regiments, who can doubt our future when he recalls the brilliant charges of the New York Sixty-ninth, and of the Minnesota First, and of the Fire Zouaves? Leonidas himself, while surveying the Persian host, that, like a troubled sea, swept onward to the pass where he stood, would have been proud of the leadership of such men. We shall rapidly recover from this discomfiture, which, after all, will serve only to nerve to yet more extraordinary exertions the nineteen millions of people who have sworn that this republic shall not perish; and perish it will not, perish it cannot, while this oath remains. When we look away to that scene of carnage, all strewed with the bodies of patriotic men who courted death for themselves that their country might live, and then look upon the homes which their fall has rendered desolate forever, we realize—what I think the popular heart in its forbearance has never completely comprehended—the unspeakable and hellish atrocity of this rebellion. It is a perfect saturnalia of demoniac passion. From the reddened waters of Bull Run, and from the gory field of Manassas, there is now going up an appeal to God and to millions of exasperated men, against those fiends in human shape, who, drunken with the orgies of an infernal ambition, are filling to its brim the cup of a nation's sorrows. Woe, woe, I say, to these traitors when this appeal shall be answered!"

XXIII.

THE SPIRIT OF VIOLENCE IN THE SOUTH.

THE Southern States, from the first stages of their rebellion against the Federal Government, put forward as a justification, the oppressions of that central power, and cited the Declaration of Independence as their defence. This assumption was indignantly denied by Northern men; in Congress and out of it an overwhelming sentiment pronounced the rebellion "causeless, wicked, and unnatural," with "no justification in the law of the country, nor in the higher law of self-protection." From this discordance sprung the passions and impulses necessary to feed the fires of discord; and watchful "guardians of Southern interests," were not slow to fan the flames to a point of lawlessness necessary to "precipitate" States into the vortex of insurrection. Success in the secession movement depended solely on the ability of the leaders to fire the popular passions to the point of hate of the North, and defiance of its association. Without a complete success in that direction, the revolution would become nerveless from inanition. A thousand devices were conceived to accomplish the desired end; and the secret history of the insurrection, if it ever shall be divulged, will be found rich in intrigue, profuse in duplicity, mighty in falsehood—all directed to the one purpose of "firing the Southern heart."

The repudiation of debts due to Northern merchants and manufacturers, became one of the earliest and most exciting facts of the Southern movement. It argued a demoralized sentiment of probity, which equally alarmed and angered the Northern people. The Southern merchants had, in exception to all commercial usage, obtained credits to an extraordinary amount, upon extraordinary time. A customer had but to say, "I am from the Cotton States," in order to obtain almost any credit desired. That secret and powerful inquisition, the "Commercial Agency," was scarcely consulted as to the Southerner's personal standing and commercial responsibility —so eager was the deluded merchant to secure a "Southern trade." The wretched list of failures in the winter and spring of 1861 ever will remain as a monument of Northern commercial temerity in the matter of Southern credits.

The spirit which found an excuse for allowing paper to go to protest, and followed the protest with a note expressing satisfaction at the refusal to pay, soon betrayed itself in a passage of "stay" laws, in the Seceded States, and in the visitations of violence upon all agents of Northern business firms who sought out the recreant debtor in hopes of obtaining some satisfaction for the overdue claim. Lawyers banded together not to receive Northern claims for collection, while the people banded together to drive away any unlucky wight who proposed to do what the lawyers refused—to collect his own accounts. The agents, however, soon "made themselves scarce," as the vulgar, but significant, announcements in the papers recorded. Tar and feathers, and an escort of a "committee of citizens" to the nearest railway station, were such inevitable results as served to rid an "indignant community" of all "Northern vagabonds" early in the year (1860.)

These occasional persecutions of collectors and agents seemed to engender an appetite for the excitement; and it became a very honorable calling for committees to spy out every man of Northern birth—to seek to inculpate him in some way, in order to allow of the usual warning "to leave." As early as February (1861) these inquisitions became so frequent, that large numbers of persons—chiefly Northern-born mechanics and tradesmen, who had found employ and a business in the South—fled for their lives, leaving behind all their possessions. To meet these refugees in Northern cities became of such frequent occurrence, in February and March, that the public almost tired of their uniform stories of injuries received and sufferings endured.

The spirit of anger was fast culminating, not in a national, or even sectional resentment, but in a species of inhuman personal malice, which served to ally that revolution to the Sepoy drama. Lawlessness towards Government soon begat lawlessness towards society—the dragon's teeth grew with fearful fecundity. The demoralization betrayed itself even in the changed tone of the secession portion of the Southern press. As an evidence, we may quote one of a great many similar notices made of General Scott—even by professedly respectable journals like the Richmond *Inquirer*. The Montgomery (Alabama) *Mail* (February 6th) contained this paragraph:

"We observe that the students of Franklin College, Georgia, burned General Scott in effigy a few days ago, 'as a traitor to the South.' This is well. If any man living deserves such infamy, it is the Lieutenant-General of the (Yankee) United States. And we have a proposition to make, thereanent, to all the young men of the South, wherever scattered, at school or college; and that is, that they burn this man in effigy all through the South, on the evening of the 4th of March next. The students of the South are an important class of our rising generation. Let them make an epoch in the history of our sunny land, to which legend, and tale, and song, shall point in after years. General Scott deserves this grand infamy. He is a traitor to the soil of his birth; false to all the principles of the Commonwealth which nurtured him; the tool, willing, pliant, and bloody, of our oppressors; and it is meet that his name should descend to our posterity as a word of execration! What say the students?"

Some notices of the war-worn veteran—who had added more glory to the American name than any man since the "Father of his Country"—were so violent and vulgar as to forbid their repetition here, even though they might reflect, with stinging severity, upon a state of society which could be pleased with such impotent malice.

To show the nature of the persecutions inflicted on those "suspected," in the revolutionary States, we shall cite a few from the numerous well-authenticated instances, that they may stand before a Christian world, as an evidence of the civilization which springs from a state of society like that which controls the Southern States of America.

An advertisement appeared in a New York daily, February 18th, (1861) as follows:

"Farming Manager.—An Englishman by birth, having had very extensive experience in breeding, raising, buying and selling of all kinds of cattle and sheep in his own country, and who has been engaged North in agriculture for three years, and South for two, is on his way to New York, having been expelled, and his property confiscated, on suspicion of being opposed to Slavery. He would like to engage with any gentleman having room to grow grain and roots, and to farm on a modern, enlightened system, not looking to corn alone. He is forty, and has a small family. Address ——."

This case was that of a person named Gardiner. He had taken a farm "on shares," near Wilmington, North Carolina. In August, September, and October, he labored assiduously and successfully, and got a good start. In the Fall he obtained about sixty dollars worth of seeds from New York, ready for his Spring planting. He was astounded, one day in February, to be arrested and thrown into prison, upon representation of the fellow whose farm he occupied, that he (Gardiner) was a "dangerous" man. Gardiner procured bail from some of his countrymen, but these men were compelled to withdraw their bond, under threats of a similar course towards themselves for being "dangerous" citizens. The matter was "compromised, out of consideration for his (Gardiner's) wife and children," by having his household goods hastily thrust on a little schooner —on which Gardiner and his family, perfectly penniless, were sent to New York. All his property and improvements passed into the hands of the good Southern Rights man who had instigated the mob, and *compelled* the authorities to the deed of violence.

Two Jersey men were hung in the vicinity of Charleston, early in February, for "suspicion of tampering with slaves." An English captain was served with a coat of tar and feathers in Savannah, in January, for having allowed a stevedore (black) to sit down with him at the dinner-table. Another Englishman, belonging in Canada, sailed on a vessel trading along coast. At Savannah, the vessel was visited by a negro having fruit to sell. On leaving, the black man asked for a newspaper, and one was given him which happened to contain one of Henry Ward Beecher's sermons. The black was caught by his master reading the "incendiary" document. Refusing to tell how he obtained it, he was ordered to the whipping-post, and flogged until he "confessed." The vessel was boarded by the authorities, and a demand made for the astonished Canadian. The captain, however, stood before him as a British subject; and, by agreeing to ship the *culprit* North, by the next day's steamer, succeeded in saving him from the mob that stood ready on the shore to lynch him. He was placed on the steamer, on the morrow, when two "officials" came forward with a writ, which they agreed not to serve if the poor fellow would pay them fifty dollars. This he gladly paid, and was suffered to depart, "out of consideration for his being a British subject." Had he been a Yankee, he would have been hung.

The following item appeared in the Eufaula (Ala.) *Express*, (February 6th :)

"A Suspicious Individual.—The worthy captain of the Home Guards arrested a man on last Tuesday, upon complaint made by one or two of our citizens. The charge was the use of improper language in regard to the acts and position of the Southern people at this time. Some of the expressions used by this traveling Yankee were, that Bob Toombs is a traitor, and that the Secessionists are thieves and robbers, and that he fully endorsed everything contained in the Knoxville *Whig*, in regard to coercion, etc. After the examination, which brought out the foregoing facts, the committee of five members of the Home Guards, appointed to investigate the matter, announced as their decision that as the individual under arrest was only guilty of using improper language, they would set him at liberty, with a request to settle his business and leave as soon as possible. An application of tar and feathers wouldn't be at all amiss in such cases. The man's name is M. A. Smith. He is traveling agent for Scovil & Mead, of New Orleans, druggists. He will bear watching. Pass him around."

Mr. Smith proceeded on his way. At Abbeville, (Ala.,) he was again "apprehended." The Vigilance Committee relieved him of his horse and buggy, $356 in money, and all his papers. Then, taking him to a grove one-half mile from town, he was *hung*. No legal proceedings were had in his case—no evidence existed as to his asserted "crime," except the newspaper's statement. He was dealt with according to the law of the super-judicial Vigilance Committee.

It has been denied that Southern men ever permitted the roasting alive of slaves, guilty of the high crime of murder of masters, or of the more heinous and diabolical nameless crime against females. Proof to the contrary, however, not only is not wanting, but is quite abundant, which goes to show that that horrible and barbarous mode of execution has been resorted to for lesser crimes than those indicated—even upon *suspicion*. A case in point was freely narrated by the Harris County (Geo.) *Enterprise*, in February. On the 14th of that month a lady named Middlebrook, being alone in her house, was alarmed, early in the morning, by the entrance of some person. "She hailed the intruder," the paper stated, who, to silence her cries, took her from her bed, and, carrying her across the yard, "threw her over the fence." This was all. No violence upon her person, no maiming—only "the fiend" abused her in a "most shameful manner." He was alarmed by two negro women, and fled. The neighborhood was aroused. The lady stated that *she believed* the perpetrator of the outrage to have been a negro man, named George. The newspaper account then states:

> "Dogs having been procured, the track was pursued to a neighboring house, where the boy George had a wife, and thence to the residence of Mr. John Middlebrook. Under these circumstances, it was thought advisable to arrest the negro, which was done, and after an investigation before a justice of the peace, he was duly committed, and placed in the jail in this place, as we thought, to await his trial at the April term of our Superior Court.
>
> "On Monday morning last a crowd of men from the country assembled in our village, and made known their intention to forcibly take the negro George from the jail, and execute him in defiance of law or opposition. Our efficient sheriff, Major Hargett, together with most of our citizens, remonstrated, persuaded, begged, and entreated them to desist, and reflect for a moment upon the consequences which might follow such a course, but without avail. Major Hargett promised to guarantee the safe-keeping of the prisoner by confining him in any manner they might suggest, and our citizens proposed to guard the jail night and day, but all to no purpose. There was no appeasing them. They rushed to the jail, and, despite of all remonstrances, with axe, hammer, and crow-bar, violently broke through the doors, and took the prisoner out, carrying him about two miles from town, where they chained him to a tree, and *burned him* to death.
>
> "We understand that the negro protested his innocence with his last breath, though repeatedly urged to confess."

This horrible record could be written of no civilized country on the globe save of the Southern States of America. How that last paragraph rings out its silent imprecation upon a state of society which would allow such a deed to be committed on its soil! These murderers were "citizens," and, of course, never were even questioned as to their crime; it was only a *suspected negro* whom they burned. This deed was committed about fifty miles above Eufaula.

Atlanta (Geo.) boasted of as violent a people as Eufaula or Abbeville. The same spirit which roasted a suspected negro would have hung a white man who might have been guilty of offence to the sensitive people. The *Intelligencer*, of Atlanta, in February, thus paragraphed the public sentiment of that locality, in regard to the editor of the Nashville (Tenn.) *Democrat*, who had pronounced Jefferson Davis a great humbug:

"If Mr. Hurley will come to Atlanta, we take the responsibility of saying that his tavern bill or his burial expenses shall not cost him anything. The only thing which strikes our astonishment is, that the people of Nashville would tolerate such a paper as the *Democrat* in their midst. General Jackson, whose bones repose within twelve miles of the City of Nashville, doubtless turned in the grave when such abominable doctrines were permitted to go forth from a Nashville paper."

These "abominable doctrines" were, loving the Union more than the newly-hatched Southern Confederacy—that was all. How many men were hung for the same crime in that delectable neighborhood, the Vigilance Committee only knew.

The statement of Mary Crawford, made public in the winter of 1861, detailed, with painful minuteness, the sad story of her husband's awful murder in Tarrant County, Texas, July 17th, 1860. The man was taken on *suspicion* of being an Abolitionist, and, after being shot, was hung. The wretched wife, informed by her two little boys (who had been with their father out to haul wood, when Crawford was seized) of their fears, had started out to learn something of her husband's fate. She had proceeded but a short distance when a party of men informed her, with indifference, that her husband was hung. The narrative read:

"They took me back to the place we had been living in. My grief, my indignation, my misery, I have no words, no desire to describe. The body was not brought to me until night, and only then by the direction of Captain Dagget, a son-in-law and partner of Turner (for whom Crawford had done much work,) who had been a friend to my husband, and was the only man of any influence who dared to befriend me. He had been away from home, and did not return until after the murder had been done. He denounced the act, and said they killed an innocent man."

The local newspaper—the *Fort Worth Chief*—thus chronicled the tragedy:

"MAN HUNG.—On the 17th instant, was found the body of a man by the name of William H. Crawford, suspended to a pecan-tree, about three-quarters of a mile from town. A large number of persons visited the body during the day. At a meeting of the citizens the same evening, strong evidence was adduced proving him to have been an Abolitionist. The meeting endorsed the action of the party who hung him. Below we give the verdict of the jury of inquest:

"'We, the jury, find that William H. Crawford, the deceased, came to his death by being hung with a grass rope tied around his neck, and suspended from a pecan limb, by some person or persons to the jurors unknown. That he was hung on the 17th day of July, 1860, between the hours of 9 o'clock A. M. and 1 o'clock P. M. We could see no other marks of violence on the person of the deceased.'"

This man Turner—a lawyer, and an owner of forty slaves—was one of those persons who arraigned Crawford in the presence of his little boys, and had borne him away from their sight to hang him. The jury took no steps, of course, to learn anything in regard to the murderers. Indeed, the act was not only justified, but, out of it, grew an organization which succeeded in whipping, banishing, and hanging over two hundred persons—three Methodist ministers included—in the course of the succeeding three months, under plea of their being "Abolition emissaries," who had instigated the burning of property, and incited negroes to run away. The report of that meeting deserves repetition, in illustration of the manner in which the slave districts care for their morals and their safety:

"At a large and respectable meeting of the citizens of Tarrant County, convened at the Town Hall, at Fort Worth, on the 18th day of July, 1860, pursuant to previous notice, for the purpose of devising means for defending the lives and property of citizens of the county against the machinations of Abolition incendiaries, J. P. Alford was called to the chair, and J. C. Terrell was appointed Secretary. After the object of the meeting was explained by Colonel C. A. Harper, the following preamble and resolutions were unanimously adopted:

"'*Whereas*, The recent attempts made to destroy several neighboring towns by fire, the nearly total destruction of one of them, coupled with the conversation and acts of one W. H. Crawford, who was hung in this county on the 17th instant, prove conclusively to us the necessity of an organized effort to ferret out and punish Abolition incendiaries, some of whom are believed to be in our county. Therefore, to discover and punish said Abolitionists, and to secure the lives and property of our citizens, be it

"'*Resolved*, That we endorse the action of those who hung W. H. Crawford in this county on the 17th instant, convinced as we are, from the evidence upon which he was hung, that he richly deserved his fate.

"'*Resolved*, That a Central County Committee be appointed by the President, consisting of seven citizens, whose duty it shall be to appoint such Committees in every precinct in the county, which sub-Committees shall confer with and report to the Central Committee the names of all suspected persons in their precincts, which persons shall be dealt with according to the pleasure of the Central Committee.

"'*Resolved*, That the members of this meeting hereby pledge themselves to support said Central Committee in the discharge of their duty in dealing with Abolitionists and incendiaries.

"'JAMES P. ALFORD, Chairman.

"'J. C. TERRELL, Secretary.'

"The Central Committee hereby notify all persons connected with or holding Abolition sentiments to leave the county forthwith, or they may possibly have cause to regret remaining."

It is probable that every one of the men persecuted were as innocent of offense as Crawford. "Abolition emissaries" were not necessary to instruct negroes how to fire houses. The "Abolitionists" were, without exception, men having a calling, and pursuing it peaceably; but, being Northerners, and living without holding slaves, were proofs conclusive of their dangerour character to the "highly respectable citizens" of Texas.*

The case of Mrs. Catharine Bottsford, as published at length in the New York *Tribune* of March 22d, afforded the age with an evidence that even in the civilized city of Charleston, South Carolina, an intelligent, honorable, and unprotected lady could be thrown into prison and be made to suffer indignities because some person had said she had "tampered with slaves."

Arthur Robinson, of New Orleans, publisher of the *True Witness*, a religious paper of the Old School Presbyterian denomination, was arrested, and thrown into prison without the usual forms of law. After laying there some time, he was taken into the criminal court for trial. The indictment, however, was so ignorantly drawn that he was set at liberty pending a second arrest. His friends managed to effect his escape up the river. He lost everything. His "crime" was, not in saying or publishing anything offensive, but a "committee"

* When Wigfall stated, on the floor of the United States Senate, that men were hanging from trees in Texas for opinion's sake, he was known to tell the truth, then, for a certainty. Lovejoy, of Illinois, in vain tried to get the case of the Methodist ministers, (one of whom was hung and others whipped,) before Congress.

having searched his premises, found "seditious" literature in his possession, and for that he was made to suffer. He would have been consigned to the State's Prison for having the Boston *Liberator* on his exchange list, had it not been for the flaw in his first indictment, and his escape from another arrest.

John Watt, a citizen of Michigan, was working near Vicksburg, Mississippi, in January. While under the influence of liquor a "committee" extracted from him "dangerous sentiments," and he was taken over the river into Louisiana and hung, and his body left hanging to the tree.

The first officer of the bark *Indian Queen* made a statement in the New York journals, March 16th, to the effect that the vessel put into St. Marks, Florida, in January—himself and his second officer both being ill of the Chagres fever. Both were sent ashore to the United States Marine Hospital at that place, for proper care, while the vessel anchored in the harbor below, to await their recovery. As soon as Florida seceded, (January 11th,) the Hospital was seized and the invalids turned out. The vessel lay at anchor about ten miles below the town. She had, as part of her crew, seven colored seamen—all able and trusty fellows. A plot was hatched to seize all these men and sell them into slavery—a judge of the Supreme (State) Court being one of the conspirators. The plot was revealed to the captain at two o'clock in the morning. He arose, hired a steamer, ran down to his vessel, and had her towed out to sea, beyond the jurisdiction of Florida. The discomfited citizens swore dreadfully over their disappointment.

The same officer stated that, a few days after the Ordinance of Secession was passed, a resident of St. Marks remarked that the South was wrong and the North right in the controversy. Whereupon, he was seized, stripped, whipped, and started "out of the country."

"Mr. H. Turner, a New Hampshire man, had for several years, spent the winter on the plantation of Woodworth & Son, near Charleston, South Carolina. Before the Presidential election, in reply to the question of a fellow-workman, he had stated that, if he held the casting vote, it should be given for

Lincoln. Two weeks after the election he was visited by two members of a "Vigilance Committee," who asked if what had been reported was true. He answered that he had made that single remark to a fellow-workman, but to no other person. A warrant for his arrest, as an incendiary and Abolitionist, was produced, and he was taken to Charleston to jail. Around the jail a mob of "citizens" gathered, demanding that the jailor should give up the prisoner to them. It was only dispersed by the horse patrol. He was allowed neither food nor water. On the afternoon of the day succeeding his arrest, he was taken before the "Vigilance Association Tribunal," for examination. Confessing, again, that he had said to the workman what was reported, he was remanded back to jail, to be passed over to the Criminal Court. The "Judge" of the Tribunal treated the prisoner with a choice lecture, chiefly composed of oaths and imprecations. He was placed in a bare cell, where the night was spent; and only on the morning of the second day's confinement was he allowed food, consisting of a small piece of black bread and a pint of bad water. For *fourteen weeks this man lay in that wretched dungeon.* At the end of that time the son of his employer came to the jail, and stated that his wages, $248, still due, should be paid him, and his release procured, if he would leave at once. This promise was gladly given. He was taken to the steamer amid the hootings and howlings of a mob, which made threats of lynching. On the way to the steamer, he called upon a watchmaker for a fine watch he had left for repairs before his arrest. The watchmaker bade him, with an oath, to leave his premises. Once on the steamer, he expected his wages, as promised; but he received nothing, and was permitted to work his passage to New York, where he arrived in a perfectly destitute condition.

Captain E. W. Rider, of the bark *Julia E. Aery*, and his son James B. Ryder, as mate, were landing a cargo at Encero Mills, Camden County, Georgia, in November, 1860, when a negro came aboard the vessel with oars to sell. None being wanted, he was sent away. He paid a second visit, and some clothes were intrusted to him to wash, upon his telling that he belonged to a Dr. Nichols, living near. That afternoon five men came to the vessel, and demanded the right to search for the negro. The captain gave permission for the search, freely, but stated that the fellow had gone ashore, taking with him some clothes to wash. The five men completed the search which, it became evident to the captain, was but a cover for the "citizens" to examine his cargo, his means of resistance, &c., as well as to discover, if possible, some "Abolition literature" by which to seize the entire crew and vessel as "dangerous to the peace of the community." The "Committee" returned on the following day, late in the evening. It had grown to fifteen in number, who proceeded to thoroughly ransack the vessel's hold. Every chest and bunker were overhauled. Nothing "dangerous" being found, the "Committee" passed on shore where, summoning the negroes who had been engaged in unloading the vessel, they examined them as to the *conversations* on the vessel. Six of them were finally most unmercifully whipped, to make them "confess." What they confessed, was not known to the captain; but, as they probably stated anything required, the mob, it soon became evident, was ready for proceedings. The captain and his son went before the "Committee" and stated that, not only had no conversation been had, but that they had positively forbidden any unnecessary communication between his men and the negroes—that one or the other of the officers always was present, to see that orders were obeyed. This did not satisfy the "Committee," and the two were taken to the jail at Jefferson, fifteen miles away. There they were again arraigned before another "Vigilance Association," and charged with being Abolitionists—a charge which both men denied as unfounded in proof. No proof being produced, they were allowed to spend that night at a hotel. A cook (black) from another vessel was produced on the succeeding morning, who stated that he had heard both white men say they were Republicans, and would have voted for Mr. Lincoln if an opportunity had offered. The black fellow who had taken the clothes to wash, was then brought forward, and he corroborated the statement of the other black man. This was deemed evidence conclusive to the "Committee," and the sentence of a public flogging was immediately decreed against both father and son. This was deemed a lenient punishment—hanging was the usual mode of treating "such scoundrels." The inhuman wretches took their prisoners to the front of the court-house, where, both being stripped to the waist and tied to a tree, they were whipped — twenty-five blows with heavy leather thongs being administered to each. The elder Ryder, being an old man, was a terrible sufferer under the horrible infliction. After "punishment" both were thrust into cells in the jail. The large crowd which witnessed the whipping enjoyed it, apparently with a real zest, as it jeered and laughed vociferously during the brutal punishment. The two men lay *fourteen days* in that jail, suffering exquisite tortures from their wounds. At the end of that time five men came, took them out, carried them to their vessel, and remained until the craft stood out to sea.

This instance of atrocious wrong was simply one of several similar cases inflicted in the same neighborhood. The civilized world may be excused for doubting evidence so inhuman; but, there is no room for disbelief when an old man's scarred back is exhibited to the pitying eye.

We may close this revolting record with the following statement made by the Cincinnati *Gazette*, of May 18th, 1861 :

"Nearly every day some fresh arrivals of refugees from the violence and ferocity of the New Dahomey bring to this city fresh and corroborative proofs of the condition of affairs in the rebel States. Many of these have come thence at the peril of their lives, and to avoid threatened death, have taken a hurried journey surrounded by thick dangers from the madmen who now fill the South with deeds of violence and bloodshed.

"The people in that section seem to have been given up to a madness that is without parallel in the history of civilization—we had almost written barbarism. They are cut off from the news of the North, purposely blinded by their leaders as to the movements and real power of the Government, and in their local presses receive and swallow the most outrageous falsehoods and misstatements.

"Yesterday, one William Silliman, a person of intelligence and reliability, reached this city, returning from a year's residence in Southern

Mississippi. He was one of a party who, in 1860 went from this city and engaged in the construction of the Mobile and Ohio Railroad.

"Mr. Silliman, for several months past, has lived in Cupola, Itawamba County, one of the lower tier of counties, two hundred miles from New Orleans, and one hundred and sixty miles from Mobile. He says a more blood-thirsty community it would be difficult to conceive. Perfect terrorism prevails, and the wildest outrages are enacted openly by the rebels, who visit with violence all suspected of loyalty, or withholding full adherence to the kingdom of Jefferson Davis. Could the full history of these outrages be written, and that truthfully, many and most of its features would be deemed incredible and monstrous, belonging to another age, and certainly to another country than our own.

"The party who is suspected of hostility, or even light sympathy, with the rebellion, is at once seized. He is fortunate if he is allowed to leave in a given time, without flogging. He is still fortunate if only a flogging is added to the order to depart. Many have been hung or shot on the spot. Mr. Silliman details five instances of the latter as having occurred among the amiable people of Itawamba County, within the past ten weeks, of several of which he was the eye-witness, a mob wreaking their vengence upon their victims under the approval of local authorities. These five men were Northerners, at different times assailed by the rebels. Three of them were strangers to all about them.

"On Saturday of last week a man was hung at Guntown, who refused to join the rebel army, and also refused to leave. He was taken to a tree in the outskirts of the village, and left hanging to a limb. He had a family in the place. Guntown is ten miles from Cupola. The same day, at Saltillo, a man was hung under similar circumstances, and still another at Vonona, where a traveller was seized in passing through the place. All these towns are within twenty miles circuit of Cupola, where Mr. Silliman resided. He says that he can recall twelve instances of killing, whipping, and other outrages thus visited upon the victims of the rebels in that vicinity, within the past two months. Many have been waiting in the hope that the storm would 'blow over,' but have, one after the other, been forced to submit or seek safety in flight."

The instances herein given are such as seemed to us to be so verified as to admit of no doubt as to their entire truthfulness. Many others made public, and some of a most outrageous character, which have been repeated to us by refugees in person, we have refrained from referring to, since a suspicious public might question the authenticity of their unsupported statements. Enough has been given to throw an historical light upon the *animus* of the Southern people engaged in the revolution. The future historian of the great rebellion will not fail to discover in that spirit, not only a key to the social state of that section of the country, but will, if he be a disciple of Schlegel, find in it an effect of a cause—which cause had sedulously, and for generations, insensibly underminded the moral sentiments of the people.

XXIV.

TREASON IN TENNESSEE.

THE history of Tennessee, during the first six months of 1861, forcibly illustrates the *spirit* of secession, proving it to be—as Johnson, Brownlow, Holt, and others have characterized it—the diabolical spirit.

The State, it will be remembered, voted (1861) for John Bell and Edward Everett for President and Vice-President—the vote being Bell, 69,274; Breckenridge, 64,709; Douglas, 11,350. Bell was the *Union* candidate, and was voted for as such. The Union sentiment, however, gave a still more emphatic expression in February (1861,) when the State voted on the question of "Convention" or "no Convention,"—resulting in a majority against a Convention to consider an Ordinance of Secession, of over *sixty thousand.* This, of course, closed the door against the designs of the Confederate conspirators, who only required a Convention to throw the State into the Confederacy, in spite of the people. But, men bent upon treason do not stand upon *ceremony.* If the people would not call a Convention, then other ways must be divised to accomplish the fell design. It was not long ere the instrument of tyranny was found. The people, and, we may say, the entire country not in the confidence of Jefferson Davis, were astounded to learn, on the morning of May 8th, that they were transferred to the keeping of a Confederate army; that an Ordinance of Secession was adopted, (to be voted on by the people, June 8th, after time enough had been allowed to place Confederate troops in every section to intimidate, overawe, arrest, and "punish" Unionists, as enemies); that, the Legislature had adopted (to go into immediate force) the Provisional Constitution of the Confederate States; thus consummating, in one dark secret session (May 6th) all that the most ardent conspirator could desire. The "League" entered into with the Confederate authorities, by which Tennessee was transferred, beyond the power of redemption, into the keeping of Jefferson Davis, was as follows:

"CONVENTION BETWEEN THE STATE OF TENNESSEE AND THE CONFEDERATE STATES OF AMERICA.

"The State of Tennessee, looking to a speedy admission into the Confederacy established by the Confederate States of America, in accordance with the Constitution for the Provisional Government of said States, enters into the following temporary Convention, agreement and military league with the Confederate States, for the purpose of meeting pressing exigencies affecting the common rights, interests and safety of said States and said Confederacy.

"*First.* Until the said State shall become a member of said Confederacy, according to the Constitutions of both powers, the whole military force and military operations, offensive and defensive, of said State, in the impending conflict with the United States, shall be under the chief control and direction of the President of the Confederate States upon the same basis, principles and footing as if said State were now and during the interval, a member of said Confederacy. Said forces, together with that of the Confederate States, to be employed for the common defense.

"*Second.* The State of Tennessee will, upon becoming a member of said Confederacy, under the permanent Constitution of said Confederate States, if the same shall occur, turn over to said Confederate States, all the public property, naval stores and munitions of war, of which she may then be in possession, acquired from the United States, on the same terms, and in the same manner, as the other States of said Confederacy have done in like cases.

"*Third.* Whatever expenditures of money, if any, the said State of

Tennessee shall make before she becomes a member of said Confederacy, shall be met and provided for by the Confederate States.

"This Convention entered into and agreed on, in the city of Nashville, Tennessee, on the seventh day of May, A. D. 1861, by Henry W. Hilliard, the duly authorized Commissioner, to act in the matter for the Confederate States, and Gustavus A. Henry, Archibald W. O. Totten and Washington Barrow, Commissioners duly authorized to act in like manner for the State of Tennessee. The whole subject to the approval and ratification of the proper authorities of both Governments, respectively."

This infamous and treacherous sale of the State, without the knowledge or consent of the people, of course sealed the fate of that Commonwealth, and thereafter Tennessee was to live in a terrorism bordering on barbarism. The invasion of the Huns, bringing fire and sword to civilized homes, was a counterpart of the invasion of Tennessee by the vagabonds of Alabama, the cut-throats of Mississippi, and the desperadoes of Texas and Arkansas.

Davis was given possession of his property May 7th, and almost immediately his turbulent hordes rushed in, to the great consternation of society, and more particularly to the Unionists, who, from that moment, lived in a state of apprehension which soon drove them into the ranks of secession, for self-protection. Thousands upon thousand accepted the order of things instated at the point of the bayonet; and when June 8th came, the vote for the Ordinance of Secession was overwhelming. A few brave souls dared to stem the tide of treason. One of these was Parson Brownlow, of Knoxville, whose paper, the *Whig*, fairly scintillated with its flashes of scorn and indignation at the betrayal of the State by the Governor and the secretly manœuvred Legislature—a body utterly without constitutional power to act upon such matters as it considered and adopted. He immediately sounded the alarum, among other things saying:

"In June we are called upon to vote for or against this Ordinance of Secession, and all its train of evils, such as enormous taxes, and the raising of fifty thousand troops! Will the people ratify it, or will they reject it? Let every man, old and young, halt and blind, contrive to be at the polls on that day. If we lose then, our liberties are gone, and we are swallowed up by a military despotism more odious than any now existing in any monarchy in Europe."

Brownlow, Maynard, Etheridge, Johnson and Nelson immediately entered the field, hoping to arouse the people to a sense of the danger impending. Johnson being in Washington, hastened home by way of Virginia, to enter upon the crusade against secession. At numerous places in the dominions of Governor Letcher he was treated with great indignity by the Virginia chivalry; but, he forebore to resent the injuries heaped upon him and his cause, not daring to jeopardize an arrest. Arrived on Tennessee soil, he at once took the stump against the tyranny inaugurated. At Elizabethtown, May 15th, an immense Union meeting was addressed by Johnson, T. A. R. Nelson, and N. G. Taylor. Other meetings rapidly followed; but the minions of the Confederacy were after the speakers; and, by June 1st, it became necessary for the Union speakers to flee from Central Tennessee. May 31st, the Louisville *Journal* published this item:

"We don't know where Mr. Etheridge is at this time, but, wherever he may be, we would warn him of the danger of his returning to Tennessee. We could give him facts, which would convince him that he can return only at the imminent risk of his life. Instructions have certainly been given by General Pillow that he shall be hung, or shot, or otherwise killed at the first opportunity. He has been keenly watched for in all direction. Men were hunting for him last night in the cars, at or near the Tennessee line."

In Eastern Tennessee the loyal sentiment was so thoroughly awakened that, when the day came (June 8th) for expressing at the ballot-box their opinions of the Ordinance and its principles, the vote was thirty-two thousand nine hundred and thirty-two—being a majority of over eighteen thousand for the Union. It was otherwise in those sections of the State where Confederate troops were gathered. The vote was:

	Separation.	*No Separation.*
Middle Tennessee, . . .	58,269	8,198
Western " . . .	29,127	6,117

making the aggregate State majority stand fifty-seven thousand six hundred and sixty-seven for "separation."

So palpably constrained was this declared vote, that the Unionists of East Tennessee gathered in mass Convention at Greenville, June 17th, (1861,) to protest against the tyranny inaugurated over them. Every county was fully represented except Rhea, as the Knoxville *Whig* said, "by delegates who, for sound practical sense, determination of will and patriotic purpose, would have done honor to any constituency." The Address adopted detailed the facts of that election—how in West and Middle Tennessee the people were overawed, bullied, persecuted, into an adoption of the Ordinance—how the Secessionists had prepared for the furtherance of their schemes even though the State had voted "No Separation"—how no provision was made for examining the returns otherwise than by a disunion Governor, whose hold on power depended upon the success of the secession programme—how "volunteers" in the secession army were allowed to vote within and *without* the State contrary to any law—how discussion was forbidden in those sections where the secession vote was triumphant, while every Union paper there was crushed out—how a military despotism was ruling in spite of the wishes and rights of the people. The Address then went on to say:

"We prefer to remain attached to the Government of our fathers. The Constitution of the United States has done us no wrong. The Congress of the United States has passed no law to oppress us. The President of the United States has made no threat against the law abiding people of Tennessee. Under the Government of the United States we have enjoyed as a nation more of civil and religious freedom than any other people under the whole heaven. We believe there is no cause for rebellion or secession on the part of the people of Tennessee. None was assigned by the Legislature in their miscalled Declaration of Independence. No adequate cause can be assigned. The select committee of that body asserted a gross and inexcusable falsehood in their address to the people of Tennessee when they declared that the Government of the United States has made war upon them.

"The secession cause has thus far been sustained by deception and falsehood: by falsehoods as to the action of Congress; by false dispatches as to battles that were never fought and victories that were never won; by false accounts as to the purposes of the President; by false representations as to the views of Union men, and by false pretenses as to the facility with which the secession troops would take possession of the Capital and capture the highest officers of the Government. The cause of secession or rebellion has no charms for us, and its progress has been marked by the most alarming and dangerous attacks upon the public liberty. In other States, as well as our own, its whole course threatens to annihilate the last vestige of freedom. While peace and prosperity have blessed us in the Government of the United States, the following may be enumerated as some of the fruits of secession.

"It was urged forward by members of Congress who were sworn to support the Constitution of the United States, and were themselves supported by the Government; it was effected without consultation with all the States interested in the slavery question, and without exhausting peaceable remedies. It has plunged the country into civil war, paralyzed our commerce, interfered with the whole trade and business of our country, lessened the value of our property, destroyed many of the pursuits of life, and bids fair to involve the whole nation in irretrievable bankruptcy and ruin. It has changed the entire relations of States and adopted constitutions without submitting them to a vote of the people, and where such a vote has been authorized, it has been upon the condition prescribed by Senator Mason, of Virginia, that those who voted the Union ticket 'must leave the State.' It has advocated a constitutional monarchy, a king and a dictator, and is, through the Richmond press, at this moment recommending to the Convention in Virginia a restriction of the right of suffrage, and 'in severing connection with the Yankees, to abolish every vestige of resemblance to the institutions of that detested race.' It has formed military leagues, passed military bills, and opened the door for oppressive taxation, without consulting the people; and then, in mockery of a free election, has required them by their votes to sanction its usurpations, under the penalties of moral proscription or at the point of the bayonet. It has offered a premium for crime in directing the discharge of volunteers from criminal prosecutions, and in recommending the Judges not to hold their courts. It has stained our statute book with the repudiation of Northern debts, and has greatly violated the constitution by attempting, through its unlawful extension, to destroy the right of suffrage. It has called upon the people in the State of Georgia, and may soon require the people of Tennessee, to contribute all their surplus cotton, corn, wheat, bacon, beef, &c., to the support of pretended governments alike destitute of money and credit. It has attempted to destroy the accountability of public servants to the people by secret legislstion, and set the obligation of an oath at defiance. It has passed laws declaring it treason to say or do anything in favor of the Government of the United States, or against the Confederate States, and such a law is now before, and we apprehend will soon be passed, by the Legislature of Tennessee. It has attempted to destroy, and, we fear soon, utterly prostrate the freedom of speech and of the press. It has involved the Southern States in a war whose success is hopeless, and which must ultimately lead to the ruin of the people. Its bigoted, overbearing and intolerant spirit has already subjected the people of East Tennessee to many petty grievances: our people have been insulted; our flags have been fired upon and torn down; our houses have been rudely entered; our families subjected to insult; our peaceable meetings interrupted; our women and children shot at by a merciless soldiery; our towns pillaged; our citizens robbed, and some of them assassinated and murdered. No effort has been spared to deter the Union men of East Tennessee from the expression of their free thoughts. The penalties of treason have been threatened against them, and murder and assassination have been openly encouraged by leading secession journals. As secession has been thus overbearing and intolerant while in the minority in East Tennessee, nothing better can be expected of the pretended majority than wild, unconstitutional and oppressive legislation; an utter contempt and disregard of law; a determination to force every Union man in the State to swear to the support of a constitution he abhors; to yield his money and property to aid a cause he detests, and to become the object of scorn and derision as well as the victim of intolerable and relentless oppression. In view of these considerations, and of the fact that the people of East Tennessee have declared their fidelity to the Union by a majority of about twenty thousand votes, therefore, we do resolve and declare:

"RESOLUTIONS.

"1. That we do earnestly desire the restoration of peace to our whole country, and most especially that our own section of the State of Tennessee should not be involved in civil war.

"2. That the action of our State Legislature in passing the so-called 'Declaration of Independence' and in forming the 'Military League' with the Confederate States, and in adopting other acts looking to a separation of the State of Tennessee from the Government of the United States, is unconstitutional and illegal, and therefore not binding upon us as loyal citizens.

"3. That in order to avert a conflict with our brethren in other parts of the State, and desiring that all constitutional means shall be resorted to for the preservation of peace, we do, therefore, constitute and appoint O. P Temple, of Knox; John Netherland, of Hawkins; and James P. McDowell, of Greene, commissioners, whose duty it shall be to prepare a memorial and cause the same to be presented to the General Assembly of Tennessee, now in session, asking its consent that the counties composing East Tennessee, and such counties in Middle Tennessee as desire to co-operate with them, may form and erect a separate State.

"4. Desiring, in good faith, that the General Assembly will grant this our reasonable request; and still claiming the right to determine our own destiny, we do further resolve that an election be held in all the counties of East Tennessee, and in such other counties in Middle Tennessee adjacent thereto as may desire to co-operate with us, for the choice of delegates to represent them in a General Convention, to be held in the town of Kingston at such time as the President of this Convention, or, in case of his absence or inability, any one of the Vice-Presidents, or, in like case with them, the Secretary of this Convention may designate; and the officer so designating the day for the assembling of said Convention shall also fix the time for holding the election herein provided for, and give reasonable notice thereof.

"5. In order to carry out the foregoing resolution, the sheriffs of the different counties are hereby requested to open and hold said election, or cause the same to be so held, in the usual manner and at the usual places of voting, as prescribed by law; and in the event the sheriff of any county should fail or refuse to open and hold said election, or cause the same to be done, the coroner of such county is requested to do so, and should such coroner fail or refuse, then any constable of such county is hereby authorized to open and hold said election, or cause the same to be done. And if in any county none of the above named officers will hold said election, then any Justice of the Peace or freeholder in such county is authorized to hold the same, or cause it to be done. The officer or other person holding said election shall certify the result to the President of this Convention, or to such officer as may have directed the same to be holden, at as early a day thereafter as practicable; and the officer to whom said returns may be made, shall open and compare the polls and issue certificates to the delegates elected."

It was not long before those Unionists and protestants against wrong were flying for their lives, and were hunted down like wild beasts. The leaders disappeared from observation, and the people could only acquiesce in a state of affairs which, in the presence of the armed minions of the Southern Confederacy, they were powerless to prevent.

XXV.

PERSECUTION OF UNIONISTS IN TENNESSEE. PARSON BROWNLOW'S STORY.

THE story of suffering in Tennessee forms one of the most painful, as it is one of the most revolting features of the rebellion. We can realize how men of one section united by no ties of relationship nor of social sympathy should fall out, and become rank enemies, but not how the people of a neighborhood could so far ignore old friendships, old associations, harmonious sympathies on social and moral questions, as to proceed to bitter extremities of violence with their neighbors who differed with them on the question of secession. That they did resort to such extremities the stories of hundreds of persecuted, exiled and ruined Unionists testify; and the fact illustrates, in a vivid light, the hateful nature of the secession sentiment.

We have already devoted a chapter to the "Spirit of Violence" in the Southern States, giving such instances of that spirit as will afford the reader much "food for thought." But, all therein stated is nothing as compared to the sufferings, the wrongs, the wretchedness, inflicted upon the men and women of Tennessee. It is a particularly unpleasant task to repeat the story of these outrages because it is so humiliating to our boasted American civilization; but, it should be repeated, over and over again, to teach American youths the inestimable value of law and order, and the repulsive nature of all revolutionary assaults upon the constituted authority. There is, too, a propriety in the recollection of those sufferings for opinion's sake, because they illustrate that trait of a truly noble human nature—power to resist wrong even unto death. The devotion of the few brave men who courted dungeons, confiscation of property, the lash and the gallows for their faith in the Union, ever will stand as examples worthy of the emulation and admiration of every lover of their country.

Parson Brownlow, after the election, (June 8th, 1861,) became the recipient of indignities from the Secessionists. His house, up to midsummer of that year, floated the American flag, though many an attempt was made to drag it down. Early in June a Louisiana regiment, *en route* for Virginia, tarried at Knoxville, awaiting transportation over the railway, then crowded beyond its capacity. Of this and other regiments which laid over at the same place, the Parson said: "During May and June a stream of whisky-drinking, secession fire, hot as hell, commenced to pour through Knoxville, in the direction of Manassas. These mean scoundrels visited the houses of Union men, shouted at them, groaned and hissed. My humble dwelling had the honor to be thus greeted oftener than any other five houses in Knoxville. The Southern papers said they were the flower of their youth. I said to my wife, if this is the flower, God save us from the rabble."

Upon one of these occasions nine members of the Louisiana regiment determined to see the flag humbled. Two men were chosen as a committee to proceed to the Parson's house to order the Union ensign down. Mrs. More (the Parson's daughter) answered the summons. In answer to her inquiry as to what was their errand, one said, rudely:

"We have come to take down that d—d rag you flaunt from your roof—the Stripes and Stars."

Mrs. More stepped back a pace or two within the door, drew a revolver from her dress pocket, and leveling it, answered:

"Come on, sirs, and take it down!"

The chivalrous Confederates were startled.

"Yes, come on!" she said, as she advanced toward them.

They cleared the piazza, and stood at bay on the walk.

"We'll go and get more men, and then d—d if it don't come down!"

"Yes, go and get more *men*—you are not men!" said the heroic woman, contemptuously, as the two backed from the place and disappeared.

Speaking of those days in June and July, the Parson said:

"Then it was that, wanting in transportation, wanting in rolling stock, wanting in locomotives, they had to lie over by regiments in our town, and then they commenced to ride Union men upon rails. I have seen that done in the streets, and have seen them break into the stores and empty their contents; and coming before my own house with ropes in their hands, they would groan out, 'Let us give old Brownlow a turn, the d——d old scoundrel; come out, and we will hang you to the first limb.' These threats toward me were repeated every day and every week, until finally they crushed my paper, destroyed my office, appropriated the building to a smith's shop to repair the locks and barrels of old muskets that Floyd had stolen from the Federal Government. They finally enacted a law in the Legislature of Tennessee authorizing an armed force to take all the arms, pistols, guns, dirks, swords and everything of the sort from all the Union men, and they paid a visit to every Union house in the State. They visited mine three times in succession, upon that business, and they got there a couple of guns and one pistol. Being an editor and preacher, I was not largely supplied. I had, however, a *small* supply concealed under my clothes! Finally, after depriving us of all our arms throughout the State, and after taking all the fine horses of the Union men everywhere, without fee or reward, for cavalry horses, and seizing upon the fat hogs, corn, fodder, and sheep, going into houses and pulling the beds off the bedsteads in day-time, seizing upon all the blankets they could find for the army; after breaking open chests, bureaus, drawers, and everything of that sort—in which they were countenanced and tolerated by the authorities, civil and military—our people rose up in rebellion, unarmed as they were, and by accident."

After that uprising, which did not occur until November 3d—when the Unionists secretly burned the bridges of the railways leading from the South and from Virginia into Eastern Tennessee—the Unionists were not suffered to escape with "civil indignities;" but were seized, shot, imprisoned, hung by scores; were driven to the mountains where they suffered from all the rigors of the winter; were rendered exiles and hunted men, whom to shoot was a duty. Of that period of suffering the Parson chiefly spoke in his various addresses to the people of the North. His story seemed incredible—it was so horrible in some of its details; yet, its authenticity none dared dispute. Persons, names, dates, places, circumstances, all were given, that not a shadow of doubt might remain. We shall reproduce so much of his narrative as will serve to give the reader a correct apprehension of the State of affairs in Tennessee during the fall and winter of 1861–62:

THE SOUTH GUILTY OF THE WAR.

"The demagogues," he said, "and the leaders of the South, are to blame for having brought about this state of things, and not the people of the North. We have intended down South, for thirty years, to break up this Government. It has been our settled purpose and our sole aim down South to destroy the Union and break up the Government. We have had the Presidency in the South twice to your once, and five of our men were re-elected to the Presidency, filling a period of forty years. In addition to that, we had divers men elected for one term, and no man at the North ever was permitted to serve any but the one term; and, in addition to having elected our men twice to your once, and occupied the chair twice as long as you ever did, we seized upon and appropriated two or three miscreants from the North that we elected to the Presidency, and ploughed with them as our heifers. We asked of you, and obtained at your hands, a Fugitive Slave law. You voted for and helped us to enact and to establish it. We asked of you and obtained the repeal of the Missouri Compromise line, which never ought to have been repealed. I fought it to the bitter end, and denounced it and all concerned in repealing it, and I repeat it here again to-night. We asked and obtained the admission of Texas into the Union, that we might have slave territory enough to form some four or five more great States, and you granted it. You have granted us from first to last all we have asked, all we have desired; and hence I repeat, that this thing of secession, this wicked attempt to dissolve the Union, has been brought about *without the shadow of a cause.* It is the work of the worst men that ever God permitted to live on the face of this earth. It is the work of a set of men down South who, in winding up this revolution, if our Administration and Government shall fail to hang them as high as Haman—hang every one of them—we will make an utter failure."

IN PRISON.

After detailing his course through the summer, and relating the incidents of the burning of bridges in November, he told of his seizure upon suspicion of having been instrumental in the incendiarism, saying:

"They wanted a pretext to seize me; and upon the 6th day of December they marched me off to jail—a miserable, uncomfortable, damp, desperate jail—where I found, when ushered into it, about one hundred and fifty Union men. There was not, in the whole jail, a chair, bench, stool or table, or any piece of furniture, except a dirty old wooden bucket and a pair of tin dippers to drink with. I found some of the first and best men of the whole country there. I knew them all, and they knew me, as I had been among them for thirty years. They rallied round me, some smiling and glad to see me, as I could give them the news that had been kept from them. Others took me by the hand, and were utterly speechless, and, with bitter, burning tears running down their cheeks, they said that they never thought that they would come to that at last, looking through the bars of a grate. Speaking first to one and then to another, I bade them be of good cheer and take courage. Addressing them, I said, 'Is it for stealing you are here? No. Is it for counterfeiting? No. Is it for manslaughter? No. You are here, boys, because you adhere to the flag and the Constitution of our country. I am here with you for no other offense but that; and, as God is my judge, boys, I look upon this 6th day of December as the proudest day of my life. And here I intend to stay until I die of old age or until they hang me. I will never renounce my principles.' "

THE HANGMEN AT WORK.

He was soon made to realize that death, as well as imprisonment, was the Unionist's lot. He said: "In the jail-yard, which was in full view from our window, we almost daily beheld a tragedy. There would drive up a horse and cart, with an ugly, rough, flat-topped coffin upon it, surrounded by fifteen to forty men, who, with bristling bayonets, as a guard, would march in through the gate into the jail-yard, with steady, military tread. We trembled in our boots, for they never notified us who was to be hanged. They came sometimes with two coffins, one on each cart, and they took two men at a time and marched them out. A poor old man of sixty-five and his son of twenty-five, were marched out at one time and hanged on the same gallows. They made that poor old man, who was a Methodist class-leader, sit by and see his son hang until he was dead, and then they called him a d—d Lincolnite Union shrieker, and said, 'Come on, it is your turn next.' He sunk, but they propped him up and led him to the halter, and swung both off on the same gallows. They came, after that, for another man, and took J. C. Haum out of jail—a young man of fine sense, good address, and of excellent character—a tall spare-made man, leaving a wife at home with four or five helpless children. They were kind enough to notify him an hour before the hanging that he was to hang. Haum at once made an application for a Methodist preacher, a Union man, to come and pray for him. They denied him the privilege; but, they had near the gallows an unprincipled drunken chaplain of their own army, who got up aud undertook to *apologize* for Haum. He said: 'This poor, unfortunate man, who is about to pay the debt of nature, regrets the course he took; he said he was misled by the Union paper.' Haum rose up, and with a clear, stentorian voice, said: 'Fellow-citizens: there is not a word of truth in that statement. I have authorized nobody to make such a statement. What I have said and done, I have done and said with my eyes open; and, if it were to be done over, I would do it again. I am ready to hang, and you can execute your purpose.' He died like a man; he died like a Union man; like an East Tennessean ought to die! As God is my judge," added the Parson, solemnly and earnestly, "I would sooner be Baum in the grave to-day, than any one of the scoundrels engaged in his murder."

THE TWO LOYAL CLERGYMEN.

The case of two venerable Baptist Clergymen, Mr. Pope and Mr. Cate, was a painfnl one, from their age and circumstances—both of which should have shielded them from the barbarous treatment they received. Brownlow, referring to this case, said: "Mr. Cate was very low indeed, prostrated from the fever, and unable to eat the miserable food sent there by the corrupt jailor and deputy marshal—a man whom I had denounced in my paper as guilty of forgery time and time again—a suitable representative of the thieves and scoundrels that head this rebellion in the South. The only favor extended to me was to allow my family to send me three meals a day by my son, who brought the provisions in a basket. I requested my wife to send also enough for the two old clergymen. One of them was put in jail for offering prayers for the President of the United States, and the other was confined for throwing up his hat and cheering the Stars and Stripes as they passed his house, borne by a company of Union volunteers. When the basket of provisions came in in the morning, they examined it at the door, would look between the pie and the bread to see if any billet or paper was concealed there, communicating treason from any outside Unionist to the 'old scoundrel' they had in jail; and when the basket went out again, the same ceremony was repeated, to discover whether I had slipped any paper in, in any way."

A HARROWING INCIDENT.

"The old man, Cate," said Brownlow, "had three sons in that jail. One of them, James Madison Cate, a most exemplary and worthy member of the Baptist church, was there for having committed no other crime than that of refusing to volunteer. He lay stretched at length upon the floor, with one thickness of a piece of carpet under him, and an old overcoat doubled up for a pillow, in the agonies of death. His wife came to visit him, bringing her youngest child, which was but a babe. They were refused admittance. I put my head out of the jail window, and entreated them, for God's sake, to let the poor woman come in, as her husband was dying. The jailer at last consented that she might see him for the limited time of fifteen minutes. As she came in, and looked upon her husband's wan and emaciated face, and saw how rapidly he was sinking, she gave evident signs of fainting, and would have fallen to the floor with the babe in her arms, had I not rushed up to her and seized the babe. Then she sunk down upon the breast of her dying husband, unable to speak. I sat by and held the babe until the fifteen minutes had expired, when the officer came in, and, in an insulting and peremptory manner, notified her that the interview was to close. I hope I may never see such a scene again; and yet, *such cases were common all over East Tennessee.*"

A CASE OF CLEMENCY.

Among others condemned to death by the drumhead court-martial which disposed of the Union prisoners, was that of a man named Hessing Self, who was informed of his fate a few hours before the time fixed for his execution. Brownlow thus related the incidents which followed: "His daughter, who had come down to administer to his comfort and consolation—a most estimable girl, about twenty-one years of age—Elizabeth Self, a tall, spare-made girl, modest, handsomely attired, begged leave to enter the jail to see her father. They permitted her, contrary to their usual custom and savage barbarity, to go in. They had him in a small iron cage, a terrible affair; they opened a little door, and the jailor admitted her. A parcel of us went to witness the scene. As she entered the cage where her father was, she clasped him around the neck, and he embraced her also, throwing his arms across her shoulders. They sobbed and cried; shed their tears and made their moans. I stood by, and I never beheld such a sight, and I hope I may never see the like again. When they had parted, wringing each other by the hand, as she came out of the cage, stammering and trying to utter something intelligible, she lisped my name. She knew my face, and I could understand as much as that she desired me to write a dispatch to Jefferson Davis, and sign her name, begging him to pardon her father. I worded it about thus:

"'HON. JEFFERSON DAVIS—My father, Hessing Self, is sentenced to be hanged at four o'clock to-day. I am living at home, and my mother is dead. My father is my earthly all; upon him my hopes are centered; and, friend, I pray you to pardon him. Respectfully, 'ELIZABETH SELF.'

"Jefferson, Davis, who had a better heart than the rest of his coadjutors, immediately responded by commuting his sentence to imprisonment."

SICKNESS AND SUFFERING.

Many other incidents were mentioned of that Life in Prison, which all served to prove the malignant and thoroughly heartless character of the Confederate authorities. Of the winter, as it passed to the living inmates, he said: "They tightened up on those of us who held out. Many of our company became sick. We had to lie upon that miserable, cold, naked floor, with not room enough for us all to lie down at the same time—and you may think what it must have been in December and January—"spelling" each other, one lying down awhile on the floor and then another taking his place so made warm. That was the way we managed, until many became sick unto death. A number of the prisoners died of pneumonia and typhoid fever, and other diseases contracted by exposure there."

A MOST REVOLTING AFFAIR.

A large jail in Greenfield—the place where Andrew Johnson resided—was, also, filled with Unionists, who were treated with even greater atrocity than those in the Knoxville prison. Brownlow mentioned the case of two men, named Fry and Nashy. Fry had a wife and six children. "A fellow from *Union*," the Parson stated, "named Leadbeater, the bloodiest and the most ultra man, the vilest wretch, the most unmitigated scoundrel that ever made a track in East Tennessee—Colonel Daniel Leadbeater, late of the United States Army, but now an officer in the Secession Army—took these two men, tied them with his own hands upon one limb, immediately *over* the railroad track in the town of Greenville and ordered them to hang *four days and nights*, and also ordered all the engineers and conductors to go by that spot slowly, in order to give passengers an opportunity to *kick* the rigid bodies and strike them with switches. And they did it! I pledge you my honor that, from the front platforms they made a business of *kicking the dead bodies as they passed by;* and the women (I will not say the ladies, for down South we make a distinction between ladies and women)—the women, the wives and daughters of men in high position, waved their white handkerchiefs in triumph, through the windows of the car, at the sight of the two dead bodies hanging there!"

A statement of this character will excite, in the reader's mind, feelings of disgust and horror. No wonder every escaped Unionist had but one wish in his heart—to wreak a *bloody* revenge on those merciless miscreants, who seemed to have taken to torture by instinct. Men who are familiar with, and practice torture upon, slaves, only have to change the objects of their malice, to become persecutors of their own fellow-citizens. Strange that the Parson saw and experienced those simple *results* of a Slave education, and yet failed to ascribe the true cause to the unheard-of atrocity meted out to the Unionists!

BARBARITIES GENERALLY PRACTICED.

"Seven miles out of Knoxville," said Brownlow, "they caught up Union men, tied them upon logs, upon blocks six or ten inches from the ground, put men upon their breasts, tying their hands and feet under the log, stripped their backs entirely bare, and then, with switches, cut their backs literally to pieces, the blood running down at every stroke. They came into court when it was in session, and when the case was stated, the judge replied: 'These are revolutionary times, and there is no remedy for anything of the kind.' He added, further:

"This is the *spirit* of secession all over the South; it is the spirit which actuates the instruments of the Confederacy everywhere. It is the spirit of murder—the very spirit of hell itself. *Can* you," he cried in an impassioned voice—"*can* you, any of you, excuse or apologize for such demons? Oh, look upon the picture before you! Hanging is even *now* going on all over East Tennessee. They shoot them down in the fields, in the streets, arresting hundreds, and shooting fifty or sixty in one instance, after they had surrendered and were under arrest. They marched between three and four hundred through the streets, some of them barefooted, and their feet bleeding, taking them to the depot and shipping them to Atlanta, Georgia, to work upon their fortifications. These men, denied water, would lift out of the mud-puddles in the street with their hands, after a rain, what they could to quench their thirst. They whip them, and, as strange as it may seem to *you*, in the counties of Campbell and Anderson they *actually lacerate with switches the bodies of females, wives and daughters of Union men—clever, respectable women.* They show no quarter to male or female; they rob their houses, and they throw them into prison. Our jails are full; we have complained and thought hard that our Government has not come to our relief, for a more loyal, a more devoted people to the Stars and Stripes never lived than the Union people of Tennessee. With tears in their eyes they begged me, upon leaving East Tennessee, to see the President, to see the army officers, to have relief sent immediately to them, and bring them out of jail."

After presenting this picture of wretchedness and wo, no wonder the speaker exclaimed:

"In God's name I call upon President Lincoln, and upon his Cabinet and army officers, to say how long they will suffer a loyal people, true to the Union and to the Government of their fathers, to suffer in this way! The Union men of East Tennessee are largely in the majority—say three to one—but they have no arms; they are in the jails of the country; they are working on rebel fortifications like slaves under the lash, and no Federal force has ever yet been marched into that oppressed and down-trodden country. Let the Government, if it has any regard for obligations, redeem that country at once, and liberate these people, no matter at what cost of blood or treasure."

DEBASED CHARACTER OF SOUTHERN MINISTERS.

Brownlow delivered in New York (May 19th) an address on the irreligious character of the rebellion. He then made public facts and incidents which proved how thoroughly the ministry of the South was demoralized by the spirit of secession. Some of his statements we may repeat.

Rev. Dr. Martin, a New School Presbyterian minister of Knoxville, was educated and graduated at the Union Theological Seminary of New York city. How he was abased by acquiescence in the revolution, the Parson stated:

"Mr. Maynard, our representative in Congress, is an elder in the New School Presbyterian Church, a scholar, and a gentleman. He had no sooner left in disguise to make his way through to take his seat in Congress, than the Rev. Joseph F. Martin made a set speech, going through the formalities of taking a text—preached an outrageous sermon, and prayed an outrageous prayer, 'that his wicked and unhallowed tracks might never again be seen or known in Knoxville.' The

The mortified wife of Mr. Maynard, (who is from the neighborhood of New York city,) who is a lady, and so regarded, in every sense of the word, an intelligent, charitable, Christian lady, shedding tears on that occasion, rose up, left the house and journeyed home; and, although she was driven out but a few weeks ago, with my wife and children, she had, to her honor and credit, never disgraced her name by visiting his vile sanctuary any more. Feeling that he had behaved in a contemptible manner, he made her a visit and apologized, saying, 'I didn't want to do it, but my elders made me do it, and I had to do it, or lose my salary and my place.' What do you think of a 'laborer in the vineyard' like that?"

Of the pastor of another Knoxville church, he related: "The pastor of the Old School Church in Knoxville, a man of education and fair talent, and until secession broke out, I thought him a gentleman and a Christian. A short time before I left, he had a special occasion to preach upon the subject of secession, and attracted a large crowd. He made the bold and open declaration that Jesus Christ was a Southerner, born on Southern soil. He did it in good faith; he did it in sincerity, however, not in truth. He said, 'Jesus Christ was a Southerner, born on Southern soil, and so were his disciples and apostles, all except Judas, and he was a Northern man.' Holding up a Bible, he said—I presume he was sober, but I would not guarantee it—'I would sooner, my brethren, announce to you a text for discussion from the pulpit out of a Bible or a Testament that I knew had been printed in hell, than out of a Bible or a Testament that was printed North of Mason and Dixon's line.' That was a part of *his* Gospel sermon on the Lord's day."

The Methodist ministry (Brownlow belonged to that persuasion) he characterized thus:

"The Methodist preachers in the South were entitled to more consideration, for there was more unanimity among them. They were nearly all, without any exception, rascals."

He thus specified one case: "Fountain E. Fitch was an old presiding elder of the Conference, a man who had been in every General Conference for thirty years. He went to Europe with Bishop Soule, and had one or two sons in the rebel army. He was a chaplain of a Nashville regiment, and made it a practice to get drunk, carrying a bottle with him; he drank to excess and swore profanely, but preached every Sunday faithfully to the soldiers. In his discourses he told them that the cause in which they were engaged—and I only give him as a specimen of all denominations—fighting for the independence of the South, fighting to keep back the abolition hordes of the North, and to repulse the hordes of Lincoln, was so good and so holy a cause, that if they died in this cause they would be saved in heaven, even without grace."

But there was one loyal man "of the cloth"—that of the Episcopal minister in Knoxville, whose case the Parson thus referred to:

"Rev. Thomas W. Hugh was a slaveholder, and a man of property. His Bishop, some months ago, furnished him with a new prayer, which did not require him to pray for the President of the United States, but substituted Jefferson Davis and the Confederate Government. Mr. Hugh, promptly but frankly, and like a man, said: 'I cannot abandon my Prayer-Book and regular form. I do not believe in the Confederacy; I do not believe in Jefferson Davis.' They turned him out and procured another pliant tool and cat's-paw, who was willing to pray for *anybody* for his victuals, his wine, and his parsonage."

GENERAL ZOLLICOFFER.

For Zollicoffer, Brownlow entertained a sincere respect. Both were Whigs—had campaigned it politically together and were, personally, friends. The rebel General did not forget old relation in his new ones—which latter we have good reason to suspect were alike painful and distasteful to him. Brownlow said:

"After my types and printing-press had been destroyed, and my office turned into a blacksmith-shop, to repair and put percussion locks on the old muskets Floyd stole, word was given to General Zollicoffer that a regiment of Texans, who were encamped a few miles out of town, had fixed up their plans to pull Brownlow's house down that night. Zollicoffer immediately gave an order that no soldier should leave camp that night, and sent a company of soldiers to guard my house, giving the ladies information of his intention. This was heralded all through the Southern Confederacy as a piece of unheard-of clemency. But I think he did nothing more than his duty. And now that Zollicoffer is dead, I must do him the credit to say that I knew him for more than twenty-five years; that I have battled with him; that he was an honest man, who never wronged another out of a cent; that he never told a lie; that he was in all respects an honorable man, and as brave a soldier as ever died in battle, and that the only mean thing he ever did, was fighting for the Southern Confederacy."

Zollicoffer was killed at the battle of Wild Cat, Kentucky, October 21st, by Colonel Fry. His death was sincerely regretted by the Unionists of Tennessee. He had been cajoled into the Confederate service; his hand, not his heart, seemed to have been the sinner.

THE BRIDGE BURNING.

The burning of bridges in East Tennessee was an act of the Unionists, to prevent the Confederates from throwing reenforcements into that section, while Garland pushed down through Cumberland Gap to protect the Unionists in their pre-arranged uprising. The story of the burning was never known until the Parson revealed it on his arrival in Nashville, late in February (1861.) The substance of his statements, at that time, was thus reported by the Louisville *Journal:*

"It appears that Chaplin Carter and Captain Fry, of one of the Tennessee regiments, in the latter part of October, made their way in disguise and over hidden paths to the house of a prominent loyalist, within eight miles of Knoxville. Here they convened about one hundred trustworthy and devoted men, to whom they represented that a Federal division was about forcing its way into the Eastern district, and that, in order to insure the success of the contemplated expedition, and prevent the reenforcement of the Confederate forces then guarding the Gap from either the West or East, they were authorized by the Federal military authorities to prepare and execute a plan for the destruction of the principal bridges on the East Tennessee and Virginia Railroad.

"Most of those present at once signified their willingness to co-operate with them, and it was accordingly arranged that parties of fifteen to twenty-five, armed and provided with the necessary combustibles, should proceed as secretly as possible to the vicinity of the bridges selected for destruction. Captain Fry, assuming the character of a Confederate contractor, professedly engaged in the purchase of hogs, under the name of Colonel Walker, traveled from point to point, personally superintending the preparations.

"So well were the plans laid, and so successfully carried out, that, although the most westerly of the doomed bridges was no less than *one hundred and seventy-five miles* from the most easterly, the guards at all of them were overpowered, and the structures fired within the same hour of the same night, that is, between the hours of eleven and twelve of the night of the 10th of November. The bridges were readily set in flames by means of ropes dipped in turpentine and stretched from end to end. Captain Fry was himself present at the burning of the Lick Creek bridge.

"The guards at that point were not only overcome, disarmed and tied, but also made to swear allegiance to the United States, upon a Bible brought along for the purpose. Captain Fry started for Southern Kentucky immediately after the burning, to return, as the conspirators all believed, in a few days, with a Federal army. His brother was afterward arrested, and hung by the rebels."

It is one of the melancholy episodes of the war that Garland and Schoepf were stayed in their advance upon East Tennessee. The way was open; and the uprising of the Unionists, with the help of the Federal forces, certainly would have given that section up to the Union. The "circumlocution office" had another way of doing the thing—of gathering a tremendous force, in the course of time—to march down upon Nashville, then to whip the rebels out of West Tennessee; then to advance into East Tennessee. The poor Unionists pined in dungeons through the weary ten months which followed before their deliverance came, by the advance of Mitchell from the South and of Morgan from Cumberland Gap. East Tennessee *should* have been in the Union, in November, 1861; and, doubtless would have been, if counter orders had not arrested a simple, straight-forward, discreet campaign. This, we believe, is now the opinion of those best qualified to sit in judgment on events in Kentucky and Tennessee.

XXVI.

THE CAMPAIGN IN MISSOURI. THE FIRST DISASTER.

THE final defection of General Price and Governor Jackson (June 12th) was followed by their calling out all the troops available to "fight the hireling Dutch," as the United States volunteers were then called. They gathered in strong force at Boonsville, whither General Lyon proceeded with all the available force at his disposition—consisting chiefly of the First, Third, and Fourth Missouri regiments volunteers, with several companies of regulars, two batteries of artillery, and several companies of Home Guards. The battle of Boonsville followed, June 17th, in which Price's forces were routed, and his camp equipage, stores, etc., captured. The Federal loss was two killed and nine wounded. General Price was not in the fight, having gone home the day previous, ill.

The Second Missouri regiment stopped at Jefferson City, where Colonel Boernstein assumed command. He issued his proclamation (June 17th,) announcing the flight of the Governor and other State functionaries, and proclaiming his purpose to co-operate with the civil and judicial authorities to preserve law and order.

On the 18th, General Lyon issued his proclamation to the people of Missouri, in which he set forth the true condition of matters as between the absconding Governor, with his treasonable coadjutors, and the General Government. He assured peace and safety to all who did not bear arms against the Government, and requested all who had been deceived into a co-operation with the treason of their late Executive, to lay down their arms, and return to their homes. He warned those in arms, however, against hoping for clemency, if they persisted in hostility against their country.

On the 18th, the Secessionists from Warsaw and vicinity attacked a body of Home Guards at Camp Cole, and dispersed them—the Guards losing twenty-three killed, twenty wounded, and thirty prisoners. The attacking force was comprised largely of Price's men, who had retired from Boonsville upon Lyon's approach.

Lyon immediately proceeded to dispose his forces so as to command the best points of occupation in the State. Siegel was pushed out toward Springfield, where he arrived June 23d. Learning that Jackson was coming down from the North with the remnant of his forces, through Cedar County, Siegel advanced to Mount Vernon to intercept his retreat. At Mount Vernon he ascertained that Price was at Neosho, and immediately resolved to use him up before striking for Jackson. With that object in view, he moved (June 30th) on to Neosho; but Price had retreated before him.

The rebels effected a combination of their forces, under Generals Parsons and Rains, at Dry Fork Creek, eight miles north of Carthage. By orders of Brigadier-General Sweeny—who had then arrived at Springfield and assumed command of the Federal forces operating in South-western Missouri—Siegel, on the morning of July 5th, pushed out to meet the enemy. His force consisted of eight companies of his own (Third) regiment, under command of Lieutenant-Colonel Hassendeubel, Missouri volunteers; seven companies of the Fifth regiment, Colonel Salomon; and eight field pieces under command of Major Backof. The enemy's force comprised State troops and Arkansas volunteers to the number of fifty-five hundred—nearly one half mounted—and a battery of five guns. An account of the battle given by one who was present, read:

"Our command was about one thousand two hundred strong, including a part of Colonel Salomon's regiment. We met the enemy in camp, in an open prairie, three miles beyond Dry Fork. We could not discover many infantry, but numbers of cavalry. Approaching within eight hundred yards, we took our position. The artillery was placed in front; we had on our left two six-pounders; in our center, two six-pounders and two twelve-pounders; and two six-pounders on our right. The enemy, who occupied the highest ground in the prairie, had in position one six-pounder on the right and left, and in his center one twelve and two six-pounders. The fight commenced at half-past nine, when large bodies of infantry began to appear. The firing of the enemy was wretched. I have seen much artillery practice, but never saw such bad gunnery before. Their balls and shells went over us, and exploded in the open prairie. At eleven o'clock we had silenced their twelve-pounder and broken their center so much that disorder was apparent. After the first five shots the two secession flags which they carried were not shown. They displayed the State flag, which we did not fire at. At about two o'clock the cavalry attempted to outflank us, on both right and left. As we had left our baggage trains three miles in the rear, not anticipating a serious engagement, it was necessary to fall back to prevent their capture. Colonel Siegel then ordered two six-pounders to the rear, and changed his front, two six pounders on the flanks, and the twelve and six-pounders in the rear, and commenced falling back in a steady and orderly manner, firing as we went. We proceeded, with hardly a word to be heard except the orders of the officers, until we reached our baggage wagons, which had approached with the two companies left in reserve. They were formed (fifty wagons) into a solid square, and surrounded by the infantry and artillery, as before. The retreat was without serious casualty until we approached the Dry Fork Creek, where the road passes between bluffs on either side. The cavalry of the enemy, eight hundred strong, had concentrated on the opposite side of the creek, to cut us off. Colonel Siegel ordered two more cannon to the right and left oblique in front, and then by a concentrated cross-fire poured in upon them a brisk fire of canister and shrapnell shell. The confusion which ensued was terrific. Horses, both with and without riders, were galloping and neighing about the plain, and the riders in a perfect panic. We took here two or three prisoners, who, upon being questioned, said their force numbered about five thousand five hundred, and expressed their astonishment at the manner in which our troops behaved.

"We proceeded, after capturing about thirty-five horses, toward Carthage. Just before entering the town, at about six o'clock, we brought up at Buck Creek, where three companies of infantry conspicuously posted themselves on the bank, while the rest, in two columns, made a small circuit around the town, which is situated near the creek. The artillery then poured in a well-directed fire upon the village. The horsemen started out in affright, and our soldiers brought them down with fearful effect. This was the heaviest charge of the whole day. No regular volley of musketry had been ordered until this time, and the Minie rifles carried their leaden messengers through man and horse with damaging effect. The enemy must have lost fully two hundred men in this skirmish. Night was approaching as we passed through Carthage. The remnant of the horsemen of the rebels were scattered in all directions; their forces were coming up in our rear, and we concluded to make for the woods on the Mount Vernon road. We could not have captured the entire force without some loss; and as we were acting without orders, thought it prudent to withdraw with our advantage.

"We took in all forty-five prisoners, some of them officers; those taken at the Dry Creek at five o'clock reported about two hundred killed, and as the heaviest fighting was done afterwards, I estimate their loss at near five hundred. Our loss up to the time I left, was eight killed and missing, and forty-five wounded. As we brought off our wounded and dead, it is probable this may reduce the mortality list.

"The rebels halted at Carthage, and hoisted the secession rag, when our artillery wheeled, and in a few minutes were in position, and firing. Shot and shell were whistling over their heads when the flag disappeared from our view. We then kept on our way to Mount Vernon, where we were ordered to rendezvous, expecting to meet General Sweeney."

This masterly retreat covered Siegel with glory, and inspired the utmost confidence among the troops for their commanders. Almost all those engaged were Germans, while the officers were largely composed of Germans and Hungarians, of large experience on European battle-fields.

That section of the State immediately became the seat of stirring movements. There the rebels gathered heavy forces from Missouri and Arkansas, preparatory to a strike for St. Louis and the Capital, Jefferson city. Lyon immediately assumed the field command—General Fremont having taken chief command of the Department of the West, July 9th. Sharp engagements of detached bodies occurred at Florida, where a rebel camp was broken up—at Forsythe, which the Federal forces occupied—at Tilton, &c.; while, on the 2d of August, Lyon fell upon Ben McCullough's advancing brigades, under command of General Rains and Colonel McIntosh, at Dug Spring, nineteen miles South-west of Springfield. The rebels withdrew before his vigorous first assault, leaving forty dead and forty-four wounded upon the field. McCullough's design was to fall upon Springfield, and, by the very enormity of his numbers, to cut Lyon's command to pieces. Lyon slowly retreated from Dug Spring to Springfield, resolved to hold it at all hazards—even if his long looked for, and earnestly called for, reenforcements from St. Louis did not arrive. If Springfield was lost, McCullough and Price might march direct upon St. Louis. New Madrid was held by the enemy, from whence the recusant Governor hoped, by aid of the Confederate forces, then centering there, to fall upon Bird Point and Cairo. August 5th, Jackson issued, from thence, his "Declaration of the Independence of Missouri"—a rather remarkable document considering that he had been deposed by the properly constituted Convention, July 31st, so that another Governor (Judge Hamilton R. Gamble) had been chosen (August 1st) in Jackson's stead. The "Declaration" was the cry of revenge and mortification, and was put forth as a rejoinder to Governor Gamble's Address and Proclamation to the People of Missouri, issued August 3d.

Price moved his brigade, July 25th—then encamped on Cowskin Prairie, in McDonald County—toward Cassville, in Berry County, where it had been arranged the forces of McCullough, Pearce, McBride, and Price should concentrate, preparatory to the march on Springfield. The junction with McCullough and Pearce's commands was effected July 28th. The First Division, under McCullough, left Cassville August 1st, taking the road to Springfield, followed by the Second Division, under Price and Pearce (of Arkansas.) The Third Division, under General Steen, started forward August 2d. It was the advance guards of this combined army which were encountered by Lyon's forces at Dug Spring. The Federal General, discovering the enormous force of the enemy—as the several divisions came up and concentrated on Crane Creek—retired before them, and managed to give them a bloody greeting before they reached their destined goal. Accordingly, his forces marched out, on the night of August 9th,* from Spring-

* Lyon marched out on the 7th, for the night attack, but found morning so near at hand when he was prepared to move from Camp Hunter, (two miles from Springfield,) that he recalled the orders and returned to town, resolved to try it again, if circumstances seemed to warrant the hazardous enterprise.

field, to encounter the rebels, then in full force at Wilson's Creek, about ten miles south of the city. The Federal disposition was to assail by two columns—one led by General Lyon in person, the other by Colonel Franz Siegel.

Lyon's conduct, in ordering this advance, has been censured as rash, and, perhaps, as influenced somewhat by pique at the neglect shown him by the commanding General at St. Louis. But, it is certain that he acted from a high and noble sense of duty. One who was present at the time, wrote: "A consultation was held, and the question of evacuating Springfield seriously discussed. Looking at it in a military view, there was no doubt of the propriety, and even necessity of the step, and many of General Lyon's officers counseled such a movement. Some favored a retreat in the direction of Kansas, while others regarded Rolla as the more desirable. General Sweeney, however, pointed out the disastrous results which must ensue upon retreating without a battle—how the enemy would be flushed and boastful over such an easy conquest, the Union element crushed or estranged from us, and declared himself in favor of holding on to the last moment, and of giving the enemy battle as soon as he should approach within striking distance. This kind of counsel decided General Lyon to remain, save his own reputation and that of the officers under him, and not evacuate Springfield until compelled."

The enemy, also, had resolved upon a night advance from Wilson's Creek camp, upon Springfield, hoping to surround it, and, by day-break, to close in upon Lyon so as to prevent his escape to Rolla. Every disposition was made for the movement—the men were under arms, with orders to march, by four columns, at nine o'clock P. M. Price, for some unexplained reason, having passed over the chief command to McCullough, the latter ordered the expedition to be given up, late at night, as the darkness was intense and a storm threatened. Lyon was not intimidated by the darkness—it rather was favorable, as it covered his passage and general disposition from the observation of pickets and scouts.

Price, in his report of the conflict, said: "About six o'clock

I received a messenger from General Rains, that the enemy were advancing in great force, from the direction of Springfield, and were already within three hundred yards of the position where he was encamped with the Second Division, consisting of about 1,200 men, under Colonel Crawford. A second messenger came immediately afterward from General Rains to announce that the enemy's main body was upon him, but that he would endeavor to hold him in check until he could receive reenforcements. General McCullough was with me when these messengers came, and left at once for his own head-quarters, to make the necessary disposition of our forces.

"I rode forward instantly toward General Rains' position, ordering Generals Slack, McBride, Clark, and Parsons to move their infantry and artillery forward. I had ridden but a few hundred yards, when I came suddenly upon the main body of the enemy, commanded by General Lyon in person. The infantry and artillery which I had ordered to follow me, came up immediately, to the number of 2,036 men, and engaged the enemy. A severe and bloody conflict ensued; my officers and men behaving with the greatest bravery, and, with the assistance of a portion of the Confederate forces, successfully holding the enemy in check.

"Meanwhile, and almost simultaneously with the opening of the enemy's batteries in this quarter, a heavy cannonading was opened on the rear of our position, where a large body of the enemy, under Colonel Siegel, had taken position, in close proximity to Colonel Churchill's regiment, Colonel Greer's Texan Rangers, and 679 mounted Missourians, under command of Lieutenant-Colonels Major and Brown.

"The action now became general, and was conducted with the greatest gallantry and vigor on both sides, for more than five hours, when the enemy retreated in great confusion, leaving their Commander-in-Chief, General Lyon, dead upon the battle-field, over five hundred killed and a great number wounded. The forces under my command have also a large number of prisoners."

This briefly alludes to the attack. Its circumstances were

so full of interest that we may refer to it more at length. An account by an eye-witness, as well as the reports of Siegel and Major Sturgis, offer all necessary information. The former said: "At eight o'clock in the evening, General Siegel, with his own and Colonel Salomon's command and six pieces of artillery, moved southward, marching until nearly two o'clock, and passing around the extreme camp of the enemy, where he halted, thirteen miles from town, and on the south side of the rebels, ready to move forward and begin the attack as soon as he should hear the roar of General Lyon's artillery. The main body of troops under General Lyon moved from the city about the same hour, halted a short time five miles west of the city, thence in a south-westerly direction four miles, where we halted and slept till four A. M., Saturday, the day of the battle. * * * * * "It was now five o'clock. The enemy's pickets were driven in; the northern end of the valley in which they were encamped was visible, with its thousand of tents and its camp-fires; the sky was cloudy, but not threatening, and the most terribly destructive of battles, compared with the number engaged, was at hand. Our army moved now toward the south-west, to leave the creek and a spring which empties in it on our left. Passing over a spur of high land which lies at the north end of the valley, they entered a valley and began to ascend a hill, moderately covered with trees and underwood, which was not, however, dense enough to be any impediment to the artillery. * * * * * *

"Meanwhile the opposite hill had been stormed and taken by the gallant Missouri First, and Osterhaus's battalion and Totten's battery of six pieces had taken position on its summit and north side, and was belching forth its loud-mouthed thunder much to the distraction of the opposing force, who had already been started upon a full retreat by the thick-raining bullets of Colonel Blair's boys. Lieutenant DuBois's battery, four pieces, had also opened on the eastern slope, firing upon a force which was retreating toward the south-east on a road leading up the hill, which juts into the south-western angle of the creek, and upon a battery placed near by to cover their etreat. * * * * * * *

"Having driven a regiment of the enemy from one hill, the Missouri volunteers encountered in the valley beyond, another fresh and finely-equipped regiment of Louisianians, whom, after a bitter fight of forty-five minutes, they drove back and scattered, assisted by Captain Lothrop and his regular rifle recruits. Totten and Dubois were, meanwhile, firing upon the enemy forming in the south-west angle of the valley, and upon their batteries on the opposite hill.

"The undaunted First, with ranks already thinned, again moved forward up the second hill, just on the brow of which they met still another fresh regiment, which poured a terrible volley of musketry into their diminished numbers. Never yielding an inch, they gradually crowded their opposers backward, still backward, losing many of their own men, killed and wounded, but covering the ground thick with the retreating foe. Lieutenant-Colonel Andrews, already wounded, still kept his position, urging the men onward by every argument in his power. Lieutenant Murphy, when they once halted, wavering, stepped several paces forward, waving his sword in the air, and called successfully upon his men to follow him. Every Captain and Lieutenant did his duty nobly, and when they were recalled and replaced by the fresh Iowa and Kansas troops, many were the faces covered with powder and dripping with blood. Captain Gratz, gallantly urging his men forward against tremendous odds, fell mortally wounded, and died soon after. Lieutenant Brown, calling upon his men to 'come forward,' fell with a severe scalp wound. Captain Cole of the Missouri First had his lower jaw shattered by a bullet, but kept his place until the regiment was ordered to retire to give place to the First Iowa and some Kansas troops.

"Just then General Green's Tennessee regiment of cavalry, bearing a secession flag, charged down the western slope near the rear upon a few companies of the Kansas Second who were guarding the ambulance wagons and wounded, and had nearly overpowered them, when one of Totten's howitzers was turned in that direction, and a few rounds of canister effectually dispersed them. The roar of the distant and near artillery now grew terrific. On all sides it was one continuous boom, while the music of the musket and rifle balls flying like an aggravated swarm of bees around one's ears was actually pleasant, compared with the tremendous whiz of a cannon ball or the bursting of a shell in close proximity to one's dignity.

"Up to this time General Lyon had received two wounds, and had his fine dappled grey shot under him, which is sufficient evidence that he had sought no place of safety for himself while he placed his men in danger. Indeed he had already unwisely exposed himself. Seeing blood upon his hat, I inquired, "General, are you badly hurt?" to which he replied, "I think not seriously." He had mounted another horse, and was as busily engaged as ever.

"The Iowa First, under Lieutenant-Colonel Merritt, and part of the Kansas troops were ordered forward to take the place of the Missouris. They fought like tigers, stood firm as trees, and saved us from utter and overwhelming defeat. General Lyon saw their indomitable perseverance and bravery, and with almost his last breath praised their behavior in glowing terms. Three companies of the Iowans were placed in ambush by Captain Granger, of the regulars. Lying down close to the brow of the hill, they waited for another attempt of the enemy to retake their position. On they came, in overwhelming numbers. Not a breath was heard among the Iowas, till their enemies came within thirty-five or forty feet, when they poured the contents of their Minie muskets into the enemy, and routed them, though suffering terribly themselves at the same time. Two Kansas companies afterward did the same thing on the eastern slope, and repulsed a vigorous attack of the enemy.

"Lyon now desired the men to prepare to make a bayonet charge immediately after delivering their next fire. The Iowas at once offered to go, and asked for a leader. On came the enemy. No time could be lost to select a leader. "I will lead you,' exclaimed Lyon. "Come on, brave men." He had about placed himself in the van of the Iowas, while General Sweeney took a similar position to lead on a portion of the Kansas troop, when the enemy came only near enough to discharge their pieces, and retired before the destructive fire of our men. Before the galling fire from the enemy, the brave General Lyon fell.

"The command now devolved upon Major Sturgis. There was no certainty that Siegel had been engaged in the fight at all, as our artillery had kept up such a constant roar that guns three miles distant were but little noticed. Under these circumstances, Major Sturgis had about determined to cross his command through the valley (the recent northern camp of the enemy) eastward, and, if possible, make a junction with Siegel on or near the Fayetteville road. Before he had time to give the necessary orders, another attack from the enemy was announced by the volleys of musketry which were heard on our right. Major Sturgis directed his attention that way, and the enemy were again repulsed.

"Captain Totten then reported his cannon ammunition nearly gone. This decided the course to be pursued, and Major Sturgis at once sent the ambulances toward the city, and Lietenant DuBois' battery back to the hill at the north end of the valley, to protect the retreat. Then, in good order, the remnant of the bravest body of soldiers in the United States commenced a retreat, even while they were victorious in battle."

Siegel was experiencing the fortunes of a reverse on the East. He had advanced so rapidly as to surprise the enemy, and, by capturing his pickets, was upon them like a whirlwind. They flew before him as he pressed his way toward the Fayetteville road, which he reached, and a fine position was secured on a hill. Having heard the firing suddenly cease in the direction of Lyon's forces, he supposed the Federal attack, like his own, to have been successful; and, that Lyon's troops were pursuing the enemy, he deemed conclusive from the large bodies of the rebels moving toward the South. He stated, in his report: "This was the state of affairs at half-past eight o'clock, A. M., when it was reported that Lyon's men were coming up the road. Lieutenant Albert, of the Third, and Colonel Salomon, of the Fifth, notified their regiments not to fire on troops coming in that direction, whilst I cautioned the artillery in the same manner. Our troops, at this moment, expected with anxiety the approach of our friends, and were waving the flag raised as a signal to their comrades, when at once two batteries opened their fire against us—one in front, on the Fayetteville road, and the other upon the hill upon which we had supposed Lyon's forces were in pursuit of the enemy, whilst a strong column of infantry—supposed to be the Iowa regiment—advanced from the Fayetteville road, and attacked our right.

"It is impossible for me to describe the consternation and frightful confusion which was occasioned by this important event. The cry, 'They (Lyon's troops) are firing against us!' spread like wildfire through our ranks; the artillerymen, ordered to fire, and directed by myself, could hardly be brought forward to serve their pieces; the infantry would not load their arms until it was too late. The enemy arrived within ten paces of the muzzles of our cannon, killed the horses, turned the flanks of the infantry, and forced them to fly. The troops were throwing themselves into the bushes and by-roads, retreating as well as they could, followed and attacked incessantly by large bodies of Arkansas and Texas cavalry. In this retreat we lost five cannon (of which three were spiked,) and the colors of the Third—the color-bearer having been wounded and his substitute killed. The total loss of the two regiments, the artillery and the pioneers, in killed, wounded and missing, amounts to eight hundred and ninety-two men."

Siegel stated, as the chief cause of the repulse, that four hundred men of the three months troops, (Colonel Salomon's regiment,) whose term of enlistment had expired, were unwilling to go into the fight, and stampeded at the first opportunity. Their defection and insubordination lost all at the critical moment.

The affair was, notwithstanding these reverses, a drawn battle. The enemy, after their last repulse by Major Sturgis, retired in confusion and prepared to retreat, fearing an advance by our troops—as would have been the case had not the artillery ammunition have given out, as reported. The rebels set fire to and consumed a large train of their stores, munitions and camp equipment, fearing their capture by the Federals. This alone proves how nearly the battle was won on the right and front. Had Siegel appeared at that opportune moment the large army of the enemy (confessed to have been 23,000 strong) would have been overwhelmed with defeat by 5,500 Federal troops.

The Federal forces, under Major Sturgis, fell back, in good order, toward Springfield—the enemy not pursuing—another proof of their own repulse. After the arrival at Springfield it was determined to fall back upon Rolla, immediately, since it was evident the enemy would soon cut off retreat in that direction. Siegel took command of the general disposition for the retreat. He was called upon to exercise all his ingenuity to get out of the net now thrown around him by the strong columns of the rebels, who well knew every rood of soil in that section. Preparations were begun for the retreat on the night of the 14th. By day-break the Federal columns were on the march toward the Gasconade. A correspondent, on the evening of the 10th, wrote: "With a baggage train five miles long to protect, it will be singular indeed, if the enemy does not prove enterprising enough to cut off a portion of it, having such a heavy force of cavalry." But, the retreat was safely effected, and the vicinity of Rolla was reached Saturday, August 19th. There the three months men were disposed for disbandment, and the gallant Iowa First was sent forward immediately to St. Louis to be mustered out of service—their term having also expired.

The official reports of the Federal losses showed them to be as follows: killed, 223; wounded, 721; missing, 292. Of the latter 231 belonged to Siegel's brigade. Of the wounded 208 were of the First Missouri, 181 of the First Kansas and 138 of the First Iowa volunteers—proving how well these regiments fought.

This disaster was followed by an inroad of the enemy, as Lyon foresaw, which soon gave them possession of that portion of the State. It cost much blood and treasure, and many months of hard campaigning to dislodge them. Had Lyon been reenforced all would have been well. Even two or three fresh regiments of infantry and one of cavalry would have filled up the ranks of the retiring three months men, and have afforded forces enough to have kept the enemy at bay until Fremont could come on in force. The loss of Springfield inflicted untold suffering upon the Unionists of that section. It was a disaster for which the country did not cease to hold Fremont responsible, although the General urged the strong plea that his men were totally unfit for the field from want of arms, transportation, &c.

Price, immediately after the retreat, moved his entire forces into Springfield, from whence he issued the following proclamation to the People of Missouri:

"Fellow Citizens: The army under my command has been organized under the Laws of the State for the protection of your homes and firesides, and for the maintenance of the rights, dignity, and honor of Missouri. It is kept in the field for these purposes alone, and to aid in accomplishing them our gallant Southern brethren have come into our State.

"We have just achieved a glorious victory over the foe, and scattered far and wide the appointed army which the usurper at Washington has been more than six months gathering for your subjugation and enslavement. This victory frees a large portion of the State from the power of the invaders, and restores it to the protection of its army. It consequently becomes my duty to assure you that it is my firm determination to protect every peaceable and law abiding citizen in the full enjoyment of all his rights, whatever may have been his sympathies in the present unhappy struggle, if he has not taken an active part in the cruel warfare which has been waged against the good people of this State by the ruthless enemies whom we have just defeated. I therefore invite all good citizens to return to their homes and the practice of their ordinary avocation, with the full assurance that they, their families, their homes, and their property shall be carefully protected.

"I at the same time warn all evil-disposed persons who may support the usurpations of any one claiming to be provisional or temporary Governor of Missouri, or who shall in any other way give aid or comfort to the enemy, that they will be held as enemies and treated accordingly.

"(Signed) STERLING PRICE,
"Major General Commanding Missouri State Guard."

This had the effect to throw into his ranks a large number of those people in the south-western portion of the State who awaited the result of this conflict before determining their allegiance. It also forced acquiescence from all settlers who did not flee with the Federal army; but even that acquiescence did not protect their farms from devastation by the hordes of veritable "cut-throats" of which the invading army was largely composed. It is certain that the army brought by McCullough into Missouri was composed almost exclusively of Texan Rangers—men as wild as Indians and as ferocious as hyenas. They never, in all their service in the Confederate ranks, were brought under subjugation to discipline. The "border ruffians" who also gathered around Price were but little better. It was of such elements that the armies of Price, Van Dorn, McCullough and Rains were afterwards composed.

XXVII.

INCIDENTS OF THE WILSON'S CREEK DISASTER.

The Iowa and Kansas troops were so full of levity on their marches that Lyon rather distrusted their steadiness and courage. He had occasion, happily, before his death, to learn to admire their heroic valor. It was in heading the charge of the Iowans that he lost his life.

When General Lyon fell he was picked up by his body-servant and one of his guard, and carried lifeless toward the ambulances, in one of which his body was placed to be conveyed to Springfield. General Sweeney received a shot in his right leg, at the same fire, and limped back to the surgeon.

Siegel, before his reverse, secured about sixty prisoners and a large number of horses. These men he made useful at a critical juncture, by making them pull his only preserved cannon off the field, after all the horses were killed.

Colonel Bates of the Iowa First, who had been confined for several days with a fever and diarrhœa, mounted his horse and attempted to go to the field of battle on the evening preceding it, but was compelled to return to town much to his regret, after marching two or three miles with the column.

Of the rebel loss nothing is known with certainty, though the terrific precision of our artillery rendered it apparent that dreadful havoc followed Captain Totten's balls and shells. A correspondent wrote: "Dr. Schenck who visited McCullough and Rains after the battle, while gathering our wounded, says their loss is much heavier than ours; that while our *dead* were comparatively few, theirs were gathered in great heaps under the trees. He says that so many of their tents were destroyed by themselves, that not less than two-thirds of them would have to bivouac under trees and by camp-fires for the night."

Of the doings of a Congressman, the same writer said: "I had not proceeded far on the eastern side of the creek when I met the son of the Honorable John S. Phelps, who had left town upon hearing the cannonading, with a few mounted Kansas troops, and not discerning the exact position of the two armies, had busied himself taking prisoners on the Fayetteville road and west of it. When I met him he had captured half a dozen, including a negro belonging to an officer in a Louisiana regiment."

Another letter writer said of General Lyon's removal from the field, that his body was lifted from its ambulance to give place to the wounded—no one surmising that it was the body of their General. It was soon recovered, however, and buried near Springfield, whence it was taken by his friends, with the consent of the rebels, and conveyed, by way of St. Louis, to Connecticut for burial.

General Lyon went into the battle in civilian's dress, except a military coat. He wore a soft hat of an ashen hue, with long fur and a very broad brim, turned up on three sides. He had been wearing it for a month; there was only one like it in the command, and it would have individualized the wearer among 50,000 men. His peculiar dress and personal appearance were well known through the enemy's camps. He received a new and elegant uniform just before the battle, but never wore it until his remains were arrayed in it, after his brave spirit had fled.

The First Kansas regiment was commanded by Colonel G. W. Deitzler of Lawrence, whose horse was pierced with four balls early in the battle. Just as his horse fell the Colonel himself received a buck-shot in his thigh, inflicting an ugly wound; but he tied a handkerchief around the bleeding limb, mounted a fresh steed, and continued to direct the regiment until he was unable to sit upright.

Every company of this superb regiment was led by "representative men"—those who knew how to meet an enemy, from having already served in many a "border ruffian skrimmage." A singular instance of coolness was betrayed by company E, Captain Clayton of Leavenworth, which went into the fight seventy-three strong and came out with but twenty-six unharmed men. The company having become separated from its regiment joined what was supposed to be the First Iowa. Captain Clayton was astounded to find, however, that he had, in truth, joined the enemy, for the regiment proved to be that led by the notorious scoundrel Colonel Clarkson, of border ruffian notoriety. The rebels, in their excitement, did not discover the identity of the Federal company. Captain Clayton, with great presence of mind, did nothing to apprise his own men of their danger; but cried out: "Boys, you are crowding here; oblique to the right." They obeyed, and were forty or fifty paces away when the rebels began to be suspicious, and one of their officers rode up and asked: "What troops are you?" "First Kansas," was the Captain's prompt reply. "Who are you?" "I am the adjutant of the Missouri Fifth." "Southern troops?" "Yes, sir," replied the adjutant, putting spurs to his horse; but in an instant Captain Clayton dragged him to the ground, and, with a cocked pistol at his breast, commanded him to give up his sword. He obeyed; but, by this time, the rebel regiment had discovered "the situation," and presented their guns. Captain Clayton still held the adjutant by the collar, directly in front of his little band, where he would be the most exposed if the rebels fired, and said: "Order your regiment not to fire." The adjutant not only refused to do this, but ordered his men to "open fire," regardless of him. He was instantly bayoneted and shot fatally. Rebel though he was, he was certainly a brave fellow. The Missourians fired upon Captain Clayton's little company, now only about forty strong, bringing down about a dozen men. The Kansas boys replied with one volley, and then ran for their lives, soon reaching one of our regiments. But for the coolness of their commander they must have been captured or quite cut to pieces.

In his report, Major Sturgis said: "The great question in my mind was—where is Siegel? If I could still hope for a vigorous attack by him on the enemy's right flank and rear, then we could go forward with some hope of success. If he had retreated, then there was nothing for us but retreat. In this perplexing condition of affairs, I summoned the principal officers for consultation. The great question with most of them was:—Is retreat possible? The consultation was brought to a close by the advance of a heavy column of infantry, from the hill where Siegel's guns had before been heard. Thinking they were Siegel's men, a line was formed for an advance, with the hope of forming a junction with him. These troops wore a dress much resembling that of Siegel's brigade, and *carried the American flag.* They were, therefore, permitted to move down the hill within easy range of DuBois' battery, until they reached the covered position at the foot of the ridge on which we rested, and upon which we had before been so fiercely assailed. Suddenly a battery, planted on the hill in our front, began to pour upon us shrapnell and canister —a species of shot not before fired by the enemy. At this moment the enemy showed his true colors. At once there commenced along our entire lines the bloodiest and fiercest engagement of the day. Lieutenant DuBois' battery on our left, gallantly supported by Major Osterhaus' battalion, and the rallied fragments of the First Missouri, soon silenced the enemy's battery on the hill and repulsed the right wing of the rebel infantry. Captain Totten's battery in the centre, supported by the Iowas and the regulars, was the main point of attack. *The enemy would frequently be seen within twenty feet of Totten's guns*, and the smoke of the opposing lines was often so confounded as to seem but one. Now, for the first time during the day, our entire line maintained its position with perfect firmness. Not the slightest disposition to give way was manifested at any point. Captain Steele's battalion, which was some yards in front of the line, together with the troops on the right and left, were in imminent danger of being overwhelmed by superior numbers—*the contending parties being almost muzzle to muzzle.* Captain Granger rushed to the rear, and brought up the supports of DuBois' battery, consisting of two or three companies of the First Minnesota, three companies of the First Kansas and two companies of the First Iowa, in quick time. These fell upon the enemy's right flank, and poured into it a murderous fire, killing or wounding nearly every man within sixty or seventy yards. From this moment a perfect route took place throughout the rebel front, while ours, on the right flank, continued to pour in a galling fire into their disorganized masses."

This saved the day from proving an overwhelming disaster, and inspired the rebels with such a wholesome dread of the Unionists' ability to hold their own—that no pursuit was made when the retreat was ordered.

A dispatch to the Rebel authorities from Little Rock,

Arkansas, August 19th, confessed the losses of the Southern army to have been—killed, 265; wounded, 800; missing, 38. This was much understated. Siegel alone captured over sixty prisoners, and safely secured them. The enemy's killed was stated by deserters and other informers to have been over *five hundred.* The dispatch said: "The enemy gave a complete surprise on the morning of the 10th, commencing on Churchill's regiment, whilst at breakfast. The regiment was thrown into confusion, but our men saddled their horses and fought bravely; they had eight killed and one hundred and fifty-eight wounded. Totten's battery opened on McCullough's headquarters with six guns. The Little Rock Pulaski artillery soon returned their fire, keeping the enemy in check till our men had time to form. General Price led the Third, and part of the Fifth regiments to McCullough's aid, and saved the day. McCullough afterward said to Price, 'You have saved me and the battle.' Churchill's regiment, Gratiot's regiment, and the Texas regiment are badly cut to pieces."

XXVIII.

GENERAL LYON.

In the death of General Lyon the National cause experienced a great loss. His services already had endeared him to the people, and his future was looked forward to with confidence, by the army and by the public. The expression of regret freely uttered by the press was reechoed by the people. Up to the date of his fall, no officer of the service had perished on the field whose loss was more sincerely regretted.

Nathaniel Lyon was a native of Connecticut, and sprung from an old and honored family. He was born in the town of Ashford (now Eastford,) Windham County, in the year 1821. His grandfather, Ephraim Lyon, was an officer in the old French war, under the command of Sir William Johnson, and also an officer in the War of the Revolution. His grandfather on his mother's side, was Lieutenant Daniel Knowlton, a brother of Colonel Thomas Knowlton, who fell at White Plains, and was with him in that action, and at the battle of Bunker Hill.

The two brothers, Thomas and Daniel Knowlton, had both distinguished themselves in the war between the Colonists and English against the French, from 1755 to 1760. At the commencement of the Revolution, we find these two brothers among the first to take the field in defense of their country, and at Bunker Hill, both the historian and the artist have contributed to place the name of Colonel Knowlton among the most prominent of those whom a grateful country will ever delight to honor.

The oft recited deeds of daring and patriotism among his ancestors, thus falling upon the ears of young Lyon from a mother's lips, fired his youthful heart, and had much to do with his choice of the profession of arms. At an early age he showed great mathematical talent and a power of combination and plan in the development of schemes, which, added to an iron will and an indomitable perseverance, thus early and unmistakably marked him as one "born to command."

He entered the West Point Military Academy in 1837, graduating in 1841, with the rank of Second Lieutenant of the Second Infantry. His first service was in the Florida Everglades—then he was transferred to the frontier. On the breaking out of the Mexican war, he was detailed to General Taylor's command, but soon followed Scott—who, it will be remembered, was compelled to take from Taylor's already meagre army, enough men to open the campaign against Vera Cruz. He followed the fortunes of the General into the Capital City, serving with distinction in every engagement up to the entrance into the Grand Plaza. In February, 1847, he was made First Lieutenant, and for gallant conduct in the battles of Contreras and Cherubusco, during August following, he was breveted Captain. On September 13th, he was wounded in the assault on the Belen gate, and in June, 1851, was promoted to a Captaincy.

After the conclusion of peace with Mexico, he was ordered to Jefferson Barracks, Missouri, preparatory to a contemplated march, overland, to California. By a change of orders from the War Department, his regiment was dispatched by ship *via* Cape Horn, and reached California soon after its acquisition by the United States. His stay in California was prolonged beyond that of most of his fellow-officers, and his time unceasingly employed in operating among the Indians, subjected to long and tedious marches, constant alarms, and frequent skirmishes, living a large portion of the time in tents, and subject to the fatigues and privations incident to a campaign in that new and hitherto unknown country, so far removed from the comforts of civilization.

After being relieved from his long service in California, he was again stationed on our Western frontier, serving most of the time in Kansas and Nebraska. He consequently became familiar with the men and measures which have so agitated the country for the last few years in that section of the country, and imbibed no special love for Slavery Propagandism. From an ardent support of a Democratic Administration he passed—as so many eminent Democrats also did—into the Free State party, to become an ardent enemy of the Buchanan *regime.* One who knew him well when he was stationed at Fort Reiley said: "He possessed great moral courage. Notwithstanding his personal bravery and his military education, he was conscientiously opposed to duelling, and no provocation could ever drive him into a recognition of the code. On one occasion he was even struck on the face. Of course, it then required much more courage to refrain from challenging his adversary than to fight him; but he adhered inflexibly to his convictions. For a time this subjected him to misapprehension, and even to contempt, among military men; but, long before his death, his fellow-officers understood and respected his position upon that subject.

The "Department of the West" after the Kansas troubles, passed under command of General Harney, whose headquarters were at St. Louis. Thither Lyon was called, upon the first appearance of trouble in the political horizon. The outrages and infamous treachery toward Government committed by Floyd and his secession coadjutors, rendered it highly necessary that the St. Louis Arsenal should be intrusted to loyal hands; and Lyon was placed in charge. Its property was preserved only by his decision, and his positive stand against treason. May 10th, he suddenly sallied out, at the head of two regiments of volunteers and a detachment of regulars, to seize the "State Guard" located close to St. Louis—taking the entire crowd prisoners, with all their artillery, camp equipage, munitions, etc. It was a bold stroke, but a masterly one; for that State camp, as he well knew, was a camp of Secessionists, whose designs were inimical to the stability or security of Government property in St. Louis. Harney was soon called upon to relinquish the chief command; and Captain Lyon, then chosen by the Missouri volunteers as their commanding General, was commissioned by the President Brigadier-General of Volunteers and assigned the chief command in Missouri—a command which he retained until July 9th, when Major-General Fremont became General-in-Chief of the Department of the Mississippi.

The rest of Lyon's history is written in the chapter devoted to the campaign which resulted in the disaster at Wilson's Creek. It is a history at once pleasureable and painful to peruse — pleasurable for the brilliant achievement of the Federal troops up to their final retreat from South-western Missouri—painful, from the death of their gallant leader, and the necessity for such a retreat as followed. One who was in Missouri, and well knew the circumstances of Lyon's last desperate dash at the overflowing ranks of the rebels, thus spoke of that last act and its disastrous termination:

"Now that the smoke begins to clear away from the battle of Springfield, it is apparent that his death was worthy of his life. He attacked the enemy with a full comprehension that the odds were fearfully against him, and that little short of a miracle could enable him to come off victorious; but he felt that the Cause demanded it; that for him to abandon Springfield without a battle, would demoralize and dishearten the Union men of South-west Missouri, and pain every loyal breast in the nation. The rebels would soon cut off his communication, and surround him; the position was not susceptible of defense against their overwhelming numbers. He had no alternative but to fall back to Rolla, or to attack the enemy. He obeyed the voice of patriotism, and went out to danger and to death on that summer morning, 'as a man goes to his bridal.' Twice wounded, he was still undaunted, and refused to obey the requests of his friends, that he should seek a less exposed position. Even after he believed the day lost, he sprang eagerly from his dead horse into a fresh saddle; at the head of a forlorn hope, dashed into the thick of the fight, and died like a true soldier. May his memory long be green in the nation's heart, and his name high in the roll of honor, among

"'The brave, who sink to rest,
By all their country's wishes blest!'"

After the battle, Lyon's body was borne back to Springfield, and thence taken to the farm of Hon. John S. Phelps, near at hand. There it was placed—by Lyon's brigade surgeon, Dr. Franklin, and by Mrs. Phelps—in a coffin, sealed, and temporarily deposited in a pit, preparatory to its removal to Rolla. But, the retreat was so rapid, and the necessities of the wounded so absorbing, that the body of the General was left for after-removal. Mrs. Phelps had it carefully buried—her husband having had to flee with the retreating Unionists. It was recovered on Friday, August 23d, by a party who obtained it under the protection of a flag of truce—General Price kindly affording every facility for the disinterment.

It was borne to Connecticut for interment, accompanied by a guard of honor, composed of several of his fellow-officers and a detachment of the St. Louis Home Guards. Everywhere on the route, where the remains tarried, they were received with civic and military honors. In New York City they lay in state for a few hours. At Eastford, his native village, they were buried, with all the honor which admiring and sympathetic friends could bestow—the Hon. Galusha A. Grow pronouncing the funeral oration. Resolutions were adopted at a large meeting of the citizens of Eastford, expressive of their consideration for the virtues and character of the deceased. We may quote one of several of the resolves adopted:

"*Resolved*, That as his fellow-townsmen, while we mourn our loss, we rejoice that we have his birth-spot among us to cheer us in steadfast devotion to our country; and we trust his grave among us will be the spot where future generations will gather, and be inspired with a noble emulation of his and the virtues of Sherman, Trumbull, Putnam, and others, who have arisen in this State, defenders of their country's flag, and supporters of its Government."

XXIX.

THE SECOND DISASTER IN MISSOURI. THE SIEGE AND FALL OF LEXINGTON.

THE seventy-two hours defense of Lexington, by twenty-seven hundred and eighty troops under command of Colonel William Mulligan, was one of the most gallant affairs of the War. Learning that Price was pushing up in strong force toward Lexington, Colonel Mulligan started, September 1st, with his Irish (Chicago) brigade, from his camp near Jefferson city—determined to hold Lexington at all hazards. If Lexington was lost it would give the rebels command of the Missouri, cutting off communication with the army in Kansas and threatening Jefferson city. As foreseen by Lyon, the rebels had, after their victory near Springfield, overrun the entire western section of the State, and so rapid were their advance toward the North and East that by September 1st the line of

Missouri river was threatened by them. Fremont ordered Mulligan forward to Lexington. Colonel Marshall's cavalry (Illinois) was to join him, with Colonel White's Home Guards, while Colonel Peabody (Thirteenth Missouri) was to fall back upon Lexington from Warrensburg if pressed by the enemy. In the meantime, General Sturgis was to move down from Kansas city with his entire disposable force (1,500) to the re-enforcement of Lexington, while General Lane was to press forward from Harrisonville and assail Price from that direction. These movements, it was thought by Fremont, would so employ the enemy as to keep him at bay until he (Fremont) could come forward with his own forces from St. Louis and vicinity.

Mulligan did his part. By a forced march of ten days his troops reached Lexington, having foraged by the way for rations. At Lexington he found Colonel Marshall with his cavalry and Colonel White's Home Guards—each command about five hundred strong. Colonel Peabody soon came in, pressed back by the enemy advancing upon Lexington from Warrensburg. The Federal troops had not long to wait, for, on the afternoon of September 11th, the rebels under Price in person appeared off the town. From Colonel Mulligan's own account of the affair,* we may quote :

"On the 10th of September, a letter arrived from Colonel Peabody, saying that he was retreating from Warrensburg, twenty-five miles distant, and that Price was pursuing him with ten thousand men. A few hours afterward, Colonel Peabody, with the Thirteenth Missouri, entered Lexington. We then had two thousand seven hundred and eighty men in garrison and forty rounds of cartridges. At noon of the 11th we commenced throwing up our first intrenchments. In six hours afterwards, the enemy opened their fire. Colonel Peabody was ordered out to meet them. The camp then presented a lively scene; officers were hurrying hither and thither, drawing the troops in line and giving orders, and the Commander was riding with his staff to the bridge to encourage his men and to plant his artillery. Two six-pounders were planted to oppose the enemy, and placed in charge of Captain Dan. Quirk, who remained at his post till day-break. It was a night of fear-

* From his Detroit speech, November 29th.

ful anxiety. None knew at what moment the enemy would be upon the little band, and the hours passed in silence and anxious waiting. So it continued until morning, when the Chaplain rushed into head-quarters, saying that the enemy were pushing forward. Two companies of the Missouri Thirteenth were ordered out, and the Colonel, with the aid of his glass, saw General Price urging his men to the fight. They were met by Company K, of the Irish brigade, under Captain Quirk, who held them in check until Captain Dillon's company, of the Missouri Thirteenth, drove them back, and burned the bridge. That closed our work before breakfast. Immediately six companies of the Missouri Thirteenth and two companies of Illinois cavalry were despatched in search of the retreating enemy. They engaged them in a cornfield, fought with them gallantly, and harassed them to such an extent as to delay their progress, in order to give time for constructing intrenchments around the camp on College Hill. This had the desired effect, and we succeeded in throwing up earthworks three or four feet in height. This consumed the night, and was continued during the next day, the out-posts still opposing the enemy, and keeping them back as far as possible. At three o'clock in the afternoon of the 12th, the engagement opened with artillery. A volley of grapeshot was thrown among the officers, who stood in front of the breastworks. The guns within the intrench-ments immediately replied with a vigor which converted the scene into one of the wildest description. The gunners were inexperienced, and the firing was bad. We had five six-pounders, and the musketry was firing at every angle. Those who were not shooting at the moon were shooting above it. The men were ordered to cease firing, and they were arranged in ranks, kneeling, the front rank shooting and the others loading. The artillery was served with more care, and within an hour a shot from one of our guns dismounted their largest piece, a twelve-pounder, and exploded a powder caisson. This achievement was re-ceived with shouts of exultation by the beleaguered garrison. The enemy retired a distance of three miles. At seven o'clock the engage-ment had ceased, and Lexington was ours again. Next morning Gene-ral Parsons, with ten thousand men at his back, sent in a flag of truce to a little garrison of two thousand seven hundred men, asking permis-sion to enter the town and bury his dead, claiming that when the noble Lyon went down, his corpse had fallen into his hands, and he had granted every privilege to the Federal officers sent after it. It was not necessary to adduce this as a reason why he should be permitted to perform an act which humanity would dictate. The request was wil-lingly granted, and we cheerfully assisted in burying the fallen foe. On Friday the work of throwing up intrenchments went on. It rained all day, and the men stood knee deep in the mud, building them. Troops were sent out for forage, and returned with large quantities of provisions and fodder. On Friday, Saturday and Sunday, we stole seven days' provisions for two thousand seven hundred men. We had found no provisions at Lexington, and were compelled to get our rations as best we could. A quantity of powder was obtained, and then large cisterns were filled with water. The men made cartridges in the cellar of the college building, and cast one hundred and fifty rounds of shot for the guns, at the foundries of Lexington. During the little respite the evening gave us, we cast our shot, made our cartridges, and stole our own provisions. We had stacks of forage, plenty of hams, bacon, &c., and felt that good times were in store for us. All this time, our pickets were constantly engaged with the enemy, and we were well aware that ten thousand men were threatening us, and knew that the struggle was to be a desperate one. Earthworks had been raised breast-high, enclosing an area of fifteen to eighteen acres, and surrounded by a ditch. Outside of this was a circle of twenty-one mines, and still further down were pits to embarrass the progress of the enemy. During the night of the 17th, we were getting ready for the defense, and heard the sounds of preparation in the camp of the enemy for the attack on the morrow. Father Butler went around among the men and blessed them, and they reverently uncovered their heads and received his benediction. At nine o'clock on the morning of the 18th, the drums beat to arms, and the terrible struggle commenced. The enemy's force had been increased to twenty-eight thousand men and thirteen pieces of artillery, They came as one dark moving mass; men armed to the teeth as far as the eye could reach--men, men, men, were visible. They planted two batteries in front, one on the left, one on the right, and one in the rear, and opened with a terrible fire, which was answered with the utmost bravery and determination. Our spies had informed us that the rebels intended to make one grand rout, and bury us in the trenches of Lexington. The batteries opened at nine o'clock, and for three days they never ceased to pour deadly shot upon us. About noon the hospital was taken. It was situated on the left, outside of the intrenchments. I had taken for granted, never thought it necessary to build fortifications around the sick man's couch. I had thought that, among civilized nations, the soldier sickened and wounded in the service of his country, would, at least, be sacred. But I was inexperienced, and had yet to learn that such was not the case with the rebels. They besieged the hospital, took it, and from the balcony and roof their sharpshooters poured a deadly fire within our intrenchments. It contained our chaplain and surgeon, and one hundred and twenty wounded men. It could not be allowed to remain in the possession of the enemy. A company of the Missouri Thirteenth was ordered forward to retake the hospital. They started on their errand, but stopped at the breast-works, 'going not out because it was bad to go out.' A company of the Missouri Fourteenth was sent forward, but it also shrank from the task, and refused to move outside the intrenchments. The Montgomery Guard, Captain Gleason, of the Irish brigade, were then brought out. The commander admonished them that the others had failed; and with a brief exhortation to uphold the name they bore, gave the word to 'charge.' The distance was eight hundred yards. They started out from the intrenchment, first quick, then double-quick, then on a run, then faster. The enemy poured a deadly shower of bullets upon them, but on they went, a wild line of steel, and what is better than steel, human will. They stormed up the slope to the hospital door, and with irresistible bravery drove the enemy before them, and hurled them far down the hill beyond. At the head of those brave fellows, pale as marble, but not pale from fear, stood the gallant officer, Captain Gleason. He said, 'Come on, my brave boys,' and in they rushed. But when their brave captain returned, it was with a shot through the cheek and another through the arm, and with but fifty of the eighty he had led forth. The hospital was in their possession. This charge was one of the most brilliant and reckless in all history, and to Captain Gleason belongs the glory. Each side felt, after this charge, that a clever thing had been done, and the fire of the enemy lagged. We were in a terrible situation. Towards night the fire increased, and in the evening word came from the rebels that if the garrison did not surrender before the next day, they would hoist the back flag at their cannon and give us no quarter. Word was sent back that 'when we asked for quarter it would be time to settle that.' It was a terrible thing to see those brave fellows mangled, and with no skillful hands to bind their gaping wounds. Our surgeon was held with the enemy, against all rules of war, and that, too, when we had released a surgeon of theirs on his mere pledge that he was such. Captain Moriarty went into the hospital, and, with nothing but a razor, acted the part of a surgeon. We could not be without a chaplain or surgeon any longer. There was in our ranks a Lieutenant Hickey, a rollicking, jolly fellow, who was despatched from the hospital with orders to procure the surgeon and chaplain at all hazards. Forty minutes later and the brave Lieutenant was borne by, severely wounded. As he was borne past I heard him exclaim, 'God have mercy on my little ones!' And God did hear his prayers, for the gay Lieutenant is up, as rollicking as ever, and is now forming his brigade to return to the field. On the morning of the 19th the firing was resumed and continued all day. We recovered our surgeon and chaplain. The day was signalized by a fierce bayonet charge upon a regiment of the enemy, which served to show them that our men were not yet completely worried out. The officers had told them to hold out until the 19th, when they would certainly be reenforced. Through that day our little garrison stood with straining eyes, watching to see if some friendly flag was bearing aid to them—with straining ear, awaiting the sound of a friendly cannonade. But no reenforcements appeared, and, with the energy of despair, they determined to do their duty at all hazard. The 19th was a horrid day. Our water cisterns had been drained, and we dared not leave the crown of the hill, and make our intrenchments on the bank of the river, for the enemy could have planted his cannon on the hill and buried us. The day was burning hot, and the men bit their cartridges; their lips were parched and blistered. But not a word of murmuring. The night of the 19th two wells were ordered to be dug. We took a ravine, and expected to reach water in about thirty hours. During the night, I passed around the field, smoothed back the clotted hair, and by the light of the moon, shining through the trees, recognized here and there the countenances of my brave men who had fallen. Some were my favorites in days gone past, who had stood by me in these hours of terror, and had fallen on the hard fought field. Sadly we buried them in the trenches. The morning of the 20th broke, but no reenforcements appeared, and still the men fought on. The rebels had constructed movable breastworks of hemp bales, rolled them up the hill, and advanced their batteries in a manner to command the fortification. Heated shot were fired at them, but they had taken the precaution to soak the bales in the Missouri. The attack was urged with renewed vigor, and, during the forenoon, the outer breastworks were taken by a charge of the rebels in force. The whole line was broken, and the enemy rushed in upon us. Captain Fitzgerald, whom I had known in my younger days, and whom we had been accustomed to call by the familiar nickname, 'Saxy,' was then ordered to oppose his company to the assailants. As I gave the order, 'Saxy, go in,' the gallant Fitzgerald, at the head of company I, with a wild yell rushed in upon the enemy. The Commander sent for a company on which he could rely; the firing suddenly ceased, and when the smoke rose from the field, I observed the Michigan company, under their gallant young commander, Captain Patrick McDermott, charging the enemy and driving them back. Many of our good fellows were lying dead, our cartridges had failed, and it was evident that the fight would soon cease. It was now three o'clock, and all on a sudden an orderly came, saying that the enemy had sent a flag of truce. With the flag came the following note from General Price:

"'Colonel—What has caused the cessation of the fight?'

"The Colonel returned it with the following reply written on the back:—

"'General—I hardly know, unless you have surrendered.'

"He took pains to assure me, however, that such was not the case. I learned soon after that the Home Guard had hoisted the white flag. The Lieutenant who had thus hoisted the flag was threatened with instant death unless he pulled it down. The men all said, 'we have no cartridges, and a vast horde of the enemy is about us.' They were told to go to the line and stand there, and use the charge at the muzzle of their guns or perish there. They grasped their weapons the fiercer, turned calmly about, and stood firmly at their posts. And there they stood without a murmur, praying as they never prayed before, that the rebel horde would show themselves at the earthworks. An officer remarked, 'this is butchery.' The conviction became general, and a council of war was held. And when, finally, the white flag was raised, Adjutant Cosgrove, of your city, shed bitter tears. The place was given up, upon what conditions, to this day I hardly know or care. The enemy came pouring in. One foppish officer, dressed in the gaudiest uniform of his rank, strutted up and down through the camp, stopped before our men, took out a pair of handcuffs, and holding them up, said, 'Do you know what these are for?' We were placed in file, and a figure on horseback, looking much like 'Death on the pale horse,' led us through the streets of Lexington. As we passed, the secession ladies of Lexington came from their houses, and from the fence tops jeered at us. We were then taken to a hotel with no rations and no proprietor. After we had boarded there for some time, we started with General Price, on the morning of the 30th, for 'the land of Dixie.'"

This disaster intensely excited the country against the commanding General of the West. It was pronounced a "reckless sacrifice of men," a "piece of bad generalship," a "reckless disregard of circumstances;" the loss of Lyon and the retreat of his forces were recalled with much bitterness; and the call became loud for Fremont's supercedure. But, it is certain that Fremont was unable to cope with all the embarrassing circumstances by which he was surrounded. He assumed command of the Department at a date when all other campaigns were already organized and in motion. He found few men, few arms, but little artillery, no transports awaiting him —all had to be created. The enemy, in the meanwhile, was in the field—armed and ready for an immediate attempt to "drive the invaders and the hireling Dutch beyond the Mississippi." He fell upon Lyon and Siegel in overwhelming force, and pressed the Federal lines back until Lexington was open before him. That Fremont, during all this advance, was alive to the peril, his almost reckless exertions to obtain arms, horses, artillery and transports, all attest; and, if he did not succeed in keeping Price out of Lexington, it is certain that he came so near accomplishing the circumvention and capture of the combined rebel forces, that the country has not hesitated to exonerate him from much, if not all, the blame at one time heaped upon him.* His suspension from command at the very moment when he was about to meet his foe, and to realize the fruits of his unquestionably well-laid schemes, was one of those military errors which seem inseparable from every great war.

XXX

THE CHARGE OF THE THREE HUNDRED.

THE charge of Fremont's "Body Guard" under Major Zagonyi, and the "Prairie Scouts" of Major Frank Ward into Springfield, is conceded to have been one of the most brilliant feats of arms of modern warfare.

* The defense of Fremont made by the Hon. Schuyler Colfax, through the columns of the South Bend (Indiana) *Register*, silenced cavil and excited sympathy for him even among those whose censures had been most severe. It was shown that, as rapidly as Fremont would fit his men for the field they were taken from him and sent to swell the ranks of the army of the Potomac—where the peril was regarded as more imminent than in Missouri. Five thousand men ready to support Mulligan were, at the very moment of their departure, counter-ordered to the East.

An interesting series of papers on "Fremont's Hundred Days in Missouri," will be found in the *Atlantic Monthly* for January, February and March, 1862.

Charles Zagonyi was a Hungarian refugee who, like so many of his countrymen, had fled to this country after the suppression of the revolution in his native country by the iron hand of the Russian Czar. His daring character brought the young officer to the notice of the invincible General Bem, by whom he was placed in command of a troop of picked cavalry for extraordinary service. His story, after that hour, up to the date of his capture by the enemy, was one of unparalleled daring. His last act was to charge upon a heavy artillery force. Over one half of his men were killed and the rest made prisoners, but not until after the enemy had suffered terribly. He was then confined in an Austrian dungeon, and finally released, at the end of two years, to go into exile in America.

Fremont drew around him a large number of these refugees from European tyranny, and found in them men of great value, in all departments of the service. Zagonyi enlisted three hundred carefully chosen men who, as a "Body Guard," served as pioneers and scouts in Fremont's advance. The exploit at Springfield was only one of many similar services for which they were designated by Fremont; but, the suspension of his command in Missouri broke up the Guard and Zagonyi withdrew from the service until his leader should again be given a command.

The Guard was mounted, and was armed with German sabers and revolvers—the first company only having carbines. The horses were all bay in color, and were chosen with special reference to speed and endurance.

The expedition to Springfield was planned, as it afterwards appeared, upon false information. Instead of Springfield being held by a small force, it was in possession of twelve hundred infantry and four hundred cavalry. Major Frank White had been ordered by General Siegel to make a reconnoissance toward Springfield — the Union army then being at Camp Haskell, south of the Pomme de Terre River, thirty-four miles from Warsaw and fifty-one from Springfield. The Major had just come in with his dashing "Prairie Scouts," one hundred and fifty-four strong, from their gallant dash into Lexington; and the order to strike out for the reconnoissance found them jaded from over service. The Major, however, put out, and was far on his way when, on the 24th (of October) he was joined by Zagonyi, who assumed command of the expedition, by order of Fremont. Zagonyi had with him one half of his Guard, provided with only one ration. The march to Springfield was to be forced, in order that the enemy should be surprised and the place secured before rebel reenforcements could reach it. The combined Scouts and Guard marched all Thursday (October 24th) night; briefly rested Friday morning, then pushed on and were before Springfield at three P. M. on the 25th—the fifty-one miles having been accomplished in eighteen hours.

Eight miles from Springfield five mounted rebels were caught; a sixth escaped and gave the alarm to the forces in the town, whose strength, Zagonyi learned from a Union farmer, was fully two thousand strong. Nothing was left but a retreat or bold dash. Zagonyi did not hesitate. His men responded to his own spirit fully, and were eager for the adventure, let it result as it would. Major White was so ill from over work that, at Zagonyi's entreaty, he remained at a farm-house for a brief rest. The Union farmer offered to pilot the Body Guard around to the Mount Vernon approach on the West—thus hoping to effect a surprise in that direction, as the enemy was, doubtless, aligned to receive the assault on the Bolivar road, on the North. Of this detour White knew nothing, and after his rest he pushed on with his guard of five men and a Lieutenant, to overtake his troops. He travelled up to the very outskirts of the town, and yet did not come up to his men. Supposing them in possession of the place, he kept on and soon found himself in a rebel camp—a prisoner. He was immediately surrounded by a crew of savages, who at once resolved to have his life. Captain Wroton, a rebel officer, only saved the Federal officer and his men from murder by swearing to protect them with his life. The blood-thirsty wretches were only kept at bay by the constant presence of Wroton.

We may quote the particulars of the charge as given by Major Dorsheimer in his most admirable papers on Fremont's Campaign, before referred to, in the *Atlantic Monthly:*

The foe were advised of the intended attack. When Major Wright was brought into their camp, they were preparing to defend their position. As appears from the confession of prisoners, they had twenty-two hundred men, of whom four hundred were cavalry, the rest being infantry, armed with shot guns, American rifles, and revolvers. Twelve hundred of their foot were posted along the edge of the wood upon the crest of the hill. The cavalry was stationed upon the extreme left, on top of a spur of the hill, and in front of a patch of timber. Sharp-shooters were concealed behind the trees close to the fence along-side the lane, and a small number in some underbrush near the foot of the hill. Another detachment guarded their train, holding possession of the county fair-ground, which was surrounded by a high board-fence.

This position was unassailable by cavalry from the road, the only point of attack being down the lane on the right; and the enemy were so disposed as to command this approach perfectly. The lane was a blind one, being closed, after passing the brook, by fences and ploughed land: it was in fact a *cul-de-sac*. If the infantry should stand, nothing could save the rash assailants. There are horsemen sufficient to sweep the little band before them, as helplessly as the withered forest-leaves in the grasp of the autumn winds; there are deadly marksmen lying behind the trees upon the heights and lurking in the long grass upon the lowlands; while a long line of foot stand upon the summit of the slope, who, only stepping a few paces back into the forest, may defy the boldest riders. Yet, down this narrow lane, leading into the very jaws of death, came the three hundred.

On the prairie, at the edge of the woodland in which he knew his wily foe lay hidden, Zagonyi halted his command. He spurred along the line. With eager glance he scanned each horse and rider. To his officers he gave the simple order, "Follow me! do as I do!" and then, drawing up in front of his men, with a voice tremulous and shrill with emotion, he spoke—

"Fellow-soldiers, comrades, brothers! This is your first battle. For our three hundred, the enemy are two thousand. If any of you are sick, or tired by the long march, or if any think the number is too great, now is the time to turn back." He paused—no one was sick or tired. "We must not retreat. Our honor, the honor of our General and our country, tell us to go on. I will lead you. We have been called holiday soldiers for the pavements of St. Louis; to-day we will show that we are soldiers for the battle. Your watchword shall be—'*The Union and Fremont!*' Draw saber! By the right flank—quick trot—march!'

Bright swords flashed in the sunshine, a passionate shout burst from every lip, and with one accord, the trot passing into a gallop, the compact column swept on in its deadly purpose. Most of them were boys. A few weeks before they had left their homes. Those who were cool enough to note it say that ruddy cheeks grew pale, and fiery eyes were dimmed with tears. Who shall tell what thoughts, what visions of peaceful cottages nestling among the groves of Kentucky, or shining upon the banks of the Ohio and the Illinois—what sad recollections of tearful farewells, of tender, loving faces, filled their minds during those fearful moments of suspense? No word was spoken. With lips compressed, firmly clenching their sword-hilts, with quick tramp of hoofs and clang of steel, honor leading and glory awaiting them, the young soldiers flew forward, each brave rider and each straining steed members of one huge creature, enormous, terrible, irresistible.

"'T were worth ten years of peaceful life,
One glance at their array."

They pass the fair-ground. They are at the corner of the lane where the wood begins. It runs close to the fence on their left for a hundred yards, and beyond it they see white tents gleaming. They are half-way past the forest, when, sharp and loud, a volley of musketry bursts upon the head of the column; horses stagger, riders reel and fall, but the troop presses forward undismayed. The farther corner of the wood is reached, and Zagonyi beholds the terrible array. Amazed, he involuntarily checks his horse. The Rebels are not surprised. There to his left they stand crowning the height, foot and horse ready to engulph him, if he shall be rash enough to go on. The road he is following declines rapidly. There is but one thing to do—run the gauntlet, gain the cover of the hill, and charge up the steep. These thoughts pass quicker than they can be told. He waves his saber over his head, and shouting, "Forward! follow me! quick trot! gallop!" he dashes headlong down the stony road. The first company, and most of the second follow. From the left a thousand muzzles belch forth a hissing flood of bullets; the poor fellows clutch wildly at the air and fall from their saddles, and maddened horses throw themselves against the fences. Their speed is not for an instant checked; farther down the hill they fly, like wasps driven by the leaden storm. Sharp volleys pour out of the underbrush at the left, clearing wide gaps through their ranks. They leap the brook, take down the fence, and draw up under shelter of the hill. Zagonyi looks around him, and to his horror sees that only a fourth of his men are with him. He cries, "They do not come—we are lost!" and frantically waves his saber.

He has not long to wait. The delay of the rest of the Guard was not from hesitation. When Captain Foley reached the lower corner of the wood and saw the enemy's line, he thought a flank attack might be advantageously made. He ordered some men to dismount and take down the fence. This was done under a severe fire. Several men fell, and he found the wood so dense that it could not be penetrated. Looking down the hill, he saw the flash of Zagonyi's saber, and at once gave the order, "Forward!" At the same time, Lieutenant Kennedy, a stalwart Kentuckian, shouted, "Come on, boys! remember Old Kentucky!" and the third company of the Guard, fire on every side of them—from behind trees, from under the fences—with thundering strides and loud cheers, poured down the slope and rushed to the side of Zagonyi. They have lost seventy dead and wounded men, and the carcasses of horses are strewn along the lane. Kennedy is wounded in the arm, and lies upon the stones, his faithful charger standing motionless beside him. Lieutenant Goff received a wound in the thigh; he kept his seat, and cried out, "The devils have hit me, but I will give it to them yet!"

The remnant of the Guard are now in the field under the hill, and from the shape of the ground the Rebel fire sweeps with the roar of a whirlwind over their heads. Here we will leave them for a moment, and trace the fortunes of the Prairie Scouts.

When Foley brought his troop to a halt, Captain Fairbanks, at the head of the first company of Scouts, was at the point where the first volley of musketry had been received. The narrow lane was crowded by a dense mass of struggling horses, and filled with the tumult of battle. Captain Fairbanks says, and he is corroborated by several of his men who were near, that at this moment an officer of the Guard rode up to him and said, "They are flying; take your men down that lane and cut off their retreat" pointing to the lane at the left. Captain Fairbanks was not able to identify the person who gave this order. It certainly did not come from Zagonyi, who was several hundred yards farther on. Captain Fairbanks executed the order, followed by the second company of Prairie Scouts, under Captain Kehoe. When this movement was made, Captain Naughton, with the Third Irish dragoons, had not reached the corner of the lane. He came up at a gallop, and was about to follow Fairbanks, when he saw a Guardsman who pointed in the direction in which Zagonyi had gone. He took this for an order, and obeyed it. When he reached the gap in the fence, made by Foley, not seeing anything of the Guard, he supposed they had passed through at that place, and gallantly attempted to follow. Thirteen men fell in a few minutes. He was shot in the arm and dismounted. Lieutenant

Connolly spurred into the underbrush and received two balls through the lungs and one in the left shoulder. The dragoons, at the outset not more than fifty strong, were broken, and, dispirited by the loss of their officers, retired. A sergeant rallied a few and brought them up to the gap again, and they were again driven back. Five of the boldest passed down the hill, joined Zagonyi, and were conspicuous for their valor during the rest of the day. Fairbanks and Kehoe, having gained the rear and left of the enemy's position, made two or three assaults upon detached parties of the foe, but did not join in the main attack.

I now return to the Guard. It is forming under the shelter of the hill. In front, with a gentle inclination, rises a grassy slope broken by occasional tree-stumps. A line of fire upon the summit marks the position of the rebel infantry, and nearer and on the top of a lower eminence to the right stand their horse. Up to this time no Guardsman has struck a blow, but blue coats and bay horses lie thick along the bloody lane. Their time has come. Lieutenant Maythenyi with thirty men is ordered to attack the cavalry. With sabres flashing over their heads, the little band of heroes spring towards their tremendous foe. Right upon the centre they charge. The dense mass opens, the blue coats force their way in, and the whole rebel squadron scatter in disgraceful flight through the corn-fields in the rear. The bays follow them sabring the fugitives. Days after, the enemy's horses lay thick among the uncut corn.

Zagonyi holds his main body until Maythenyi disappears in the cloud of rebel cavalry; then his voice rises through the air: "In open order—charge!" The line opens out to give play to their sword-arm. Steeds respond to the ardor of their riders, and quick as thought, with thrilling cheers, the noble hearts rush into the leaden torrent which pours down the incline. With unabated fire the gallant fellows press through. Their fierce onset is not even checked. The foe do not wait for them—they waver, break and fly. The Guardsmen spur into the midst of the rout, and their fast-falling swords work a terrible revenge. Some of the boldest of the Southrons retreat into the woods, and continue a murderous fire from behind trees and thickets. Seven Guard horses fall upon a space not more than twenty feet square. As his steed sinks under him, one of the officers is caught around the shoulders by a grape-vine, and hangs dangling in the air until he is cut down by his friends.

The rebel foot are flying in furious haste from the field. Some take refuge in the fair-ground, some hurry into the corn-fields, but the greater part run along the edge of the wood, swarm over the fence into the road, and hasten to the village. The Guardsmen follow. Zagonyi leads them. Over the loudest roar of battle rings his clarion voice—

"Come on, Old Kentuck! I'm with you!" And the flash of his sword-blade tells his men where to go. As he approaches a barn, a man steps from behind the door and lowers his rifle; but before it has reached a level, Zagonyi's sabre-point descends upon his head, and his life-blood leaps to the very top of the huge barn-door.

The conflict now raged through the village—in the public square, and along the streets. Up and down the Guards ride in squads of three or four, and wherever they see a group of the enemy, charge upon and scatter them. It is hand to hand. No one but has a share in the fray.

There was at least one soldier in the Southern ranks. A young officer, superbly mounted, charges alone upon a large body of the Guard. He passes through the line unscathed, killing one man. He wheels, charges back, and again breaks through, killing another man. A third time he rushes upon the Federal line, a score of sabre-points confront him, a cloud of bullets fly around him, but he pushes on until he reaches Zagonyi—he presses his pistol so close to the Major's side, that he feels it and draws convulsively back, the bullet passes through the front of Zagonyi's coat, who at the instant runs the daring rebel through the body; he falls, and the men, thinking their commander hurt, kill him with a dozen wounds.

"He was a brave man," said Zagonyi afterwards, "and I did wish to make him prisoner."

Meanwhile it has grown dark. The foe have left the village and the battle has ceased. The assembly is sounded, and the Guard gathers in the *Plaza*. Not more than eighty mounted men appear: the rest are killed, wounded, or unhorsed. At this time one of the most characteristic incidents of the affair took place.

Just before the charge, Zagonyi directed one of his buglers, a Frenchman, to sound a signal. The bugler did not seem to pay any attention to the order, but darted off with Lieutenant Maythenyi. A few moments afterwards he was observed in another part of the field vigorously pursuing the flying infantry. His active form was always seen in the thickest of the fight. When the line was formed in the *Plaza*, Zagonyi noticed the bugler, and approaching him said: "In the midst of battle you disobeyed my order. You are unworthy to be a member of the Guard. I dismiss you." The bugler showed his bugle to his indignant commander—the mouth-piece of the instrument was shot away. He said: "The mouth was shoot off. I could not bugle viz mon bugle, and so I bugle viz mon pistol and sabre." It is unnecessary to add, the brave Frenchman was not dismissed.

I must not forget to mention Sergeant Hunter, of the Kentucky company. His soldierly figure never failed to attract the eye in the ranks of the Guard. He had served in the regular cavalry, and the Body-

Guard had profited greatly from his skill as a drill-master. He lost three horses in the fight. As soon as one was killed, he caught another from the rebels: the third horse taken by him in this way he rode into St. Louis.

The Sergeant slew five men. "I won't speak of those I shot," said he—"another may have hit them; but those I touched with my sabre I am sure of, because I felt them."

At the beginning of the charge, he came to the extreme right and took position next to Zagonyi, whom he followed closely through the battle. The Major, seeing him, said :

"Why are you here, Sergeant Hunter? Your place is with your company on the left." "I kind o'wanted to be in the front," was the answer.

"What could I say to such a man?" exclaimed Zagonyi, speaking of the matter afterwards.

There was hardly a horse or rider among the survivors that did not bring away some mark of the fray. I saw one animal with no less than seven wounds—none of them serious. Scabbards were bent, clothes and caps pierced, pistols injured. I saw one pistol from which the sight had been cut as neatly as it could have been done by machinery. A piece of board a few inches long was cut from a fence on the field, in which there were thirty-one shot-holes.

It was now nine o'clock. The wounded had been carried to the hospital. The dismounted troopers were placed in charge of them—in the double capacity of nurses and guards. Zagonyi expected the foe to return every minute. It seemed like madness to try and hold the town with his small force, exhausted by the long march and desperate fight. He therefore left Springfield, and retired before morning twenty-five miles on the Bolivar road.

Captain Fairbanks did not see his commander after leaving the column in the lane, at the commencement of the engagement. About dusk he repaired to the prairie, and remained there within a mile of the village until midnight, when he followed Zagonyi, rejoining him in the morning.

I will now return to Major White. During the conflict upon the hill, he was in the forest near the front of the rebel line. Here his horse was shot under him. Captain Wroton kept careful watch over him. When the flight began he hurried White away, and, accompanied by a squad of eleven men, took him ten miles into the country. They stopped at a farm-house for the night. White discovered that their host was a Union man. His parole having expired, he took advantage of the momentary absence of his captor to speak to the farmer, telling him who he was, and asking him to send for assistance. The countryman mounted his son upon his swiftest horse, and sent him for succor. The party lay down by the fire, White being placed in the midst. The rebels were soon asleep, but there was no sleep for the Major. He listened anxiously for the footsteps of his rescuers. After long weary hours, he heard the tramp of horses. He arose, and walking on tiptoe, cautiously stepping over his sleeping guard, he reached the door and silently unfastened it. The Union men rushed into the room and took the astonished Wroton and his followers prisoners. At daybreak White rode into Springfield at the head of his captives and a motley band of Home Guard. He found the Federals still in possession of the place. As the officer of highest rank, he took command. His garrison consisted of twenty-four men. He stationed twenty-two of them as pickets in the outskirts of the village, and held the other two as a *reserve.* At noon the enemy sent a flag of truce, and asked permission to bury their dead. Major White received the flag with proper ceremony, but said that General Siegel was in command and the request would have to be referred to him. Siegel was then forty miles away. In a short time a written communication purporting to come from General Siegel, saying that the rebels might send a party under certain restrictions to bury their dead: White drew in some of his pickets, stationed them about the field, and under their surveillance the Southern dead were buried.

The loss of the enemy, as reported by some of their working party, was one hundred and sixteen killed. The number of wounded could not be ascertained. After the conflict had drifted away from the hill-side, some of the foe had returned to the field, taken away their wounded, and robbed our dead. The loss of the Guard was fifty-three out of one hundred and forty-eight actually engaged, twelve men having been left by Zagonyi in charge of his train. The Prairie Scouts reported a loss of thirty one out of one hundred and thirty: half of these belonged to the Irish Dragoons. In a neighboring field an Irishman was found stark and stiff, still clinging to the hilt of his sword, which was thrust through the body of a rebel who lay beside him. Within a few feet a second rebel lay, shot through the head.

This was the first and the last exploit of the Guard. They returned, soon after, to St. Louis, along with Fremont. Their rations and forage were denied them and they were disbanded —ashamed of their soiled and ragged garments, and humiliated at their usage. Such are the fortunes of those at the mercy of opposing factions of the same service.

XXXI.

BOMBARDMENT OF THE PORT ROYAL FORTS.

SEVENTY vessels sailed and steamed out of Hampton Roads, on the morning of Tuesday, October 29th, stretching out to sea, then heading for the South. It was a fleet of conquest, bearing one of the most superb armaments that ever floated in American waters. Frigates, sloops-of-war, and gunboats were mixed in with stately ocean steamers; while these had in tow nemerous small craft—all loaded to their fullest capacity with war *materiel.* Their destination was a mystery, even to those on board, except to those in whose hands the direction of that vast expedition was entrusted. The country speculated in vain as to whither it would move—Charleston, Savannah, New Orleans, Beaufort (S.C.,) Bull's Bay—all being named as probable points of attack. This suspense was not cleared up until November 10th, when it became known, through rebel sources, that the Port Royal forts were ours.

The particulars of the bombardment of these forts are very interesting. It was one of the most imposing spectacles of the war—not so sublimely wild as the bombardment of the New Orleans forts, but very novel and magnificent as a naval demonstration.

The vessels of the squadron arrived off Kibben Head (Port Royal Harbor entrance) during the night of Sunday and the day of Monday, November 3d and 4th. The gunboats immediately commenced their soundings, to verify their old surveys of the channel. The rebel fleet, of five small vessels, under command of Commodore Tatnall, late of the United States Navy, put out from one of the estuaries, and engaged the reconoitering and surveying boats. After a sharp passage the rebels retired—evidently impressed with the smallness of his means to cope with such antagonists. The forts on Hilton Head and Bay Point kept silence, nor did any land batteries open, to betray their whereabouts to the fleet.

To draw their fire, and determine the order of attack, the gunboat *Mercury*, under Captain Gilman, chief of the Engineer Corps, was dispatched "along shore" to reconnoitre. Several of the vessels of war during the day dropt so far into the harbor, as to tempt the enemy to "show his teeth," which he did in a sharp manner, betraying a heavy battery on Hilton Head (afterwards discovered to be a well-appointed fort,) and two batteries on the opposite shores. The Union gunboats and the batteries kept up a fire for about two hours, when Commodore Dupont (in command of the Naval force of the expedition) signalled the boats out of the fight.

Wednesday morning was fixed upon as the moment for the reduction of the batteries; but, the flag-ship, *Wabash*, grounded on Fishing Rip shoal, and did not get off until too late for tide-flow, which her heavy draught required, in order safely to clear the bar and shoals.

Thursday (November 7th) was the momentous day. The morning was one of the most beautiful of Southern latitudes. A gentle breeze broke the clear water's face into ripples, as if the Naiades were smiling at the tragedy which portended. Butterflies fluttered through the air, and the songs of Southern birds broke the stillness with their waves of melody. The vessels of war reposed in quiet just beyond the reach of the enemy's guns, while beyond swung the transports at anchor, containing fifteen thousand troops, as an audience, to witness in safety the sublime combat of artillery.

At half past nine the vessels began to move into battle—in most novel and exciting disposition. The order as arranged was to sail in singly—the flag-ship *Wabash* first; each vessel to follow in its allotted succession, Passing slowly up stream, the starboard guns were to pour their fire into the two batteries (or forts) on the Bay Point side—passing down stream, on the return, the battery (or fort) on Hilton Head, was to receive the fire. The vessels, thus sailing in an ellipse, passed in and out of range of the enemy's stationary guns, dealing, as they passed in close range, a fearful shower of shot and shell.

The first shot was fired by the Hilton Head fortification (Fort Walker,) as the *Wabash* steamed within range, at twenty-six minutes past nine, A. M. Three shots were thus fired. Then the Bay Point battery opened, when the *Wabash* responded with a terrific broadside. Her batteries consisted of twenty-six guns to the side, and a heavy pivot-gun fore and aft. These literally rained their iron shower on the lesser rebel fort. No attention was paid to Fort Walker. The flag-ship steamed slowly up stream, keeping the enemy under fire about twenty minutes, when she winded the line, turning southward, and, steaming down stream, gave Fort Walker her entire attention, passing within eight hundred yards of the Fort, which showed itself to be a very powerful work, mounting very heavy and superior guns, whose fire proved them to be not only improved ordnance, but well served.

The other vessels followed the same order of action. The *Susquehanna*, *Pawnee*, *Seminole*, *Bienville*, *Pocahontas*, *Mohican*, *Augusta*, and the gunboats *Ottawa*, *Seneca*, *Unadilla*, *Pembina*, and *Vandalia* joined in the fray, firing shell with great rapidity and precision, and making the battery vocal with their practice. The rebels fought their guns with a desperate coolness, and fired with a rapidity really surprising under the circumstances. In Fort Walker, against which the Federals directed their chief efforts—the Confederate gunners were stripped to the waist, and worked like furies. Their officer in command, Brigadier-General Drayton, was efficient, cool, and stubborn, but what could withstand that fearful hail?

Around the course the stately messengers of destruction moved, never faltering, never failing to come up to the work with exhaustless fury. The smaller gunboats obtained a position close into shore where the fort guns were enfiladed, while the *Bienville* sailed in, at the second round, close to the fort, and gave her tremendous guns with such fearful effect that the enemy's best guns were soon silenced, but not until the vessel had been well spotted with the enemy's shot. The *Wabash* also came to a stand, at the third round, about six hundred yards from the fort. That moment decided the day. No human power could face such a death-storm, and the enemy suddenly fled, taking to the woods in the rear with such haste as allowed no time for any to gather up even the most prized of their goods.

The firing ceased at a few minutes past two P. M.—the battle having thus been waged with stubborn fierceness for over four hours. Discovering that the enemy had probably evacuated, Commander Rodgers—aid to Flag Officer Dupont—went ashore in the *Mercury* to find the enemy really gone. With his own hands he hauled down the rebel colors and flung the Stars and Stripes to the breeze. Then followed such a shout from the watching thousands as must have made appalling music for the Southern heart. Fort Walker had fallen and South Carolina was "invaded." The "dastard Yankee" had opened a way into her very vitals.

A reporter wrote, of the effects of the Federal bombardment:

"The effects of our fire were to be seen on every hand in the work. On the line along the front, three guns were dismounted by the enfilading fire of our ships. One carriage had been struck by a large shell and shivered to pieces, dismounting the heavy gun mounted upon it, and sending the splinters flying in all directions with terrific force. Between the gun and the foot of the parapet was a large pool of blood, mingled with brains, fragments of skull and pieces of flesh, evidently from the face, as portions of whiskers still clung to it. This shot must have done horrible execution, as other portions of human beings were found all about it. Another carriage to the right was broken to pieces, and the guns on the water fronts were rendered useless by the enfilading fire from the gunboats on the left flank. Their scorching fire of shell, which swept with resistless fury and deadly effect across this long water pond, where the enemy had placed their heaviest metal, *en barbette*, without taking the precaution to place traverses between the guns, did as much as anything to drive the rebels from their works, in the hurried manner I have before described. The works were ploughed

41

up by the shot and shell so badly as to make immediate repairs necessary.

"All the houses and many of the tents about the work were perforated and torn by flying shell, and hardly a light of glass could be found intact, in any building where a shell exploded. The trees in the vicinity of the object of our fire, showed marks of heavy visitations. Everything, indeed, bore the marks of ruin. No wonder, then, that the rebels beat a hasty retreat. I can, and do, cheerfully bear testimony to the gallant and courageous manner in which the rebels maintained their position under a hot fire, and fought at their guns when many would have fled."

Another correspondent wrote:

"The road the rebels took was strewn for miles with muskets, knapsacks, blankets, cartridge-boxes and other valuables that they had thrown away in their flight. They had retreated across the island to Seabrook, a distance of half a dozen miles, where they took boat for Savannah. Even the wharf at Seabrook was strewn with valuables, carried even so far and abandoned at the last moment. The troops who were in charge of this fort, and who certainly fought most gallantly, were the Twelfth regiment of South Carolina volunteers, under Colonel Jones, and the Ninth South Carolina volunteers, commanded by Colonel Haywood, and a battalion of German artillery, under Colonel Wagener. They had in the fort about 1,300 men in all—enough to serve all the guns in the most efficient manner. They had also a field battery with 500 troops stationed at a point a short distance above Hilton Head, where they anticipated our transports would undertake to send troops to attempt a flank movement for the assistance of the navy. On the opposite side of the river they had 400 men. It cannot be denied that the resistance was as gallant as the final panic was complete; but the hardest fighting on the rebel side was all done by the German artillery, they being the last to leave the fort, which they did not do until long after the greater part of the valiant Palmetto 'Chivalry' had taken to the woods to save their precious necks.

"They had spiked but one gun, a most valuable rifled cannon, which they temporarily disabled with a steel spike, which can with difficulty be extracted. The other guns were, most of them, columbiads of the very largest size, one hundred and thirty-pounders, and of the most admirable finish, being the finest and latest productions of the Tredegar Works, Richmond, and fully equal to any guns owned by the North. There were twenty-three of these guns in the fort.

"The fortification is of most admirable construction, evidently planned and built under the superintendence of a thoroughly able engineer, and is one of the strongest works of the kind in the whole country. Our losses were: ten killed; twenty-five wounded."

As was anticipated, the fate of Fort Walker decided that of the opposite fortifications. The two batteries were that night abandoned without further struggle, and at daylight in the morning the Stars and Stripes floated over both the two points and St. Philip's Island. The works there were two well-constructed earth-works, the one on Bay Point mounting twenty-one heavy columbiads, and the other mounting four columbiads.

It was a noticeable fact, that the large store of powder found was of the best *English* make—that many of the projectiles were of *English* make—that several of the rifled guns were of *English* manufacture.

The abandoned fort and adjacent islands were immediately occupied by the troops on the transports. The islands and forts on the north side of the harbor were occupied Friday morning. In a few days Beaufort was a Federal city, and the Sea Islands around were soon sending their treasures of cotton once more to the "outer world."

XXXII.

INCIDENTS OF THE CAPTURE OF THE PORT ROYAL FORTS.

General Drayton, the rebel officer in command at Fort Walker, was brother of Captain Drayton, in command of the *Pocahontas*, gunboat. The case certainly afforded a painful verification of the truth that, in the war, "brother was arrayed against brother."* Captain Steedman, of the *Bienville*, gunboat, was a South Carolinian. He fought his vessel with remarkable skill and fury, as did also Captain Drayton the *Pocahontas.*

After the ships had made one round, and sailed their fiery circle once, the order of battle was changed; certain ones of the gunboats dropped out of their assigned places, having discovered that they could take up a raking position which would enable them to remain stationary, and still keep up a rapid and galling fire on the fort. So, henceforth, the other attacking ships moved in a single line, the *Wabash* still leading.

Four of the gunboats ran into the bight of the river, to the north of the Fort, where they were enabled to keep up an enfilading fire, that completely raked the entire fortifications of Fort Walker, and distressed the enemy exceedingly. These gunboats were the *Ottawa*, *Curlew*, *Seneca*, and *Unadilla.* They were afterward joined by the *Pocahontas.*

Very many of the shot from the shore batteries were aimed high, especially at the *Bienville*, and other steamers having the walking-beam of the engine high above the deck, the object being to cripple the engine, and thus render the vessel unmanageable, so that she might drift on the shoals and become an easy prey. In these attempts they were not successful in a single instance, for not one of our ships, save the *Penguin*, which was immediately taken care of by one of our own boats, was injured in her steam works, so as to be disabled for a single instant.

The rebels regarded the destruction of the fleet as certain—their powerful guns being relied upon to sink any hull which should come in their way. In some of the letters found, half finished, in the officers' quarters, the utter destruction of the entire expedition was considered so positively assured, and their belief in the ability of their batteries to put an effectual quietus upon the pretentions of Lincoln's fleet was so perfect, that, in one or two of the documents, the writers lamented the

* Among other cases cited, is that of the sons of the venerable John J. Crittenden. One was a Major-General in the rebel service—the other was Brigadier-General in the Union army.

necessity they should be under of sending the ships to the bottom, when the Confederates were so much in need of ships. It was taken for granted that the tremendous execution to be done by their heavy guns, would perforate the hulls of our ships, and send them instantly to the bottom. Having this confident expectation, the rebels looked eagerly after every fire to see some of our ships go down. They especially concentrated their guns on the *Wabash*, and, as the prisoners afterward informed our men, were much surprised that she persisted in remaining afloat. When the ships had all passed their battery in safety for the first time, had "peppered them well," and had all escaped without apparent injury, the astonishment was great, and the universal impression began to prevail that there was some mistake.

For the second time the fleet came steaming down; for the second time the Federals poured in their terrible fire, dismantling guns, shattering buildings, and stretching in death numbers of men; and for the second time the fleet passed on in safety, showing not the slightest sign of any intention of going to the bottom.

By this time, a new element began to mingle with the feelings of the rebel garrison. With astonishment and wonder that they had not yet sunk any of the opposing vessels, began to mingle a large, a very large proportion, of doubt whether they *could* do it.

Without paying more attention to the barking of the battery at Fort Beauregard, on Bay Point, than to pitch them an occasional shot, merely to let them know they were not forgotten, for the third time the ships rounded their circular track, and came slowly down to pay their respects again. Again was the whole fire of the fort concentrated on the *Wabash*, and afterward, in turn, on each one of the vessels, as they passed, in a fiery procession, before the shore, delivering with the utmost coolness and the most exact precision, their murderous fire, running even nearer than before, firing more effectually than ever, yet again steaming away unharmed, and turning the point for still another round.

The utmost consternation now took full possession of the rebels, and, in an uncontrollable panic, they fled with precipitation. The panic at Bull Run was not more complete; indeed, not half so much so, for the rebels in their mortal terror ran for the woods without stopping for anything whatever. The left in their tents hundreds of dollars of money, gold watches, costly swords, and other valuables, showing that their fear was uncontrollable and complete.

The flight, observed first from the little gunboat *Mercury*, was communicated by her to the flag-ship, and then was immediately telegraped to all the fleet.

When our men took possession on Bay Point, they discovered a characteristic trick of the enemy, which most luckily failed to succeed. The Secession flag was hauled partly down, and the halyards were connected with an ingenious percussion-cap apparatus, so arranged that the complete hauling down of the flag would explode the cap, which was intended to ignite a train of powder connected with the powder magazine. By some unforeseen accident, a quantity of sand was thrown over part of the train of powder, so that although the cap exploded and fired a part of the powder, and blew up a neighboring house, it did not communicate with the magazine, and little harm was done.

The *Wabash* fired, during the entire action, nine hundred shots, being all eight, nine, ten, and eleven-inch shells, with the exception of a few rifled-cannon projectiles of a new pattern, and which were used simply as a matter of experiment. The *Susquehanna* fired five hundred shots, the *Bienville* one hundred and eighty-five, and the average of the gunboats and the other smaller ships may probably be set down at one hundred and fifty each. There were, in all, sixteen vessels engaged on our side, and, probably, from all of them were fired not far from 3,500 shot and shell at the two forts, Walker and Beauregard, the four-gun battery, and Tatnall's, and the three steamers.

On almost every vessel, after the fight, the men were called aft and publicly thanked by their respective Captains. On the

Bienville, particular mention was made and special thanks returned, in presence of the ship's company, to William Henry Steele, a boy not fourteen years old, who conducted himself with distinguished bravery. He was powder-boy; and not only never flinched nor dodged a shot, but when two men were killed at his gun, he did not turn pale, nor cease, for an instant, his duties, but handed the cartridge he had in hand to the gunner, stepped carefully over the bodies, and hastened below for more ammunition.

Thomas Jackson, coxswain of the *Wabash*, was struck by a shot, which so nearly cut his leg off as to leave it hanging by a small portion of the muscle and skin. Partially rising and leaning painfully against a gun, Jackson glanced at his mangled limb, and, in an instant perceived its helpless condition. Feeling behind his back in his belt, where seamen always carry their knives, he drew his sheath-knife from its leathern scabbard, and deliberately began to saw away at his leg. He was borne below by his mates; and afterward asked continually how the fight was going, saying, "I hope we'll win it, I hope we'll win." In two hours he died; his last words being a wish for victory, and a word of thanks that he had been able to do something for the honor of the "dear old flag."

The *Wabash* was struck thirty-five times. One shot below the water-line started a bad leak. Another almost cut away the mainmast. Her rigging was badly cut up. Her handling was very effective. She was, at no time, in a position to be raked by the enemy's guns. She escaped with remarkable good fortune, considering that, as the flag-ship, she was the enemy's special target.

The *Bienville* was particularly exposed—having approached nearer the shore than any other vessel. But five shots struck her, and only one doing any serious injury. One columbiad solid shot struck her on the starboard bow, killing two and wounding three of her crew.

The *Penguin* was struck in her steam-chest, but no person was injured by the escaping steam. She was immediately towed out of action by the *Isaac Smith* tug-boat, which, though not a fighter, was everywhere in the midst of shot and shell, ready for towing off any disabled ship.

The *Pawnee* was struck nine times. The *Mohican* also received a number of shots. These two were the most cut-up of any of the smaller vessels of the fleet. The *Ottawa*, *Seneca*, *Vandalia*, *Seminole*, *Susquehanna*, *Pocahontas*, and *Augusta*, all were several times hit, but none were disabled. This apparent lack of execution, when the shots so many times struck the vessels, arises from the fact that, either the rebels aimed high, for the purpose of breaking the walking-beams, and so crippling the engines of such of our vessels as could thus be disabled; or not deeming it possible that we would have the temerity to engage them at six hundred yards instead of two or three miles, the guns were all sighted for the longest range, and they consequently carried over, and clear of the hulls of our ships, and only cut the upper rigging.

The enemy left Fort Walker so hurriedly that their private effects, indeed, everything were wholly abandoned. The Federal troops found everything just as they left them. Dinner tables were set, and good food ready for the hungry fighters. The amount of stuff found was astonishing. All was taken possession of by our forces, and, with the exception of a few articles taken as mementoes of the occasion, everything was turned over to the proper officers. Quite a number of elegant swords and pistols, saddles, etc., were found, and distributed among the deserving.

The appearance of the old flag on the Game Cock State was hailed by enthusiastic cheers from the men of war, and caught up by the transports. Cheer after cheer went round the harbor, bands played patriotic tunes, and every one felt most gay and festive. The effect on the men when the flag waved aloft, was differently and curiously manifested. Some cheered lustily, while others were choked with their emotions. Some wept with joy, the tears rolling down their cheeks as large as peas, whilst others were much excited at once more seeing the colors of the Federal Union waving over South Carolina's traitorous soil.

XXXIII.

THE FALL OF FORTS HENRY AND DONELSON.

THE sudden change of programme in the conduct of the war in the West during February was owing to the fine stage of water in the rivers and to the proven efficiency of the gun-boats. Anticipating an advance up the Cumberland and Tennessee rivers the Confederates had erected two strong fortifications near the Tennessee line—Fort Henry on the Tennessee river and Fort Donelson, a powerful defense, on the Cumberland, near Dover. These structures were well constructed, mounted heavy and numerous guns, were well flanked by rifle pits, and, beside their regular garrison, had heavy supporting field forces constantly within reach. It was their powerful character which induced Grant to desist from his first essay up the Tennessee.

A movement against them, if successful, would at once force the rebel lines of defense far to the South, and render Bowling Green and Nashville an easy conquest. Whether to General Halleck, Commodore Foote, General Grant, or Mr. Lincoln belongs the credit of first conceiving the campaign, we do not know. That it was well planned and brilliantly executed, the history of the war proves.

An order (February 1st) promulgated by General Grant, placed his forces on a footing of active service. It was as follows:

"HEAD-QUARTERS DISTRICT OF CAIRO,
CAIRO, Feb. 1st, 1862.

"For temporary government the forces of this military district will be divided and commanded as follows, to wit:

"The First brigade will consist of the Eighth, Eighteenth, Twenty-seventh Twenty-ninth, Thirtieth and Thirty-first regiments of Illinois Volunteers, Schwartz's and Dresser's batteries, and Stewart's, Dollin's, O'Harnet's, and Carmichael's cavalry. Colonel R. J. Oglesby, senior Colonel of the brigade, commanding.

"The Second brigade will consist of the Eleventh, Twentieth, Forty-fifth and Forty-eighth Illinois infantry, Fourth Illinois cavalry, Taylor's and McAllister's artillery. (The latter with four siege guns) Colonel W. H. L. Wallace commandimg.

"The First and Second brigades will constitute the first division of the district of Cairo, and will be commanded by Brigadier General John A. McClernand.

"The Third brigade will consist of the Eighth Wisconsin, Forty-ninth Illinois, Twenty-fifth Indiana, four companies of artillery, and such troops as are yet to arrive, Brigadier General E. A. Paine commanding.

"The Fourth brigade will be composed of the Tenth, Sixteenth, Twenty-second, and Thirty-third Illinois and the Tenth Iowa infantry; Houtaling's battery of light artillery, four companies of the Seventh and two companies of the First Illinois cavalry; Colonel Morgan commanding.

"General E. A. Paine is assigned to the command at Cairo and Mound City, and Colonel Morgan to the command at Bird's Point. By order of

"U. S. GRANT, Brigadier General Commanding.

"JNO. A. RAWLINS, Assistant Adjutant-General."

The advance—McClernand's two brigades—from Cairo, commenced by transports, February 3d, passing directly up the Tennessee river, and disembarking on the 4th four miles north of Fort Henry. The iron-clad gunboats of Commodore Foote's fleet were already there. Upon the arrival of the troops three of the boats steamed up to reconnoiter and "feel of" the batteries. The enemy gave them a warm reception, fully showing his position and force. Reenforcements pressed up almost hourly from below, until Grant's force, by February 6th, was equal to any emergency. February 5th the General returned from the advance to Paducah to bring up General Smith's division, then at that point, 7000 strong. These all debarked at a favorable point, on the 6th, near the Fort.

But the activity of Foote anticipated the slower movements of the army. He steamed up, February 6th, passing around Painter's Creek Island—which lay over on the west side of the Tennessee, directly in front of Fort Henry. The enemy had neglected to obstruct that passage.

The boats emerged above the Fort, only one mile away, having the stream in their favor. The gunboat *Cincinnati*, (the "flag ship,") Commodore Foote on board, opened the fight, slowly advancing directly down upon the fort, followed by the *St. Louis*, *Carondelet*, *Essex*, *Conestoga* and *Lexington*. The Fort replied with a furious and well served fire from heavy guns. The boats floated down until within three hundred yards of the enemy's embrazures, when headway was stopped and a close quarter action ordered. The fire was perfectly appalling for a few minutes succeeding, when at 1.40 the enemy's flag struck and the Fort was won. Its commander, General Lloyd Tilghman of Kentucky, (formerly of the United States Army,) surrendered unconditionally, with his staff and artillerists, (sixty.) The rebel infantry encamped near the Fort fled at the first fire, abandoning even their dinner—leaving Tilghman to do his work alone. The rebels also had three gunboats which fled hastily up the river. The Fort mounted seventeen guns—most of them thirty-two and thirty-four-pounders rifled, and one, a superb ten-inch columbiad. The rebel loss was five killed and ten badly wounded. Why Tilghman surrendered, with only two guns disabled, our forces could not see. Commodore Foote received his sword, when General Tilghman said: "I am glad to surrender to so gallant an officer." Foote's notable reply was: "You do perfectly right, sir, in surrendering; but you should have blown my boats out of the water before I would have surrendered to you!"

The *Cincinnati* was hit by thirty-one shots—some of them passing through her. The *Essex* was disabled by a heavy ball, which entered her side forward port, cut through the bulkhead and squarely through one of her boilers. The escaping steam scalded to death the two pilots in the house above and injured more or less all on board, including Commander Porter. His aid, S. B. Brittan, was killed at his side by a shot. The *Essex*, after the disaster, was allowed to float down stream beyond the range of the guns. Her loss was six killed, seventeen wounded, and five missing.

Grant's forces were in the Fort one half hour after its surrender. A delay of the attack by the gunboats until Grant could have invested the place, doubtless would have given the Union army the entire force of rebel infantry which so hastily fled across to Fort Donelson.

This capture opened the way for an immediate descent on Fort Donelson. The pursuit of the retreating forces was rapid, and resulted in the capture of eight brass guns and thirty-three prisoners. Three gunboats pushed on up the river disabling the railway bridge across the Tennessee and Danville, and securing considerable quanty of commissary stores, wagons and army supplies found at the bridge. The entire property secured by the day's work was valued at about two hundred thousand dollars. The gunboats returned on the 10th, having succeeded in reconnoitering as far up as Florence, and in capturing and destroying a number of steamers used by the enemy as transports.

The rebels hastened to reenforce Fort Donelson. Generals Pillow, Floyd and Buckner were all there with their respective brigades, besides the regular garrison of the fortress, composed of artillerists from Columbus and the Mississippi river forts below. Outlying fortifications were thrown up, and rifle pits thrown out flank and rear. With this force and disposition it became evident that the reduction of the Fort would be a bloody affair, at best.

Commodore Foote with five boats started down the Tennessee immediately after the capture of Fort Henry, proceeding to Cairo to recruit and repair damages. On the night of February 11th he started for the Cumberland river.

The investment of Fort Donelson was complete by the 12th —McClernand's division having the Federal right wing and General Smith's the left, while Foote's gunboats commanded the river and assaulted the works from the front. The powerful river batteries were his chief point of attack. Six gunboats went into the fight February 14th before three P. M., the flag boat *St. Louis* leading. A severe contest followed of an hour and a half duration—the enemy using every possible exertion to overcome their water antagonists. They were so far successful as to shoot away the wheel of the *St. Louis* and the rudder of the *Louisville*, while all the boats were riddled with shot. The *St. Louis* alone received fifty solid balls in and through her mail and upperworks. The firing of the vessels was fearfully destructive—much of the time some of the boats being within four hundred yards of the batteries. The enemy were completely driven from most of the guns, but three guns kept up the contest bravely so long as the ironclads were within range. Fifty-four men were killed and wounded on the boats. The enemy's loss was not ascertained. The *Tyler* and *Conestoga* (not iron-clad) were disabled early in the fight.

The particulars of the fight are so full of interest, as showing the tremendous power of modern enginery of war, that we may quote from the account of one present during the terrific conflict:

"At two P. M. (Feb. 14th) precisely the signal was given from the flag-ship to get under weigh, and in a few moments we were slowly steaming up the river. We had proceeded perhaps a fourth of a mile when a single report, emanating from the upper battery of the Fort, greeted us, and notified us that the rebels were awaiting us in savage expectation. On we went, however, not a sound escaping from our crafts, except the slow puffing of the escape pipes and the cheery plashing of the paddle wheels, while the enemy were busy awaking the dormant echoes with their cannonading, and agitating the swollen waters with their shot and shell, scattered in promiscuous profusion all around us. When we had sailed up to within a mile of the Fort, the Flag Officer let go his starboard bow rifle, and we followed him with ours; then the *Pittsburg* and *Carondelet* followed suit, and the ball was really opened in earnest. Our first shots fell short; but a little more elevation of the guns remedied the failing, and the next round saw our balls dropped into uncomfortably close proximity to their batteries. From this time to the end of the action there was not a lull in the steady and constant firing from our boats, nor was there a moment when the whole of the enemy's front was not a steady stream of fire. In order to get the best view of the action, I stationed myself upon the upper deck, and just as near in the wake of the pilot house as possible, taking my chances at getting a sight of what was going on in front by abbreviated peeps and squints around the corners, and hurried stares through the look-out holes which the considerate carpenter had left for the optical accommodation of the pilots. The flag-ship *St. Louis* took the advance, and was hugging the western shore; then came our own (the *Louisville*), then the *Pittsburg* and *Carondelet*, in order, and as near side by side as was possible in a river scarcely wide enough for two boats to pass each other. In this order we formed a straight battery of twelve guns in front, while the two gunboats *Conestoga* and *Lexington*, followed in our wake, pouring in their quota of missiles from their bow columbiads at a safe distance. We could see nearly every one of our shots take effect within or near the rebel batteries, the more deadly and certain as we slowly steamed up toward them. Thus we proceeded side by side, our fire never slackening or our determination faltering until we arrived within three hundred yards of the lower battery. At this time the enemy's shot and shells were screaming through the air or ravaging our sides and decks without cessation, while ours were divesting them of their more exposed batteries, ploughing up their hill-sides aad decimating their camps in terrible haste. I saw one large shell from the *Louisville* fall and explode directly under one of their guns, sending a score of rebel soldiers to their long homes, demolishing the battery and scattering those not killed or wounded in indecent haste to the nearest covers. When we had attained the last named position, viz. within three hundred yards of their works, we stopped our headway, and when the boats were motionless we poured in our last and most destructive fire. It really seemed at this time that the quintessence of destruction was contained in those twelve great iron thunderers. With each discharge a rebel gun was silenced, at each broadside a host of frightened rebels would scud up the hill to a place of safety behind the upper earthworks, and all but two of the lower guns had ceased to deal us their destruction. Now a new battery of one hundred and twenty-pound guns opened upon us from the left and rear of the first works. We were within point blank range, and the destruction to our fleet was really terrible. One huge solid shot struck our boat just at the angle of the upper deck and pilot house, perforated the iron plating, passed through the heavy timbers and buried itself in a pile of hammocks just in front and in a direct line with the boilers. Another, a shell, raked us from bow to stern, passed through the wheelhouse, emerged, dropped and exploded in the river just at our stern. Then a ten-inch solid shot entered our starboard bow port, demolished a gun carriage, killed three men and wounded four others, traversed the entire length of the boat, and sunk into the river in our wake. Then a shell came shrieking through the air, striking fair into our forward starboard port, killing another man and wounding two more, passed aft, sundering our rudder chains, and rendering the boat unmanageable. Now we were compelled to drop astern, and leave the scene of action; but our gunners sent their respects to the rebels as long as their fire could be the least effective; and, so far as we were concerned, the battle was over.

"The last battery was the one that put the finishing stroke to the fleet. One of the enemy's shells entered and exploded directly in the pilot house of the *St. Louis*, killing the pilot and wounding Flag Officer Foote severely in the leg. Two of the shots entered the *Pittsburg* below the guards, causing her to leak badly, and it is probable that she will sink before morning. Another entered the *Carondelet*, killing four men and injuring eight others. By this time three of the boats were disabled, and then the signal was given to back out and return to our anchorage. The enemy's lower battery was silenced, however, and only the two one hundred and twenty-pounders on the hill were playing upon us, and it is universally conceded that if we had had ten minutes more time Fort Donelson would have shared the fate of Fort Henry, and the Cumberland river been opened and divested of its rebel embargo."

Fort Donelson was thus described by one on the ground: "This Fort takes its name from the Andrew Jackson Donelson family of Tennessee. Its construction was commenced in May last. No better position for defense could have been selected at any point on the Cumberland as yet passed by us. It is on a fine slope a hundred and fifty feet high, in a very slight bend, on the right hand side of the Cumberland, one hundred and seven miles from the mouth of the river, and nearly two hundred from Cairo. It mounts sixteen guns. There are three batteries—the first about twenty feet above the water, consisting of six guns, thirty-two and sixty-four-pounders; the second about equal in strength, located about sixty feet above this; and the third on the summit of the hill, mounting four one hundred and twenty-eight-pounders. The trenches in the vicinity of each battery are unusually deep. The earth works are not less than six feet thick, braced by heavy logs. The rebel camp is behind the hill, and cannot be reached from the gunboats by shot or shell."

The gunboats having been disabled, General Grant resolved not to await their repair, and prepared at once to assault and reduce the rebel stronghold. His army was rapidly strengthened by five detachments from General Hunter's (Kansas) Department, and by all the available regiments of the Western States. The investment of the fort was completed by assigning the Federal center to General Lew Wallace's division.

The gunboats withdrew Friday afternoon, (14th.) That night was spent in getting the brigades in position. Early on

Saturday morning (15th) the enemy opened on the Federal right (McClernand's division) by a sharp fire on Colonel Lawler's Eighteenth Illinois regiment. All of Ogleby's brigade was quickly engaged. The brigades of Wallace and McArthur soon came into the fight, which, by ten o'clock, became very furious. General Wallace sent four regiments to McClernand's support, viz.: the Seventeenth and Twenty-fifth Ken tucky and Thirty-first Indiana, with the Forty-fourth Indiana as a reserve.

The troops on the right were disposed as follows: First, McArthur's brigade, consisting of the Ninth, Twelfth and Forty-first Illinois, having temporarily attached the Seventeenth and Nineteenth Illinois. Next came Ogleby's brigade, the Eighth, Eighteenth, Twenty-ninth, Thirtieth and Thirty-first Illinois, and Schwartz's and Dresser's batteries. Next, Colonel W. H. L. Wallace's brigade, the Eleventh, Twentieth, Forty-fifth and Forty-eighth Illinois, and Taylor's and McAlister's batteries.

These three brigades composed McClernand's division, and bore the brunt of conflict. Upon that point the rebels pressed with the utmost tenacity, and the deeds of valor there performed by both parties form one of the most splendid, though bloody, records of the entire war. McClernand's men exhausted their ammunition entirely, and, finally, were called from the field to recuperate and obtain reenforcements. With this returning movement a counter movement was made by the charge of Smith's entire division upon the enemy's works. The charge was so furious as to bear all before it, and Smith's men occupied the entire works of the rebels on the left. Grant announced this to McClernand, ordering his advance. This was then made, in a brilliant manner, and the enemy was forced back within his works on the Federal right. Thus the Union army found themselves in a position to carry the enemy's main work by assault, on the morning of Sunday.

But, no such service was required of the elated and brave fellows whose achievements during the Saturday's contest covered them with glory. At a very early hour General Simon

Buckner, the senior rebel General in the fortification, sent out to obtain an armistice preliminary to arrangements of terms of honorable capitulation. Grant replied that nothing but unconditional and immediate surrender would answer—that he was prepared for the assault and should soon carry the works by the bayonet. Grumbling at the discourtesy (!) shown him, Buckner unconditionally surrendered with his force of nearly 15,000 men.

Upon entering the premises it was found that Generals Pillow and Floyd, with their troops, had flown. During the night they had, at a council of war, declared their purpose to leave by the three steamers still at the landing above Dover. Pillow said he would not surrender—Floyd said it never *would* do for *him* to fall into Federal hands; and so Buckner, the unfortunate ex-chief of the Kentucky State Guard, was forced to do the deed—to give up his arms and submit to the tender mercies of the Government which he had betrayed. The flight of Floyd and Pillow was the theme of much amusing comment by the Northern forces. The escape of the great "chief of thieves" was certainly greatly deplored, for if any rebel among the conspirators deserved the halter more than another, that man was John B. Floyd, Mr. Buchanan's Secretary of War.*

The armament of the Fort and water batteries consisted of forty-four guns, most of them of superior make and heavy calibre. About 17,000 stand of small arms were taken, and an immense amount of stores — among which were twelve hundred boxes of beef, showing that the rebels had resolved to stand a siege before giving up. Floyd's and Pillow's men, in crossing the river, pitched all superfluous arms and baggage into the stream. A Louisiana cavalry company made its way, during the darkness, up the river, and thus escaped. Pillow and Floyd made direct for Clarksville.

* This surrender was the occasion of a pretty sharp correspondence among the Confederates; and Johnson had to "explain" to his government. Buckner felt that he was made the scape-goat for greater rogues than himself.

The following table exhibits the losses of the Union regiments that were engaged in the battle :

	Killed.	*Wounded.*
Eighth Illinois	56	196
Ninth Illinois	36	160
Eleventh Illinois	71	180
Twelfth Illinois	35	109
Seventeenth Illinois	4	20
Eighteenth Illinois	45	60
Twentieth Illinois	21	118
Thirtieth Illinois	19	71
Thirty-first Illinois	40	200
Forty-first Illinois	17	130
Forty-ninth Illinois	10	30
Twelfth Iowa	3	24
Second Iowa	38	160
Fourteenth Iowa	6	50
Fifty-eighth Ohio	—	3
Taylor's Battery	1	4
Total	401	1,515
Prisoners taken		250

Making a total Union loss of 2,166. The rebel loss in killed and wounded and prisoners is estimated at 15,700.

As was expected these rapid strokes of the Union army astounded and disconcerted the enemy. His boasted strongholds at Bowling Green and Columbus were quickly abandoned ; Clarksville was soon deserted, and Nashville temporarily occupied by the fast retreating rebels. But, the operations of the gunboats on the Tennessee river promised to cut off retreat by the South, and Nashville was therefore soon given up without a struggle—the enemy falling back upon Murfresboro, then upon Chatanooga, and finally upon Corinth, where Johnson and Beauregard determined to await the shock of the combined Federal armies, and thus decide the fate of the Mississippi Valley.

XXXIV.

INCIDENTS OF THE BATTLE BEFORE FORT DONELSON.

THE enemy's assault was in force upon the morning of Saturday. McClernand's division not only was the Federal weak point, but the ground was so contracted that but one regiment of the Unionists could be brought to bear on the assailed point. As a consequence, the slaughter was fearful. But no troops ever fought with less idea of giving way.

The first regiment to receive the enemy's onslaught, was the Eighteenth Illinois, Colonel Lawler, Oglesby's brigade. This regiment fought until their ammunition was all expended, when the Eighth Illinois walked into their places, commanded by Lieutenant-Colonel Frank L. Rhodes—Colonel Oglesby acting as commander of the First Brigade. The remaining regiments of the brigade rendered such assistance as the nature of the ground would admit. The Thirtieth Illinois, Lieutenant-Colonel E. S. Dennis, commanding, supported Schwart's Missouri battery, posted on the right, and the Thirty-first Illinois, Colonel John A. Logan, supporting Dresser's Illinois battery, posted on the left of the brigade position.

The enemy struck for the batteries, over which a most sanguinary struggle ensued. Every horse was killed at Schwartz's guns, and most of the artillerists. Logan's regiment defended the guns until it had lost the Colonel, Lieutenant-Colonel, acting-Major, seven Captains, and a proportionate number of lower grade officers and men, either killed or disabled! The battery was finally surrounded, and Captain

Cook drew off the skeleton of the fine regiment—leaving the guns in the enemy's hands. A reporter present wrote of that terrible struggle :

"The Eighteenth regiment seems to have resisted the severest storm. Against their ranks the Rebels directed their heaviest fire, but instead of falling back they advanced to the very face of the enemy, and there stood in the very jaws of death, with scarcely a prospeet that a single one would escape.

"For three hours these regiments, numbering scarcely 3,000 men held their ground against the whole rebel garrison. At one time the Eighteenth being partially flanked, was exposed to a cross-fire of both musketry and artillery, but our right wing, securing the rebels' left, at once relieved them. At this critical moment Colonel Lawler fell. Captain Bush, acting Lieutenant-Colonel, assumed command, but was soon wounded.

"Captain Crane was shot dead, Captain Lawler was mortally wounded, Lieutenants Mansford and Thompson killed, Captains Dillon and Wilson and Lieutenants Kelly and Scanlon wounded, so that the daring Egyptian regiment stood before an overwhelming fire almost without officers They fell in heaps dead and wounded. Companies were bereft of Captains and Lieutenants, Captains almost bereft of Companies.

"The three other regiments did their duty nobly. Colonels Oglesby, Marsh, and Logan dashed along the ranks, waving their hats and cheering their men to the conflict. 'Suffer death, men,' cried Logan, 'but disgrace never. Stand firm,' and well they heeded him. Many fell dead and wounded. Among the latter were Colonel Logan and Lieutenant-Colonel White. Oglesby's and Marsh's regiments fought desperately, losing like other regiments, an undue proportion of officers.

"Colonel Oglesby displayed coolness and courage that have elicited the highest praise, and served well in stimulating his men. Never, perhaps, on the American Continent has a more bloody battle been fought. An officer who participated and was wounded in the fight, says: 'The scene beggars decription. So thickly was the battle-field strewn with bead and wounded, that he could have traversed acres of it, treading, at most every step, upon a prostrate body.'

"The rebels fought with desperation, their artillerists using their pieces with most fearful effect. On either side could be heard the voices of those in command cheering on their men. The four Illinois regiments held their ground full three hours. Nearly one third had been killed or wounded, yet the balance stood firm."

But they had to give way before the tremendous odds precipitated against them, composed of some of the choicest troops in the Confederate army. Slowly the Unionists fell backward, the shattered regiments being covered by Colonel W. H. L. Wallace's brigade, composed of the Eleventh, Twentieth, Forty-fifth and Forty-eighth, commanded respectively by Lieutenant-Colonel Hart, and Colonels Marsh, Smith, and Haynie, and by Arthur's brigade. Colonel Croft's brigade, from General Lew Wallace's division, also went into the fight. These united forces succeeded in staying the rebel advance—which really was an effort to turn the Federal right wing, and thus offer a means for the garrison's retreat.

The assault of the enemy's works on the Federal left by General Smith's division, as already stated, gave the Union forces the upper hand. It was a brilliantly-conducted affair. General Lanman, with the Second Iowa, Fifty-second and Twenty-fifth Indiana, and Seventh Iowa, was commissioned to the work. These fine regiments advanced in solid column up to the enemy's outer line of defences, when they broke column, and with a yell leaped into the rebel rifle-pits. The contest was brief, but bloody. The enemy flew to the second line of defences, dreadfully cut to pieces by the fire of the four regiments, which had been reserved. Lanman was accompanied by General Smith in person, whose invincible courage made heroes of his men.

The correspondence between Buckner and Grant was rather humorous than otherwise. It read as follows :

"HEADQUARTERS, FORT DONELSON, Feb. 18, 1862.

"SIR—In consideration of all the circumstances governing the present situation of affairs at this station, I propose to the commanding officer of the Federal forces, the appointment of Commissioners to argue upon terms of capitulation of the forces at this post under my command. In that view I suggest an armistice until twelve o'clock to-day.

"I am, very respectfully.

"Your obedient servant,

"S. B. BUCKNER,

"Brigadier-General, C. S. A."

"To Brigadier-General U. S. GRANT, commanding United States forces, near Fort Donelson.

"HEADQUARTERS ON THE FIELD, FORT DONELSON, Feb. 16, 1862.

"To General S. B. BUCKNER:

"SIR—Yours of this date, proposing an armistice and the appointment of Commissioners to settle on the terms of capitulation, is just received.

"No terms, except unconditional and immediate surrender, can be accepted.

"I propose to move immediately on your works.

"I am very respectfully, your obedient servant,

"U. S. GRANT,

"Brigadier-General Commanding."

"HEADQUARTERS, DOVER, Tenn., Feb. 16, 1862.

"Brigadier-General U. S. GRANT, U. S. A.

"SIR—The distribution of the forces under my command, incident to an unexpected change of commanders, and the overwhelming force under your command, compel me, notwithstanding the brilliant success of the Confederate arms, to accept the ungenerous and unchivalrous terms which you propose.

"I am, sir, your servant,

"S. B. BUCKNER,

"Brigadier-General, C. S. A."

"Ungenerous and unchivalrous terms which you propose!" Injured gentleman! He doubtless expected to have General Grant give him a horse and escort to the nearest rebel stronghold—to have his men supplied with a half-eagle each and rations for three days, with sundry other comforts, to enable them to fight somewhere else! It took a good many reverses to teach the insolent, unprincipled, and ungenerous men, who wore Confederate epaulettes, that the North and Northern soldiers were no longer their humble servants, but their superiors in good manners as well as in arms.

We should not omit the following good thing which emanated from the Frankfort (Ky.) *Commonwealth*, in view of the rather dubious character of the Southern conquests on Kentucky soil:

"MY DEAR REBS: I now take my pen in hand for the purpose of holding communion with you through the silent medium of pen and paper. I have just learned that the lines are now open as far as Fort Donelson, in Tennessee, and I avail myself, with alacrity, of the opportunity now presented of resuming our correspondence. Your many friends in this section, would like to be informed on various topics—for instance:

"How are you, any how?

"How does 'dying in the last ditch,' agree with your general health?

"How is the 'Constitution' down your way?

"Do you think there is any Government?

"How is 'King Kotting?'

"Is Yancey well, and able to eat his oats?

"When will Buckner take his Christmas dinner in Louisville?

"Is Lloyd Tilghman still hanging Union men in the first district?

"Is Floyd still '*rifling*' cannon and other small arms?

"How is Pillow's 'last ditch,' and when will he gratify his numerous friends by 'dying' in the same?

"How is the 'Southern heart?'

"Are you still able to whip five to one?

"What is your opinion of the Dutch race?

"Did the recognition of the S. Confed. by England and France benefit you much?

"Where is the 'Provisional Government' of Kentucky, and what is it kept in?

"Where is the Louisville-Nashville-Bowling Green-Courier now published? Say!

"And lastly, what do you think of yourselves any how?

"A prompt answer will relieve many anxious hearts.

"Yours in a horn, A LINCOLN MAN.

"United States. Feb. 18th, 1862."

XXXV.

THE BATTLE OF PITTSBURGH LANDING.

Pressed out of Kentucky by the flank movements up the Cumberland and Tennessee rivers, the rebels fell back upon Clarksville, deserting their boasted stronghold at Bowling Green, and, soon after, their reputed "Gibraltar," at Columbus—all without a musket being fired against them. The fall of Donelson compelled Johnston to *recede* to Nashville; and, from thence, to the South, as rapidly as was consistent with the Southern idea of "retiring." Buell came down with his well-organized divisions, occupying Nashville, and preparing to move from thence down upon the enemy, wherever he was to be found. Thomas' fine division was recalled from its work upon East Tennessee (alas for it!) and Mitchell was drawn from Bowling Green. Andrew Johnson was instated as Military Governor of Tennessee. Grant moved forward from Donelson direct to the South, by the Tennessee river, designing to strike into Northern Alabama and Mississippi, and break the railroad connections with Memphis and the East. This would flank and turn Memphis, compelling its evacuation, while the very centres of the Cotton States would be open to invasion.

In order to counteract this invasion, which promised to swoop up the Confederacy with a grand completeness, the rebels bent their whole energies to oppose the progress of the Federal army. General A. Sidney Johnston, as Commander-in-Chief, and Beauregard, as second in command, called to their aid the redoubtable General Bragg, with his well-drilled army, from Pensacola; Price and Van Dorn, with their wild brigades from Arkansas and Texas; Breckenridge, with his well-ordered brigades of recusant Tennesseans and Kentuckians; Pillow and Floyd with their forces of Mississippians and Virginians; Cheatham and the Reverend General Polk, with their well-drilled brigades from the line of the Mississippi. Hardee, Hindman, and others, were also detailed to the rebel lines, which were centered around Corinth, Mississippi. To fill up the ranks to a number equal to the work in hand of staying the Federal progress, a conscription was enforced, by which great numbers of those who had not borne arms against the Union, were forced into the service. Corinth was fortified. Memphis was strengthened by the strengthening of the defences above it. Every appearance seemed to indicate that the decisive struggle for the possession of the Mississippi Valley was at hand.

The Federal Government appreciating the greatness of the emergency, prepared for it by ordering Buell to join Grant at Savannah, thence to move direct against Corinth, while the indefatigable Mitchell "sky-rocketted" down upon Huntsville,

Decatur, etc., to cut off the railway and river communication with the East. Halleck was given the command in chief of the combined forces—thus to bring all the Federal military resources in the West to the work in hand.

It was not until late in March that Buell's divisions began to move out of Nashville toward Savannah and Pittsburgh Landing, on the Tennessee river—there to join Grant's forces, already on the ground, for the advance against Corinth. Buell's forces consisted of the superbly-equipped divisions of Nelson, Thomas, Wood, McCook, Negeley and Crittenden—Mitchell going South toward Huntsville, by way of Murfreesboro' and Fayetteville. Grant's forces comprised the divisions of McClernand, Lew Wallace, W. H. L. Wallace, Prentiss, Hurlburt, and W. T. Sherman, with most ample equipments, artillery, etc. All of these forces were Western men—there being not a single regiment in that combined army from East of the Alleghanies.

To prevent the unity of the forces of Grant and Buell was the suddenly conceived design of Johnston. With the usual success, the rebel commander ascertained the plans and disposition of the Federals, and prepared to strike a blow at once on Grant's divisions, advanced to Pittsburgh Landing and located in a semi-circle around the landing, as a centre. If Grant could be beaten back before Buell could reinforce him, the rebels were sure of being able then to overmatch Buell; and, if he was forced back, the way was again opened to recover the ground lost in Tennessee and Kentucky. Immense forces, a steady hand, a daring will might accomplish all, and these Johnston had.

Grant, advancing his forces over the Tennessee, only awaited the coming up of Buell's divisions to assail the enemy intrenched at Corinth. Sherman's division had the extreme advance, left wing, supported by General Prentiss; McClernand held the left centre; W. H. L. Wallace (commanding General Smith's forces) held the left right; Hurlburt's fine brigades formed the reserve; General Lew Wallace's division was stationed at Crump's Landing, forming the Federal extreme right wing.

The skirmishes of Friday and Saturday (April 4th and 5th) chiefly with the enemy's cavalry, kept Sherman's men on the alert. Friday the Federal pickets were driven in on the main line of the division, with a loss of one Lieutenant and seven men, when Sherman ordered a charge. The rebel cavalry were, in turn, driven five miles, with no small loss. Saturday the rebels again made a bold push at the lines, in considerable force, and retired after a warm reception. These advances were but reconnoissances to test the Federal spirit and to locate his lines.

The pickets were again driven in at an early hour on the morning of Sunday (April 6th)—a day the rebels always seemed to choose for fight when the choice lay with them. Sherman immediately ordered his entire division to arms, as, also, did Prentiss his division—both commanders, it is ascertained, being suspicious of the impending attempt of the enemy, in force. The troops stood under arms for an hour, when, no heavy firing occurring, the General and his staff rode to the front. The enemy's sharpshooters picked off Sherman's orderly, standing near the General. This shot, and others which rapidly followed, came from a thicket lining a small stream, flowing north into the Tennessee. Along this stream Sherman's line was stretched. Sherman observed that, in the valley before him, the enemy was forming. He said, in his report:

"About eight A. M., I saw the glistening bayonets of heavy masses of infantry to our left front, in the woods beyond the small stream alluded to, and became satisfied for the first time that the enemy designed a determined attack on our whole camp. All the regiments of my division were then in line of battle at their proper posts. I rode to Colonel Appler and ordered him to hold his ground at all hazards, as he held the left flank of our first line of battle, and I informed him that he had a good battery on his right and strong supports to his rear. General McClernand had promptly and energetically responded to my request, and had sent me three regiments which were posted to protect Waterhouse's battery and the left flank of my line."

This shows that there was no surprise. McClernand was informed, as early as half-past six, of the enemy's presence, and had placed his troops in order of battle. The same with Prentiss and Hurlburt—both of whom were ready before the assault on Sherman's front.

It would be impossible, in the space of even a lengthy chapter, to detail the movements and events which followed on that most momentous day. A book alone would suffice to tell the story in detail.* The first news dispatched of the battles which reached the North, gave a graphic, and, in the main, a correct description of the two days' struggle. It, we may quote :

"PITTSBURG, *via* FORT HENRY, April 9th, 3:20 A. M.

"One of the greatest and bloodiest battles of modern days has just closed, resulting in the complete rout of the enemy, who attacked us at daybreak, Sunday morning.

"The battle lasted without intermission during the entire day, and was again renewed on Monday morning, and continued undecided until four o'clock in the afternoon, when the enemy commenced their retreat, and are still flying toward Corinth, pursued by a large force of our cavalry.

"The slaughter on both sides is immense.

"The fight was brought on by a body of three hundred of the Twenty-fifth Missouri regiment, of General Prentiss' division, attacking the advance guard of the rebels, which were supposed to be the pickets of the enemy, in front of our camps. The rebels immediately advanced on General Prentiss' division on the left wing,† pouring volley after volley of musketry, and riddling our camps with grape, canister and shell. Our forces soon formed into line, and returned their fire vigo-

---

* See "Pittsburgh Landing and the Investment of Corinth," in Beadle's series of "American Battles,"—where a 12mo. of 100 pages, is devoted to the subject.

† This account, in common with most all others made by newspaper reporters, was incorrect in the particulars of the enemy's first advance. The reader will find the correct statement of the first assault given in our own version above.

rously; but by the time we were prepared to receive them, they had turned their heaviest fire on the left center, Sherman's division, and drove our men back from their camps, and bringing up a fresh force, opened fire on our left wing, under General McClernand. This fire was returned with terrible effect and determined spirit by both infantry and artillery along the whole line, for a distance of over four miles.

"General Hurlburt's division was thrown forward to support the center, when a desperate conflict ensued. The rebels were driven back with terrible slaughter, but soon rallied and drove back our men in turn. From about nine o'clock, the time your correspondent arrived on the field, until night closed on the bloody scene, there was no determination of the result of the struggle. The rebel regiments exhibited remarkably good generalship. At times engaging the left with apparently their whole strength, they would suddenly open a terrible and destructive fire on the right or center. Even our heaviest and most destructive fire upon the enemy did not appear to discourage their solid columns. The fire of Major Taylor's Chicago artillery raked them down in scores, but the smoke would no sooner be dispersed than the breach would again be filled.

"The most desperate fighting took place late in the afternoon. The rebels knew that if they did not succeed in whipping us then, that their chances for success would be extremely doubtful, as a portion of General Buell's forces had by this time arrived on the opposite side of the river, and another portion was coming up the river from Savannah. They became aware that we were being reenforced, as they could see General Buell's troops from the river-bank, a short distance above us on the left, to which point they had forced their way.

"At five o' clock the rebels had forced our left wing back so as to occupy fully two-thirds of our camp, and were fighting their way forward with a desperate degree of confidence in their efforts to drive us into the river, and at the same time heavily engaged our right.

"Up to this time we had received no reenforcements. General Lew. Wallace failed to come to our support until the day was over, having taken the wrong road from Crump's Landing, and being without other transports than those used for Quartermasters' and Commissary stores, which were too heavily laden to ferry any considerable number of General Buell's forces across the river, those that were here having been sent to bring up the troops from Savannah. We were, therefore, contesting against fearful odds, our force not exceeding thirty-eight thousand men, while that of the enemy was upward of sixty thousand.

"Our condition at this moment was extremely critical. Large numbers of men panic-stricken, others worn out by hard fighting, with the average percentage of skulkers, had struggled toward the river, and could not be rallied. General Grant and staff, who had been recklessly riding along the lines during the entire day, amid the unceasing storm of bullets, grape and shell, now rode from right to left, inciting the men to stand firm until our reenforcements could cross the river.

"Colonel Webster, Chief of staff, immediately got into position the heaviest pieces of artillery, pointing on the enemy's right, while a large number of the batteries were planted along the entire line, from the river-bank north-west to our extreme right, some two and a half miles distant. About an hour before dusk a general cannonading was opened upon the enemy from along our whole line, with a perpetual crack of musketry. Such a roar of artillery was never heard on this continent. For a short time the rebels replied with vigor and effect, but their return shots grew less frequent and destructive, while ours grew more rapid and more terrible.

"The gunboats *Lexington* and *Tyler*, which lay a short distance off, kept raining shell on the rebel hordes. This last effort was too much for the enemy, and, ere dusk had set in, the firing had nearly ceased, when night coming on all the combatants rested from their awful work of blood and carnage."

Then followed a list of the leading officers known to have been killed or wounded. It was meager, but gave names enough to plunge the country into mourning. Over Congress it threw a shadow which was betokened by the silence reigning in the halls after the news was received. That splendid army of the Union comprised some of the country's bravest spirits among its commanders, and all dreaded to read the lists which were hourly looked for after the receipt of the first news. The dispatch added: "There has never been a parallel to the gallantry and bearing of our officers, from the commanding General to the lowest officer. General Grant and staff were in the field, riding along the lines in the thickest of the enemy's fire during the entire two days of the battle, and all slept on the ground Sunday night, during a heavy rain. On several occasions General Grant got within range of the enemy's guns, and was discovered and fired upon. Lieutenant-Colonel McPherson had his horse shot from under him when alongside of General Grant. General Sherman had two horses killed under him, and General McClernand shared like dangers; also General Hurlburt, each of whom received bullet-holes through their clothes. General Buell remained with his troops during the entire second day, and with General Crittenden and General Nelson, rode continually along the lines encouraging the men."

This refers specially to the first day's battle which closed, leaving the enemy in the camps held in the morning by the Federal troops. No wonder that Beauregard—Johnston being among the enemy's fearful list of slain—telegraphed a victory to the Confederate arms. To have given the Federal advance a staggering blow—to be permitted to feast his half-fed troops on Federal rations, and to rest their dirty limbs on Federal blankets, in Federal tents, was indeed a victory for them, even if the morrow should find them hurled back in confusion upon their intrenchments and reserves at Corinth.*

The second day redeemed the disasters of the first. Buell's forces were marching in divisions, six miles apart. The advance (Nelson's brigades) reached Savannah on the 5th. There Buell arrived in person, on the evening of the same day. Crittenden's division came in during the evening. Hearing the terrific cannonading, Buell surmised its meaning and ordered forward Nelson's division at a quick march, without its train. Ammen's brigade arrived at the opportune moment, when Grant's forces were being slowly but surely pressed to the river's bank after their whole day's struggle. The fresh brigades immediately crossed and walked to the front. This arrival gave the wearied men fresh heart, and caused the enemy to fall back. The residue of Nelson's division came up and crossed the ferry early in the evening. Crittenden's division came on by steamers from Savannah. The batteries of Captains Mendenhall and Terrell, of the regular service, and Bartlett's Ohio battery, also came up. McCook's division, by a forced march, arrived at Savannah during the night of the 6th, and pushing on immediately, reached the Landing early on the morning of the 7th.

* As one of the "humors of the campaign," we may mention that the Memphis *Appeal* charged the Monday's defeat of the rebels to the *whiskey found, the night before, in the Federal tents!*

Buell's divisions, taking the Federal left wing, opened the day's work, soon after five o'clock, when Nelson's division moved forward upon the enemy's pickets, driving them in. The rebel artillery opened at six o'clock on Nelson's lines.

Grant gave the right Federal wing to General Lew Wallace's fine division of fresh men, which had arrived at eight o'clock on the evening of Sunday. Sherman's broken brigades again assumed the field, taking position next to Wallace. On the right the attack commenced early after daybreak, by Thompson's artillery, which opened on a rebel battery occupying a bluff to the front and right of Wallace's First brigade.

The battle soon became general. The enemy, during the night, had been reenforced to the utmost extent consistent with the safety of his defenses at Corinth, and was, therefore, prepared for a desperate conflict. It was evident, from his fighting that, if victory was won by the Union army, it must be at a fearful loss of life. But, the Federals—officers and men—were resolved upon victory even at a sacrifice of half their numbers, and they went into the fight with astonishing alacrity.

Wallace's position on the extreme right was one of great responsibility. But, he was the right man in the right place. He had for his coadjutor the really unconquerable Sherman, whose skeleton of a division was then as ready for the fray as if over one half of its numbers was not able to answer the roll call. Observing that his right was well protected by an impassable swamp formed by a creek, (Snake,) and discovering that the rebel left was open for a demonstration, Wallace determined to press it, if possible turn it. For that purpose, he stated in his report: "It became necessary for me to change front by a left half-wheel of the whole division. While the movement was in progress, across a road through the woods at the southern end of the field we were resting by, I discovered a heavy column of rebels going rapidly to reenforce their left, which was still retiring, covered by skirmishers, with whom mine were engaged. Thompson's battery was ordered up and shelled the passing column with excellent effect, but while so engaged he was opened on by a full battery planted in the field just beyond the strip of woods on the right. He promptly turned his guns at the new enemy. A fine artillery duel ensued, very honorable to Thompson and his company. His ammunition giving out in the midst of it, I ordered him to retire, and Lieutenant Thurber to take his place. Thurber obeyed with such alacrity, that there was scarcely an intermission in the fire, which continued so long and with such warmth as to provoke the attempt on the part of the rebels to charge the position. Discovering the intention, the First brigade was brought across the field to occupy the strip of woods in front of Thurber. The cavalry made the first dash at the battery, but the skirmishers of the Ninth Missouri poured an unexpected fire into them, and they retired pell-mell. Next the infantry attempted a charge; the First brigade easily repelled them. All this time my whole division was under a furious cannonade, but being well masked behind the bluff, or resting in the hollows of the woods, the regiments suffered but little."

This affair only stayed the advance for a brief period. The cleared field in front was intersected by a willow-fringed stream. Over this the First and Second brigades now pressed. The skirmishers in action all the way cleared the rise, and grouped themselves behind the ground-swells within seventy-five yards of the rebel lines. As the regiments approached them, suddenly a sheet of musketry blazed from the woods, and a battery opened upon them. About the same instant, the regiments supporting his left fell hastily back. To save his flank a halt was ordered. The wavering battalions soon recovered, when the two brigades pressed on with fixed bayonets. The rebels fell back into the woods, thus abandoning their first positions, which the Federals now held.

Fortune, however, wavered for a moment on the left of Wallace's well won position. Sherman advanced under cover of the three guns of the Chicago Light artillery, (Company A, Lieutenant P. P. Wood commanding,) until the line of McClernand's old camp was gained, on the Corinth road. There he first met Buell's column of veterans—such troops as only a military commander of the truest instincts can produce. Their steadiness and precision inspired the new recruits of Sherman's brigades with great confidence and enthusiasm. Willich's famous regiment advanced upon the enemy lurking, in heavy force, in a thicket of water-oaks. The reception by the enemy compelled even the invincible Indiana Thirty-second to retire before it. The fire of musketry was perfectly astounding, and Colonel Willich came from the wood with sadly riddled ranks. It was evident that *there* was to be the great struggle of the day. Into the thicket, to support Buell's forces, Sherman now led his men. He says: "The enemy had one battery close to Shiloh, and another near the Hamburg road, both pouring grape and canister upon my column of troops that advanced upon the green point of water-oaks. Willich's regiment had been repulsed, but a whole brigade of McCook's division advanced beautifully, deployed and entered this dreaded wood. I ordered my Second brigade, then commanded by Colonel T. Kilby Smith, (Colonel Stuart being wounded,) to form on its right, and my Fourth brigade, Colonel Buckland, on its left, all to advance abreast, with the Kentucky brigade before mentioned, (Rosseau's.) I gave personal direction to the twenty-four-pounder guns, whose fire soon silenced the enemy's guns to the left, and at the Shiloh meeting House. Rosseau's brigade moved in splendid order steadily to the front, sweeping everything before it, and at four P. M. stood upon the ground of our original front line. The enemy was then in full retreat."

This states a splendid achievement in very modest terms. It was one of the most severe and hotly contested sections of the field, where Beauregard commanded in person and was supported by the divisions of Bragg, Polk and Breckenridge.

Thus far for the fortunes of the Federal right. The center, under McClernand's command, was engaged from the first moment with great obstinacy. Finding Buell gaining ground on the left, while the right was slowly advancing, the enemy threw his greatest strength in several assaults upon the center, hoping to force it and thus retrieve the day. But McClernand's men were invincible. Hurlburt's somewhat thinned, but still resolute ranks moved up to his support, taking his left. There the obstinacy of the fight, at times, was not paralleled on the field. The two contestants seemed equally resolved not to yield a rood of ground. One who was present, on this portion of the field, wrote:

"It now became evident that the rebels were avoiding the extreme of the left wing, and endeavoring to find some weak point in the lines by which to turn our force, and thus create an irrevocable confusion. It is wonderful with what perseverance and determination they adhered to this purpose. They left one point but to return to it immediately, and then as suddenly would, by some masterly stroke of generalship, direct a most vigorous assault upon some division where they fancied they would not be expected. The fire of our lines was steady as clock-work, and it soon became evident that the enemy almost considered the task they had undertaken a hopeless one. Notwithstanding the continued rebuff of the rebels wherever they had made their assaults, up to two o'clock they had given no evidence of retiring from the field. Their firing had been as rapid and vigorous at times as during the most terrible hours of the previous day, yet not so well confined to one point of attack."

Hurlburt's forces, Second and Third brigades, were also doing great service in another part of the field, on the left, where, by their undaunted bravery, they contributed to the complete success of the day. Hurlburt thus chronicled the doings of his brigades:

"The Second brigade led the charge ordered by General Grant until recalled by Major-General Buell. The Third brigade was deeply and fiercely engaged on the right of General McClernand, successfully stopping a movement to flank his right, and holding their ground until the firing ceased. About one o'clock of that day, (Monday,) General McCook having closed up with General McClernand, and the enemy demonstrating in great force on the left, I went, by the request of General McClernand, to the rear of his line to bring up fresh troops, and was engaged in pressing them forward until the steady advance of General Buell on the extreme left, the firmness of the center, and the closing in from the right of Generals Sherman and Wallace determined the success of the day, when I called in my exhausted brigades, and led them to their camps. The ground was such on Sunday that I was unable to use cavalry. Colonel Taylor's Fifth Ohio cavalry was drawn up in order of battle until near one o'clock in the hope that some opening might offer for the use of this arm. None appearing, I ordered the command to be withdrawn from the reach of shot."

Wallace, after having forced the rebels back into their centre, pushed in upon them again by an oblique movement. This exposed his right flank, temporarily, when the Confederates suddenly threw their cavalry upon the right. The Twenty-third Indiana and one company of the First Nebraska, kept the enemy at bay until reserves came up, when a most obstinate conflict followed, and the rebels, bringing six or seven regiments immediately forward—their aim being to cut Wallace off from the army line, and thus "bag him," as Prentiss was bagged the day previous. As an evidence of fighting done there, we may recur to the words of the General:

"Pending this struggle, Colonel Thayer pushed on his command, and entered the woods, assaulting the enemy simultaneously with Colonel Smith. Here the Fifty-eighth Ohio and Twenty-third Indiana proved themselves fit comrades in battle with the noble Nebraska First. Here also the Seventy-sixth Ohio won a brilliant fame. The First Nebraska fired away its last cartridge in the action. At a word the Seventy-sixth Ohio rushed in and took its place. Off to the right, in the meanwhile, arose the music of the Twentieth and Seventy-eighth Ohio, fighting gallantly in support of Thurber, to whom the sound of rebel cannon seemed a challenge no sooner heard than accepted.

"From the time the wood was entered, forward was the only order. And step by step, from tree to tree, position to position, the rebel lines went back, never stopping again—infantry, horse and artillery, all went back. The firing was grand and terrible. Before us was the Crescent regiment of New Orleans; shelling us on the right was the Washington Artillery, of Manassas renown, whose last stand was in front of Colonel Whittlesey's command. To and fro, now in my front, then in Sherman's, rode General Beauregard, inciting his troops, and fighting for his fading *prestige* of invincibility. The desperation of the struggle may be easily imagined.

"While this was in progress, far along the lines to the left the contest was raging with equal obstinacy. As indicated by the sounds, however, the enemy seemed retiring everywhere. Cheer after cheer rung through the woods. Each man felt the day was ours.

"About four o'clock, the enemy to my front broke into rout, and ran through the camps occupied by General Sherman on Sunday morning. Their own camp had been established about two miles beyond. There, without halting, they fired tents, stores, etc. Throwing out the wounded, they filled their wagons full of arms, (Springfield muskets and Enfield rifles,) ingloriously thrown away by some of our troops the day before, and hurried on. After following them until nearly nightfall, I brought my division back to Owl Creek, and bivouacked it."

Buell, with Nelson's and Crittenden's divisions, pressed into the enemy's right as obstinately as Wallace had pressed their extreme left. Buell thus briefly states the important services of his command:

"Ammen's brigade, which was on the left, advanced in good order upon the enemy's right, but was checked for some time by his endeavor to turn our left flank, and by his strong center attack in front. Captain Terrell, who, in the mean time, had taken an advanced position, was compelled to retire, leaving one caisson, of which every horse was killed or wounded. It was very soon recovered. Having been reenforced by a regiment from General Boyle's brigade, Nelson's division again moved forward, and forced the enemy to abandon entirely his position. This success flanked the enemy at his second and third batteries, from which he was soon driven, with the loss of several pieces of artillery by the concentrated fire of Terrell's and Mendenhall's batteries, and an attack from Crittenden's division in front. The enemy made a second stand some eight hundred yards in rear of this position, and opened fire with his artillery. Mendenhall's battery was thrown forward, silenced the battery, and it was captured by Crittenden's division, the enemy retreating from it. In the mean time, the division of General McCook on the right, which became engaged somewhat later in the morning than the division on the left, had made steady progress, until it drove the enemy's left from the hotly-contested field. The action was commenced in this division by General Rosseau's brigade, which drove the enemy in front of it from his first position, and captured a battery. The line of attack of this division caused a considerable widening of the space between it and Crittenden's right. It was also outflanked on its right by the line of the enemy, who made repeated strong attacks on its flanks, but was always gallantly repulsed. The enemy made his last decided stand in front of this division, in the woods beyond Sherman's camp."

Johnston having been killed, Beauregard was in chief command. Everywhere along his lines rode that leader, striving by appeal, command, exposure of his own person, to arrest the tide of defeat, but to no purpose.* The steady flank advances of the Federal wings—the solidity of their centre, rendered it necessary to "retire," if he would not be cut off entirely from retreat. His baffled and somewhat dispirited brigades fell back slowly, gathering, in good order, in upon the Corinth road, which, in all the fortunes of the two day's fight, had been carefully secured from any approach of the Unionists. The retreat has been described as a rout, but such it was not to any great degree. Some regiments threw away their arms, blankets, etc., from exhaustion, and a reckless disregard of orders; while the great numbers of killed, wounded and exhausted, so absorbed even the transport wagons, as to compel the enemy to leave behind much of his camp equipage and some of his guns.

The pursuit was feeble. The nature of the woods restrained the cavalry in their movements, and rendered them comparatively useless. Three thousand finely-mounted fellows had waited, for two days, an opportunity to ride into the conflict; and the order, late in the day of Monday, to pursue and harass the enemy, gave them but a brief service. The infantry pushed forward only for a mile or two. Colonel Wagner's brigade of General Wood's division, arrived late in the day, and was given the order to advance to the front for the pursuit; but Buell knew so little of the topography of the country that he considered it hazardous to penetrate too far into the enemy's midst. This neglect to press the retreating foe gave

* To show what importance Johnston attached to the impending battle, we may quote from his address to his army, dated April 3d:

"SOLDIERS: I have put you in motion to offer battle to the invaders of your country, with the resolution, discipline and valor becoming men fighting, as you are, for all worth living and dying for. You can but march to a decided victory over *agrarian mercenaries*, sent to subjugate you and to despoil you of your liberties, property and honor.

"Remember the precious stake involved! Remember the dependence of your mothers, your wives, your sisters and your children on the result! Remember the fair, broad, abounding lands, the happy homes that will be desolated by your defeat! The eyes and hopes of eight millions of people rest upon you!" etc., etc.

them the poor consolation of pronouncing their effort to stay the Federal advance a success, and thereupon a victory. The press of the South quite generally heralded it as a great triumph for the Confederates! They needed some crumb of comfort to console them for the loss of Island No. 10, which General Pope's masterly strategy and Commodore Foote's "irrepressible" guns gave to the Federal arms, with all its garrison, armaments, stores, etc., on the morning of the 8th of April.

XXXVI.

INCIDENTS OF THE PITTSBURGH LANDING BATTLE.

THE field was strewn with the wounded and the dead. No time offered for the wounded to be cared for by their fellows, though, on the second day, as the Unionists advanced, the surgeons came on and did their duty manfully and well. Friend and foe were treated alike. Captain Jackson, of General Grant's staff, wrote: "The field presented a sorry spectacle. It extended over a distance of five miles in length and three-quarters of a mile in width. This space was fought over twice, in regular battle-array, and many times in the fluctuating fortunes of the different portions of the two armies. It was covered with dead and wounded. Where the artillery had taken effect, men lay in heaps, covering rods of ground, mingled in wild masses of mangled horses, broken gun-carriages and all the dread *debris* of a battle-field. Where our men had made their desperate charges, the bodies lay in rows as they had received the bayonet, constituting, at particular points, parapets of flesh and blood, over which a battle might have been fought, as over a breast-work. Not a tree or a sapling in that whole space which was not pierced through and through with cannon-shot and musket-balls, and, if we may believe the accounts, there was scarcely a rod of ground on the five miles which did not have a dead or wounded man upon it."

The struggle was of that character which made men forgetful of self. Every man seemed infused with only one thought, to kill as many as possible. One who was on the ground wrote of this obstinacy of both parties:

"On Sunday, especially, several portions of the ground were fought over three and four times, and the two lines swayed backward and forward, like advancing and retreating waves. In repeated instances, rebel and Union soldiers, protected by the trees, were within thirty feet of each other. The rebels derisively shouted 'Bull Run,' and our men returned the taunt by crying 'Donelson.' Many of the camps, as they were lost and won, lost again, and retaken, received showers of balls. At the close of the fight, General McClernand's tent contained twenty-seven bullet-holes, and his Adjutant's thirty-two. Chairs, tables, mess-pans, camp-kettles, and other articles of camp furniture were riddled. In the Adjutant's tent, when our forces recaptured it, the body of a rebel was found in a sitting position. He had evidently stopped for a moment's rest, when a ball struck and killed him. In one tree I have counted sixty bullet-holes. Another tree, not more than eighteen inches in diameter, which was in front of General Lew Wallace's division, bears the mark of more than ninety balls, within ten feet of the ground. On Sunday, Company A, of the Forty-ninth Illinois, lost from one volley twenty-nine men, including three officers; and, on Monday morning, the company appeared on the ground commanded by a Second Sergeant. General McClernand's Third Brigade, which was led by Colonel Raith, until he was mortally wounded, changed commanders three times during the battle. On Monday morning, one of General Hurlburt's regiments (the Third Iowa) was commanded by a First Lieutenant, and others were in command of Captains."

Such statements would be discredited were they not confirmed by those of other writers who have visited the field. They serve to prove how appalling must have been the slaughter, and yet out of the awful picture how the one great fact stands forth in a halo of glory—that of the courage of the Northern men! Such courage has its elements of sublimity which would immortalize any other people. But of Americans *it is expected*, and therefore, will not especially be noted by writers on the war. The correspondent above referred to says of the personal bearing and hair-breadth escapes of some of the commanders:

"General Grant is an illustration of the fortune through which some men, in the thickest showers of bullets, always escape. He has participated in two skirmishes and fourteen pitched battles, and is universally pronounced, by those who have seen him on the field, daring even to rashness; but he has never received a scratch. At four o'clock on Sunday evening, he was sitting upon his horse, just in the rear of our line of batteries, when Captain Carson, the scout who had reported to him a moment before, had fallen back, and was holding his horse by the bridle, about seven feet behind him—a six-pound shot, which flew very near General Grant, carried away all Carson's head, except a portion of the chin, passed just behind Lieutenant Graves, volunteer aid to General Wilson, tearing away the cantle of his saddle, cutting his clothing but not injuring him, and then took off the legs of a soldier in one of General Nelson's regiments, which were just ascending the bluff.

"About the same hour, further up to the right, General Sherman, who had been standing for a moment, while Major Hammond, his chief of staff, was holding his bridle, remounted. By the prancing of his horse, as he mounted, General Sherman's reins were thrown over his neck, and he was leaning forward in the saddle, with his head lowered, while Major Hammond was bringing them back over his head, when a rifle-ball struck the line in Major Hammond's hand, severing it within two inches of his fingers, and passing through the top and back of General Sherman's hat. Had he been sitting upright it would have struck his head. At another time a ball struck General Sherman on the shoulder, but his metallic shoulder-strap warded it off. With a third he was less fortunate, for it passed through his hand; but now he has nearly recovered from the wound. General Sherman had three horses shot under him, two with three balls each, and the last with two. It is the universal testimony that he manœuvered his troops admirably, and that he is the hero of the battle. His nomination to a Major-Generalship is a deserved tribute to one of the best officers in our service.

"General Hurlburt had a six-pound shot pass between his horse's head and his arm; a bullet passed through his horse's mane, and one of his horses was killed under him. Lieutenants Dorchester and Long, of his staff, each had several bullets and pieces of shell strike their clothing. Lieutenant Tesilian, of General McClernand's staff, had his clothing perforated by five balls, without receiving a wound. Major Hammond, of General Sherman's staff, had his cap cut by two bullets, and his boots by two, and two horses shot under him, but he escaped uninjured. A private in the Seventeenth Illinois had two of his front teeth knocked out by a bullet, which, though it entered his mouth, did him no further injury. A rifle-ball struck the temple of another private, near his right ear, passed through his head, and came out near the left ear; but he is recovering. Lieutenant Charles Provost, of the First Nebraska, received a bullet in the clasp of his sword-belt, and was afterward knocked down by the windage of a cannon-ball, but was not injured."

Of Buell's conduct, one of his men wrote in these enthusiastic terms: "I wish you could have seen the gallantry, the bravery, the dauntless daring, the coolness of General Buell. He seemed to be omnipresent. If ever man was qualified to command an army, it is he. He is a great, a *very* great General, and has proved himself so; not only in organizing and disciplining an army, but in handling it. General Buell had his horse shot under him. Captain Wright, his Aid, had the visor of his cap touched by a ball."

The fighting of not only regiments, but of individuals, afforded so many instances of remarkable courage, devotion and endurance, as to make the record one of extraordinary though painful interest. "Each man fought," said one of the newspaper correspondents from the bloody field, "as if success or defeat depended on his own right arm; and charge after charge was made upon the rebels to regain the ground we had lost. They stood firm as a rock; and though our artillery often swept down their ranks and left fearful gaps in their columns, they manifested no trepidation, nor did they waver for a moment. The living supplied the place of the dead. The musket that had fallen from a lifeless hand was seized at once, and the horrid strife swept on as before. The force of the enemy appeared increasing, and where the greatest havoc was made, there the strongest opposition was shown. Hand-to-hand contests were innumerable. Every struggle was for life. Quarter was asked on neither side, and the ground drank up the blood of hundreds of brave fellows every hour. Men lost their semblance of humanity, and the spirit of the demon shone in their faces. There was but one desire, and that was to destroy. There was little shouting. The warriors were too much in earnest. They set their teeth firm, and strained every nerve to its utmost tension. Death lost all its terrors, and men seemed to feed upon the sight of blood."

Of such ghastly features is the "grim front of war;" only the reality is more painful, more horrible than words can express. Men to contemplate it with serenity must be demons indeed, or else they must be mastered by emotions higher and nobler than love of life or self—the love of a cause which Heaven consecrates.

One of General Buell's manœuvres, characteristic of his off-hand and reliable way of meeting exigencies, is happily illustrated in the following:

"They were advancing in great force to turn our left and capture our transports and supplies, when Buell, becoming aware of their intentions, made preparations to receive them. About half a mile above the Landing are two large ridges running back from the river. The ridge next to the Landing is the highest. Buell placed a battery on each of the ridges, and between them he placed a brigade of infantry. The troops were ordered to lie down. He then ordered the lower battery to fire on the enemy and make a show of retreating in confusion, so to draw the rebels on. On came the rebels pell-mell, yelling at the top of their voices, 'Bull Run! Bull Run!' thinking to frighten us. As soon as the rebels came in range, the lower battery, agreeably to orders, opened fire, retreated, and took a position in the rear of the upper battery. The rebels, seeing our men retreating, charged up the hill and took possession of the battery. The rebels, in the mean time, were not aware of our troops being in the hollow below them. At this moment the signal was sounded, and the whole brigade rose to their feet and poured a deadly fire of rifle-balls into the ranks of the rebels, cutting them down by scores. At this favorable moment, also, the upper battery poured in a perfect storm of grape and canister shot. The rebels reeled and staggered like drunken men, and at last broke and fled in every direction, leaving the ground strewed with dead and dying."

The losses of the Union forces in the two days struggle have been set down at 13,508, distributed as follows:

GRANT'S ARMY.

DIVISIONS.	KILLED.	WOUNDED.	MISSING.	TOTAL.
1—General McClernand,	251	1,351	236	1,848
2—General W. H. L. Wallace,	228	1,033	1,163	2,424
3—General Lew Wallace,	43	257	5	305
4—General Hurlburt,	313	1,449	223	1,985
5—General Sherman,	318	1,275	441	2,034
6—General Prentiss,	196	562	1,802	2,760
Total,	1,349	5,927	3,870	11,356

BUELL'S ARMY.

DIVISIONS.	KILLED.	WOUNDED.	MISSING.	TOTAL.
2—General McCook,	95	793	8	896
4—General Nelson,	90	591	58	739
5—General Crittenden,	80	410	27	517
Total,	265	1,794	93	2,152
Grand Total,	1,614	7,721	3,963	13,508

That of the enemy in killed and wounded was much greater than the Union loss. Of the rebel losses no authentic data probably ever will be furnished. The Sunday's fight they could report upon and not upon that of Monday, where they were compelled to leave their dead upon the field, from which they were driven. After Monday's fight, General McClernand's division buried the remains of six hundred and thirty-eight rebels left upon the field, General Sherman's, six hundred, General Nelson's, two hundred and sixty-three, and Colonel's Thayer's brigade of General Lew Wallace's division, one hundred and twenty-three. These were the only commands from which returns were received; but the most of the other divisions and brigades buried a proportionate number. The rebels must have lost four thousand killed, by the most moderate estimate. After the battle, Captain Russell of the Sixth Ohio counted the bodies of one hundred and twenty-six rebels, lying where they fell, upon a strip of land less than one-fourth of a mile long, and fifty yards in width. Eleven of them, in front, had fallen nearly in line, about five paces apart, and were evidently skirmishers. Colonel Thayer of the First Nebraska, in another portion of the field, opposite General Sherman's division, counted thirty-seven dead rebels, side by side, who had evidently been killed while in line of battle, by a single volley. Sixty-eight were counted in front of the ground held by the Forty-eighth Ohio, and eighty-five in front of the Seventy-second Ohio. A detail of men from General McCook's division buried in a single trench one hundred and forty-seven, including three Lieutenant-Colonels and four Majors. A tabular statement published in the Memphis *Argus*, April 24th, confessed to nine hundred and twenty-seven killed, four thousand four hundred and seventy-one wounded and three hundred and sixty-one missing. As this statement was but fragmentary, and "daily additions were being made to the list," it was only valuable for showing what regiments were in the engagement. They were (so far as named :) One hundred and fifty-fourth Tennessee; Fifteenth Tennessee; Blythe's "Mississippi;" Breckenridge's brigade; Eleventh, First, Thirteenth and Fourth Louisiana; Second, Fourth, Forty-seventh, Sixth, First, Twenty-second, Thirteenth, Fifth, Twentieth, Nineteenth, Twenty-eighth, Forty-fifth and Thirty-third Tennessee; Twentieth, Twenty-second, Twenty-fifth and Sixteenth Alabama; First and Thirteenth Arkansas; Seventh Kentucky; Fifteenth and Twenty-second Mississippi; First Missouri; Polk's, Banks' and Stamford's batteries; Forrest's cavalry, &c., &c. Several companies of Texan rangers were also engaged in the fight.

Bearing on the enemy's losses we may cite the dispatch of Beauregard to Adjutant-General Cooper, of the Confederate army establishment. That dispatch was intercepted by General Mitchell in his rapid and unexpected descent on Huntsville, Alabama, where the telegraph office was seized. In its freshly-booked business file was found the following :

"CORINTH, April 9th.

"*To General Samuel Cooper, Richmond, Va.* :

"All present probabilities are that whenever the enemy moves on this position he will do so with an overwhelming force of not less than vrzole xriy lohkjnap men, by wna ahc vkjlyi hate nqhkl lorite xrmy lohkjnap yx31 wlrmqj mna phia may possibly shrakj ran xyc pnejcrlo nghkl xrlly 5a lohkjnap vhmy. Can we not be reinforced xrhn dyvgzilhaj nive. If defeated here cy thjy lov vrjq mnt 3yc nap dchqn4te hki wnkjy whereas we could even afford to lose for a while wonilyjlha nap inmzu5yl for the purpose of defeating qkyt4j nive, which would not only insure us the valley of the Mississippi, but our independence.

P. G. T. BEAUREGARD."

The "astronomer General" was not long in deciphering this. He had studied the laws of refraction and reflection too long to be baffled by this *divertisement.* Here is the translation:

"CORINTH, April 9th.

"*To General Samuel Cooper, Richmond, Va.:*

"All present probabilities are that whenever the enemy moves on this position he will do so with an overwhelming force of not less than eighty-five thousand men. We can now muster only about thirty-five thousand effective (men.)* Van Dorn may possibly join us in a few days with fifteen thousand more. Can we not be reenforced from Pemberton's army? If defeated here we lose the Mississippi valley, and probably our cause; whereas we could even afford to lose for a while Charleston and Savannah, for the purpose of defeating Buell's army, which would not only insure us the valley of the Mississippi but our independence.

P. G. T. BEAUREGARD."

This tells a woeful story of losses, for it is certain that, in the attack of Sunday, forty-five thousand men were engaged; while in that of Monday, at least seventy-five thousand men were brought into the field. The General doubtless considered a large portion of his command *non-effective* from exhaustion, demoralization, desertion and sickness.

---

* Beauregard's dispatch announcing to his Government the tidings of the second day's battle, read:

"We have gained a great and glorious victory. Eight to ten thousand prisoners and thirty-six pieces of cannon. Buell reenforced Grant and we retired to our intrenchments at Corinth, which we can hold. Loss heavy on both sides."

No matter if the "eight to ten thousand prisoners" actually was about one-third of that number—no matter if his own losses in prisoners were immense—no matter if his losses of artillery *exceeded* the number given as captured by him; these facts were only for "private circulation"—those given in the dispatch were for the public. The confessions to the Adjutant-General was the key-note to the truth. But that was only for the private, official ear.

XXXVII.

A DIGRESSION.

VICTORIES of the most signal character followed so rapidly, one after the other during the latter part of April and the early part of May, (1861,) that the public expressed disappointment if each morning's paper did not contain its usual "display" of big type announcing another great conquest. Small affairs, where but ten or fifteen thousand troops were engaged, attracted but little attention. It was only the bombardment and fall of Fort Macon; the bombardment and fall of Fort Pulaski; the bombardment of Forts Jackson and St. Philip and the fall of New Orleans; the evacuation of Yorktown and the pursuit of the rebel grand army toward Richmond; only these that were the street talk, so insatiable was the public for heavy blows. Look at the record of news for one week, as gleaned from the files of the leading journals:

SUNDAY, April 27.—Received news that the advance guard, under General Halleck, had attacked and driven back a body of rebels which acted as rear guard of the rebel post of Corinth. Date of fight, April 24th. Lieutenant Gwinn, of the United States Navy, in command of the Tennessee river fleet, led a land expedition to Bear Creek Bridge, of the Memphis and Charleston Railroad, destroyed two spans of the bridge, each one hundred and ten feet, about five hundred feet of trestle work, and half a mile of the rebel military telegraph line. The rebels hastily retreated after a short skirmish.

MONDAY, April 28.—Received news of the capture of New

Orleans. The surrender was formally made on Saturday, April 26th. General McClellan captured a lunette fortification in front of Yorktown, driving the rebels out at a charge. This capture was also effected on Saturday, April 26. General Banks reported our troops in possession of Stanton, Virginia, Saturday, April 26th.

WEDNESDAY, April 30.—Received news that a cavalry reconnoissance met a foraging party outside of Monterey, near the Mississippi border, and, after a skirmish, in which five rebels were killed, including one Major, captured nineteen prisoners, putting the rest to flight. Major Duncan, of General Canby's staff, with a small force, obtained a victory over the Texan rebels in New Mexico, routing them entirely after a spirited fight.

THURSDAY, May 1.—Received the news that a skirmish had taken place within a few miles of Corinth, between one of the advance brigades of General Halleck's army and the rebels. The Union army was victorious. Date of fight, April 29th.

FRIDAY, May 2.—Received news that the forces of General Halleck had a skirmish with the rebels at Purdy; drove them through the town, which the Union troops took possession of, burnt two bridges, and ran a locomotive into the river. This action cut off all communication between Corinth and the North. Date of action, April 30th.

Received intelligence through rebel sources, that Fort Macon had been surrendered, after a lengthy bombardment. Date of surrender, April 26th.—General Mitchell telegraphed that his forces had skirmished with and routed the rebels at Bridgeport, Ala., capturing the place. Date of fight, Wednesday, April 30th.—General Halleck reported that Major Hubbard, with one hundred and fifty of the First Missouri volunteers, had defeated Colonels Coffee and Stearnweight, with a force of six hundred Indians, at Neosho, capturing sixty-two prisoners and seventy-six horses. Date of conflict, Saturday, April 26th.

SATURDAY, May 3.—General Mitchell reports that after his skirmish of Wednesday, his troops crossed from the island to the mainland, captured two cannon and their ammunition. The rebels retreated in great confusion, without again offering battle.—The evacuation of Corinth reported in the South. No official account thereof received from our troops.—Baton Rouge reported once more in the possession of the Union troops.

SUNDAY, May 4.—Received full particulars of the battle of Camden, or South Mills, under General Reno, reported by the rebels as a victory for their forces. It has since proved to have been a defeat.—The arrival of the *Santiago de Cuba* brings intelligence of the capture of the rebel steamer *Isabel*, or *Ella Warley;* capture of the schooner *Bee*, capture of a schooner without a name, etc.—The arrival of the *Empire City* reports the capture of the contraband steamer *Nostra Signora de Regla.*—The captured rebel steamers *Bermuda* and *Florida* arrived at Philadelphia on Saturday, May 3d.

SUNDAY EVENING, May 4.—Yorktown evacuated by the rebels. General McClellan reports his forces in possession of the ramparts, guns, ammunition, camp equipage, *everything*, and his troops in full pursuit of the retreating rebels.—Gloucester in possession of the Union troops. General Paine made a reconnoissance to Farmington, Mississippi; met, fought with and defeated four thousand five hundred rebels, and captured the position, some prisoners, their tents, camp equipage, etc. The cavalry in pursuit of the retreating rebels. Date of fight, May 3d.—An artillery reconnoissance destroyed two trestle bridges, and some track of the Memphis and Charleston Railroad, at Glendale, Mississippi. Date, May 3d.

All this in one week. Yet one of the leading journals, with an impudence that bordered on the sublime, stated (in the middle of May) that "what the Union cause now most needs is a striking victory, which shall at once prove the superiority of the Federal arms, and thus demonstrate *toward* a final triumph." Can meanness go farther than this? The London *Times* said, early in June, that it was ascertained the Union victories, if such were ever won, were only obtained by *forcing* the Federal soldiers into battle by planting cavalry behind them to cut down any regiment that flinched! The malignancy of the Southern mind found a fit counterpart in the contemptible meanness of the English heart, for through all our gigantic struggle against treason and conspiracy to overthrow the Union, the English press—with one or two honorable exceptions—sedulously misinterpreted, scoffed, maligned and ridiculed the progress of the Federal arms and the measures of the Federal Government. So much for a "great and chivalrous nation!" History will point to her in scorn as the embodiment of hypocrisy, dishonor and malice. The people of the United States can afford to await their time to redress the insults heaped upon them by a people whose very existence depends in so large a measure upon American products and money. A bitterness has grown in the American heart, toward the old enemy, during the progress of the war for the Union, which it will take more than one generation to forget. *There never will be a satisfied people on these shores, until British insolence and ingratitude is thoroughly and permanently punished.*

In saying this we simply interpret a sentiment which every intelligent American knows to exist. Let those who are wise read the "signs of the times" aright, and be prepared for a conflict for supremacy which will as surely come as that British insolence has an existence. The Great Republic has only fought half the fight for human liberty, and popular Government, in repressing the Southern rebellion: the other half is to be fought with those enemies of the Republic in Europe who presume to sit in judgment on our affairs; to say what we shall and shall not do—as if they were the arbiters of the destinies of the American Continent. The Nineteenth Century must witness the complete supremacy of the American Union in the affairs of this Continent, without fears of foreign "intervention" or dictation, or it must witness the downfall of popular Government. The century has no other issue.

XXXVIII.

BOMBARDMENT OF FORTS JACKSON AND ST. PHILIP, AND THE FALL OF NEW ORLEANS.

THE conflict with the forts guarding the approach to New Orleans, added to the lustre of American arms, and afforded another demonstration of the immense superiority of fleets over land defenses. The first official announcement from the scene of the contest was as follows:

"To the Hon. GIDEON WELLES, Secretary of the Navy.

"I have the honor to announce that, in the providence of God, which smiles upon a just cause, the squadron under flag-officer Farragut, has been vouchsafed a glorious victory and triumph in the capture of the city of New Orleans, Forts Jackson, St. Philip, Livingston and Pike, the batteries above and below New Orleans, as well as the total destruction of the enemy's gunboats, steam rams, floating batteries (iron-clad,) fire-rafts, and obstructions, booms and chains. The enemy, with their own hands, destroyed from eight to ten millions of cotton and shipping. Our loss is thirty-six killed and one hundred and twenty-three wounded. The enemy lost from one thousand to fifteen hundred, besides several hundred prisoners. The way is clear, and the rebel defenses destroyed from the Gulf to Baton Rouge, and, probably, to Memphis. Our flag waves triumphantly over them all. I am bearer of dispatches.

(Signed) "THEODORUS BAILEY."

This most important announcement was dated at Fortress Monroe, May 8th, 1862. It filled the hearts of loyalists with rejoicing and sent dismay into the hearts of the revolutionists. It was just cause for rejoicing, opening, as it virtually did, the Mississippi river to commerce, and depriving the rebels of their most important metropolis. Recognizing its importance, the Confederates had so fortified the approaches as to deem the city safe, and they looked forward to the Federal struggle with their forts and obstructions, with a satisfaction not at all repressed. The New Orleans papers were defiant and derisive until the sudden knowledge (April 26th) that the Federal gunboats were approaching the city, when dismay sent the over-confident and boastful press into the most painful condition of wounded pride.

The story of the struggle by which the Union forces under General Butler were placed in possession of the capital, forms one of the most novel and deeply interesting chapters of the war. We will recur to it with as much brevity as is consistent with completeness.

The success of the expeditions against Hatteras, Port Royal and the North Carolina coast inspired the Navy Department with new zeal in the prosecution of its plans for the reduction of New Orleans. It secretly organized an immense fleet of gunboats, mortars and transports, giving the fleet command to Commodore D. G. Farragut, and the mortar flotilla to Captain D. D. Porter; while an expeditionary corps of land forces was placed under command of Major-General B. F. Butler. The destination of the fleet and flotilla was kept a secret for some time, though by March 20th it became generally understood that New Orleans was its point of combined operations. Butler's forces centered at Ship Island early in March. Brigadier-General Phelps assuming command, awaiting the superior officer's arrival. The fleet arrived at Ship Island late in March; the bomb flotilla and transports rapidly followed, bearing an armament of mortars, the strength of which exceeded that brought to bear upon Sebastopol.

This concentration at once threatened Mobile and New Orleans. The rebels immediately deserted Pensacola, which they had fortified with so much labor and cost—the land forces under Bragg hastening to reenforce Johnston and Beauregard at Corinth, and the artillerists from the forts going to strengthen the garrisons in the forts guarding Mobile and New Orleans. The forts, Navy-yard, dry dock, store houses, barracks and marine hospital at Pensacola were abandoned, April 6–9th. On the night of the latter day they were fired by the coast guard and consumed. This left no "enemy in the rear" to attend to, and all attention was directed to the work in hand against the forts commanding the approaches to New Orleans.

The fleet and flotilla gathered, during the middle of April, in the Mississippi River, ten miles below Fort Jackson. The novel expedient was then resorted to of painting the vessels with *mud*—the more effectually to hide them from the enemy's sight. The masts were afterwards rigged out with bushes and ever-greens, thus quite successfully *masking* their proportions. It was only by the smoke of the Federal guns that their location could be marked by the enemy. Under the leafy covert of the river banks the mortar-boats fought, when the bombardment finally opened, in comparative security, sending their fearful thirteen-inch shells into the Fort (Jackson) with precision, without offering any target for a return fire. The mud-paint and bush-masque were a "Yankee trick," for which the rebels were not prepared.

The bomb flotilla was prepared for the bombardment by the 17th. The rebels sent fire rafts, in large numbers, down the river, hoping to destroy some of the Union boats, but they were uniformly *suppressed* by a ball or two from one of the rifled guns. "The mortar fleet sent the first missile howling over the water," wrote a correspondent, "towards Fort Jackson at precisely half-past nine on the morning of Friday, April 18th. It is called Good Friday in the calendar of the Church, although anything but a good day for the rebels. Our schooners lay partly hidden from the enemy behind the trees and under the brushwood of a dense swamp which stretches along the right bank of the river. With a curious display of ingenuity, they baffled the eyes of the enemy still further by dressing up their masts and rigging with the branches of green withes and leaves, which so confounded them with the woods that at a distance they could scarcely be distinguished. The rebel gunners learned only from the wreaths of smoke which curled above the seeming forest the temporary position of their assailants. This will be pronounced a Yankee trick, doubtless, by our secession critics and their sympathetic friends abroad, or else, that it was borrowed from Macbeth's enemies, when 'Birnam wood did come to Dunsinane.'

"The distance of the foremost vessel from the Fort was three thousand three hundred and forty yards, and the three divisions of which the fleet was composed engaged in the fire alternately, each division firing for four hours and then resting for eight. The rate of fire generally observed was, one shell from each mortar of the division every ten minutes. As Fort Jackson replied with considerable rapidity and vigor, you may conceive the noise of the thunder, which was continued for six days and five nights.

"Fortunately, our schooners were mostly out of the range of Fort Jackson, and only within range of Fort Philip; but, even from the latter, nothing but rifled guns and mortars were at all dangerous. Fortunately again, the enemy had few of these customers to send us, and we fought comparatively secure. Many of our vessels were struck, in the course of the long engagement, but only one of them was severely injured, and only two of their men severely wounded."

The firing of the bomb and gunboats having apparently done but indifferent service in disabling the forts, Commodore Farragut determined to "run their fire" and make for the city without waiting for the reduction of the formidable defenses. All night long of the 23d the vessels of the squadron were arranging for the perilous attempt, and were on the way by three A. M. Captain Porter, in his report, said:

"We commenced the bombardment of Fort Jackson on the 18th, and continued it without intermission until the squadron made preparations to move. The squadron was formed in three lines to pass the forts. Captain Bailey's division composed of the following vessels, leading to the attack on Fort St. Philip, viz.: *Cayuga*, *Pensacola*, *Mississippi*, *Oneida*, *Varuna*, *Katahden*, *Kineo* and *Wissahicon*. Flag Officer Farragut leading the following (second line): *Hartford*, *Brooklyn* and *Richmond*; and Commander Bell leading the third division composed of the following vessels: *Sciota*, *Iroquois*, *Pi nola*, *Winona*, *Itasca* and *Kennebec*.

"The steamers belonging to the mortar flotilla were to enfilade the water battery commanding the approaches; mortar steamers *Harriet Lane*, *Westfield*, *Owasco*, *Clifton* and *Suanee*, and the *Jackson* towing the *Portsmouth*. The vessels of the squadron were rather late in getting weigh and into line; and did not get fairly started until 3:30 A. M. The unusual bustle apprised the garrison that something was going on.

"In an hour and ten minutes after the vessels had weighed anchor, they had passed the forts, under a most terrific fire, which they returned with interest. The mortar fleet rained down shells upon Fort Jackson to try and keep the men from the guns, while the steamers of the mortar fleet poured in shrapnel upon the water battery commanding the approach at a short distance, keeping them comparatively quiet. When the last vessel could be seen, amid the fire and smoke, to pass the battery, signal was made to the mortars to cease firing, and the flotilla steamers were directed to retire from a contest that would soon become unequal."

This alludes only incidentally to that extraordinary "running the muck." From a *resume* of the eventful passage, we may quote: "Just before dawn the squadron was discovered approaching by the enemy. The fury with which it was attacked is proved by the tremendous exertions our vessels were compelled to make in order to carry through their purpose. At first the rebel fleet endeavored only to check their progress, while the two forts poured incessant volleys upon them; but presently the action became closer and more involved, and mainly confined to the river. Hollins' 'ram,' the *Manassas*, although it afterward turned out a helpless and feeble fabric, served the rebels well for a time. It not only engaged Commodore Farragut's flag-ship, the *Hartford*, but also succeeded in forcing a fire raft upon her, from which she narrowly escaped destruction. 'I thought it was all up with us,' said the Commodore in a letter describing the event to

Captain Porter. The flames were, however, extinguished in time to save the ship, and the 'ram' betook itself to other errands of destruction. The floating battery *Louisiana*, which lay moored not far from Fort Jackson, also occasioned great inconvenience. Its firing was well directed, and its metallic sides were found to be quite impenetrable. Other 'rams' emulated the *Manassas*, and attacked our gunboats with considerable effect. The *Varuna*, gallantly commanded by Captain Boggs, was broken in pieces by their repeated onsets, but before her own destruction she made her name memorable by disabling and destroying no less than six of the rebel craft. Five of these were set in flames by the *Varuna's* shell and run ashore, and another was shattered and forced to surrender. The intrepid tenacity of the *Varuna*'s officers and crew is best illustrated by the fact that her last broadside, which beat in the sides of the ram *Morgan*, was fired while the gun-carriages on her upper deck were already settling in the water. During this time our other gunboats were not idle. Nine of them, together with the sloops-of-war, fought their way up the river, and gradually widened the space between themselves and the forts. A few were beaten back, having received injuries to their machinery which rendered them incapable of proceeding. The *Itasca*, for example, is said to have received thirteen shots under her water line, beside having her boiler destroyed. But a sufficient number passed to secure the success of the expedition. Even at the last moment, the rebels maintained the struggle. Some of their steamers, which had been spared on condition of surrendering, broke away and renewed the fight at other points. Finally, the 'ram' *Manassas*, after the engagement had virtually ended, and when the Union squadron was seeking an anchorage, bustled up after them, and fired a shot or two at the *Richmond*. The *Mississippi* turned swiftly to resent the insult, when, as if fearful of the consequences of its temerity, the 'ram' immediately ran ashore, was deserted, and was forthwith pounded to fragments by three heavy broadsides from its pursuer.

"The conflict was a short one, lasting only an hour and a

half at the most. By half-past five in the morning our success had been achieved, and the destiny of New Orleans decided. It was a result which the rebels never had anticipated, and which could never have been obtained except by the most devoted and unshrinking bravery. The consternation of the people of New Orleans was all the greater for the confidence they had cherished. After this decisive action only the merest show of resistance was offered at the fortifications intended for the immediate protection of the city. The fleet lay before New Orleans on the morning of the 25th. The inhabitants seemed possessed with a frenzy of rage and apprehension. They were destroying all accessible property, the rebel General Lovell having set the example by burning his own goods. The officer sent on shore by Commodore Farragut was received by the people, whom their Mayor afterward characterized as 'gallant and sensitive to all that can affect their dignity and self-respect,' with brutal and ferocious demonstration of insult. In spite of this and similar actions, the dignity of our own mission was sustained, and the quiet occupation of the city by our forces was duly carried into effect."

Farragut announced his success in the following rather laconic epistle to the commander of the flotilla:

"DEAR PORTER: We had a rough time of it, as Boggs will tell you, but, thank God, the number of killed and wounded was very small, considering. This ship had two killed and eight wounded. We destroyed the ram in a single combat between her and the old *Mississippi*, but the ram backed out when she saw the *Mississippi* coming at him so rampantly, and he dodged her and ran on shore, wherupon Smith put two or three broadsides through him and knocked him all to pieces. The ram pushed a fire-raft on to me, and in trying to avoid it I ran the ship on shore. He again pushed the fire-raft on me, and got the ship on fire all along one side. I thought it was all up with us, but we put it out and got off again, proceeding up the river, fighting our way. We have destroyed all but two of the gunboats, and these will have to surrender with the forts. I intend to follow up my success and push for New Orleans and then come down and attend to the forts, so you hold them in *statu quo* until I come back. I think if you send a flag of truce and demand their surrender they will yield, for their intercourse with the city is cut off. We have cut the wires above the Quarantine and are now going ahead. I took three hundred or four hundred prisoners at

Quarantine. They surrendered and I paroled them not to take up arms again. I could not stop to take care of them. If the General will come up to the bayou and land a few men or as many as he pleases, he will find two of our gunboats there to protect him from the gunboats that are at the forts. I wish to get to the English Turn, where they say they have not placed a battery yet, but have two above, nearer New Orleans."

Captain Boggs' account of his exploit deserves notice. We give the material portions of his report:

"Sir: I have the honor to report that, after passing the batteries with the steamer *Varuna* under my command, on the morning of the 24th, finding my vessel amid a nest of rebel steamers, I started ahead, delivering her fire both starboard and port at every one that she passed. The first on her starboard beam that received her fire appeared to be crowded with troops. Her boiler was exploded and she drifted to shore. In like manner three other vessels, and one of them a gunboat, were driven ashore in flames and afterwards blew up.

"At six A. M. the *Varuna* was attacked by the *Morgan*, iron-clad about the bow, commanded by Beverley Kennion, an ex-naval officer. This vessel raked us along the port gangway, killing four and wounding nine of the crew, butting the *Varuna* on the quarter and again on the starboard side. I managed to get three eight-inch shell into her abaft her armor, as also several shot from the after rifled gun, when she dropped out of action partially disabled.

"While still engaged with her another rebel steamer, iron-clad, with a prow under water, struck us on the port-gangway, doing considerable damage. Our shot glanced from her bow. She backed off for another blow, and struck again in the same place, crushing in the side, but by going ahead fast the concussion drew her bow around, and I was able with the port guns to give her, while close alongside, five eight-inch shells abaft her armor. This settled her, and drove her ashore in flames. Finding the *Varuna* sinking, I ran her into the bank, let go her anchor, and tied up to the trees.

"During all this time the guns were actively at work, crippling the *Morgan*, which was making feeble efforts to get up steam.

"The fire was kept up until the water was over the gun-trucks, when I turned my attention to getting the wounded and crew out of the vessel. The *Oneida*, Captain Lee, seeing the condition of the *Varuna*, had rushed to her assistance, but I waved her on, and the *Morgan* surrendered to her, the vessel in flames.

"I have since learned that over fifty of her crew were killed and wounded, and she was set on fire by her commander, who burned his wounded with his vessel. I cannot award too much praise to the officers and crew of the *Varuna* for the noble manner in which they supported me, and their coolness under such exciting circumstances, particularly when extinguishing fire, having been set on fire twice during the action by shells.

"In fifteen minutes from the time the *Varuna* was struck she was on the bottom, with only her topgallant forecastle out of water. The officers and crew lost everything they possessed, no one thinking of leaving his station until driven thence by water."

The forts followed the fate of the city. A demand was made by Captain Porter for their surrender, immediately after the passage up of Commodore Farragut's squadron; but, the commanding officer, Colonel Higgins, refused to give up, particularly as he regarded himself able to hold the position for a time longer against Porter's bombs. Porter preferred to await the coming up of Butler's forces from the land side, to invest and carry the works by storm. Aware of this approach of the land forces, the commanding officer in the main fortress, together with General J. R. Duncan, commanding the coast defenses, and W. B. Renshaw,* commanding the rebel "navy," accepted the terms of capitulation extended by Captain Porter.

The forts finally surrendered, as stated, April 28th. Porter, in his account of the interview with the rebel officers, reflected in severe terms upon the want of honor in one commander J. K. Mitchell, who, while the negotiations for the surrender were transpiring, towed above the fort, with his three steamers, an iron floating battery of sixteen guns. This was set on fire and sent adrift to come down upon the *Harriet Lane*, on board of which the articles of capitulation were being arranged. Porter said: "While drifting down on us the guns, getting heated, exploded, throwing the shots above the river. A few minutes after the floating battery exploded with a terrific noise, throw-

---

* This Renshaw was one of the Lieutenants in command at Pensacola Navy Yard, in 1861; and, in conjunction with Captain Farrand, he betrayed that important property into the hands of those with whom he had been, for some time, conspiring. His release, on "parole," was a great mistake, since it recognized him as an ordinary belligerent. He should have been held, to be tried for high treason.

ing the fragments all over the river, and wounding one of their own men in Fort St. Philip, and immediately disappeared under water. Had she blown up near the vessels she would have destroyed the whole of them." It is well to know that Porter thrust the scoundrels into close quarters when he obtained possession of their persons a few hours afterward. They ought to have been instantly tried by court-martial and shot for their rascality. In doing as they did, the rebels on board the steamers only expressed their own disregard for all the rules of civilized warfare. They courted savage treatment, and should, in strict justice, have had it; but, in consonance with the general course pursued toward the Southern prisoners, they were treated with lenity.

The forts, after capitulation, were turned over to General Phelps. Porter said of their condition: "Fort Jackson is a perfect ruin. I am told that over one thousand eight hundred shells fell in and burst over the centre of the fort. The practice was beautiful. The next fort we go at we will settle sooner, as this has been hard to get at. The naval officers sunk one gunboat while the capitulation was going on, but I have one of the others, a steamer, at work, and hope soon to have the other."

XXXIX.

INCIDENTS OF THE CAPTURE OF FORTS JACKSON AND ST. PHILIP, AND THE FALL OF NEW ORLEANS.

BEFORE our bombardment of the forts began, the commanders of the British and French men-of-war lying in the river expressed a desire to visit the enemy, of course to examine his preparations. The Commodore readily granted their request. When they returned, they assured him that it was of no use for him to attempt the capture of New Orleans in that direction; it could not be done with wooden vessels. The brave old tar replied: "I was sent here to make the attempt. You may be right, but I came here to take New Orleans—to pass the forts—and *I shall try it on!*"

Of the fire-rafts sent down on the 18th and 19th, to destroy our fleet, a reporter present at the scene, wrote: "Our men had an opportunity to test, in a practical manner, their means for destroying fire-rafts, and they proved to be an admirable success. A turgid column of black smoke, arising from resinous wood, was seen approaching us from the vicinity of the forts. Signal lights were made, the varied colors of which produced a beautiful effect upon the foliage of the river bank, and rendered the darkness intenser by contrast when they disappeared. Instantly a hundred boats shot out towards the raft, which now was blazing fiercely, and casting a wide zone of light upon the water. Two or three of the gunboats then got under way and steamed boldly toward the unknown thing of terror. One of them, the *Westfield*, Captain Renshaw, gallantly opens her steam valves, and dashes furiously upon it, making the sparks fly and timbers crash with the force of her blow. Then a stream of water from her hose plays upon the blazing mass. Now the small boats lay alongside, coming up helter-skelter, and actively employing their men. We see everything distinctly in the broad glare—men, oars, boats, buckets, and ropes. The scene looks phantom-like, supernatural; intensely interesting, extremely exciting, inextricably confused. But, finally, the object is nobly accomplished. The raft, yet fiercely burning, is taken out of range of the anchored vessels and towed ashore, where it is slowly consumed. As the boats return they are cheered by the fleet, and the scene changes to one of darkness and repose, broken occasionally by the gruff hail of a seaman when a boat, sent on business from one vessel to another, passes through the fleet. We have a contempt for fire-rafts. They have proved, like many other things, to be 'weak inventions of the enemy.'"

Fort Jackson, as stated by Captain Porter, was greatly shattered by the appalling fire of the flotilla and fleet. The drawbridges were completely destroyed; the cisterns were demolished; the casemates and passages were filled with water, the levee having been cut away. The platforms for tents were destroyed by the fire of shells. All the casemates are cracked from end to end, and in some places the roofs are completely broken, and frequently masses of brick have been dislodged. Four guns were dismounted, and eleven carriages and traverses injured. The outer works of the fort are cracked from top to bottom, in several places admitting daylight freely. It is computed that 3,339 shells were thrown into the ditches and overflowed parts of the fort; 1,080 shells exploded in the air over the fort; 1,113 mortar-shells were counted on the sloping ground of the fort and levee, and eighty-seven round shot. Altogether 7,500 shells were fired. One shell passed through the roof of the water battery magazine, but did not explode. On the parapet were fourteen new graves.

Porter, when told, at the conference on board the *Harriet Lane*, that the rebel "gentlemen 'of the navy" had fired and let loose the iron battery, signalled to his captains to look out for their ships, and then quietly went on with the conference, telling the rebel colonel who was on board with him, that "we could stand the fire and blow-up, if he could." That speech has the true ring of the old "Essex" Porter, who fought one of the most desperate battles known to history, and whose spirit is evidently alive in this descendant of his.

During the conflict the much heard of ram *Manassas*—with which Commodore Hollins achieved his sole exploit by running into the *Brooklyn* when she ventured into the river in the fall of 1861—again made its appearance, but only to its own dire destruction. It was so well "peppered" that it came drifting helplessly down stream on fire and in a sinking condition. Whether her crew remained on board, to be roasted or parboiled according to their place in the ship, or whether they escaped, is not known. Commodore Porter, who had an eye for a joke, did his best to preserve that specimen joke of the rebels; he clapped a hawser round it and tried to tow it to the bank, but the ridiculous affair gave a puff, blew a few harmless flakes of flame into the eyes of the laughing tars who were endeavoring to surround it, and sunk.

Among other things destroyed by the rebels at New Orleans, was their monster and really formidable floating battery—the *Mississippi*—upon which the Southern people had founded high hopes of success to their cause. She had been seven months in course of construction, employing five hundred men the whole time, and would have been finished in three weeks. Her length was two hundred and seventy feet, her depth sixty, and her armament was to have been twenty rifled guns. The frame of the hull was made of Georgia pine, nine inches thick. Over the wood were placed three plates of rolled iron, making the thickness of the armor alone four inches and a half. She was 5,000 tons burden, and her motive power consisted of three propellers, which were calculated to give her a speed of eleven knots an hour. Two millions of dollars are said to have been expended in building her. Some of the prisoners, taken in the gunboats, stated that she was intended to break up the blockade and then cruise in the Gulf and near Havana for prizes.

A pleasing incident occurred when the Federal frigate *Mississippi* struck the levee shore at "Algiers" in her effort to swing around. A large and boisterous crowd collected, and sought to provoke the officers and men by their remarks. The Captain, to drown their noise, called the band and bade them strike up Hail Columbia. Involuntarily, as it were, the rabble ceased howling, and instinctively some of the old men in the throng raised their hats in acknowledgment of the strains which from their youth had inspired them.

Two Irishmen came alongside Captain Woodworth's vessel on her way up stream, with milk and eggs to sell. The Captain, to enjoy a joke, offered to pay them for what was purchased in Confederate scrip. "Be gorra!" said Pat, "I thought yez was gintlemen, and paid for what yez wanted. Divil a bit of money have I seen for a year, and Confederate scrip has brought the wife and children to starvation almost." He was paid in the coin of Uncle Sam, when he broke out: "Hurrah for the ould flag! They wanted to make me fight against it, but I never have fought and I never will fit for 'em." And he turned the money in his hand, examining it curiously, as a child might a newly-acquired toy.

A correspondent wrote of the appearance of the city: "I was impressed with the remarkably desolate appearance of the city. All the warehouses were shut, and there was not a vessel, save those of the squadron, to be seen anywhere. As soon as the fleet, in its victorious advance, swept away the defenses at La Chalmette, a few miles below, and appeared before the city, the deluded people burned all the shipping, and quantities of sugar, tobacco and cotton. The work of destruction was complete. More than forty vessels—steamers, schooners, ships—and immense piles of cotton, were fired at the same time, and the levee was a line of flame. The scene is described as being terrible. The mob took advantage of the occasion to plunder, and a panic of the wildest description raged. I saw the effects of this wanton sacrifice of property in the half-burned and submerged hulls of several vessels, and the charred planks of the wharves on both sides of the river. Several heaps of cotton were still ablaze."

The mob was only learned to cease its violence and taunts by the strong hand of Butler's soldiers. A day or two after the United States flag was hoisted over the public buildings, some persons assembled before the Mint, and tore the colors from the staff, trampling upon them. The *Pensacola*, then lying opposite, discharged a round of grape into the crowd, killing one man and dispersing the others. When Butler assumed martial control over affairs the fellow who tore the flag down (one Mumford) was taken, tried and hung in sight of a vast assembly, while his sentence was placarded over the city. That summary disposition of one incorrigible traitor had the capital effect to render treason much less popular. The women of the city—including its leading "ladies"—were, however, so malignant, and impudent in their malignancy, as to omit no occasion to bestow upon the Federal officers and soldiers alike their utmost scorn by words and acts. Oaths, imprecations, indecent epithets and spitting in faces were everywhere meted out to the quiet and gentlemanly fellows who were distributed over the city as a guard. Butler finally put a stop to this feminine and disgraceful state of affairs by ordering the enforcement of a local law which assumed all females to be "women of the town" who were guilty of public indecorum: all such were to be consigned to the calaboose. There was very little female treason visible after that order. It was that order which so horrified Johnny Bull as to compel a leading faction in Parliament to demand English "interference" in our affairs, to put a stop to such outrages upon helpless women!

There were found, safely stored in the Custom House, at least $50,000 worth of bells of all descriptions, from the ponderous cathedral bell to the smallest size of hand-bells. These had been contributed in response to the proclamation of Beauregard for gun metal, and were to have been worked up in the Algiers foundries. The "patriotic" churches, planters and schools which had contributed these bells to "the cause" must have relished the joke exceedingly when they were made to chime melodiously for a Yankee victory. Unlike Tennyson's poetical bells, they rang in the Old and rang out the New order of things.

Commodore Farragut's politeness was of a nature to excite a smile for its significance. April 26th he dispatched to "His Honor, the Mayor of New Orleans," the following polite *request:*

"Your Honor will please give directions that no flag but that of the United States will be permitted to fly in the presence of this fleet, so long as it has the power to prevent it; *and as all displays of that kind may be the cause of bloodshed*, I have to request that you will give this communication as wide a circulation as possible."

This so injured the feelings of the Mayor that "His Honor" immediately made it the subject of a special message to the City Council. Faragut's politeness evidently was of the overpowering kind.

The day previous (April 25th) the Commodore dispatched Captain Bailey to the Mayor to demand the unconditional surrender of the city—the hauling down of the Louisiana flag from the City Hall and of the Confederate flag from the Custom House, Post-office and Mint—to require the raising of the United States flag on all these places. The Mayor called in General Lovell, commander-in-chief of the rebel forces, for the defense of the city. As stated by "His Honor," in his message to the Common Council, immediately convened: "General Lovell refused to surrender the city or his forces, or any portion of them; but accompanied his refusal with the statement that he should evacuate the city, withdraw his troops, and then leave the city authorities to act as they might deem proper." Whereupon the Mayor confessed that he was placed in a pretty predicament: as a *civil* magistrate how could he surrender the city to a hostile force? He asked the Council's advice, and, in the end, addressed a very impertinent note to the considerate Commodore, stating that brute force had power to do as it pleased, and might come and take the city.

It remained for Butler to teach "His Honor" good manners by sending him to the North to spend the summer in a less treason-tainted atmosphere than that of New Orleans. Butler proved to be a capital physician for all the ills which afflicted the sensitive souls of the Southern "copper-heads." He soon brought order, peace, security, industry, commerce out of that chaos of treason and rebel ruffianism. Was it for that service to law and order that the foreign interventers demanded his recall?

XL.

SECESSION ATROCITY ON THE FIELD.

A FACT made apparent early in the contest, was the shocking cruelty practiced upon Federal prisoners, by the rebels. Parson Brownlow explicitly stated, that troops passed home from the battle-field of Bull Run, armed with Yankee skulls, teeth, finger-bones, etc., as trophies, and exhibited them to their delighted friends as an Indian would have shown his scalps, in evidence of his valor. The same statement was made by various authorities, and was discovered to be true upon the reoccupation of the field by McClellan's advance. Residents in and around Manassas confessed freely that the wounded were bayoneted, and their bodies left, in many instances, unburied—that all our dead soldiers were stripped of clothing and property almost as soon as the retreat commenced—that numbers were buried face downward, to express the fiendish disregard of the rules of civilized warfare, which the rebels saw proper to exercise upon many occasions. The Southern army teamsters frequently referred to the fact, that they used Yankee skulls for tar-pots, slung under the wagons by two strings. Women were found in the Shenandoah valley wearing amulets, made of Yankee finger and toe-bones. The women of Winchester were remarkable for their profanity in everything regarding the "Yankee." Even the daughter of General Taylor—the once beautiful and dashing Bessie, who married Colonel Bliss, and, after his decease, wedded a physician living in Winchester—scarcely refrained from vulgar rudeness and malice toward the men and officers of the Union army. Everywhere, throughout Virginia, the spirit of secession seemed allied to the spirit of evil: men, women, and even children alike were possessed of a malignancy of heart, that argued anything but civilization and self-respect.

The Lynchburg (Va.) *Republican* told a story, illustrative of the indifference entertained by Southern gentlemen toward Northern friends. It may be repeated:

"Just before the war broke out, and before Lincoln's proclamation was issued, a young Virginian named Summerfield was visiting the city of New York, where he made the acquaintance of two Misses Holmes, from Waterbury, Vt. He became somewhat intimate with the young ladies, and the intercourse seemed to be mutually agreeable. The proclamation was issued, and the whole North thrown into a blaze of excitement. Upon visiting the ladies one evening, and at the hour of parting, they remarked to Summerfield that their present meeting would probably be the last; they must hurry home to aid in making up the overcoats and clothing for the volunteers from their town. Summerfield expressed his regret that they must leave, but at the same time especially requesting them to see that the overcoats were well made, as it was his intention, if he ever met the Vermont regiment in battle, to kill one of them and take his coat. Now for the sequel. Virginia seceded. The Second Vermont regiment, a portion of which was from the town of Waterbury, was sent to Virginia. The battle of Manassas was fought, in which they were engaged, and so was Summerfield. During the battle S. marked his man, not knowing to what State he belonged; the fatal ball was sped on its errand of death; the victim fell at the flash of the gun, and upon rushing up to secure the dead man's arms, Summerfield observed that he had a fine new overcoat strapped to his back, which he determined io appropriate to his own use. The fight was over, and Summerfield had time to examine his prize, when, remarkable as it may appear, the coat was marked in the lining with the name of Thomas Holmes, and in the pockets were found letters, signed with the name of the sister, whom Summerfield had known in New York, and to whom he had made the remark we have quoted, in which the dead man was addressed as brother. The evidence was conclusive—he had killed the brother of his friend, and the remark which he had made in jest had a melancholy fulfilment. We are assured this narrative is literally true. Summerfield now wears the coat, and, our informant states, is not a little impressed with the singularity of the coincidence."

"Is not a little impressed with the singularity of the coincidence!" No feeling of regret for the shooting of the brother of those in whose family he had been a guest—no compunctions of conscience against robbing the dead of goods made up with hands which he had once pressed in friendship! No! Southern enmity forbade any such "sentimental qualms;" Southern honor and the Southern cause alike demanded that a Northerner should be regarded as a savage, and treated as such.

The massacre at Guyandotte, Virginia, illustrated this spirit of secession atrocity. There a troop of Union cavalry was quartered, when the rebels, secretly informed of the fact by the residents of the town, made a sudden descent upon the place. An indiscriminate slaughter of the Federals followed, in which the people of Guyandotte—including the women—joined. But about forty escaped of the two hundred cavalrymen—many of whom were shot by the Guyandotte people as they were trying to escape by swimming the river. This bloody act was followed by a just retribution. The town was reduced to ashes by the Unionists, who quickly gathered to avenge the atrocious conduct of citizens whom they had respected.

The Southern "muse," of course, made itself heard during the contest. If the poetry was detestable as poetry, it was never lacking in the spirit which comes of the intense emotions of hate and scorn. The following is one of the best effusions made public. It first appeared in a Virginia paper:

Whoop! the Doodles have broken loose,
Roaring round like the very deuce!
Lice of Egypt, a hungry pack,
After 'em, boys, and drive 'em back.

Bull-dog, terrier, cur and lice,
Back to the beggardly land of ice;
Worry 'em, bite 'em, scratch and tear
Everybody and everywhere.

Old Kentucky 's caved from under,
Tennessee is split asunder,
Alabama awaits attack,
And Georgia bristles at her back.

Old John Brown is dead and gone!
Still his spirit is marching on,
Lantern-jawed, and legs, my boys,
Long as Apes from Illinois!

Want a weapon? Gather a brick!
Club or cudgel, or stone or stick;
Anything with a blade or butt,
Anything that can cleave or cut.

Anything heavy, or hard, or keen!
Any sort of a slaying machine!
Anything with a willing mind,
And the steady arm of a man behind.

Want a weapon? Why, capture one!
Every Doodle has got a gun,
Belt and bayonet, bright and new,
Kill a Doodle, and capture *two!*

Shoulder to shoulder, son and sire!
All! call all! to the feast of fire!
Mother and maiden, and child and slave,
A common triumph, or a single grave.

Rebel atrocities were renewed at the campaign before Richmond. Such evidence was obtained as left no doubt upon the minds of even the most ardent sympathiser with the rebels, that there were men in the Confederate army capable of almost any atrocity. A letter from a member of the Eighth New Jersey volunteers, gave the following painful relation of the indignities heaped, at the battle of Williamsburg, upon our wounded officers and men, whom the varying fortunes of the struggle, for a brief period, placed in their possession:

"Major Ryerson fell bravely. No words can do more than justice to his coolness and courage. Unfortunately we were not able to get his body off the field in the pressure of the engagement. Some of the enemy came across him, and with their usual brutality and worse than heathen barbarism, stripped him of all he had about him, save his shirt and pants. They did the same with Lieutenant-Colonel Van Lear's body (of the Sixth New Jersey volunteers). In fact they served all in the same way, turning out the pockets of every stricken soldier they met. Nor did they stop at this robbery of the dead. They perpetrated savage outrages upon them, bayoneting the wounded and breaking in the skulls of the dead with the butts of muskets, until the brain laid entirely bare upon the earth beside the body! This is fearful to recount—almost too shocking. But it is true. And I give it to show to those who laud southern honor, chivalry and nobleness, what southern honor and chivalry and nobleness consist in. I dare not longer dwell on this. My feelings of indignation might lead to language unbecoming a Christian. Though, in truth, no language to express disgust and contempt of such deeds as I have recounted could well be too strong."

This horrible statement was more than confirmed by the correspondent of the New York *Times*, who wrote from the field: "Major Ryerson, of the New Jersey brigade, fell wounded in the action of Monday, and two officers who undertook to carry him from the field were shot in the attempt. A couple of privates then sprang to his assistance, but he advised them to leave him for their own safety, telling them that he was not dangerously injured, and had nothing to fear from the enemy; but when the field was searched the next day for the dead, he was found lying among them, with six bayonet wounds in his breast, his ears slit, and his body nearly stripped of clothing." The Comanches would not have done worse. It was wonderful that, seeing these things, the Federal troops did not seek to retaliate, but, in no single instance, are we aware of any other than the most humane and considerate treatment being meted out to wounded rebel prisoners in our hands. Occasionally threats were uttered by the men of particular regiments, some of whose wounded members had suffered outrage and murder at the hands of the villains, who comprised full one-half of the rebel army. Thus, a member of the New York Sixteenth said, in writing of the Williamsburg fight: "It is hardly necessary to say that officers and men are very much exasperated by the barbarous conduct of some of the rebels—bayoneting the dead, cutting the throats of the wounded, and, in one instance, beating with the butt of a musket the skull of a drummer-boy, who had received a wound which might well be presumed to be mortal. 'This war ought to have been one of extermination from the first,' was read, recently, either in a rebel newspaper, or in some of the choice specimens of literature left in the camps. The army of the Potomac is quite ready to accept that rule; possibly to press it. Certainly I should pity any rebel who should ask a favor of the men of the Sixteenth New York.'"

Occasionally, also, a villain here and there got his deserts. Two notorious "bush-whackers," named Koehl and Weimer, were hung at Sutton, Virginia, having been convicted of murder. These barbarous wretches, during the latter part of the summer of 1861, caught a poor boy who had been driving a Government team alone on the road. They inhumanly cut off his head with a scythe, and disemboweled him; and, in their fiendish joy, boasted that they had killed one Yankee. They were captured, convicted of the murder, and executed. Their unusual brutality was fully proven at the trial.

We could multiply instances of this painful character, but have given enough to answer our purpose, viz.: to show that a thirst for revenge was one of the inspiring motives which filled and fired the Southern heart. It will take two generations of prosperity to banish from such breasts the evil effects of the passions engendered in the brief struggle for "Southern Independence."

XLI.

ANECDOTES AND INCIDENTS.

WE find at our disposal an immense number of excerpts, illustrative of the facts and humors of the service. Our volume would scarce contain them all. We have already given many of the incidents which transpired on certain fields; and will, now, reproduce such as seem to possess more than a passing interest.

The *music* of bullets and balls is referred to frequently in accounts of battles. A soldier, critical in musical intonation and the graduation of scales, gave us these notes, explanatory and commentary on the "performances" of the death-dealing messengers:

"It is a very good place to exercise the mind, with the enemy's picket rattling close at hand. A musical ear can study the different tones of the bullets as they skim through the air. I caught the pitch of a large-sized Minie yesterday—it was a swell from E flat to F, and as it passed into the distance and lost its velocity, receded to D—a very pretty change. One of the most startling sounds is that produced by the Hotchkiss shell. It comes like the shriek of a demon, and the bravest old soldiers feel like ducking when they hear it. It is no more destructive than some other missiles, but there is a great deal in mere sound to work upon men's fears.

"The tremendous scream is caused by a ragged edge of lead, which is left on the shell. In favorable positions of light, the phenomena can sometimes be seen, as you stand directly behind a gun, of the clinging of the air to the ball. The ball seems to gather up the atmosphere and carry it along, as the earth carries its atmosphere through space. Men are frequently killed by the wind of a cannon-shot. There is a law which causes the atmosphere to cling to the earth, or which presses upon it with a force, at the surface, of fifteen pounds to the square inch; does the same law, or a modification, pertain to cannon-balls in flight? I do not remember of meeting with a discussion of the subject in any published work. It is certainly an interesting philosophic question."

A good story is related of Colonel Merideth, of the Nineteenth Indiana volunteers, regarding his principles and practice in *dodging bullets.* It runs: "At the Lewisville skirmish, the Colonel was at the head of his men, as they were formed in line of battle, under the fire of the enemy. As the shells exploded over them, his boys would involuntarily duck their heads. The Colonel saw their motions, and, in a pleasant way, exhorted them, as he rode along the line, to hold up their heads and act like men. He turned to speak to one of his officers, and at that moment an eighteen-pounder shell burst within a few yards of him, scattering its fragments in all directions. Instinctively he jerked his head almost to the saddle-bow, while his horse squatted with fear. 'Boys,' said he, as he raised up and reined his steed, 'you MAY dodge the large ones!' A laugh ran along the line at his expense, and after that no more was said about the impropriety of dodging shells."

There is power in music to send men into the fray with the wild *abandon* which inspires them in the dance. At the battle of Williamsburg, Heintzelman's brigade for some time withstood the terrific shock of the assault of the enemy, fully numbering three men to his one. Worn out with fighting, it was evident that he must give way if reenforcements did not come up to his relief. At that critical and anxious moment, Brigadier-General Berry, of Maine, came in sight, with his fine brigade, upon a run. Heintzelman huzzaed with gratitude. He ran to the nearest band, *and ordered it to meet the coming regiments with "Yankee Doodle," and to give them marching time into the field with the "Star-Spangled Banner."* A wild "hurrah!" went up from the army, and, with a yell that was electric, three regiments of Berry's brigade went to the front, formed a line nearly half-a-mile long, and commenced a volley firing that no troops on earth could stand before—then, at the double-quick, dashed with the bayonet at the rebel army, and sent them flying from the field into their earthworks, pursued them into the largest of them, drove them out behind with the pure steel, and then invited them to retake it. The attempt was repeatedly made, and repeatedly repulsed. The count of the rebel dead in that battery, at the close of the fight, was fearful evidence of the tenacity of the Northern troops. They were principally Michigan men who did this work. The equilibrium of the battle was restored.

This tenacity of the Northern troops was illustrated on many a field. Read our account of the Ball's Bluff disaster, of the Missouri campaign, of the Pittsburg Landing struggles, where our men seemed to court death. The same virtue was more splendidly illustrated in the six days struggle (June 27th–July 2d) of McClellan's army in its retreat for realignment on the James River. The history of modern warfare does not present an instance of greater endurance, heroism, devotion to orders and desire for the close quarters of deadly conflict. It was an almost ceaseless struggle of life and death, wherein men freely walked into the fire to leave on the ground one half of their numbers. The General who could educate his men up to that point of duty possesses elements of greatness even though his campaigns should prove failures.

At Bull Run, prior to the "panic," the men, as a general thing, fought splendidly. The records of that two days battle are alive with deeds of true heroism—some of which we already have recounted, (see pages 178–187.) One incident, not there recurred to, deserves mention, bringing out in bold relief as it does the prowess of men brought up in the forest and familiar with danger from their childhood.

"On the evening previous to the battle of Sunday, two of the Minnesota boys took it into their heads to forage a little, for amusement as well as eatables. Striking out from their encampment into the forest they followed a narrow road some distance, until, turning a bend, five secession pickets appeared not fifty yards distant. The parties discovered each other simultaneously, and at once leveled their rifles and fired. Two of the Confederates fell dead, and one of the Minnesotians, the other also, falling, however, but with the design of trapping the other three, who at once came up, as they said, to 'examine the d—d Yankees.' Drawing his revolver, the Minnesotian found he had but two barrels loaded, and with these he shot two of the picket. Springing to his feet, and snatching his saber bayonet from his rifle, he lunged at the survivor, who proved to be a stalwart lieutenant, armed only with a heavy sword. The superior skill of the Southerner was taxed to the utmost in parrying the vigorous thrusts and lunges of the brawny lumberman: and for several minutes the contest waged in silence, broken only by the rustle of the long grass by the roadside and the clash of their weapons. Feigning fatigue, the Minnesotian fell back a few steps, and as his adversary closed upon him with a cat-like spring, he let his saber come down on the head of his antagonist, and the game was up. Collecting the arms of the secessionists, he returned to the camp, where he obtained assistance, and buried the bodies of his companion and his foes in one grave."

An equally exciting story is told of a member of the Tenth Massachusetts, who was taken prisoner at the battle of Fair Oaks. A guard of two Alabamians was placed over him temporarily. Seeing a New York regiment approaching, the Massachusetts man concluded to "*secede*." He "pitched into" his guards, knocking down and disarming both of the Southern gentlemen before they were aware of the Yankee's design. But Yankee was not then ready to leave. A wounded comrade was placed on a rude litter and the two Alabamians were made to bear the burden into the New York ranks.

The women of the South proved, at times, more unconquerable enemies than the men. Their unbridled tongues ran to a vocabulary of epithets and passion perfectly astonishing to the Northern men, who had been led to believe that a Southern woman was a superior creature. Our troops learned, in their campaigns, that the spirit of secession made demons of men and furies of women, and few of them will return home to entertain respect for the females of the South who unsexed themselves to prove their scorn of "the Yankees."

How brightly the story of the war is illuminated by the sacrifices of many of the women of the North! As nurses—as beneficiaries and directors of relief and supply associations—as ministers of hope to the hospital and the camp—their record is one to make Northern men rejoice to claim them as mothers, sisters, wives and friends. It will be a precious volume that relates their good deeds and blessed ministrations. From the noble Sisters of Mercy to the humble, self sacrificing woman who toiled alone to do something for her beloved ones in the field, it is one ceaseless story of a devotion over which the angels must have rejoiced. May the book of their deeds be written!

After the battle at Pittsburg Landing, great numbers of persons flocked to the vicinity of the conflict to look after their dear ones dead or wounded. Many affecting stories were related. A lady in search of her boy, reported "wounded," examined all the hospitals to find her treasure. She passed through the various wards, and saw none whom she could recognize as her boy. After looking in vain, and scanning closely every countenance, she was about to retire in sorrow and disappointment, when a poor emaciated lad — a mere shadow of humanity—who had severely suffered from fever and disease, feebly uttered, Mother! The lady turned and looked upon the poor sufferer, but could see no likeness of her boy, who so recently had left home in the bloom of youth and health. Again the lad feebly articulated, Mother! The tears started from the eyes of the good woman, as she thought of her own boy. A gentleman standing near—a Mr. S——, of New York—said: "Madame, I can see a likeness of you in that boy; it must be your son." The mother asked his name, and with scarcely strength enough to speak, he managed to utter almost inarticulately his name, when the lady saw it was her boy. The gentleman who narrated this, added: "This is a sample of many such cases, the result of the fevers to which the unacclimated are incident."

Another painfully interesting incident is related of the manner in which Mrs. Pfieff, the wife of Lieutenant Louis Pfieff, of Chicago, who was killed at Pittsburg Landing, was enabled to find her husband's body. No person, when she arrived on the field, could inform her where her husband's body was buried; and after searching among the thousands of graves for half a day, she was about to abandon the pursuit in despair.

Suddenly she saw a large dog coming toward her, which she recognized as one which had left Chicago with her husband. The dog seemed delighted to find her, and led her to a distant part of the field, where he stopped before a single grave. She caused it to be opened, and found the body of her husband. It appears, by the statements of the soldiers, that the dog was by the side of the Lieutenant when he fell, and remained with him till he was buried. He then took his station by the grave, and there he had remained for twelve days, until relieved by the arrival of his mistress, only leaving his post long enough each day to procure food. This is a well authenticated incident, and will go far toward relieving the race of dogs from the odium which some would attach to their species.

A woman was regularly commissioned *Major* for her services on the field. Governor Yates, of Illinois, recognized the eminent and beneficent labors of Mrs. Reynolds, of Peoria, wife of Lieutenant Reynolds, (Company A, Seventeenth Illinois volunteers,) by conferring on her the commission. The lady accompanied her husband through the greater part of the campaign through which the Seventeeth passed, sharing with him the dangers and privations of a soldier's life. She was present at the battle of Pittsburg Landing, and, like a ministering angel, attended to the wants of as many of the wounded and dying soldiers as she could, thus winning the gratitude and esteem of the brave fellows by whom she was surrounded. Governor Yates, hearing of her heroic and praiseworthy conduct, presented her with a commission as Major in the Army —the document conferring the well-merited honor being made out with all due formality, and having attached the great seal of the State.

Among some of the most painful experiences of the war, were those wherein Northern men were first made familiar with the dark side of the institution of Slavery. Throughout the South, where the Union forces penetrated, slaves and masters were, of necessity, forced upon the attention of the troops. The negro, longing for freedom, would seek our lines for safety, and, to prevent such desertion the master would resort to even more rigorous measures than usual—inflicting punishments which were, indeed, well calculated to inspire terror and to repress effort to escape. In a few instances only were these shocking brutalities toward slaves properly punished. General Butler—himself a life-long friend and supporter of the institution of Slavery—was called upon to consider a case, upon his first assumption of power in New Orleans. It at once so shocked him, as to induce the exercise of all his power in its punishment. The case was this:

A citizen of New Orleans (one William T. Hunter) had his house visited, by order of the military authorities, to discover the store of arms, etc., known to be secreted on the premises. Hunter being absent, his wife directed a negro woman to show the guard over the house, which she did. Arms, tents, etc., were found. Hunter soon returned, to find that not only were the "contraband" articles gone, but that the negro woman had followed the guard away. Mrs. Hunter had, however, recovered the slave—who, it would appear, simply followed the *cortege* away out of curiosity, and would soon have returned of her own accord. Hunter, however, resolved to "punish" his servant property for her *crime.* Taking down the heavy whip used for negro whipping, he beat the woman cruelly over the head. Tiring of this, he took her down into the back-yard, to "the block," to which she was chained—Mrs. Hunter herself fastening the shackles.

"The husband and wife then threw the servant down upon her back, fastened her hands to the feet of another servant, who was forced to hold the girl out to her full length. The girl was then subjected to head-shaving; her clothes were next removed, and Hunter beat the exhausted creature with the horsewhip *until he was too tired to stand. He then called for a chair, sat down, and finished his brutal beating in a sitting posture.* The screams of the sufferer attracted the attention of the neighborhood. One neighbor sent intelligence of what was transpiring to General Butler. Before word reached the General the monster had flayed the back of his slave until it became raw—*washed her down with brine*, threw her into a wagon, and, at nine o'clock at night, conveyed her to the parish prison, with the pleasing information that the rest of the beating—to the extent of three hundred lashes—would be inflicted in the morning."

Butler was horrified at that early lesson of the "rights of masters over slaves." He ordered Hunter, his wife and the slave woman into his presence early on the following morning, and, with his own eyes, beheld the shocking sight—a human being, a woman—beaten almost into a jelly for no greater crime than running down with the crowd, to the Federal quarters. Butler gave the villain—who was one of the "most respectable citizens" of the city—such a talk as the case demanded, and ended by committing the inhuman creature to Fort Jackson. Hunter demurred to the incarceration saying he had brought along with him a physician to prove that he had been sick for six months. Butler sternly remarked that all the *proof* he wanted was in that woman's back—if Hunter was able to flog a human being in that manner he was strong euough to suffer punishment for it. "And be careful," said the irate General, "that you behave yourself perfectly, for I shall order *you* to be flogged and your back to be washed down with brine if any insolence is offered." And the fellow was marched off to Fort Jackson while the slave was taken from her mistress—who was one of the leading *ladies* of New Orleans—and turned over to the Thirteenth Connecticut regiment as a laundress.

This case greatly excited the indignation of the New Orleans people, who saw in it "an invasion of their constitutional rights"—that Butler should have dared to incarcerate a citizen for simply beating his slave! He had a right to beat her, under the laws of the State; and, in sitting in judgment on the case, Butler had exceeded his authority and had set a dangerous precedent! Perhaps he did exceed his authority and sit in judgment on a case belonging to the civil authorities; but even B. F. Butler was a "higher law" man when emergencies required, and, what was strange, the "conservatives" in Congress did not call for an inquiry into the matter, nor demand the General's recall! Had he been some "abolition" General, instead of an old "Hard Shell" Breckenridge Democrat, Butler would have seen the lightning and heard the thunder of several Congressmen whose labors were chiefly devoted to the end of securing to outlaws, assassins, thieves and traitors "constitutional rights." Nero fiddled while the torch was applied to Rome, but Rome had no Senators base enough to prate of the "constitutional rights" of the incendiaries and emissaries enforcing the orders of a monster. There was no Vallandigham there—alas for the memory of Nero!

We have before us, in a letter from an officer in an Indiana regiment serving in Arkansas in May, 1862, a little incident of adventure and experience which may be quoted. He says:

"Yesterday my heart was fearfully agitated by a sight I shall never forget. We traveled eight miles, and stopped for breakfast at a rich planter's house. While breakfast was preparing I heard one of the soldiers remark that in a certain cabin there was a woman with a chain around her neck. I walked to the cabin, opened the door, and saw that which made my heart sick. A woman in chains! It is true she was *yellow* in complexion. There *was* negro blood in her veins. She was a quadroon, with regular features. 'Who placed this chain around your neck?' 'That man.' 'What man?' 'The owner of this place.' 'What did he do it for?' 'For running away; I am not his; I was stole from St. Louis. Oh, do save me and my little boy. He gave me three hundred lashes last night. The dear Lord save me. Look at my feet.' I looked. There was blood upon her ankles and feet as it had trickled down her person. I sent for the master; he came. 'Take that chain from that woman's neck.' He hesitated. '*Take it away!*' The chain was removed. I have done this on my own responsibility. I suppose I have violated the law, and made myself liable to be tried by court-martial, and perhaps cashiered."

"Made myself liable to the law." Then *the law* does give a man the right to place chains on a woman's neck, to whip her with three hundred lashes, and to punish those who gainsay that right? The answer is, *it does!* Let Christian men, who have respect for the law, see to it that, in the new order of things which must follow the struggle for the Union's life, the *right* of a man to flay a woman alive, at his pleasure, may be made one of the things of the past.

www.ingramcontent.com/pod-product-compliance
Lightning Source LLC
LaVergne TN
LVHW020112110826
845151LV00001B/137